Children's Syntax

D1493675

Blackwell Textbooks in Linguistics

Children's Syntax

An Introduction to Principles and Parameters Theory

Martin Atkinson

BLACKWELL
Oxford UK & Cambridge USA

First published 1992

Blackwell Publishers
108 Cowley Road
Oxford OX4 1JF
UK

Three Cambridge Center
Cambridge, Massachusetts 02142
USA

British Library Cataloguing in Publication Data
A CIP catalogue record for this book is available from the British Library.

Library of Congress Cataloging-in-Publication Data
Atkinson, Martin.
    Children's syntax : an introduction to principles and parameters theory / Martin Atkinson.
       p.   cm. — (Blackwell textbooks in linguistics ; 5)
    Includes bibliographical references (pps. 297–312) and index.
    ISBN 0–631–17267–X (acid-free paper). — ISBN 0–631–17268–8 (pbk. : acid-free paper)
    1. Language acquisition.   2. Principles and parameters (Linguistics)   3. Grammar, Comparative and general—Syntax.
I. Title. II. Series.
P118.A79 1992
401′.93—dc20   91–44373
                                                     CIP

Typeset in 10 on 11½ pt Sabon
by TecSet Ltd, Wallington, Surrey
Printed in Great Britain by T. J. Press Ltd, Padstow, Cornwall

This book is printed on acid-free paper

Contents

Acknowledgements

I am grateful to the University of Essex for granting me leave of absence from teaching and administrative duties during the academic year 1990–1. Without this leave, it is unlikely that the book would have been started, let alone finished.

Because of my own inefficiency in producing and distributing copies of the typescript, I have not been able to benefit from the comments and criticisms of friends and colleagues – no doubt these will follow. However, it would be remiss to fail to note the beneficial influence that such people have had on my thinking about the issues to which the book is devoted. Andrew Radford has, perhaps unwittingly, taught me a great deal about syntactic theory as well as being a good friend and supportive colleague. Keith Brown, Peter Carruthers, Vivian Cook, Roger Hawkins, Mike Jones, Iggy Roca and Andy Spencer have all taken time to discuss important issues with me, the quality of their observations more than compensating for the brevity of our interaction.

Several doctoral students have been particularly helpful, not just because in choosing to write dissertations on interesting topics, they forced me to read material of which I would otherwise be ignorant, but also because they were enthusiastic enough to persuade me to maintain some intellectual impetus through a period when my principal duties were administrative. They are Abdallah Al-Harbi, Gao Chang-Fan, Síle Harrington, Asma Moubaideen, Mark Newson, Anjum Saleemi and Liu Yuan.

The staff of Blackwell Publishers have been exceptional in their encouragement, support and professionalism. Philip Carpenter displayed admirable patience and confidence as I staggered to the end of my 'administrative period' with the book still no more than a remote possibility. Andrew McNeillie dealt with editorial preparation in a most helpful and efficient manner. Margaret Hardwidge performed as fine a piece of copy-editing on the original typescript as I have ever seen.

Finally, the continued love of my family has been a source of constant encouragement (and occasionally, when the going has been tough, wonder) to me. The book is dedicated to Angela, Ben, Dan, Sarah and Jo.

Introduction

How is it that children who have been brought up in an English-speaking environment come to judge that the string of words in example (1) does not comprise a well-formed sentence?[1]

(1) *John wants Mary to photograph himself

This question takes on added significance if we assume, as seems plausible, that such children are not standardly presented with explicit information about the status of this string of words. Nor is it possible to advert to a suggestion that the 'meaning' (1) would express is unintelligible and that this semantic incoherence is what accounts for the child's judgement. If (1) *were* well-formed, it would unambiguously express the proposition that an individual named John desires that a photograph of himself be produced by a second individual named Mary. Such a proposition is immediately sensible, a point which is reinforced by the observation that the translation of (1) into Icelandic is well-formed and expresses just this proposition (Higginbotham, 1985, p. 551).

A second question: how is it that an English-speaking child succeeds in retreating from the overgeneral application of certain syntactic processes? The examples in (2) – (4), illustrating the Dative Alternation, indicate that a subset of English verbs can appear in two distinct environments:

(2) a. John gave a present to Mary
   b. John gave Mary a present

(3) a. John sent a present to Mary
   b. John sent Mary a present

(4) a. John told a story to Mary
   b. John told Mary a story

However, it is well known that some verbs which might be expected to behave identically to these do not do so:

(5) a. John said something horrible to Mary
   b. *John said Mary something horrible

That children often produce forms similar to (5b) at some point in their development is widely attested (Bowerman, 1978; Pinker, 1989); so, again, if we assume that their linguistic environment does not provide them with the appropriate 'tuition', our question becomes urgent.

Consideration of questions such as these has been instrumental in the development of *linguistic nativism*, the view that the child approaches first language acquisition equipped with innate cognitive structures which, in conjunction with linguistic experience, determine a mature system of mental representation. It is access to this system which enables the adult English-speaker to consistently make the judgements illustrated in (1) – (5), and it is the contribution of the innate structures to bridge the gap between linguistic experience and the mature system.

It is tempting to believe that we must all be nativists of some sort by now: the arguments developed by Chomsky and his associates in the context of first language acquisition, briefly illustrated above, and by Fodor in philosophy of mind have carried the day. While the remnants of radical empiricism and its psychological offshoot, behaviourism, continue to protest occasionally (e.g. Harris, 1989), if ever there was a lost cause, this is surely it. Quite simply, the nativists have had *arguments*, admittedly based on defeasible premises, whereas the other lot have had *dogma*. The arguments have often been solidly located in reflections on first language acquisition, and the exciting thing has been that they have not been restricted to supporting a nebulous sort of nativism of the type '*something* must be innate, or we couldn't explain . . .' Rather, they have attempted to tell us something about *what* must be innate, and have claimed that it is rather specific: in the case of language, so specific as probably not to play a direct role in other aspects of human cognitive development.

All of this is fine, but the developmentalist, perhaps trained as a psychologist, can still have a dilemma. This is because linguists keep changing their theories, which are often technical and quite hard to understand. For those who are not linguists, it is extremely difficult to keep up with even the general mood of the changes, and there is perhaps the temptation to think: 'Do those guys really know what they're up to? Is it worth my while to try to find out what they're up to?' To encapsulate the dilemma, we might note that it is now commonplace to assume that in the course of first language acquisition, the child develops a grammar which comprises a system of rules. It is only since the late 1960s that developmentalists began seriously to adopt this perspective, and in the train of forty years of behaviourism, it met with considerable resistance. What is someone who has gone through a transition to seeing things in this light to make of the statement in Chomsky (1987a, p. 15): 'There are no rules at all, hence no necessity to learn rules'?

I believe that it is appropriate for developmentalists to be familiar with the work of linguists and the implications of this for their own interests. The ambitious response to the Chomsky statement is to be intrigued by it and to want to know more; something has happened in linguistic theory that more people working in language acquisition might benefit from knowing about. Chomsky (1986a, p. 5) makes the observation:

During the past 5–6 years, . . . efforts have converged in a somewhat unexpected way, yielding a rather different conception of the nature of language and its mental representation, one that offers interesting answers to a range of empirical questions and opens a variety of new ones to enquiry while suggesting a rethinking of the character of others. This is what accounts for an unmistakable sense of energy and anticipation – and also uncertainty – which is reminiscent of the period when the study of generative grammar in the modern sense was initiated about 30 years ago.

It is important to be clear that the changes to which Chomsky refers here are internal to the development of generative grammar; they have occurred *within* a nativist perspective. Elsewhere (1987b, p. 23) he says:

The second conceptual shift is more theory-internal than the first, but . . . it is in many ways a more radical departure from the tradition than the earlier one that initiated the development of generative grammar. . . . [It] provides us with a conceptual framework which is quite new and sharply different from anything that preceded.

Such statements convey Chomsky's perception that, from about 1980, there have been some fundamental changes within the variety of generative grammar he and his colleagues have developed, and that these have implications for a range of issues. Central among these is that of accounting for first language acquisition, and a major aim of this book is to justify, in this context, the optimism and excitement (and uncertainty) that is apparent in the above remarks.

The recent history of the interaction between research in linguistic theory and the empirical study of first language acquisition is, in some respects, puzzling. Between the mid-1960s and the mid-1970s, there appeared a number of accounts of the earliest stages of syntactic development which acknowledged the influence of linguistic theory and which adopted the spirit, if not always the letter, of its pronouncements. Such painstakingly researched contributions as Bloom (1970), Bowerman (1973) and Brown (1973) appeared on everyone's language acquisition reading list, and it seemed that a clear paradigm for the conduct of research in this area was well established. But this turned out not to be so, and by the middle of the 1970s, the era of producing grammars which were intended to capture the regularities in early child speech was effectively over. This was not because the authors referred to above and others had resolved the outstanding problems; rather, the difficulties which they confronted appeared to yield only to *ad hoc* and uninsightful manoeuvres, and an air of pointlessness came to surround the enterprise (see Atkinson, 1982, for discussion of this predicament).

The next decade saw a majority of language acquisition researchers lose contact with serious syntactic work, diverting their energies to semantic, pragmatic and other issues. A consequence of this was a fragmentation of the field, as workers, freed of the discipline of linguistic theory, invoked an ever-increasing range of 'cognitive' constructs to account for naturalistic and experimental data. As Pinker (1984, p. 2) succinctly puts it:

> . . . developmental psycholinguists' attention turned away from using child language data to illuminate the process of language acquisition and turned towards characterizing children's language in its own terms, without regard to how the child ever attains adult linguistic proficiency (witness the popular use of the term 'child language' for the field that used to be called 'language acquisition').

The mid-1980s witnessed the beginnings of a second period in which linguistic theory has supplied conceptual apparatus that has guided research in language acquisition studies, and it is no accident that this new *rapprochement* coincides with the maturation and dissemination of the novel ideas to which Chomsky refers. It would be misleading to suggest that the bulk of language acquisition researchers are now working within this novel paradigm, but a significant number are, and their activities are spiced with a definite sense of progress. After a decade in the wilderness, the question of how small children master the structural intricacies of their native language is firmly re-established as a central issue in acquisition research, and the belief that we at last have the tools to move towards a genuine explanation of this unique achievement is difficult to resist.

The most straightforward way to persuade the reader of the exciting nature of these developments is to offer a systematic presentation of some of the theories and findings which have emerged in the last few years, and the book attempts to do this. In pursuing this aim, it should serve as a useful introduction to the primary literature for students following advanced courses in first language acquisition or for graduate students embarking on their research careers. However, I believe that it is necessary to interleave with this primary goal two additional intentions.

The first of these is to provide a measure of contextualization. For readers who are not familiar with the linguistic developments which will be our prime concern, it is important to see them in the light of what they have replaced. As suggested above, there may be some developmentalists who despaired of linguistic theory's contribution to the problems in which they were interested in the 1970s and whose acquaintance with the theoretical literature stopped there. For such readers to appreciate the nature of the current theoretical framework, it is essential to be able to contrast this with what went before. In particular, it is important to grasp the character of the linguistic theory embraced by acquisition theorists in this earlier period, and to address the question directly as to why this now seems inappropriate.

Second, as well as seeking to evaluate the details of individual studies, I believe that it is important to develop a perspective on the status of the whole programme. While I share the optimism which this research is generating, there remain fundamental issues which are unclear. Where appropriate, I do not retreat from raising these issues and attempting to get some grasp on the available options.

In pursuing these two intentions, the book goes beyond what would normally be expected from an introductory treatment. No attempt has been made to separate expository, critical and evaluative discussion, although, as briefly described below, some sections of the book clearly have one flavour or another. Inclusion of these non-expository sections should ensure that what follows will be of some interest to the specialist.

Chapter 1 introduces informally a framework for developing theories of first language acquisition in terms of the four-component model of learnability theory. The four components (hypothesis-space or learner, data, learning procedure and criterion for acquisition) are discussed in some detail and the feasibility of obtaining formal results within this framework is illustrated. The classic work of Gold (1967) is summarized, along with an assessment of its empirical significance, and some of the most important results of Osherson and his colleagues (Osherson, Stob and Weinstein, 1986) are briefly introduced.

Chapter 2 gives an outline of the linguistic theory which informed acquisition research in the 1960s and 1970s in terms of the framework outlined in chapter 1. This theory is what is often referred to as the Standard Theory of Chomsky (1965). Formal learnability theory has been implemented in this context (Wexler and Culicover, 1980; Morgan, 1986), and the chapter includes discussion of the significance of this work. The difficulties (conceptual and empirical) arising within the Standard Theory assumptions are introduced as providing the motivation for subsequent developments.

Chapter 3 presents, within the same scheme of conceptualization, the Principles and Parameters model of syntactic structure which guides much current work in theoretical syntax. It is the shift from Standard Theory to the Principles and Parameters account to which Chomsky refers in the passages cited earlier. Accordingly, this chapter is of central importance to the book, and it seeks to achieve three aims. First, it offers an overview of the Principles and Parameters model, explicitly comparing it with Standard Theory. Such an overview cannot, of course, constitute a comprehensive introduction to a complex and developing model of linguistic structure, but the reader should at least be in a position to appreciate the appropriate contrasts (some recent developments in the model are discussed in chapter 10). Second, it sets out the implications of this model for a theory of first language acquisition. Third, it raises a series of questions which will recur in later parts of the book.

With the Principles and Parameters model in place, chapters 4, 5 and 6, which are largely expository, constitute case studies of particular phenomena which have received attention within this model. Chapter 4 is devoted to phonetically null elements (particularly subjects), starting with discussion of linguistic accounts and moving on to developmental studies. Chapter 5 concentrates on Binding Theory and the Governing Category Parameter, introducing the important Subset Principle of Wexler and Manzini (1987) and providing an answer to the question we raised in connection with example (1). This chapter addresses developmental issues at a theoretical level, but does not include extensive discussion of studies of children. In chapter 6 this is put right, when I summarize and evaluate a range of empirical studies of the Binding

Principles and other grammatical phenomena. This chapter also raises important methodological questions which are again illustrated by experimental studies.

Chapter 7 focuses on the relationship between lexical representations and syntactic representations, and on the manner in which this is mediated by the Projection Principle. The previous three chapters presuppose that the child has access to representations formulated in terms of grammatical categories and finesse the questions of the origins of these categories and how the child's linguistic experience engages them. This issue requires clarification of what Chomsky (1981) refers to as 'epistemological priority'. The major possibility considered is that the emergence of syntactic representations relies on a process of 'semantic bootstrapping' (Pinker, 1984). Alternations of argument structure, as illustrated by (2)–(5) above and extensively investigated by Pinker (1989), are also discussed in this chapter, as is the notion of 'syntactic bootstrapping' proposed by Landau and Gleitman (1985).

Chapters 8 and 9 are more evaluative than what has gone before. Any theory of first language acquisition has to include an account of the procedures whereby a child moves from one system of representation to another in the acquisition process. Views on such procedures will have already appeared in earlier chapters, but chapter 8 submits the issue of developmental mechanisms to close scrutiny. Learning and triggering as candidate procedures are introduced and defined, and their role in general conceptual development is discussed with particular reference to the factors raised in Fodor (1981). Once clear definitions are available, it is possible to consider systematically how, if at all, the proposals of previous chapters mesh with these procedural notions. Maturation, as an alternative to externally guided developmental mechanisms, is introduced and its explanatory role in acquisition discussed.

Chapter 9 raises the crucial question of the necessity to constrain parameterization. An advantage claimed for Principles and Parameters Theory, when compared to Standard Theory, is that it offers a more constrained model of linguistic description and renders the child's task in acquiring a grammar more tractable. The chapter discusses several ways (substantive and procedural) in which it might be possible to develop a constrained theory of parameterization and evaluates their plausibility.

One particularly provocative suggestion for constraining parameterization is that it might be restricted to the properties of functional categories (for example, determiners and verbal inflectional categories). Chapter 10 introduces recent linguistic discussion of these and summarizes Radford's (1990a) claim that children at the earliest stages of syntactic development lack functional categories entirely. The juxtaposition of functional parameterization with Radford's position raises a set of intriguing questions, which are discussed in a somewhat speculative way.

The speculative tone is carried over into chapter 11, which, as well as containing a summary of the major conclusions of the book, offers and defends an overview of the acquisition of syntax.

Two final comments are in order. First, the focus in this book is almost exclusively on syntactic development. Exceptions to this consist of passing references to morphology and rather more systematic discussion of one aspect of semantics in chapter 7. The reasons for this are not hard to fathom. There is the issue of my own competence, but, more notably, the conceptual shift away from rule-based systems has to date been more intensively pursued in syntax than in other areas of linguistic study (for a suggestion that it might not be appropriate to extend it to phonology, see Bromberger and Halle, 1989).

Second, I must offer a word of encouragement to the non-linguist. Some of the analyses of linguistic phenomena with which we shall be concerned, while often deliberately avoiding a range of complex issues, are still quite abstract. Coupled with the fact that data from children are often conspicuously absent in the discussion and only cursorily summarized when they do appear, this might lead to understandable doubts about relevance. I take it as axiomatic that an understanding of acquisition requires a grasp of what is acquired, and I believe that linguists working within Principles and Parameters Theory are developing stimulating ideas on what this is. If we are to make contact with recent acquisition work, it is essential that we have some familiarity with the linguistic concepts. A book which went into considerable detail about the ages of samples of children, their mean lengths of utterance, the numbers of utterances having particular characteristics and so on might (or might not) be fun to write, but it is not this book. I am concerned to introduce a way of thinking about first language acquisition which leads us to formulate new questions and approach well-known developmental phenomena in a novel way. I firmly believe that this way of thinking will take on increasing importance as our understanding deepens, and it will certainly outlive the details of any analysis contained in the following chapters. The message is not to despair at technical details; the general shape of arguments is much more important.

1 Laying the Foundations

Introduction

There is a variety of ways in which an understanding of the remarkable process of first language acquisition has been pursued.

The first, and most obvious, strategy is to collect language data from children of different ages. Then, armed with some basic descriptive vocabulary, it is possible to sketch the emergence of linguistic capacities. Such a procedure was widely adopted in the classic diary studies conducted during the late nineteenth century and the first half of the twentieth century, and the results of these are often rich in descriptive insight (see Ingram, 1989, for sympathetic discussion and references). Subsequent large-scale surveys like McCarthy (1954), producing detailed statistics on utterance length, emergence of the parts of speech, etc., also fall within this characterization, and have, on occasion, provided the basis for more theoretically driven investigations.

What such approaches have in common (of course, there are many different emphases in individual studies) and what distinguishes them from alternatives considered below is their *descriptive* nature. There is little attempt in such work to *explain* the process of first language acquisition and the linguistic vocabulary employed is itself not derived from an explicit theory of language structure. Nor, with one or two notable exceptions (e.g. de Laguna, 1927), are the descriptions embedded within a psychological framework, and the reasons for this are not difficult to discern. Particularly throughout the later part of the period in question, the study of mental structures and their development was anathema to mainstream psychology, which was very much in the thrall of behaviourism. From this perspective, how children come to use and understand a language was not a special achievement – like all other aspects of development, it was a process of habit formation under the moulding influences of a supportive environment. True, the habits were complex and no one knew how to tell the story about their emergence in detail; but habits they were, and the belief that the apparatus needed to account for the establishment of simple habits in laboratory experiments was extendible in principle to the first language acquisition situation was firmly established in the relevant community.[1]

As everyone with interests in this area now knows, this orthodoxy was well and truly demolished by Chomsky (1959) in his famous review of B. F. Skinner's *Verbal Behavior* (1957).[2] Chomsky offered a very different conception of language, whereby it constitutes a mentally represented body of implicit knowledge which might be only indirectly related to what a speaker says and understands. Once this emphasis was established, the way was open for the development of a different approach to first language acquisition, one in which the investigator starts from the supposition that the child is developing mental structures along the lines suggested by linguists, and uses these suggestions to structure his or her investigations. From this perspective, the relationship between data – utterances the child actually produces, for example – and the account which is the outcome of the investigation becomes less transparent. As in all scientific enquiry, the data to which the investigator pays attention are now largely determined by the theoretical framework adopted; nor is it necessary to account for all data within such a circumscribed set. Acknowledgement of a complex causal relationship between the underlying representational system and the overt products of that system provides a licence to set certain problematic aspects of data aside, pending a deeper understanding of this relationship.

Naturally, some care is necessary at this point, as the licence alluded to must not be such as to admit only those data which fit theoretical predilections, and an important methodological question in contemporary linguistic and developmental research is that of how to place the appropriate constraints on this process. As I have already admitted that data from children will play a supportive rather than regulative role in this book, I might with some justification be accused of adopting a too liberal stance on this issue, but for now all we need to note is that this second way of approaching our problem-domain is distinguished from the first in terms of its theoretical and explanatory commitment. The move from descriptive to explanatory frameworks is often identified with scientific progress, so there is nothing unusual about this shift in emphasis.

Somewhat surprisingly, there is a third style of enquiry in which data from children play *no* systematic role. Given the assumption that a system of mental representation emerges in the child, the details of this again being supplied by linguistic theory, it is possible to enquire theoretically into the conditions under which this would be *possible*. Of necessity, this involves the development of a general framework for thinking about how systems with specific characteristics could emerge, and this in turn pushes us in the direction of formulating and exploring the consequences of a range of auxiliary assumptions. At this level, we are no longer dealing with what children actually do at any point in their development. Instead, we are investigating a series of hypothetical questions with the general form: if the acquired system is of such-and-such a nature, if the child's environment has such-and-such properties, if . . ., would the system be acquirable in principle? It should be immediately apparent that the questions formulated in connection with examples (1) – (5) in the Introduction arise in adopting this perspective.

A significant proportion of this book is concerned with research into language acquisition of this third type. In this respect, it focuses on issues in *learnability* and *the logical problem of language acquisition*. However, it must be borne in mind that if this sort of research is to be of anything more than formal significance, it must make contact with what is known about the actual stages through which children pass in acquiring the different aspects of their native language. Accordingly, research of the second type – empirical work with children which is informed by linguistic speculation – will also be a major theme. Ideally, there will be a symbiotic relationship between these two enterprises; in practice, the flow of ideas has tended to be asymmetric, with learnability considerations stimulating work with children. However, the mood of optimism and excitement, alluded to in the Introduction, is to some extent inspired by the two sorts of enquiry coming together and beginning to support each other. The remainder of this chapter is devoted to the development and exemplification of an appropriate framework for studying questions of learnability.

1.1 A Learnability-Theoretic Framework

We begin by considering an example which is some way removed from first language acquisition. It will, however, serve to introduce a set of important concepts in a rather straightforward fashion and will also be of some importance in a different context in chapter 8.

A topic which has exercised psychologists over the years is that of concept learning. In the laboratory, the typical concept-learning experiment is structured along the following lines. First, the experimenter (E) decides on the identity of the concept he wishes a subject (S) to learn. Normally, this concept will be some logical combination of a small set of perceptual attributes, for example, SQUARE AND GREEN or CIRCLE OR BLUE. E further decides on a set of stimuli, some of which will instantiate the concept and others of which will not. If the concept is to be SQUARE AND GREEN, it would be reasonable for the stimuli to be cards containing geometrical figures which vary in shape and colour and perhaps number. If variations in number are included, then number will be an irrelevant stimulus attribute for this particular concept. Finally, E decides on the identity of a response which S must produce in the presence of the concept and withhold in its absence. Again, it is standard for this response to be the uttering of a nonsense syllable, say *nurg*; alternatively, S could simply be asked to sort the stimulus cards into two piles, those which are nurg and those which are not nurg.

With the experiment set up in this way, concept learning now proceeds. S is confronted with the first card in the set and invited to respond to it (by saying *nurg* or not, by placing it in the left- or right-hand pile, as the case may be). When S has responded, E provides feedback on the correctness of the response, and S moves on to the next card. The whole set of cards is treated in this way, then shuffled and the process is repeated. After a certain number of runs through the pack, S is consistently correct. At this point, S is said to have learned/acquired the concept.

Now, it is instructive to reflect on the various features of this experimental situation. First, E provides S with *data* in the form of the stimulus cards and feedback on correctness; each such datum can be seen as a pair (s, r), where s is a specification of the stimulus attributes of the card as perceived by S, and r can have the values *yes* or *no* depending on whether the feedback confirms or disconfirms the stimulus as an instance of the concept. Second, *E* determines, usually before the onset of the experiment, a *criterion of learning/acquisition*; only after going through the whole pack *n* times without errors will *S* be deemed to have learned/acquired the concept.

Attempts to produce theoretical accounts of what goes on in such situations have seen *S* as proceeding via *hypothesis testing* (see Fodor, 1975, for extensive discussion). That is, for any presentation of a stimulus, *S* has one or more 'live' hypotheses, e.g. *nurg* = CIRCLE AND RED, *nurg* = TRIANGLE OR TWO, which are confirmed or disconfirmed by the evidence provided by *E*'s feedback. But such accounts take it for granted that *S* has available a *set of hypotheses* to test, i.e. *S* comes to the experiment already equipped with a *hypothesis space* from which the hypotheses to be tested are selected. If this much is plausible, we need to go one step further and note that *S* must also have available a *procedure* for selecting hypotheses. There is ample evidence from the literature on concept learning to show that some hypotheses are more readily adopted than others, so we might be tempted by the view that the hypotheses submit to some sort of ordering with the procedure in question being sensitive to this.[3] Irrespective of the correctness of this view, *some* procedure for selecting hypotheses needs to be assumed.

The preceding discussion has identified four components in what we take to be the standard account of concept learning in the laboratory. These are: (1) a hypothesis space (equivalently, a learner); (2) data available to the learner; (3) a procedure by means of which the learner selects hypotheses; and (4) a criterion for learning.[4] The question we now pursue is whether language acquisition can be conceptualized in these terms.

1.2 Identification in the Limit

The earliest work of linguistic significance developed within the framework of the previous section is Gold (1967). He presented a set of learnability paradigms characterized by his notion of identification in the limit and, since virtually all subsequent formal work in this area builds on Gold's results, it is important to have a grasp of these. To achieve this, we shall consider each of the four components of the framework in turn.

For Gold, the hypothesis space with which the learner is equipped consists of *languages*, i.e. sets of sentences, and the learner's task is to determine to which of these languages he or she is being exposed. Thus, an implementation of the Gold paradigm will involve the specification of such a set of languages.[5]

What data are available to the learner in proceeding with this task? Gold assumes that time is quantized into discrete moments and that a datum is presented at each such moment; two importantly distinct paradigms are determined by making different assumptions about what a datum consists of.

The first of these yields *text presentation*. According to this, a sentence from the target language is presented at each moment in time. This condition restricts the available data to *positive instances* from the language. Additionally, *any* sentence in the target language will eventually appear in a data sequence. Equivalently, for any sentence in the target language, there is some finite time at which that sentence has been presented to the learner. Satisfaction of these two conditions, then, provides a definition of legitimate data sequence for text presentation.

The second mode of presentation is *informant presentation*. In this mode, at any instant of time a sentence from the target language *or a non-sentence* is presented along with the correct information about its status. In this condition, therefore, the learner is exposed to both *positive and negative instances* from the target language together with an indication of which category they belong to. Again, a legitimate data sequence is further constrained by the requirement that all sentences *and all non-sentences* eventually appear. It is important to clearly distinguish informant presentation from a situation in which a learner is presented with non-sentences which are *not* labelled as such. This latter situation represents one aspect of what Chomsky (1965) refers to as *degeneracy* in the data available to the child and intuitively is likely to be a hindrance for the learner. Informant presentation, on the other hand, is likely to be helpful.

We need not dwell too long on the details of procedures for selecting hypotheses (languages). We can assume that the languages constituting the hypothesis space are *enumerated* in some order or other, so that it makes sense to talk of a first, second, etc. language in the enumeration. Selection of hypotheses is then determined by this enumeration in the following way. When the learner is presented with the first sentence, he selects the first language in the enumeration and checks whether this sentence belongs to it. For text presentation, if it does, he adopts this first language as his hypothesis and awaits the second sentence; if it does not, he moves on to the second language in the enumeration and checks this. This process continues until he finds a language which includes the first sentence. This is then the hypothesis that he carries forward to the second sentence. For the second sentence, the procedure is repeated with the current language first being checked for whether it includes this sentence. If it does, this language is retained for the third sentence; if it does not, the learner proceeds through the enumeration until he finds a language which contains this second sentence *as well as the first sentence*. For informant presentation, we can easily imagine the parallel procedures, which differ only in that some data are such that they must be excluded from the hypothesized language.

Finally, we come to the acquisition criterion and it is this, *identification in the limit*, which gives the set of paradigms its name. The intuition behind this notion is transparent. If we are to say that a learner has succeeded in identifying the target language, the following situation should obtain: there should be some finite time at which the learner's hypothesis corresponds to the target language and at no time after that should this hypothesis change. Subject to obvious caveats about the continued acquisition of vocabulary, this appears to correspond reasonably closely to what we understand by the acquisition of a natural language, i.e. the child goes through a process of approximating more and more closely to the language of his or her environment and at some point this process stabilizes. At this point, we say that the child has acquired the language.

We can now proceed to some informal definitions on the basis of the above. The account we have given of the data available to the learner defines the notion of *legitimate data sequence for L*, where L is a language. In the case of text presentation, any sequence of sentences from L such that for every sentence in L, there is some finite position in the sequence at which it appears satisfies our definition. For informant presentation, a legitimate data sequence for L consists of any sequence of sentences from L and non-sentences, suitably annotated to show which is which, so long as for any sentence or non-sentence, there is a finite position in the sequence at which it appears. We now say that a language L is identifiable in the limit from data sequence S if there is some finite time at which the learner's hypothesis stabilizes on L when presented with S. More importantly, L is identifiable in the limit *tout court* if it is identifiable in the limit from *any* legitimate data sequence. Thus, for L to be identifiable in the limit requires a guarantee that the learner's hypothesis will stabilize on L no matter what order the data are presented in.[6] Note that this definition is applicable to both text and informant presentation.

Of course, we also need to consider a learner equipped with a set of hypotheses (languages) $\mathbf{L} = \{L_0, L_1, L_2, \ldots\}$, since this is a crucial element of the paradigm we are discussing. We say that such a set of languages is identifiable in the limit if each language in the set is itself identifiable in the limit, i.e. if any legitimate data sequence from L_i is presented, where L_i belongs to **L**, the learner's hypothesis will stabilize on L_i after some finite time. Again, this definition applies to both text and informant presentation. We shall now consider an illustration of these ideas.

1.3 An Illustration of the Identification in the Limit Paradigm

The example to which this section is devoted is by now a standard way of illustrating the sort of result that can be obtained using Gold's framework. As well as being implicit in his own original treatment, it is discussed in Wexler and Culicover (1980), Morgan (1986), Atkinson (1990) and Hammond (1990). Furthermore, it provides a first look at the sort of problem which motivates the Subset Principle of Wexler and Manzini (1987) – this will be of central concern to us in chapter 5. It is, therefore, of something more than illustrative interest. Some have felt that its significance extends even further, and this is something to which we shall briefly attend in the next section.

Consider, then, a learner confronted with the problem of identifying a language drawn from the set $\mathbf{L} = \{L_1, L_2, L_3, \ldots\}$ where the $L_i (i \geqslant 1)$ are as in (1):

(1) $L_1 = \{a, aa, aaa, \ldots\}$
    $L_2 = \quad \{aa, aaa, \ldots\}$
    $L_3 = \qquad \{aaa, \ldots\}$
    etc.

Here, each language has a single 'word' *a* and grammatical sentences consist of strings on this 'word'. L_1 contains *all* such strings, L_2 contains all such strings except *a*, L_3 all such strings except *a* and *aa*, and so on. There is an infinite number of languages in **L**.

In terms of the framework of the previous section, the languages in (1) constitute the hypothesis space available to the learner. Regarding data, we assume text presentation. Recall that what this means is that only grammatical sentences are presented and that for any grammatical sentence, there is some finite time in any legitimate data sequence at which it appears. Assume that the learning procedure is one in which a hypothesis is rejected when it cannot accommodate a new datum and that when this happens, a new hypothesis is selected according to the rule in (2):

(2)   set *i* in the hypothesis L_i as the length of the *shortest* string presented so far.

It is easy to see that this procedure provides a guarantee that the learner will eventually select the correct language and, once selected, this language will remain the learner's hypothesis throughout further data presentation. Why is this?

Assume for the sake of argument that L_5 is the presented language. Eventually, in any legitimate data sequence *aaaaa* will be presented and, at this point, will take over as the shortest string presented so far. Therefore, the rule in (2) will select L_5 at this point. Furthermore, no subsequent datum will be shorter than *aaaaa* – this string may itself be re-presented as the notion of legitimate data sequence does not rule out repetitions, but this will not cause the hypothesis to be changed – i.e., once L_5 is selected, it will remain the learner's hypothesis thenceforth. Obviously, this reasoning can be generalized to any language in **L**, so we can conclude that this class of languages is identifiable in the limit from text presentation.

It is noteworthy that each of the languages in **L** is *infinite*, and we might be tempted to believe that classes of languages, some of which are *finite*, will always be identifiable under these conditions. But this is not so, as is indicated by the class of languages $\mathbf{L}^* = \{L_0, L_1, L_2, L_3, \ldots\}$ defined as in (3):

(3) $L_0 = \{a, aa, aaa, aaaa, \ldots\}$
       $L_1 = \{a\}$
       $L_2 = \{a, aa\}$
       $L_3 = \{a, aa, aaa\}$
       etc.

Here, only L_0 is an infinite language, consisting of all strings on the 'word' *a*; each of the other languages contains a finite number of strings on this 'word'. Now consider what happens when $\mathbf{L}^*$ constitutes the learner's hypothesis space.

Again, we assume text presentation, and in this case we cannot define a procedure for the rejection and selection of hypotheses which will guarantee that the learner selects and retains the correct language after some finite time.

Think about how this might be done by producing a rule along the lines of (2). Such a rule could be 'conservative' and sensitive to the lengths of presented strings in a way similar to (2). In this case, longest strings appear to be important for identifying languages, so we might be attracted by the rule in (4):

(4) set i in L_i as the length of the *longest* string which has appeared in the data sequence so far.

This is fine, so long as the presented language is one of the *finite* languages. If, for example, the learner is being exposed to L_7, eventually *aaaaaaa* will be presented; at this point (4) will select L_7 and no subsequent datum will lead to this hypothesis being modified. But now suppose that the presented language is L_0, the infinite language. L_0 has no longest string and at any point in a data sequence, there will always be a string longer than any presented so far which has not yet appeared. Accordingly, while (4) will produce hypotheses and modify these as the data are presented, it will never stabilize on any one hypothesis; specifically, it will never stabilize on L_0.

What alternative to (4) might there be? We have labelled (4) 'conservative', and we might consider a 'non-conservative' strategy along the lines of (5):

(5) set i in L_i at 0.

Obviously, this strategy does stabilize on a particular hypothesis – there is no scope for changing hypotheses in its formulation. So long as the target language is L_0, this is not problematic; indeed, it is correct to say that L_0 is identified in the limit in such a system. Recall, however, that what is at issue is not identification in the limit of individual languages but of *classes* of languages; in this system, the finite languages are never hypothesized, let alone identified.

So, neither the 'conservative' nor the 'non-conservative' strategy guarantees identification in the limit for this class of languages. In fact, there is no learning procedure that yields this guarantee, not even systematic enumeration. To see this, assume that the languages in $\mathbf{L}^*$ are enumerated in some fashion and that hypothesis selection is governed by this enumeration. Consider two possibilities: (i) L_0 precedes some finite language L_n in the enumeration; (ii) every finite language precedes L_0 in the enumeration. Clearly, any enumeration satisfies either (i) or (ii). So now assume that in fact (i) is the case and that L_n is the target language. Because L_0 precedes L_n in the enumeration and because it is consistent with any data sequence drawn from L_n, it will be selected when it is reached. Further, no subsequent data from L_n will cause it to be rejected, with the result that L_n will be incorrectly identified as L_0. Alternatively, consider option (ii) with L_0 as the target. In this case, because an infinite number of finite languages precedes L_0 in the enumeration, the learning procedure will continue to change its hypothesis and there will be no finite time at which it chooses L_0. So L_0 will not be identified in the limit. The upshot of this is that no enumeration will yield the required guarantee and we must accept the conclusion that $\mathbf{L}^*$ is not identifiable from text.[7]

It is instructive to see how this situation is dramatically altered if we move to informant presentation and allow the learner access to negative instances labelled as such. Consider again L^* with hypothesis selection determined by the rule in (6):

(6)   set i in L_i initially at 0; if l is the length of the shortest presented non-sentence, set $i = l - 1$.

To see how this works, consider first the case where L_0 is the target. In these circumstances, there are no non-sentences to present, so the hypothesis, initially L_0, is maintained at this value, i.e. L_0 is successfully identified in the limit. What if the target language is one of the finite languages? In this situation, there will be non-sentences presented and, given our assumptions about legitimate data sequences, eventually the shortest of these will appear. At this point, (6) will set i at the appropriate value and no subsequent datum will modify this value, i.e. each of the finite languages is also successfully identified in the limit. We see, then, that increasing the amount of information available in the data can have a quite striking impact on learnability, a point of considerable significance which will be explored further in Section 1.5 and in chapter 2.

This section has illustrated how it is possible to demonstrate that specific, abstract learning problems, suitably specified, are or are not tractable. Of particular significance is the relationship between the languages in L^*, which are not identifiable from text. In an intuitively clear sense, L_0 – the single infinite language – is more general than any of the finite languages, and part of the problem we have identified is that of a learner being unable to retreat to a more specific hypothesis having adopted one which is too general. This issue will arise again in a linguistically much more interesting context when we discuss the Subset Principle in chapter 5.

1.4 Is the Illustration Empirically Significant?

Is the example from the previous section of more than illustrative significance? To assess this, it is necessary to take a short, informal excursion into formal grammar theory.

Largely under the impetus of the development of generative grammar, the 1950s and 1960s witnessed developments in the study of the mathematical properties of grammars of various types (see, for example, Chomsky, 1963; Miller and Chomsky, 1963). These were particularly concerned with *rewrite systems* which were familiar to linguists from their work with context-free and context-sensitive phrase-structure grammars.

For our purposes, we can assume that any rewrite system contains an alphabet of symbols which can be partitioned into two subsets, a *non-terminal vocabulary* and a *terminal vocabulary*. Readers of this book will be familiar with this as the distinction between those symbols which are expanded or rewritten in phrase structure trees (S, NP, V, etc.) and those symbols which appear at the ends of branches of such trees (typically lexical items and grammatical morphemes), but the study of formal grammar merely requires two disjoint vocabularies. Additionally, within the non-terminal vocabulary, there is a designated symbol (typically S for 'sentence') which initiates any derivation. Derivations are produced by applying *rules* to symbols and it is the *type* of rules included in a system which determines what sort of rewrite system we have.

Specifically, we might first impose no constraints on the rules, allowing any rule to appear in a system which rewrites any string of symbols from the two vocabularies as any other string of symbols. If a system contains rules of this type, it is an *unrestricted rewrite system* (URS).

Second, we can restrict rules so that only single symbols from the non-terminal vocabulary are rewritten at any point in a derivation.[8] However, other symbols may appear in the statement of such rules, and when they do, they constitute a *context* for the rewriting of the symbol. To illustrate, adopting the convention that capital letters correspond to non-terminal vocabulary and lower case letters to terminal vocabulary, the rules in (7) are of this type:

(7)   a. $abABc \rightarrow abCDBc$

   b. $aC \rightarrow abc$

Example (7a) rewrites the non-terminal A as the string of non-terminals CD so long as it is preceded by the string of terminals ab (a left context) and followed by the mixed string Bc (a right context). Example (7b) rewrites the non-terminal C as the string of terminals bc when it is preceded by the single terminal a with no conditions on what follows it – the right context is empty.

For reasons which should be obvious, rules of this type are referred to as *context-sensitive rules* and a rewrite system which contains such rules and no unrestricted rewrite rules is known as a *context-sensitive grammar* (CSG). Note that any context-sensitive rule is also an unrestricted rule – it legitimizes the rewriting of a string of non-terminals and terminals as another such string – so it follows that any CSG will also be a URS. There will, however, be URSs which are not CSGs, namely those containing unrestricted rewrite rules which are not context-sensitive rules.

The next restriction is to allow only rules which rewrite single non-terminal symbols irrespective of context. Following the conventions introduced above, the rules in (8) are of this type:

(8)   a. $A \rightarrow BCD$

   b. $B \rightarrow CaA$

Example (8a) permits the single non-terminal A to be rewritten as the string of non-terminals BCD wherever it appears in a derivation; (8b) allows B to be rewritten as the mixed string CaA anywhere. Rules like those in (8) are known as *context-free rules* and any system containing rules of this type (with no context-sensitive or unrestricted rules) is known as a *context-free grammar* (CFG). Again, it is easy to see that any CFG is also a CSG (all contexts are empty), but there will be CSGs which are not CFGs – those which contain any rules with non-empty contexts.

Finally, we can impose a restriction on the string which appears as a result of the application of a context-free rule, requiring it to contain at most *one* non-terminal symbol. Neither rule in (8) satisfies this condition, but those in (9) do:

(9)   a. $A \rightarrow bcBcb$

    b. $B \rightarrow cd$

Example (9a) rewrites the single non-terminal A as a string containing the single non-terminal B along with preceding and following terminals; (9b) replaces the single non-terminal B by a string of terminals which, of course, contains *at most* a single non-terminal.

Rules satisfying this condition have a variety of names, but we shall refer to them as *finite-state rules*. A system containing rules of this type, and none of those we have introduced earlier, is known as a *finite state grammar* (FSG). Once more, it is clear that any FSG is a CFG since the rules of an FSG are simply context-free rules with an additional restriction; but there will be CFGs which are not FSGs, specifically those containing rules like those illustrated in (8).

What we have so far, then, is four classes of rewrite systems and an informal demonstration that a relationship of proper inclusion holds between them. That is, if we refer to the classes of unrestricted rewrite systems, context-sensitive grammars, context-free grammars and finite state grammars as G_0, G_1, G_2 and G_3 respectively, our discussion has indicated that (10) holds:

(10) $G_3 \subset G_2 \subset G_1 \subset G_0$

Here $\subset$ represents set-theoretic proper inclusion.

Alongside these classes of rewrite systems, we can consider the classes of languages which can be generated by such systems. Given the distinction between terminal and non-terminal vocabularies, it is easy enough to define the notion of *terminated derivation* as one to which no further rules apply and that of *terminal string* as the last line of a terminated derivation consisting entirely of terminal symbols. Thus, with a rewrite system specified, we can consider the set of terminal strings produced by that system as the language generated by it. The classes of languages generated by rewrite systems of particular types can then be referred to as L_0, L_1, L_2 and L_3, paralleling the notation introduced for types of grammars above. L_0 is the class of languages that can be generated by unrestricted rewrite systems – the *recursively enumerable languages*; L_1 is the class of languages that can be generated by context-sensitive grammars – *the context-sensitive languages*; L_2 is the class of languages that can be generated by context-free grammars – the *context-free languages*; and L_3 is the class of languages that can be generated by finite state grammars – *the finite state languages*.

From the set-theoretic relationship between grammar types in (10), we can see that a relationship of inclusion holds between these classes of languages, i.e. where $\subseteq$ represents inclusion, (11) obtains:

(11) $L_3 \subseteq L_2 \subseteq L_1 \subseteq L_0$

This is because any language in, say, L_3 is generated by a grammar in G_3. But any grammar in G_3 is also in G_2, so the language in question is also in L_2. Similar reasoning applies to any pair in (11).

In fact, it is possible to strengthen the inclusions in (11) to proper inclusions by demonstrating the existence of languages which belong to L_i but not to L_{i+1} ($0 \leqslant i \leqslant 2$), but it would take us too far afield to go into this here. So, we can replace (11) by (12):

(12) $L_3 \subset L_2 \subset L_1 \subset L_0$

This is simply a statement of what is often referred to as the *Chomsky Hierarchy*, and it is customary to represent this in a 'doughnut' fashion as in (13).

(13)

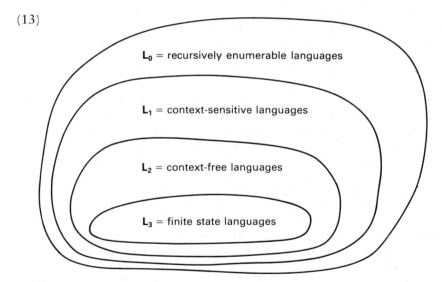

Why should this be of any interest in the present context?

If we return to the class of languages L^* from the previous section, it is easy to show that each of these is a finite state language. Take one of the finite languages in L^*, say $L_4 = \{a, aa, aaa, aaaa\}$, and consider a grammar which contains the single non-terminal symbol S, the single terminal symbol a, and the rules in (14):

(14) $S \rightarrow a$
 $S \rightarrow aa$
 $S \rightarrow aaa$
 $S \rightarrow aaaa$

This is a finite state grammar, since each of the rules allows a single non-terminal symbol to be rewritten as a string containing at most one non-terminal symbol, and obviously a similar grammar can be produced for any of the finite languages in $\mathbf{L}^*$. What about the single infinite language $L_0 = \{a, aa, aaa, \ldots\}$? A finite state grammar, again employing just a single non-terminal symbol S, that will generate this language appears in (15):

(15) $S \rightarrow aS$
 $S \rightarrow a$

The first rule here is recursive and guarantees that the grammar can generate arbitrarily long strings, but it is also a finite state rule since the right-hand side contains only a single non-terminal symbol.

From the above, it follows that $\mathbf{L}^*$ is a subset of the set of finite state languages. But now note that if a certain set of languages is not identifiable in the limit on a specific set of assumptions, any superset of this set of languages will also have this property – if there is no effective strategy for searching through a set of hypotheses, this situation will not be improved by extending the set.[9] So the set of finite state languages is also not identifiable from text presentation. And of course the same goes for the larger classes in the Chomsky Hierarchy, and we can conclude that none of L_0, L_1, L_2 or L_3 is identifiable in the limit from text.

The question of whether text presentation is an appropriate assumption in the context of natural language acquisition is an issue we shall consider in the next section. For now, let us assume that it is and pursue the consequences of the above conclusion. Given the Chomsky Hierarchy, a question that immediately arises is: where, if anywhere, does the class of possible natural languages fit? This was a question which was largely inspired by Chomsky's (1957) demonstration that English is not a finite state language and Postal's (1964) claims that constructions exist in the Amerindian language Mohawk which show that this language is not context-free. Such observations might be taken to entail that the class of possible natural languages is at least a superset of the class of context-free languages, in which case non-identifiability of this class from text follows by the above reasoning. If learnability is equated with identification in the limit, we conclude that the class of possible natural languages is not learnable from text. But this class is learnable, as is witnessed repeatedly by small children. Something has gone wrong.

The argument of the previous paragraph only proceeds on the basis of a number of contentious assumptions, and we shall attend to some of these in the next section. Here, we shall point to one step in the argument which can be resisted: it is mistaken to seek to identify the class of possible human languages with some concentric circle in (13). Most obviously, the class of finite state languages, and therefore each of the other classes, properly includes the class of *finite cardinality languages* – those languages which contain only finite numbers of sentences. Indeed, above we presented a finite state grammar for the language L_4 which is just such a finite cardinality language. Now, there is every reason to believe that no finite cardinality language is a possible human language – all languages which have been investigated provide some means for embedding structures recursively, thereby ensuring that they contain an infinite number of well-formed sentences (the consequences for learnability of restricting the learner's hypothesis space so as to exclude finite cardinality languages are briefly discussed in Section 1.6). From this it immediately follows that the class of possible natural languages cannot be assigned a position on the Chomsky Hierarchy.[10]

The fallacy, then, in attempting to draw conclusions about learnability from the formal properties of grammars is in the assumption that the class of possible human languages can be characterized in rather simplistic mathematical terms. It seems more plausible to suggest that their ultimate characterization is going to be biological, and there is no reason to believe that biological criteria will give rise to systems which are easily accommodated in a hierarchy which is founded on mathematical criteria (for more detailed discussion of this issue, see Lasnik, 1981; Berwick and Weinberg, 1982; for instances of being seduced by mathematical criteria, see Levelt, 1974; Gazdar, 1982).

This section has pursued one sense in which the abstract illustration of the previous section might have been significant in a more general context. Our conclusion is that to see such significance would be misguided. We now turn to ways in which the Gold paradigm might present a misleading picture.

1.5 The Empirical Status of the Identification in the Limit Paradigm

Our learnability framework includes four components, and the identification in the limit paradigm makes explicit assumptions about each of these. This section discusses these assumptions with a view to assessing the role they might play in a plausible theory of first language acquisition.

Consider first, then, the hypothesis space. It would, of course, be possible to assume that there is *no* a priori delimitation of this space with the child approaching first language acquisition totally uninformed as to the nature of the systems he or she will encounter. Such a view might be ascribed to the programme of linguistic description envisaged by American structuralists, in so far as this embodied an account of first language acquisition. For example, Bloomfield (1933, p. 20) says:

> The only useful generalizations about language are inductive generalizations. Features which we think ought to be universal may be absent from the very next language that becomes accessible.

Such a perspective, echoed by Joos's (1957) notorious remark that 'languages could differ from each other without limit and in unpredictable ways', suggests that any attempt to impose substantive constraints on the child's hypothesis space is doomed to failure. The affinities between this approach and psychological behaviourism can be readily appreciated by noting that the latter perceived language acquisition as not involving any specialized representational capacity or developmental mechanisms; rather, it was just another species of learned behaviour and as such was to be accounted for by simple learning principles. These principles were assumed to be operative within an initially uninformed organism; consequently, any similarities in acquired systems would simply reflect the nature of the learning principles. It is no accident that when neo-behaviourist psychologists such as Osgood (1963) discovered the methods and results of the American structuralist tradition, they saw it as amenable to a behaviourist interpretation.[11]

One of the earliest achievements of the approach to linguistics inspired by Chomsky was to demonstrate the descriptive poverty of the methodologically guided structuralist approach. With this demonstration came the insistence that the child approaches language acquisition equipped a priori with knowledge about the general form of language. This a priori knowledge is, from our perspective, nothing more than a specification of a hypothesis space which simultaneously delimits the child's options as far as language acquisition is concerned and also makes such acquisition possible. The arguments leading to this conclusion will be a constant theme throughout this book.[12]

What should the hypotheses comprising the hypothesis space consist of? In the simple illustrations of the Gold paradigm we have considered, these have been languages, construed as sets of sentences, but as soon as we take seriously the view that the hypothesis space is mentally represented in the child, the inappropriateness of this suggestion is apparent. To see this, we have only to consider what we are committed to when we assert that someone is a speaker of English. From a mentalist perspective, we obviously wish to identify this condition with the person being in a certain mental state. However, the content of this mental state does not correspond to a listing of all the possible sentences in English. As already observed, the number of sentences in any natural language is infinite and minds, ultimately brains, have finite capacities. To see the child, embarking on language acquisition, as initially provided with a set of (infinite) sets of sentences is, if anything, even more bizarre.

Indeed, identifying English with a set of sentences is itself a somewhat dubious strategy if we adopt Chomsky's view (1980, 1986a) that languages, understood in this way, are epiphenomenal and not amenable to scientific investigation. Chomsky (1986a) distinguishes E-languages from I-languages, the former being sets of sentences, somehow construed, with the 'E' suggesting 'external', and the latter corresponding to systems of mental representation, the 'I' indicating 'internal'. He says (p. 26):

> The technical concept of E-language is a dubious one . . . languages in this sense are not real-world objects but are artificial, somewhat arbitrary, and perhaps not very interesting constructs. In contrast, the steady state of knowledge attained and the initial state S_0 [what we are here calling the initial hypothesis space – MA] are real elements of particular minds/brains . . .

Thus, I-languages constitute the proper domain for scientific linguistic study.

What, then, are we to make of the claim that someone is a speaker of English? This now becomes a sociopolitical assertion which could be recast as follows: the person in question has an internal system of representation (an I-language), the overt products of which (utterance production and interpretation, grammaticality judgements), in conjunction with other mental capacities, are such that that person is judged (by those deemed capable of judging) to be a speaker of English. From this perspective, it is, of course, natural that individuals with different I-languages can be judged to be speakers of the same E-language, a situation which should give rise to no puzzlement.

Returning, then, to our question of what a speaker of English mentally represents, it is an I-language, or, in more traditional terminology, a *grammar*. If this appears an appropriate answer for this question, it also provides the basis for an answer to the question about the initial hypothesis space. This must now consist of a delimitation of a class of possible grammars. Proposals on the exact form this takes are hypotheses about the nature of what Chomsky and his associates refer to as *Universal Grammar* (UG), and chapters 2 and 3 will explore evolving interpretations of this notion within generative grammar. The task of the child is that of selecting one (or more) of the possible grammars supplied by UG. This process takes place in the context of *primary linguistic data*, and we now turn to this component of the Gold paradigm.

As already indicated, Gold considered two modes of data presentation to a learner, text presentation and informant presentation. These have an important property in common: a guarantee that if the learner waits around long enough, each possible datum (grammatical sentence in the case of text, sentence or non-sentence in the case of informant) will appear in a legitimate data sequence. Before discussing the plausibility of this assumption for the natural language learner, we shall first attend to what distinguishes the two modes.

That the distinction between them is formally important has already been illustrated by our simple example in Section 1.3: L^* is not identifiable in the limit from text, but is so identifiable from informant. Which of the modes, if either, is appropriate for the situation confronting the child?

Recall first that we have previously distinguished informant presentation from another way in which non-sentences may be involved in the child's linguistic environment. Chomsky (1965) makes much of the degenerate nature of the data available to the child, and part of what he means by this is that the child is surrounded by utterances which are not tokens of well-formed sentences in the adult language.[13] But such utterances are *not* labelled for the child as inappropriate strings in the language, and are to be clearly distinguished from the non-sentences contemplated in informant presentation. Indeed, whereas we have seen that informant presentation facilitates language identification, it is intuitively clear that the phenomenon Chomsky has in mind could only hinder this process. Chomsky (1980) draws an analogy with the task of an initially uninformed observer attempting to induce the rules of chess, when the players occasionally break the rules without giving any indication that they are so doing. Whether ill-formed sentences unlabelled as such do form a significant part of the child's linguistic environment is, in fact, disputed

(Newport, Gleitman and Gleitman, 1977), but it is worth noting that only a small number of aberrations of this kind might render the child's task considerably more difficult.

Putting this issue aside, is there evidence that the child's situation is more akin to informant presentation than to text presentation? The answer which is generally accepted is that there is not. First, it is incontestable that adults do not systematically provide tokens of ill-formed sentences explicitly informing children of their ill-formedness, this being the situation that corresponds most closely to informant presentation. Additionally, informant presentation requires that *all* non-sentences appear at some point in a legitimate data sequence, and clearly this is not a situation that children enjoy.

It may none the less be the case that children are provided with *some* information about ill-formedness of a less direct kind. If this is so, we ought to know about it, even if it does not amount to full-blown informant presentation. A number of possible indirect sources of negative evidence were considered in a classic study by Brown and Hanlon (1970). These included correction contingent on the child's utterances being grammatically ill-formed, negative reinforcement of the child's ill-formed utterances, and failure of the adult to comply with the child's desires when these were expressed using ill-formed constructions. Their well-known conclusions were that none of these factors seemed to be sensitive to grammatical ill-formedness and could not therefore be construed as providing the child with indirect negative evidence.[14]

Furthermore, when overt correction does appear, the child being corrected appears to be remarkably resistant to its intended effects. An oft-cited example, reported by McNeill (1966), is (16):

(16)   CHILD: Nobody don't like me.
       MOTHER: No, say 'Nobody likes me'.
       CHILD: Nobody don't like me.
       (dialogue repeated eight times)
       MOTHER: Now listen carefully, say 'Nobody likes me'.
       CHILD: Oh! Nobody don't likes me.

A rather different conception of indirect negative evidence is formulated by Chomsky (1981), where he maintains that if the child's current grammar predicts as occurring certain structures which do not occur, the child may conclude that these are ill-formed and modify his or her grammar accordingly. Chomsky expresses optimism that a language-learning model utilizing this assumption could be developed and, indeed, Oehrle (1985) and Lasnik (1985) have taken some preliminary steps in this direction (see also Saleemi, 1990, forthcoming). The vast majority of workers in language acquisition, however, have been sufficiently impressed by the observations ruling out labelled negative data, that the view that the child's situation more closely approximates text presentation is taken as virtually axiomatic. This *No Negative Data Assumption* will play an important role in subsequent chapters.

Let us return now to what text and informant presentation have in common in the Gold paradigm.

The assumption that a child has access to all sentences (or sentences and non-sentences) in a language during the course of first language acquisition can clearly not be sustained, and the identification in the limit paradigm is empirically most implausible at this point. Given the infinite nature of any possible human language, it is transparent that such systems are acquired on the basis of only a fragment of the possible evidence, and Hornstein and Lightfoot (1981) see this as one of the crucial respects in which the data available to the child are deficient. While the observation that the child must acquire a system with infinite capacity on the basis of a finite corpus of data is correct, it is not clear that this of itself constitutes an argument for a highly specific UG as part of the child's innate endowment. In particular, all that is at issue here is the specification of an inductive mechanism which can formulate rules on the basis of the observation of regularities in a corpus, and there is no reason in principle why the data-analytic procedures of the American structuralists should not have this property.[15]

More interesting is the suggestion that the set of utterances to which children are exposed has properties over and above finiteness; specifically, its members are *simple* in some sense, and this simplicity facilitates the language acquisition task, reducing the need for a priori constraints. This proposal is a particularization of a more general claim that the data available to the learner are *ordered*, and before evaluating it, it will be useful to see an illustration of its formal power.

Recall $\mathbf{L}^*$ from Section 1.3 and the demonstration that this class of languages could not be identified from text. Text was, of course, understood in a particular way when we defined a legitimate data sequence. Now consider a more constrained definition of this notion, whereby sentences from the target language in $\mathbf{L}^*$ are presented in order of increasing length. For the finite languages, once all of the sentences have appeared, the sequence returns to the shortest sentence and begins again. It is easy to see that the procedure for selecting hypotheses in (17) will ensure identifiability in the limit for $\mathbf{L}^*$:

(17)   set i in L_i initially at 0; if any presented sentence is not longer than its predecessor in the sequence, reset i at the length of the predecessor.

If the target language is L_0, the initial hypothesis will never be modified as the presented sentences will continue to increase in length, i.e. L_0 will be identified in the limit. If, however, the target language is one of the finite languages, say L_3, a legitimate data sequence for this language will be as in (18):

(18)   ⟨a, aa, aaa, a, aa, aaa, a, . . . ⟩

As soon as the fourth sentence in this sequence is encountered, (17) will operate, and i will be set to 3. Subsequent operations of (17) will leave this setting unchanged, so L_3 will be identified in the limit, as will any other of the finite languages in the set. Thus, we see that it is possible to code information about the identity of the target language into the sequence of presented sentences, thereby ensuring learnability for classes of languages which are not learnable if weaker assumptions are made about the data (for further discussion, see Wexler and Culicover, 1980; Morgan, 1986).

So much for the power of order in the data; what of simplicity? First, it should be noted that those who have proposed that ordered data in acquisition will be useful (e.g. Levelt, 1975; Brown, 1977) have not been in a position to offer the sort of demonstration illustrated by the above example. Rather, they have assumed, without substantial argument, that simple data at the early stages will facilitate first language acquisition. This assumption is associated with at least two problems, one empirical, the other conceptual.

The empirical problem arises once we begin to push the notion of simplicity. What exactly do supporters of this position have in mind? A relevant study was conducted by Newport, Gleitman and Gleitman (1977). These authors developed a number of syntactic criteria against which they could measure the characteristics of the speech addressed to children by their mothers and compare it to adult-directed speech. Interestingly, they found that the speech of one adult to another was *simpler* than the child-directed speech on each of these measures. Of course, it is possible to dispute the validity of the criteria used by Newport et al., but the fact remains that one important study which analytically addressed the question of simplicity in the speech directed to young children failed to find any evidence for it.

The conceptual problem is of wider scope and raises a very general issue for much of what we are discussing in this chapter. It depends on the following argument. Suppose that, in fact, the data available to the child are simple and that what this means is that they do not display the full extent of structural complexity found in the target language. Another way to put this would be to say that the *information* about the structure of a language contained in a sequence which is restricted to contain simple data is not as great as that contained in an unrestricted data sequence. Demonstrably, children acquire their native language and, from the present perspective, they do this on the basis of information with which they are supplied a priori – i.e. constraints on the hypotheses they are capable of entertaining – and information contained in the data to which they are exposed. The position advocated by Brown, Levelt and others says that the extent of a priori knowledge necessary can be reduced by paying attention to the simplicity of the data available to the learner. But it should be obvious that if the protagonists are agreed on the endpoint of development, and there is no suggestion that they are not, this conclusion is quite misguided. To offer a simple arithmetic analogy, the position requires that in the equation (19), we can reduce a, reduce b and still get c:

(19) $a + b = c$

In fact, what follows from the observation that data are simple is that commitments to innate factors become *more* and not less necessary (for further discussion of this argument, see Wexler, 1982). Note that this observation is entirely consistent with our discussion of the identifiability of L^* above. In that case, no ill-defined notion of simplicity was at issue in the ordering of data; rather, the ordering in the data was explicitly encoding information about the identity of the target language.

Despite the negative tone of the preceding remarks, we must continue to acknowledge that the idea of a data sequence containing all possible data is preposterous. Furthermore, we must take account of the fact that most of the language addressed to children, while perhaps not syntactically simple in any definable sense, does consist of *short* utterances, a fact that must be recognized in the assumptions we make in a plausible model of first language acquisition (see Sections 2.3, 2.4 and 9.3 for further relevant discussion).

Let us now consider procedures for the selection of hypotheses from the hypothesis space. In the abstract illustrations which have appeared earlier, two sorts of procedures have been considered. One of these, exemplified by (2), (6) and (17), construed the learning procedure as a *function* from data sequences to hypotheses. Thus, consider (2), repeated here as (20):

(20)　set i in L_i as the length of the shortest string which has appeared in the data so far.

This can be recast as a function in the following way. For any string s, let $l(s)$ designate the length of s. For any sequence of strings $\langle s_1, s_2, \ldots, s_n \rangle$, let $F(\langle s_1, s_2, \ldots, s_n \rangle) = min\ (l(s_1), l(s_2), \ldots, l(s_n))$, where *min* is a function which has as value the smallest of a set of positive integers. Then the learning procedure in (20) is represented by the function G in (21):

(21)　For any data sequence, $S = \langle s_1, s_2, \ldots, s_n \rangle$, $G(S) = L_{F(S)}$.

G is a function from data sequences to hypotheses, and it should be clear that it has exactly the same consequences as the statement in (20).

The other notion we have considered is that of a learning procedure operating via an enumeration of hypotheses from the hypothesis space, and, in the case of $\mathbf{L}^*$ not being identifiable from text, we showed that this conclusion was derivable even if we assumed such an enumeration of hypotheses. It would be inappropriate here to go into the technicalities underlying these ideas, but one point of interest which is readily apparent suggests that the learning procedures we have utilized are not particularly plausible from an empirical perspective.

To see the problem, consider again (20) and its functional formulation in (21). This requires that the learner must be in a position to determine whether the current datum *is* the shortest in the whole data sequence. But, in order for this to be possible, it is necessary for the learner to have available all previous data in the sequence; in other words, such a learning procedure requires *complete memory* for previous data. Transferring this to first language acquisition immediately highlights its implausibility. The suggestion that children remember (in such a way as to have access to) all previous utterances to which they have been exposed is not one we are likely to be attracted by.

Similar reservations hold of enumeration as a learning procedure. Recall that what is supposed to happen here is that the learner tests incoming data against an ordered set of hypotheses, moving on to the next hypothesis whenever the current hypothesis fails to accommodate a datum. The rejection of a hypothesis in this way is clearly *local* in that it is occasioned by a single datum which is currently available. However, the selection of a new hypothesis is constrained by having to deal not only with the current datum but also with *all previous data*. That this latter is necessary is clear; without it, the hypothesis selection mechanism would constantly be at the mercy of local factors and in accommodating these, it might well fail to be consistent with earlier presented data. So the success of enumeration depends again on the availability of all previous data (see Section 2.3 for discussion of this within a linguistically more interesting context).

There is one further factor which should temper any enthusiasm we might feel for the learning procedures we have met so far. This is that they involve *comprehensive* switches from one hypothesis to another, and it is difficult to see a role here for the *gradual* approximation to the correct system, which intuitively appears to characterize first language acquisition. Again, this issue will receive more attention in Section 2.3.

The final component of the Gold paradigm is the criterion for acquisition – identifiability in the limit itself – and here we can be brief. First, it seems that *something* along these lines must be appropriate for the child, i.e. there is some point in the child's development at which the linguistic system is established with a particular form and from that point onwards there are no significant modifications. Other criteria for acquisition can be readily conceptualized. For example, we could contemplate a learner who, having selected the correct hypothesis, subsequently abandons it but is guaranteed to return to it after some finite time. But it is not at all clear why we should take such a possibility seriously. For discussion of a range of options, see Wexler and Culicover (1980), Osherson, Stob and Weinstein (1982, 1986). In Sections 2.3 and 2.4, we shall discuss an alternative which remains in the spirit of identifiability in the limit.

Of rather more concern is the role of the 'limit'. In Gold's system, the only requirement is that there should be *some* finite time at which the learner converges on the correct hypothesis, but, of course, children appear to manage this in a relatively short time without exhibiting much variation among themselves. This latter observation is particularly noteworthy if the data to which they are exposed vary significantly (if, in Gold's terms, they are exposed to radically different data sequences). It therefore appears necessary to impose some relatively fixed limit on the time by which convergence must have taken place, a condition which amounts to satisfying what Pinker (1979) refers to as the Time Constraint.

In this section, we have surveyed the various components of the identifiability in the limit model and raised some of the difficulties which arise when we attempt to match it to the natural language acquisition situation. None of this should be seen as critical of Gold's work or of work developing from it. In introducing the framework he did, he made it possible to conceptualize first language acquisition in a novel manner and to focus attention on a number of fundamental questions. Also, of course, he demonstrated the feasibility of producing results within this framework.

One feature of subsequent work, building on that of Gold and largely conducted by Osherson and his colleagues, has been to manipulate the assumptions of the Gold model to produce a rich variety of learning systems.

Some of these manipulations are specifically designed to produce empirically more plausible systems. In the next section, we shall briefly consider some of the more interesting of these.

1.6 Alternative Learning Models

The four components of acquisition models are as in (22):

(22)   a. a hypothesis space
      b. data available to the learner
      c. a procedure for selecting hypotheses
      d. a criterion for acquisition

It is possible to manipulate assumptions under each of these headings and we have already sketched some of the consequences of doing this. Thus, we have considered the hypothesis spaces defined by **L** and **L*** in Section 1.3 and those comprising the Chomsky Hierarchy in Section 1.4. Text and informant presentation comprise different assumptions about data, and procedures for selecting hypotheses outlined earlier have included some simple functions and enumeration. Finally, at the end of the previous section, we briefly mentioned the possibility of adopting different assumptions about the criterion for acquisition.

In a series of publications, Osherson and his colleagues have described a large number of learning paradigms by systematically modifying one or more of the assumptions in (22) while keeping the others constant (see Osherson and Weinstein (1982), Osherson, Stob and Weinstein (1982, 1984, 1986)). This work is highly technical, relying extensively on concepts from the mathematical theory of recursive functions and computability, so I shall not attempt a detailed summary of it here. However, it is possible to convey the general tenor and some of the more significant results informally.

The sort of conclusion in which Osherson et al. are interested is one where the class of sets of languages which can be learned on one set of assumptions regarding (22b, c and d) is properly contained in the class which can be learned on a different set. In showing that **L*** is identifiable in the limit from informant presentation but not from text presentation, we changed the assumption under (22b) in such a way as to yield a larger class of identifiable sets of languages.[16]

Consider, then, (22c) and ways in which we might modify assumptions about the learning procedure. In the previous section, we gave an example to show how one such procedure could be construed as a function, and this functional emphasis is adopted by Osherson et al. throughout their work. A restricted class of functions is known as the *computable* functions, the idea being that these are the functions for which a finite computational device can be guaranteed to produce the value of the function for any argument. If minds (or brains) are finite computational devices – the orthodox stance in cognitive science – and if a learning theory is embodied in a mind, it is plausible to suggest that the learning procedure included in that learning theory should correspond to a computable function.

Is the restriction to computable learning procedures interesting? It is, because Osherson et al. are able to prove that it is *restrictive* in the sense that there are classes of languages which are learnable by non-computable functions but not learnable by computable functions. Note that the proof of this requires that other assumptions in the learning model, namely assumptions about data and the acquisition criterion, remain constant.

More interestingly, we noted above (Section 1.4) that no natural language is a finite cardinality language. It is plausible, therefore, to assume that the child's hypothesis space does not admit such languages as candidate natural languages. In terms of Osherson et al.'s approach, this can be captured by restricting learning functions to those which never take a finite cardinality language as value.

Does this restriction on learning procedures have implications for classes of learnable languages? Obviously it does if the class of languages in question contains one or more finite cardinality languages; these languages will now never be identified. Intriguingly, however, it also has consequences for the learnability of classes of languages all of whose members contain infinite numbers of sentences. There are classes of languages with this property which are learnable by a computable learning function but are not learnable by a computable learning function which never hypothesizes a finite cardinality language. What this means is that if, as seems plausible, the child's hypothesis space does not admit finite cardinality languages, this restricts the classes of *infinite* languages that can be identified; such a consequence is not intuitively obvious.

Turning now to data, in the previous section we discussed the possibility that children are exposed to non-sentences which are not labelled as such, suggesting that such a situation might have serious implications for language learning. Osherson et al. explore this issue by introducing the notion of a *noisy text*, which is characterized by a finite number of non-grammatical intrusions. Our intuition that such intrusions would be significant is confirmed by the conclusion that there are classes of languages which are learnable on (standard) text but not on noisy text. Again, it is important to note that this proof requires other assumptions in the learning model to remain constant.

Again in the previous section, we considered the implausibility of the assumption regarding text presentation that for every well-formed sentence in the target language, there is a finite time at which that sentence appears in a data sequence. Abandoning the assumption commits us to texts being *incomplete* in the sense that there are well-formed sentences in the language which do not appear in them. Osherson et al. formally define this notion of incomplete text and are able to show that there are classes of languages which are learnable from complete text but not from incomplete text. Note how this interacts with the conceptual problem raised in the previous section for the view that the data available to the child are 'simple'. The Osherson et al. result shows that if languages are to be learned from incomplete text, they must be constrained over and above whatever constraints are necessary for learning from standard text. But such constraints are no less than constraints on the hypothesis space, and from the perspective adopted here, this amounts to an enrichment of the child's innate endowment.

Finally, it is worth drawing attention to a result proved in Osherson et al. (1984), since the idea will appear again in a different context in chapters 3 and 10. The result is that, given a particular set of assumptions in the learning model, the class of languages which can be learned by that model is *finite*. Osherson et al. are tempted by the view that their assumptions are empirically plausible, and are therefore disposed to the conclusion that the class of possible natural languages is finite. What assumptions are necessary to derive this rather strong conclusion?

There are three of these, one concerned with the data and two with the learning procedure. The assumption about data is mercifully straightforward and simply subscribes to language acquisition proceeding on noisy text. Regarding the learning procedure, this is assumed to be *local* in the sense already introduced in the previous section. There we noted the implausibility of a learning procedure having access to all previous data, and the locality assumption appearing in this proof simply formalizes this by placing a finite bound on the number of previous data which the procedure may consult. Finally, the procedure is *conservative* in that it will not modify its hypothesis without appropriate evidence that it should do so.[17] Certainly, none of these assumptions is immediately implausible and the result that such a learning model can only identify a finite class of languages is therefore significant.

1.7 Summary

In this chapter, we have introduced a general, abstract framework for considering the acquisition of language. This four-component framework will underlie a great deal of the subsequent discussion in this book.

We have also investigated, in an informal way, some of the results which have been obtained within this framework in the theory of learnability. The point of this was twofold: first, to show how it is possible to come to definite conclusions on the learnability or non-learnability of a class of objects (languages) once the assumptions within the framework are in place; second, to comment on the gap between the assumptions which were made in the earliest work in this tradition and the actual situation in which children acquiring their first language find themselves, and to discuss some of the factors involved in closing this gap. Formal learnability will appear again in Sections 2.3 and 2.4, where it will be linked much more closely to the work of linguists than anything we have seen in this chapter. However, the remainder of the book will rely on the learnability emphasis not so much for formal analysis, but to enable us to raise, and in some cases throw light on, a wide range of empirical problems in first language acquisition.

2 Standard Theory and Language Acquisition

Introduction

The Standard Theory of transformational generative grammar (henceforth ST), usually seen as having its most representative formulation in Chomsky (1965), was a reference point for a generation of research into language acquisition. This research, represented by such detailed grammatical descriptions as appear in Bloom (1970), Brown (1973) and Bowerman (1973), adopted (and sometimes adapted) the formalisms developed by linguists, and attempted to chart the syntactic development of children in terms of a series of grammars.

This chapter offers a brief presentation of ST and discusses the sense in which it was intended to contribute to an understanding of language acquisition. Because our interest is in conveying the general character of the approach, in particular its reliance on *rules*, there is no attempt to be comprehensive. Illustrative examples will be sufficient for our purposes, and the reader who is interested in having a wider overview is referred to one of the many textbooks which broadly adopt this perspective (e.g. Akmajian and Heny, 1975; Culicover, 1976).

Following on from the considerations of the previous chapter, it is of considerable interest that the theory of language acquisition advocated in ST has been formally interpreted in terms of learnability. The chapter continues, then, with an outline of the work of Wexler and his colleagues on the learnability of transformational grammars and of subsequent developments within this framework, due to Morgan (1986).

Finally, we shall discuss some of the reasons for the abandonment of ST, which can also be seen as motivations for the Principles and Parameters approach introduced in the next chapter. Of course, the transition from one theory to another was not instantaneous, and students of linguistics will no doubt be familiar with labels such as Extended Standard Theory and Revised Extended Standard Theory. Interested readers are referred to Newmeyer (1980) for detailed discussion of the evolution of the theoretical ideas.

2.1 Standard Theory

Like all versions of generative grammar within this tradition, ST is multi-
stratal, recognizing a number of *levels* of linguistic description. The overall
organization of these levels is as in (1).

(1)

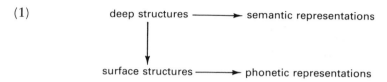

The arrows linking the various components in this schematization indicate that
one level of representation is *derived* from another, and such derivations are
mediated in each case by *rules*. Central to our concerns is the relationship
between deep structures and surface structures and this particular mapping is
achieved by a set of *transformational rules*. We return to the nature of these
rules below. While Chomsky (1965) is not concerned with the remaining links
between levels in (1), the presupposition is that they too are mediated by
systems of rules, a set of rules of semantic interpretation in the case of the deep
structure-semantic representation mapping (see Katz and Fodor, 1963; Katz
and Postal, 1964, for early attempts to formulate such rules), and a set of
phonological rules linking surface structures to phonetic representations (see
Chomsky and Halle, 1968, for the classic account of this part of the theory, as
it was understood during the 1960s).[1] Thus, once deep structures are in place,
different rule components will derive the remaining levels of linguistic representation. How is the set of deep-structures itself defined?

Again, this is achieved by a set of rules, principally a set of *context-free*
phrase-structure rules (see Section 1.4). To illustrate, we can consider some of
the possibilities for predicate phrases not involving transformational rules,
italicized in the examples in (2):

(2) a. The boy *ran*
     b. The boy *kissed the girl*
     c. The boy will *put the book on the table*
     d. The boy may *believe that the girl loves the dog*
     e. The boy *wants to marry the girl*

These predicate phrases can all be generated and assigned appropriate
structures by the phrase-structure rules in (3), so long as these are supplemented by other phrase-structure rules for expanding NP, PP and S:

(3) a. VP → V
     b. VP → V – NP
     c. VP → V – NP – PP
     d. VP → V – C – S
     e. VP → V – to – VP

Thus, assuming the additional rules in (4), we can generate (2c) with the structure in (5):[2]

(4)   a. S → NP – AUX – VP
      b. NP → D – N
      c. PP → P – NP

(5)

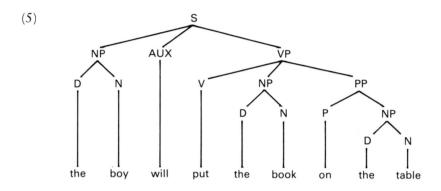

It is easy to see that all the rules in (3) and (4) satisfy the condition on context-free rules introduced in section 1.4 – they each involve the rewriting of a single non-terminal symbol by a string made up of terminal and non-terminal symbols.

One important feature of these rules appears in (3d, e); since S and VP will allow further expansions involving V, this ensures the possibility of *recursive embedding* in the phrase-structure component of the grammar. This was a significant difference between ST and the account offered in Chomsky (1957) – in the latter, the recursive property of grammars was located in the transformational rules.

It is clear that, in themselves, rules expanding VP along the lines of (3) are inadequate. In particular, they contain no way of restricting the co-occurrences of verbs and complements; supplemented by the rules in (4), they would allow as well-formed sentences the examples in (6):

(6)   a. *The boy *ran that the girl loves the dog*
      b. *The boy *kissed to marry the girl*
      c. *The boy *wanted*

To deal with this problem, which had been tentatively approached using context-sensitive rewrite rules in earlier formulations, Chomsky introduced *subcategorization rules* into the grammar which had the effect of elaborating symbols denoting lexical categories in terms of the syntactic environment in which they appeared. Thus, the configuration produced by (3b), i.e. (7), is developed by a subcategorization rule applied to the V to yield (8).

(7)

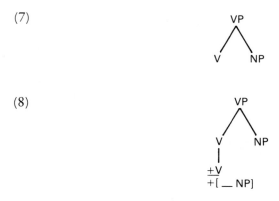

(8)

The significance of this *complex symbol* introduced under V is that it restricts the class of lexical items which can be substituted in this position to those which are verbs (+V) and which require a direct object (+[___NP]), i.e. transitive verbs.

Substitution into such configurations is governed by the information contained in a *lexicon* which is a repository of idiosyncratic properties of lexical items, i.e. all those properties which cannot be predicted by general rule. Accordingly, there will be a lexical entry for *kiss* which, as well as specifying its phonological and semantic properties, also contains the information in (9):

(9) *kiss*: [+V, +[___NP]]

Lexical items can then be entered into structures by a Lexical Insertion Rule subject to the restriction that the subcategorization frame of the item being inserted should not be distinct from the subcategorization information specified at the appropriate point in the configuration. This will enable *kiss* to be inserted under V in (8) but will prohibit, e.g. *put*, which will have a lexical entry including the information in (10):

(10) *put*: [+V, +[___NP – PP]]

We can see, then, that deep structures are defined on the basis of a fairly complex set of operations, with the overall organization of this component of the grammar being organized as in (11).

(11)

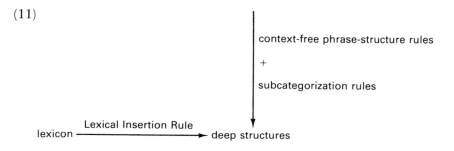

What we have in (11) is a schematic representation of the organization of the *base* of an ST grammar, and what is important for our purposes is the clear emphasis in this notion on *rules*: phrase-structure rules, subcategorization rules and a rule of lexical insertion. As we shall see in the next chapter, none of these survives in more recent versions of generative grammar.

Turning now to the relationship between deep and surface structures, we have already noted that this too is mediated by rules. A fundamental claim in Chomsky (1957) was that phrase-structure rules (context-free or context-sensitive) could not generate a wide range of syntactic structures in economical and insightful ways. His response to this was to assume that natural language grammars also contain rules of a different formal type, transformational rules, which operate on the configurations produced by phrase-structure rules to yield surface structures, and this innovation is carried into ST.[3]

The rules of the base can be conceived of as rules which *build* structures of certain kinds, whereas transformations, as their name suggests, transform these structures into other structures. It follows that there are two things that need to be specified in the statement of a transformational rule: the class of structures to which it applies; and the class of structures which it produces. The first of these is achieved by stating a *structural description* for the rule, an abstract characterization of a class of structures; the second involves specifying a *structural change*. Let us illustrate these notions using the example which has probably received more attention than any other, that of the English passive.

Consider the active – passive pairs below:

(12) a. The boy will kiss the girl
      b. The girl will be kissed by the boy

(13) a. The boy will kiss the girl on his birthday
      b. The girl will be kissed by the boy on his birthday

(14) a. Unfortunately, the boy will kiss the girl
      b. Unfortunately, the girl will be kissed by the boy

These examples illustrate the 'core' active–passive relationship, and also make it clear that peripheral material in the sentence (*unfortunately, on his birthday*) does not affect this relationship. They suggest a formulation of the Passive transformation along the lines of (15):[4]

(15) $X - NP - AUX - V - NP - Y - by - \Delta - Z$
     SD: 1   2   3   4   5   6   7   8 9
     SC: 1   5 $3+be$ $4+en$ ϕ 6   7   2 9

In (15), the SD is a specification of a set of structures to which the rule applies. For the rule to apply, the terminal string in such a structure must be such that it can be exhaustively segmented into nine portions. The first of these can be anything at all (X is a variable), the second must be an NP, the third must be an AUX, and so on. So consider (16), which we assume is generated by the base component.

(16)

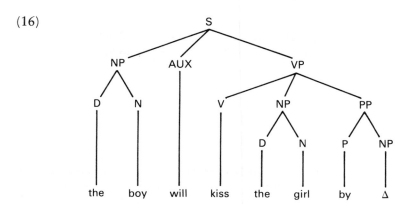

The terminal string in (16) can be segmented as in (17):

(17) ϕ |the boy| will| kiss| the girl| ϕ | by | Δ | ϕ

Here ϕ signifies the *empty string*, and we can note the following identifications with respect to the structure in (16): ϕ is an X since X is a variable satisfied by any string, *the boy* is an NP, *will* is an AUX, *kiss* is a V, *the girl* is an NP, ϕ is a Y, *by* just is *by*, Δ just is Δ, and ϕ is a Z. Thus the nine terms in the SD are satisfied by this structure and the rule applies.

Now consider the SC. This says that term 1 in the SD is unaffected by Passive, term 2 is replaced by term 5, term 3 is modified by *be* being adjoined to AUX, term 4 is modified by the passive morphology *-en* being adjoined to V, term 5 is deleted in its original site, terms 6 and 7 are unaffected, term 8 is replaced by term 2 and term 9 is unaffected. Applying the rule to (16) involves performing these various operations and yields (18):[5]

(18)   The girl will+be kiss+en by the boy

Morphological rules convert *kiss+en* to *kissed* in the mapping from surface structure to phonetic representation, and we successfully derive (12b). Obviously, this operation generalizes to the examples in (13) and (14), since *unfortunately* and *on his birthday* simply fill the variable slots in the SD of Passive and are therefore unaffected by the rule as required. Granted that (15) achieves the desired results, we might be suspicious of its complexity, a point to which we shall return in the final section of this chapter.

As a second example, let us briefly consider the rule of Dative Shift, as exemplified in (19) and (20):

(19)   a. John gave the book to Mary
        b. John gave Mary the book

(20)   a. John bought a present for Mary
        b. John bought Mary a present

While this alternation has exceptions, such as that noted in (5) in the Introduction, it is reasonably productive and this productivity could be captured by including a transformational rule in the grammar along the lines of (21):

(21) $X - V - NP - \{to, for\} - NP - Y$
       SD: 1   2   3   4   5   6

       SC: 1   2   5 ϕ 3   6

The effects of this rule should be fairly transparent – it switches the order of the direct and indirect object (terms 3 and 5) and deletes the preposition (term 4). But the question immediately arises as to how we are to prevent this rule applying inappropriately to structures which satisfy its SD. For example, as things stand, it will apply to the structure underlying (22a) and thereby incorrectly predict the well-formedness of (22b):

(22)   a. John donated a book to the library
       b. *John donated the library a book

One way in which this could be avoided would be to include information in the lexical entries of individual verbs, indicating rules which exceptionally do not apply to them. Thus *donate* could be marked in the lexicon as [−Dative Shift] and a condition imposed on (21) indicating that the V appearing in the SD must not carry this feature.

Many more examples of transformational rules were formulated and explored within ST. For our purposes, however, it is sufficient to have established that such rules, collectively constituting the *transformational component* of the grammar, could perform a variety of operations, including movement and deletion, could refer to specific morphological and lexical elements, and could be associated with conditions which limited their productivity. Again, we shall see that all of these complications are swept away in the theory of the next chapter.

So far, we have concentrated on the *form* of the rules which comprise the components of ST. A further issue concerns how the rules in a component interact with each other, specifically whether or not their application needs to be *ordered*. We can see the case for ordering in connection with the two transformational rules we have formulated here. The crucial question concerns the derivation of a sentence such as (23):

(23)   Mary was given a book by John

By assumption, both Passive and Dative Shift will apply in the derivation of this sentence, and it is easy to see that Dative Shift must apply first. The deep structure which underlies this sentence is roughly along the lines of (24):[6]

(24)   John gave a book to Mary by Δ

If Passive applies to this structure first, we would derive (25):

(25) A book was given to Mary by John

This is fine, but now Dative Shift cannot apply to this structure since no NP intervenes between the V and *to*, and such an NP is required by the SD of Dative Shift. Consequently, there is no way to derive (23) on these assumptions.

If, however, Dative Shift applies first to (24), we derive (26):

(26) John gave Mary a book by Δ

Subsequent application of Passive then yields (23). But now it might seem that another problem arises: how are we to derive (25) if Dative Shift precedes Passive? This is answered by noting a further property of transformational rules in ST, their optionality or obligatoriness.

We can accommodate the data in (23) and (25) by assuming that Dative Shift is ordered before Passive and that in addition Passive is obligatory whereas Dative Shift is optional. Thus, we derive (23) by first applying the optional Dative Shift and then the obligatory Passive; we derive (25) by eschewing the option on Dative Shift and only applying Passive. We shall see in Section 2.5 that there are reasons to be wary of including information about ordering and an optional/obligatory distinction in the theory of grammar.

Finally, we should note one aspect of ordering which does survive in more recent work. We observed above that the ST base allows for the generation of embedded structures via the recursive property of some of the phrase-structure rules. Thus, the base will present the transformational component with configurations like those schematized in (27).

(27)

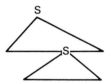

Suppose we wish to generate the sentence in (28):

(28) Mary is believed to be loved by Bill by John

Such a sentence involves one S embedded inside another, and both verbs are passives. On our current assumptions, the deep structure for (28) will be along the lines of (29), where the bracketing indicates the embedded clause:

(29) John believes [Bill to love Mary by Δ] by Δ

The Passive transformation must apply twice to this structure. Does it matter whether it applies in the embedded clause or matrix clause first? Suppose we apply it first in the matrix clause. This will give (30):

(30) Bill is believed [to love Mary by Δ] by John

But then *Bill* is in subject position in the matrix clause, and no further application of Passive is possible to move *Mary* to this position, since the SD for the rule is not satisfied by (30). Alternatively, suppose Passive applies first in the embedded clause. This will yield (31):

(31)   John believes [Mary to be loved by Bill] by Δ

Now the SD in (15) is satisfied, so Passive can apply again in the matrix clause to derive (28).

What we have seen in this simple example is an argument for the *Principle of the Cycle*, a condition on the application of transformational rules, which requires that they apply first (in whatever order is specified) to the most deeply embedded S, then the next most deeply embedded and so on.[7]

This concludes our sketch of ST. Of particular importance is the rule-based nature of each component, and I have attempted to give some idea of the formal nature of the different types of rules. Additionally, we have seen that as well as having their operation constrained by the Principle of the Cycle, transformational rules may be ordered with respect to each other and may be optional or obligatory. We now move to discussion of the status of this theory of grammar with respect to first language acquisition.

2.2 Standard Theory and the Theory of Language Acquisition

If what is involved in being linguistically competent is possessing a mental structure of which an ST grammar provides a model, a pressing question is that of how such a structure could develop in a child. Part of the answer to this question in Chomsky (1965) is that the child approaches the task already supplied with non-trivial information about the nature of the target grammar. Before looking at the form this information takes, we shall consider the arguments for this general perspective.

Chomsky (1965) contains one of the first systematic attempts to formulate a *poverty of the stimulus argument*. At its most general, such an argument maintains that the child's linguistic environment does not provide an appropriate data base for the induction of knowledge of grammar. The specific formulation of this offered by Chomsky refers to the *degenerate* nature of this environment, a property which is intended to encapsulate a number of features, including the presence of ill-formed sentences, false starts, hesitations, etc.

Whether the child's linguistic environment is significantly degenerate in this sense is an issue we have already raised in Section 1.4, and we shall not pursue it further here. Subsequent interpretations of degeneracy (for example, Hornstein and Lightfoot, 1981), have focused on the *insufficiency* of the data available to the child and it is examples of this type with which we embarked on this book. To appreciate fully the issues involved, let us consider a further example in some detail.

The examples in (32) are well-formed *wh*-questions in English:

(32)   a. Who does John believe Bill kissed *e*?
       b. Who does John believe *e* kissed Mary?

Here *e* merely indicates the position which is interrogated in each case, and it is not to be pronounced. The appropriateness of this non-theoretical characterization is indicated by 'full' answers to the questions as in (33), where the italicized expressions supply the information requested:

(33)   a. John believes Bill kissed *Mary*
       b. John believes *Bill* kissed Mary

The generalization we (or the child hearing such sentences) might draw is that in English it is legitimate to question either subject or object position in the complement of a verb like *believe*.

A feature of (32) and (33) is that the complements are not introduced by the complementizer *that*. If we now consider examples including *that*, we can see that questioning of the object position inside the complement is still possible, with (34b) being the 'full' answer to (34a):

(34)   a. Who does John believe that Bill kissed *e*?
       b. John believes that Bill kissed *Mary*

Putting this observation alongside the generalization we have formulated for constructions in which *that* does not appear, we (or the child) might be attracted by the suggestion that the presence of *that* is irrelevant for *wh*-question formation. But we (and the child) would be wrong, as (35) indicates:

(35)   a. *Who does John believe that *e* kissed Mary?
       b. John believes that *Bill* kissed Mary

Example (35a) is not a well-formed question in English, despite the fact that (35b) would be a perfectly well-formed answer to it if it were.

Assuming now that every native speaker of English is familiar with the observations just made, how did this familiarity come about? It is perhaps reasonable to suppose that children are exposed to well-formed examples illustrating the above constructions. Such examples suggest the generalization we were briefly tempted by and which we saw to be incorrect. In particular, if the child's language acquisition procedures enabled him or her to formulate generalizations based on the distributions of certain words in syntactic contexts, this generalization would be the obvious one in the absence of information to indicate its incorrectness.

Obviously, if the child were explicitly informed that (35a) is ill-formed, this would indicate the inappropriateness of the generalization, but we have taken it as uncontroversial that explicit information about ill-formedness is not supplied by the child's environment. Alternatively, we might suppose that the child, seduced by the generalization, has occasion to utter something like (35a), and this leads an adult to correct him; but we have seen that this sort of indirect negative evidence is also probably not available on a systematic basis. Furthermore, to my knowledge, the error in (35a) is not attested in the development of English-speaking children, so the situation which would lead to the presentation of indirect negative evidence does not exist either. If this is correct, we must conclude that the English-speaking child actually avoids the generalization suggested by the data, and it is such plausible, but non-occurring, errors in acquisition which are of particular interest in the present context.[8]

How might we ensure that a child will not be attracted by certain generalizations? This is easy to answer in principle: by maintaining that the initial hypothesis space is constrained in such a way as to ensure that hypotheses which have the generalizations as consequences are illegitimate. If they are illegitimate, they will never be considered by the child and we will have an account of how it is that certain errors can be avoided. The postulation of a set of constraints on the initial hypothesis space constitutes a theory of Universal Grammar (UG), and ST adopts a specific view on the nature of this construct.

ST maintains that the rules appearing in the various components of the grammar are defined on sets of *substantive universals*. These include grammatical categories (N, V, etc. and their phrasal projections) and grammatical features (+V, +[__NP], etc.) in the syntactic component, phonological distinctive features in the phonological component and semantic primitives of some kind in the semantic component. These sets belong to UG, and the child is assumed to approach language acquisition already equipped with them.

Additionally, the rules themselves appear in designated formats. Thus, in the base, there are context-free phrase-structure rules and, while individual languages can differ in the particular rules they employ, the general form of these rules is fixed by UG (see Section 1.4 for discussion of what this form takes). Again, transformational components are made up of transformational rules which have a format specified in UG, satisfying empirically justified constraints on legitimate structural descriptions and structural changes.[9] These constraints allow a degree of variation, so different grammars may include different rules, but these variations are limited by the conditions on the general form of such rules (see the next section for discussion of this in a learnability context). Additionally, as outlined in the previous section, the application of rules may be subject to ordering constraints, partially determined by the Principle of the Cycle, and rules may be optional or obligatory.

Finally, the overall organization of a grammar of this type is taken to be fixed by UG. Each such grammar consists of a set of context-free phrase-structure rules and a lexicon, these constituting the base. Structures produced by the base are input to a transformational component which mediates a mapping between deep and surface structures. These provide inputs to the interpretive semantic and phonological components respectively. Taken together, the constraints on the general form of rules of different types and on the overall organization of a grammar constitute a set of *formal universals.*

So far, then, the picture of language acquisition schematized in (36) is suggested.

(36)

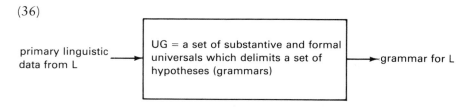

But (36) is perhaps too ambitious in requiring primary linguistic data in conjunction with the universals to determine a *single* grammar. In principle, it is more likely that a *range* of grammars will be compatible with any set of data. In response to this possibility, the acquisition schema is modified so that UG also contains an *evaluation measure* (EM). The task of this is to rank grammars, all of which are compatible with the primary linguistic data, enabling the child to select the one which is most highly valued according to some criterion or other. Taking account of this additional factor yields the schema in (37).[10]

(37)

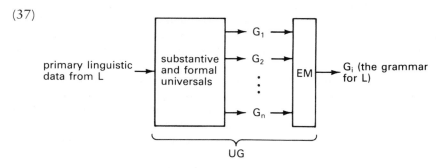

It is important to be clear on the sense in which (36) and (37) comprise a theory of language acquisition. Putting aside the issue of whether the specific contents proposed for UG are correct, one obviously inappropriate feature of these schemas is their total lack of a developmental dimension, i.e. there are no claims about the *stages* through which children go in acquiring their native language. They provide an *instantaneous* model of language acquisition in which children are assumed to have simultaneous access to the full range of primary linguistic data with the correct grammar for the language emerging from the interaction of UG and this full set of data. This is obviously not an attractive idealization for anyone interested in understanding the *course* of acquisition. Whether it is appropriate in the context of seeking an explanation for the *fact* of acquisition is a difficult issue which I shall not pursue here.[11]

It is straightforward to see the sort of account we derive if we remove the idealization, particularly as models derived in this way are what have guided empirical and learnability research based on ST. Quite simply, we can construe the child as moving through a series of grammars, each of which is constrained by the contents of UG under the influence of a non-instantaneous environment. This is represented in (38) (for simplicity, I do not include the EM in (38) – strictly speaking this should be seen as operative at each stage, leading to a most highly valued grammar).

(38)

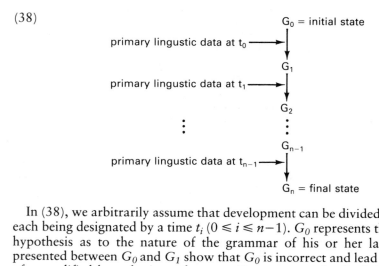

In (38), we arbitrarily assume that development can be divided into n stages, each being designated by a time t_i $(0 \leqslant i \leqslant n-1)$. G_0 represents the child's first hypothesis as to the nature of the grammar of his or her language. Data presented between G_0 and G_1 show that G_0 is incorrect and lead to acceptance of a modified hypothesis, and so on. G_n represents the final (mature) state. Each of the G_i $(0 \leqslant i \leqslant n)$ is constructed according to the constraints specified in UG.

There are several remarks to make about this proposal which make clear its incompleteness as a theory of language acquisition. First, we have said nothing about the nature of the data available to the child at particular points which lead to modification of the hypotheses. Second, we have said nothing about the process of hypothesis-modification beyond noting that a new hypothesis will be subject to the constraints specified in UG, i.e. we have indicated the population of the hypothesis space but not how this population is searched. Finally, in assuming that all grammars in the series are constrained in the same way, we have committed this account to the Continuity Hypothesis (Pinker, 1984), a hypothesis which can be questioned and which will play an important role in later sections of this book (see particularly Sections 8.4, 10.4 and chapter 11).

Having made these observations, we can now formulate this account in terms of the four-component learnability model of chapter 1 as in (39):

(39)   a. a set of possible grammars, where this construct is constrained by the contents of UG;

b. primary linguistic data, where this notion remains unexplicated within the theory;

c. hypothesis selection and testing, where the details of this procedure are not supplied by the theory;

d. some notion of identification.[12]

An obvious weakness of (39) is the imprecision in (b), (c) and (d), and we shall now discuss an important attempt to rectify this situation which also makes significant contact with the ideas introduced in chapter 1.

2.3 Learnability and Standard Theory: Degree-2 Learnability

Wexler and Culicover (1980), developing earlier work by Wexler and his associates (e.g. Hamburger and Wexler, 1973, 1975), is an impressive attempt to bring the concepts of formal learnability theory, introduced in the previous chapter, to bear on the question of the acquisition of transformational grammars. This section offers an informal account of the way in which this programme was implemented, and we shall see that it includes specific proposals on (39b, c, d) from the previous section.

Taking note of the fact that an ST grammar consists of a transformational component defined on a context-free base, it is easy to derive a negative result. Assume that the class of transformational languages generated by such grammars is L_T, and that transformational components are sets of transformational rules satisfying certain formal conditions which allow for identity transformations, i.e. transformations which have no structural effects. It follows that L_T is at least co-extensive with L_2, the class of context-free languages. Why is this? Simply because for every context-free base, we can consider the transformational grammar which is obtained by adding a single identity transformation to this base. The language generated by this grammar will be a member of L_T, so any member of L_2 will be a member of L_T. Exactly the same result follows if we allow *empty* transformational components. In these circumstances, any context-free grammar will also be a transformational grammar, viz. that consisting of the context-free grammar with an empty transformational component, and again L_2 is provably contained in L_T.

Now recall that in Section 1.4 we noted that any superset of a class of unlearnable languages is itself unlearnable so long as the other components of the learnability model are held constant. This enabled us to conclude that L_2 is unlearnable from text, and we can immediately see that the same conclusion follows for L_T.

Because of this, Wexler and Culicover resolved to exploit the bi-stratal nature of syntactic representations in ST by setting questions of the learnability of the base to one side and concentrating on the transformational component itself.[13] Focusing on sets of transformational rules, then, with certain auxiliary assumptions, it is possible to show that transformational components are *functions*, and it is feasible to investigate their acquisition within the context of *function learnability*.[14]

Formally, a function is a pairing of values from two sets, one referred to as the domain of the function and the other as its range. In order to be a (total) function, such a pairing must be everywhere defined in its domain, i.e. if F is a function from A to B and a is a member of A, then there is some b in B such that $F(a) = b$. Additionally, a function must be single-valued, i.e. if $F(a) = b$ and $F(a) = c$, then $b = c$, for any a in A.

Consider now an abstract learning situation in which a learner is being presented with a function from some antecedently given set and has access to an enumeration of this set as in (40):

(40) $F_1, F_2, F_3, \ldots, F_n, \ldots$

Presentation of the function amounts to a data sequence of argument–value pairs, with a guarantee that for any such pair there is some finite time at which it appears in the data sequence. Thus, if the target function is F_i, one legitimate data sequence could commence as in (41):

(41) $\langle\langle a_j, F_i(a_j)\rangle, \langle a_k, F_i(a_k)\rangle, \ldots$

It is easy to see that the class of functions in (40) is identifiable after some finite time using the enumeration to guide the hypothesis selection procedure. The learner is presented with the first datum, say $\langle a_j, F_i(a_j)\rangle$ and selects the first function in the enumeration, F_1. He applies F_1 to a_j, the first member of the datum, and tests whether $F_1(a_j) = F_i(a_j)$, the second member of the datum. If this equality obtains, he adopts F_1 as his hypothesis and awaits the second datum; if it does not, he moves to F_2 and tests $F_2(a_j)$ against $F_i(a_j)$, and so on. As the target function is somewhere in the enumeration, he is guaranteed eventual success on the first datum, although, of course, such success does not entail that he has at that stage selected the correct function. The second datum is dealt with in exactly the same way, except that the hypothesis now selected must yield the correct value not only on this datum but also on the first datum. And so the process goes on. Eventually, the target function will be selected, and from that point onwards no subsequent datum can lead to its rejection, i.e. the target function is successfully identified.

Obviously, the above reasoning applies to any target function in the initial set, so we can assert that any class of enumerable functions can be identified from data sequences consisting of argument–value pairs which satisfy the stated constraints.

We now return to transformational components viewed as functions, and see what is involved in translating the above discussion into this arena. The obvious question concerns their domain and range. In ST, deep structures are input to the transformational component and surface structures result. Thus, the two sets linked by a transformational component are a set of deep structures and a set of surface structures, and our discussion of function learnability suggests that we need to consider pairings from these two sets as appropriate data for the learner. Finally, it is possible to argue that, with certain technical assumptions which we will not go into, the class of possible transformational components can be enumerated. Thus, the conditions required for function-learnability are satisfied and we have the conclusion that the model in (42), fashioned on the four-component approach of the previous chapter, yields a positive learnability result:

(42)   a. a set of transformational components satisfying certain conditions to guarantee their status as functions and their enumerability;

      b. a legitimate data sequence consists of deep structure–surface structure pairs, where for any such pair, there is a finite time such that it appears in the sequence by that time;

      c. hypotheses are rejected on errors and selected by reference to an a priori enumeration of transformational components;

      d. the criterion for learning is the functional equivalent of identification in the limit.

This model works in the sense that any of the transformational components in (42a) will be identified to the criterion (42d) on the basis of any data sequence consistent with (42b) by reference to the procedure in (42c). As this is a positive result, why not stop here?

The discussion in the previous chapter should have prepared the reader for the answer to this question: the empirical plausibility of the assumptions on which this model is based is extremely low in a number of respects. First, the learning procedure requires enumeration and, as we have noted, this calls for access to all previous data in a data sequence. The idea that the child, when confronted with a novel sentence, can consult his or her memory and access all previous pairings of deep and surface structures is quite unacceptable. Second, enumeration involves the rejection and selection of transformational components wholesale, and this would appear to allow for the child's development to display massive discontinuities. While the idea that children do 'reorganize' their grammars in certain ways does have some support (Bowerman, 1982), the sort of discontinuity countenanced by wholesale switches in transformational components might be expected to lead to constant, readily observable discontinuities: these do not occur in language development. Third, the assumption about data sequences is clearly inappropriate. We can be confident that the data sequences to which children are exposed do not come with a guarantee that every possible deep structure–surface structure pair will eventually be presented. Furthermore, again echoing discussion in the previous chapter, there is reason to believe that the data which are presented are restricted, at least as far as length is concerned.

For these reasons, Wexler and Culicover are not impressed by the positive result, and perceive the need to develop an alternative. This alternative leads to their famous degree-2 learnability proof.

To approach an understanding of this, we should first note what is retained from the function-learnability framework. This is: (i) a focus on transformational components regarded as functions; (ii) the view that children are exposed only to positive data which come as pairs of base structures and surface *strings*, i.e. (b, s) pairs.[15] However, enumeration is rejected as a learning mechanism in favour of a procedure which has the attractive feature of 'gradualness'.

Consider a child who currently holds the hypothesis that the transformational component of the target language is T_C. The child is presented with a datum (b, s) and applies T_C to b. There are two possible outcomes to this: either $T_C(b) = s$, in which case T_C remains unchanged; or $T_C(b) \neq s$, requiring a change in hypothesis. That changes are only occasioned by this outcome is a commitment to the position that learning only takes place on *errors*. In fact, since such an error has to appear in the *string* – an error in the *structure* which does not manifest itself in the string will not lead to hypothesis modification – learning takes place on a subset of errors, *detectable errors*.

When a detectable error occurs, the child can modify T_C in one of two ways. First, he can throw out a transformation that applied in the derivation of $T_C(b)$. Second, he can go to a pool of transformations which is provided in the specification of the hypothesis space and add one of these to T_C to yield $T_{C'}$. The transformations available for hypothesization are those which ensure that $T_{C'}(b) = s$.[16] Transformations are rejected or hypothesized on an equiprobable basis, and as the sets from which rejection and hypothesization take place are finite, there is a non-zero probability that correct decisions will be made.

It should be readily apparent that this learning procedure overcomes the conceptual objections to enumeration. Here, no access to earlier data is involved in hypothesis modification, and there is a clear sense in which hypotheses are changed gradually as new data are encountered. Note, though, that there is a price to pay for this, a price which is a consequence of enumeration being the most powerful learning procedure possible in the sense that it will guarantee learnability if any alternative procedure can. Whereas enumeration is 'cumulatively more and more correct', with any new hypothesis being required to account for all the data accommodated by the previous hypothesis as well as the new datum, the Wexler and Culicover procedure carries no guarantee that, in dealing with a new datum, a new hypothesis is not performing less well than its predecessor on earlier data in the sequence. The procedures of rejection and hypothesization of transformations will, on occasions, make mistakes by throwing out a correct transformation or hypothesizing an incorrect one.

An immediate consequence of this is that the class of transformational components which is function-identifiable under enumeration no longer has this property with the modified learning procedure. If identification is to be restored, it is necessary to restrict the class of possible transformational components, and what this amounts to is restricting the class of possible transformations.[17]

Now consider the other empirically implausible aspect of function identification under enumeration identified above, its assumption about data sequences. In the modified learning procedure, learning (hypothesis modification) takes place only on detectable errors. If progress is to be made towards the correct transformational component, it is therefore important that *such detectable errors should occur*, i.e. that data on which they are revealed are presented. As a first step to ensure this, Wexler and Culicover assume that at any point in a data sequence, *any* datum has a non-zero probability of occurring. But now the following observations become crucial.

We refer to the number of S-nodes (not counting the topmost one) appearing in a base structure as the *degree* of the datum to which this base structure belongs. Thus, there are degree-0 data which contain no sentential embedding, degree-1 data which contain a single embedded S, and so on. For any finite n, the number of data of degree less than or equal to n is finite; this is not so for data of degree greater than n, since there are infinitely many sentences in any language. If any datum has a non-zero probability of occurring at any point in a data sequence, it follows that the probability of the learner being presented with any datum of degree less than or equal to n is bounded away from zero. This is not the case for data of degree greater than n; because these are infinite in number, they must include items for which the probability of their being presented at any time can be arbitrarily close to zero.[18]

We can now see that a number of probabilistic measures are in play: the probability of selecting a transformation from the available pool when a detectable error occurs, the probability of rejecting a transformation which has applied in a derivation yielding a detectable error, and the probability of a datum which reveals a detectable error being presented. If the learner is to converge on the correct transformational component, there must be some chance of correctly selecting or rejecting a transformation and this requires detectable errors to occur with probabilities which are not vanishingly small; if such errors occur only on data of high degree, the probability of such data being presented will be extremely small and the learner's opportunities to learn will be few and far between. Furthermore, if an error is detectable only on complex data, there will be a large number of transformations involved in the derivation of such data and the chances of a learner choosing a correct transformation to discard will be correspondingly reduced – recall that all transformations in a derivation leading to a detectable error are equiprobable candidates for rejection.

The reasoning of the previous paragraph highlights the attractiveness of being able to ensure that detectable errors will occur on reasonably simple data, and the strategy now is to impose this as a condition on a learnability theory for transformational components. But notice that to say that any error in a learner's transformational component will be detectable on data of degree $\le n$ for some finite n is equivalent to saying that learning can take place on data sequences which consist *entirely* of data of degree $\le n$, i.e. data sequences which are 'simple' as far as degree of embedding goes. Now, by the argument introduced on p. 25, we should expect such 'simplification' in data to require compensation at some other point in the model. There are therefore *two* reasons for the Wexler and Culicover model requiring a retreat from the class of transformational components which are function-learnable under enumeration: first, we now have a 'weaker' learning procedure; second, the new procedure must be able to succeed with data sequences which are 'simple'.

There is not space here to do more than gesture towards the constraints on transformations which are necessary to ensure learnability under these new assumptions. Linguistically, one of the most interesting is the Binary Principle, which restricts the structural description of a transformation operating in the transformational cycle to the current S and material in the immediately included S. Its learnability motivation is rather obvious in the context of the previous discussion: if an incorrect transformation applying on, say, the topmost S of a structure could affect deeply embedded material, the error induced by this transformation would only be detectable on data exhibiting the required amount of embedding. But we have seen the case for errors being detectable on 'simple' data.

The Binary Principle is a locality constraint on the operation of transformational rules and bears striking similarities to Subjacency, a condition on movement formulated independently of learning-theoretic considerations by linguists working within the Revised Extended Standard Theory (see Chomsky, 1973, for an early formulation, and chapter 3 below for discussion of this within the Bounding module of Principles and Parameters Theory). This convergence on similar constraints from descriptive and learnability perspectives is seen by Wexler and Culicover as particularly significant, and chapter 6 of their book is devoted to providing descriptive support for some of the constraints their theory requires.

Of the further twenty or so constraints required by the degree-2 proof, among the most important are The Freezing Principle, which forbids transformations from applying to configurations not independently produced by the base rules – a node dominating such a configuration is 'frozen' – and the Raising Principle which prevents material dominated by a node which has been raised from being affected by a subsequent transformation. With this set of constraints, Wexler and Culicover are able to prove degree-2 learnability where *learnability* now has a probabilistic interpretation, a necessary consequence of the introduction of the range of probabilistic concepts briefly outlined above. What this amounts to is that for any p $(0 < p < 1)$, there is a finite time at which the probability of the learner having the correct transformational component is greater than or equal to $1 - p$. Obviously p can be arbitrarily close to 0, so the probability of being correct can be arbitrarily close to 1.[19] The conclusion of the degree-2 proof now states that the class of transformational components, subject to the various constraints, is learnable from data sequences consisting of (b, s) pairs of degree less than or equal to 2.

The theory outlined above has been subjected to criticism from a number of directions. Williams (1981b) takes issue with some of the constraints from a linguistic perspective and Pinker (1979, 1981) raises doubts about the learning procedure. Most seriously, perhaps, the assumption that a learner has access to (b, s) pairs is predicated on some rather inconclusive deliberations about the child's ability to construct a significant number of base structures on the basis of semantics, i.e. the (b, s) assumption may be *too strong* in certain respects. Arguably, in other respects it is *too weak*, in that it requires the child's data to consist of mere surface *strings* with no structural information included. Morgan (1986) has developed an alternative system based on the assumption that the child has access to aspects of surface *structure*, and we shall consider his account and his reasons for preferring it in the next section.

2.4 Learnability and Standard Theory: Degree-1 Learnability

In the previous section and in chapter 1, we have seen numerous examples of where modifications in one component of a learnability model lead to an adjustment in the assumptions made in another component. In this section, we shall consider another such example, where the modifications take place *within* one component. What we shall see is that if the data available to the learner are enriched in one respect, then they can be impoverished in another while preserving learnability of transformational components.

Morgan (1986) adopts the *Bracketed Input Hypothesis*, according to which the child's data consist of sequences of base structure–surface *bracketing* pairs. This contrasts with Wexler and Culicover's model, with a surface bracketing replacing a surface string as the second element of a datum.[20]

It is fairly easy to see the impact of this assumption on the learnability problem. Because Wexler and Culicover's system only allows the learner access to surface strings, misadjunction errors in the child's transformational component are non-detectable. For example, suppose that (43) is an abstract base structure.

(43)

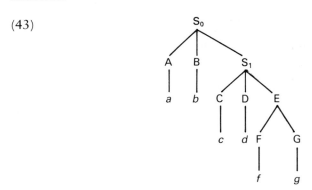

Suppose further that the target grammar contains a transformation which operates on the S_0 cycle, raising E and adjoining it as a right sister of a.[21] This will yield (44).

(44)

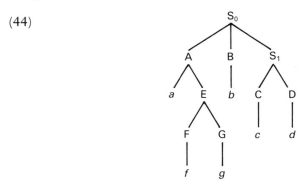

Thus, in the target grammar, if no further transformations apply, *afgbcd* will be a surface string. Now suppose the child has hypothesized a rule which raises E on the S_0 cycle but adjoins it as a left sister of *b*. Applying this rule to (43) gives (45).

(45)

```
                              S₀
                    ┌─────────┼─────────┐
                    A         B         S₁
                    │        ╱ ╲       ╱ ╲
                    a       E   b     C   D
                           ╱ ╲        │   │
                          F   G       c   d
                          │   │
                          f   g
```

Assuming again that no further transformation applies, *afgbcd* will be a surface string and there will be no detectable error. Consequently, the learner will have no basis for modifying the hypothesis. If, however, the structure in (43) were embedded under a higher S, and a transformation which appears in both the target grammar and the child's grammar were to apply on this topmost cycle raising *B*, a detectable error would occur, as only *b* would be raised in the target grammar whereas *fgb* would be raised in the child's grammar. Thus, a degree-2 datum would reveal the error.[22]

Now suppose that the learner has access to surface bracketings rather than surface strings; (44) and (45) will no longer be equivalent, as they will be represented as (46) and (47) respectively:

(46) [[*a* [*fg*]] *b* [*cd*]]
(47) [*a* [[*fg*] *b*] [*cd*]]

The misadjunction error will be revealed on the degree-1 datum with the base structure in (43).

The above example is, of course, merely illustrative, and does not constitute a proof of degree-1 learnability. Just as with Wexler and Culicover's proof of degree-2 learnability, the degree-1 proof is complex, requiring the postulation of an extensive set of constraints on transformational rules, and I shall not attempt to summarize it here. More important for my purposes is the general principle which the demonstration illustrates: by enriching the data to include information about bracketing, Morgan is simultaneously able to impoverish it, so that learnability is assured even if a data sequence consists entirely of degree-0 and degree-1 instances.[23]

An obvious question to ask at this stage is whether the assumption of bracketed input is empirically plausible. We have seen (note 15) that Wexler and Culicover dismiss this possibility, but Morgan recruits a range of evidence in its favour. First, he asks whether information about bracketing is available in principle in the input. Several perspectives suggest that it might be. For example, as reported by Newport, Gleitman and Gleitman (1977), a significant part of the child's input consists of well-formed *phrases* which are not presented in sentential contexts. A mother saying *in the garden* in response to her child's question about the whereabouts of daddy, might be providing clues to justify the partial bracketing in (48) where this phrase occurs in a sentence:

(48)   Daddy is [in the garden]

Alternatively, prosodic cues involving post-phrase pauses and phrase-final vowel lengthening are well-attested phenomena (Cooper and Paccia-Cooper, 1980) and Morgan presents evidence suggesting that these are exaggerated in the speech addressed to children.

Of course, the mere existence of such information does not guarantee that children *represent* the utterances they hear in terms of it, but studies reported by Read and Schreiber (1982), employing a partial repetition task, indicate that children of seven and eight find it much easier to identify complex subjects than simple subjects (such as pronouns) for the purposes of the task. Subsequent experimentation suggested that canonical phrasal prosody was the most important factor underlying this result. Naturally, caution is justified since the children in this study were already linguistically sophisticated.

Finally, even if information about bracketing is available and is represented, this does not establish that it is *utilized* in acquisition. The pursuit of this issue is difficult, since it is not possible to study the consequences of systematically withholding such information from the child. Morgan reports work on the learning of artificial languages by adults, which shows that such learning is facilitated by supplying consistent information (prosodic, morphological or semantic) about phrasal structure with exemplars from the language. As he notes, such results are at best suggestive of the usefulness of bracketing information in the acquisition of syntax by small children.

In this and the previous section, we have sampled some of the positive learnability results derived within assumptions which approximate to those of ST. We have also seen how these studies have made some efforts to establish contact with empirical constraints on acquisition. However, such contacts are somewhat programmatic, and one is left admiring the formal sophistication which has gone into the development of the learnability proofs, but conscious of the considerable gap which exists between this work and empirical work with children. To some extent, this may be an inevitable consequence of the complexities of ST, and in the final section of this chapter, we shall look at some of the issues which have led to its extensive revision.

2.5 The Demise of the Standard Theory

From the late 1960s, ST came under pressure from a variety of sources. Most notable of these was that arising from considering the theory as providing a satisfactory account of language acquisition. Chomsky (1987a, p. 15) encapsulates the difficulty when he says:

> In essence, the problem is that there are too many rule systems. Therefore, it is hard to explain how children unerringly select one such system rather than another.

To get some perspective of what the issue is here, let us return to (15), a formulation of the Passive transformation from Section 2.1, repeated here as (49):

(49) $X - NP - AUX - V - NP - Y - by - \Delta - Z$
SD: 1   2   3   4   5   6   7   8   9
SC: 1   5 $3+be$ $4+en$ ϕ 6   7   2   9

Recall that this rule is an instantiation of a general schema for 'transformational rule' supplied by UG. It would appear that this schema must permit reference to specified lexical and morphological forms such as *by*, *be* and *-en*, and we might legitimately ask whether such forms are themselves limited by some implicit statement of UG or whether reference to them is unrestricted. Additionally, (49), as well as performing two adjunctions of new material (*be* and *-en*), performs two movements, taking term 5 to the position of term 2 and term 2 to term 8. So the schema must permit two adjunctions and two movements: does it permit larger numbers of adjunctions and movements, and if so, is there some finite limit on the number of operations such rules can perform? Further questions of this type can be raised (see van Riemsdijk and Williams, 1986, pp. 34–5, for a more comprehensive list), but these will serve to illustrate the nature of the difficulty to which Chomsky refers. It is clear that adoption of rules such as (49), whatever their descriptive merits, runs the risk of vastly inflating the set of possible rules the child has to consider.

The same point can be made in connection with the phrase-structure rules of the base. If these are merely constrained to be context-free rules, then the examples in (50) will be candidates for the child's grammar:

(50)   a. $S \rightarrow VP - PP$
       b. $VP \rightarrow N - NP$
       c. $PP \rightarrow P - P - P - P - P$

Each of the rules in (50) involves the rewriting of a single non-terminal symbol as a string of symbols, so their status as context-free phrase-structure rules is impeccable. But we would be amazed if, in studying a language, we found ourselves resorting to such rules: (50a) says that a sentence can be well-formed without containing a nominal which refers to what the sentence is 'about'; (50b) says that a verb phrase can be well-formed without containing a head verb; and (50c) says that a prepositional phrase can be well-formed while containing five prepositional heads, none of which has a complement. Rules such as these are just so much garbage which the child must none the less consider and reject along with much more plausible rules if our current conception of UG is correct.

Observations of this type, while strongly suggesting that the view of UG as partly a system of rule schemas is misguided, do not conclusively demonstrate that this emphasis is wrong. It is not inconceivable that an account of acquisition could be produced which had the child searching a hypothesis space populated by rule systems, the vast majority of which were never selected. It is therefore useful to have available a further type of argument which renders the perspective even less plausible.

Recall from chapter 1 (p. 24) the No Negative Data Assumption and consider in the light of this the Dative Shift transformation (21), repeated as (51) with the inclusion of a diacritic rule feature to account for those verbs which do not undergo it:

(51)
$$X - V[+\text{Dative Shift}] - NP - \{to, for\} - NP - Y$$

SD:	1	2	3	4	5	6
SC:	1	2	5	ϕ	3	6

Although this rule is less complex than (49), it introduces a further descriptive possibility in so far as the UG schema for transformational rules must allow for the possibility of diacritic rule features, but this is not what concerns us here. If the rule is to work, verbs must be appropriately categorized as [± Dative Shift]. How is this achieved? For [+Dative Shift] there is no problem of principle, since the child may well hear a verb such as *give* occurring in the two relevant contexts, this being sufficient to fix the value of the feature.[24] However, for [−Dative Shift] if there are no negative data, the child will never receive the information to justify classifying a verb in this way. It seems that any rule such as (51) which includes a diacritic rule feature depends crucially on the presence of negative information in the child's environment.

Two other aspects of ST alluded to in Section 2.1 fall foul of similar observations: rule ordering and the optional/obligatory distinction. Consider rule ordering first, and the evidence that might lead a linguist to suggest that two rules are ordered. Typically, this evidence will consist of observations like those in (52):

(52) a. $DS \rightarrow \ldots \rightarrow R_1 \rightarrow R_2 \rightarrow \ldots \rightarrow SS_1$
       b. $DS \rightarrow \ldots \rightarrow R_2 \rightarrow R_1 \rightarrow \ldots \rightarrow {}^*SS_2$

The schematic derivations in (52a.b) involve applications of two rules, R_1 and R_2. In (52a), R_1 applies before R_2 and the result is a well-formed surface structure SS_1; in (52b), the rules apply in the reverse order, and the result is an ill-formed surface structure ${}^*SS_2$. Crucially, in deciding that R_1 is ordered before R_2, the linguist relies on the information that SS_2 is ill-formed. But the No Negative Data Assumption denies the child access to this information. It follows that if the No Negative Data Assumption is correct, the child has no way of determining that rules are ordered in a particular way. It is therefore inappropriate for UG to make this option available.[25]

Consider the optional/obligatory distinction in a similar way. Evidence which might lead a linguist to suggest that R_1 is optional and R_2 obligatory is schematized in (53):

(53)   a. $DS \rightarrow \ldots \rightarrow R_1 \rightarrow SS_1$
     b. $DS \rightarrow \ldots\ldots\ldots \rightarrow SS_2$
     c. $DS \rightarrow \ldots \rightarrow R_2 \rightarrow SS_3$
     d. $DS \rightarrow \ldots\ldots\ldots \rightarrow {}^*SS_4$

Here, (53b) represents exactly the same derivation as (53a), except that R_1 does not apply. The resulting SS_2 is well-formed, indicating that R_1 is optional. However, in (53d), which is exactly like (53c) except that R_2 does not apply, the result is the ill-formed $^*SS_4$. So R_2 must apply to guarantee a well-formed surface structure, i.e. R_2 is obligatory. But, again on the No Negative Data Assumption, the child has no access to information about the ill-formedness of SS_4 and thus has no way of determining that a rule is obligatory, and the optional/obligatory distinction has no place in UG.[26]

From a rather different perspective, the evaluation measure, which was seen as an important part of UG in ST, never took on a serious explanatory role in acquisition studies. Even within linguistic theory, Williams (1987, p. vii) refers to the 'failure, on the part of grammarians, to make any progress in understanding grammar selection with this 'evaluation metric.' The only general component of the evaluation metric that ever received any real scrutiny was 'shortness' of grammars, and this failed in such pervasive ways that it became tedious to mention it.'[27] Of course, the evaluation measure would only have a role so long as UG was producing a set of candidate grammars each consistent with the primary linguistic data. With the suspicions about highly expressive rule systems that we are beginning to voice, it becomes more plausible to consider acquisition as a more deterministic process in which UG is so constrained that the number of candidate grammars at any stage is perhaps reduced to one. In such circumstances, the evaluation measure has no part to play (cf. Section 8.2).

Finally, the descriptive largesse which we have hinted at in this section was carried over into empirical studies of language acquisition. The classic studies of the period (Bloom, 1970; Bowerman, 1973; Brown, 1973) adopted the readily understandable goal of writing grammars which would account for children's syntactic knowledge at various stages in their development. A great deal of ingenuity was displayed in producing and justifying rule systems, but, as argued extensively in Atkinson (1982), these rule systems often bore tenuous relationships to their ancestors in linguistic theory. As Pinker (1984, p. 2) puts it:

> It turned out to be nearly impossible to determine which grammar best fit a corpus of child speech . . . especially since the rules in the grammars proposed often contained arbitrary mixtures of adult syntactic categories, ad hoc syntactic categories, semantic features, phonological features, and specific words.

In short, not only was the descriptive extravagance adopted, but it was also extended to a point where adherence to ST was fairly notional. The tools of linguistic theory were often little more than a notation for producing a reasonably economical description of a corpus of child speech, and, as mentioned in the Introduction, the task of accounting for the child's acquisition of grammar was lost sight of.

2.6 Summary

In this chapter, we have looked at the Standard Theory of Chomsky (1965) from a variety of perspectives. We began by offering an overview of the major components of the theory, emphasizing its reliance on rule systems. This was followed by a presentation of the theory of language acquisition within which ST is embedded. This account, incorporating the Language Acquisition Device, is familiar in outline to many psychologists and other non-linguists. Along with developing the ST account of the contents of UG, we also discussed the idealization to instantaneous acquisition, and presented a schematic account of the model which appears most natural if this idealization is removed.

ST presents serious learnability problems, and we have sketched how some of these have been approached in the degree-2 and degree-1 learnability proofs. In the theory we are going on to consider, learnability in a formal sense will not intrude as a central issue, but in chapter 9, we shall have occasion to reconsider the complexity of the data necessary for acquisition. Finally, we have drawn attention to some of the difficulties which have been raised for the ST account of language acquisition and have hinted that the way to deal with these might involve a move away from richly expressive rule systems. The next chapter will be an extensive development of these hints.

3 Principles and Parameters Theory

Introduction

In this chapter, we shall outline the ideas which inform much contemporary research in syntactic theory. These ideas were given their first systematic expression by Chomsky in his 1979 Pisa Lectures, a modified form of which appeared as Chomsky (1981). The title of this work, *Lectures on Government and Binding*, led to the approach being known as Government-Binding Theory or GB, but as Chomsky (1987b, pp. 14–15) makes clear, government and binding are only two of the theoretical concepts assumed in the approach, albeit particularly central ones. Chomsky indicates that Principles and Parameters Theory (henceforth PPT) more accurately captures the content of the account, and we adopt this title throughout this book.

Before embarking on this outline, a preliminary remark is in order. PPT has two properties which create difficulties for us. First, it has a complex deductive structure which means that individual phenomena are explicated by reference to a number of interacting systems. Proposals which may appear *ad hoc* when introduced in the context of a particular construction often have ramifications in other parts of the grammar, and it is only by taking full account of these that the explanatory force (or inappropriateness) of specific proposals can be properly appreciated. Obviously, in one chapter, it is not possible to do justice to this perspective. I shall return briefly to the notion of deductive structure in chapter 8, but readers who are unfamiliar with the theory would undoubtedly benefit from consultation of van Riemsdijk and Williams (1986), Radford (1988a) or Haegeman (1991). Second, the theory continues to develop, with far-reaching ideas being pursued on a number of fronts. This is particularly true of research into the properties of functional categories, and, because of the significance of this for acquisition, it is discussed separately in chapter 10. For this chapter, I have tried to restrict myself to reasonably stable aspects of the theory with occasional additional references in footnotes. The major goal of the chapter is to contrast PPT with ST, and I believe that this can be done without pretending to offer a definitive overview.

After some basic structural notions are introduced in the first section, the next three sections contain the core of the theory. The first of these focuses on the *levels of representation* acknowledged by the theory, the second on the *modular* nature of the account and the *principles* operative in each module, and the third on the need for *parameterization* within individual modules. In the course of this presentation, I shall attempt to pay particular attention to the claim that PPT does not embrace descriptively rich *rule systems*.

The final section focuses on PPT as a theory of language acquisition along the lines of the four-component learnability model of chapter 1. This will lead us to formulate a set of questions which will inform much of the subsequent discussion in the book.

3.1 Some Fundamental Notions

There are a few basic structural ideas which are widely employed in PPT, cropping up in definitions in a number of distinct parts of the theory. As a result, it would not be appropriate to introduce them in connection with a specific module. To make the discussion in subsequent sections as accessible as possible, this brief section introduces these ideas in a preliminary way.

First among them is *maximal projection*. This is already intelligible in the context of ST, where phrase-structure rules produce such partial structures as those in (1).

(1)

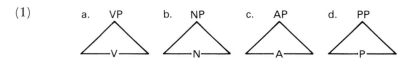

In (1), we can describe the configurations in terms of a lexical category (V, N, A, P) *projecting* into a phrasal category (VP, NP, AP, PP) and of the phrasal categories being *projections* of the lexical category.[1] If we consider a slightly fuller, but still partial, structure, as in (2), we can say that while the N projects into NP, it does not project to any higher position in the structure, since moving up from NP takes us into the system of V-projections.

(2)

Thus, in (2), NP is the *maximal projection* of N. Of course, the use of 'maximal' here suggests that there are also non-maximal projections of lexical categories. This was not the case in ST, but, as we shall see in Section 3.3, non-maximal projections play an important role in the X-bar module of PPT. For our purposes here, all that is necessary is to identify the maximal projection of X with XP, acknowledging that the force of 'maximal' will be dealt with later.

The notion of maximal projection appears in one of the standard definitions of *c-command* (constituent-command), although not in the original definition of Reinhart (1976). C-command is a relation defined on nodes in structural representations, and a version of Reinhart's definition appears in (3):

(3)   A node α c-commands a node β iff (i) α does not dominate β and (ii) the first *branching node* dominating α also dominates β.

Thus, if we consider the simple structure in (4), the statements in (5) are all true with this definition of c-command.

(4)

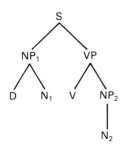

(5)   a. D c-commands N_1
      b. N_1 c-commands D
      c. NP_1 c-commands VP, V, NP_2 and N_2
      d. VP c-commands NP_1, D and N_1
      e. V c-commands NP_2 and N_2
      f. NP_2 c-commands V
      g. N_2 c-commands V, since VP is the first *branching* node dominating N_2 and this dominates V.

An alternative definition of c-command, relying on maximal projection and first formulated by Aoun and Sportiche (1983), appears in (6):

(6)   A node α c-commands a node β iff (i) α does not dominate β and (ii) for every maximal projection γ, if γ dominates α then γ also dominates β.

With respect to this definition and the structure in (4), all the statements in (5) remain true except for (5g). Since NP_2 is a maximal projection, it prevents N_2 from c-commanding any node outside it.

Confusingly, despite the fact that both (3) and (6) are offered as definitions of c-command, they are in fact definitions of *different* relations, both of which are coherent given the primitive ideas of branching node and maximal projection. Acknowledging this, Chomsky (1986b, p. 8) proposes that the relation defined in (6) should be referred to as *m-command*, c-command being reserved for Reinhart's definition.[2] Despite this, it is common practice in the literature to refer ambiguously to c-command, disambiguation being achieved by referring to Reinhart or Aoun and Sportiche where necessary.

The important issue concerns which, if either, of these notions is important in the theory of grammar.[3] Because Aoun and Sportiche's definition plays a major role in what follows, we shall reserve c-command for this. Any use of the branching node definition will be explicitly indicated.

One place where Aoun and Sportiche c-command is important is in the definition of our last preliminary concept, *government*. A definition of this concept which will serve our preliminary purposes appears in (7):[4]

(7) A node α governs a node β iff (i) α c-commands β and (ii) no maximal projection intervenes between α and β.

To illustrate, consider again the structure in (4) and the nodes governed by NP_1. Statement (5c) holds that NP_1 c-commands VP, V, NP_2 and N_2, therefore, given condition (i) in (7), these are the candidates for governed nodes. However, the maximal projection VP intervenes between NP_1 and all of V, NP_2 and N_2, *blocking* government of these nodes. But V not only c-commands NP_2; it also governs it. Thus, government is a stricter notion than c-command, requiring that a governor and a governee should share dominating maximal projections. Government is probably the single most important structural relation in the theory which we are about to present, playing a central role in a number of modules.

Terminology which is related to c-command and government is *c-command domain* and *government domain*. The former simply refers to the set of nodes in a structure which are c-commanded by a specified node and the latter to those nodes which are governed by it. Armed with these preliminary concepts, we can now turn to the substance of PPT.

3.2 Linguistic Levels

In PPT, the overall organization of a grammar is as in (8).

(8)

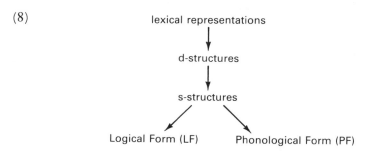

Each of the labels in (8) refers to a linguistic level, and representations at that level satisfy a number of principles which we shall consider in the next section. Additionally, the levels are linked, as indicated by the arrows, and the nature of the mappings establishing these links can also be seen as embodying simple principles. In this section, we shall provide some initial motivation for postulating these levels and say something about how they are distinguished from the levels recognized in ST, as schematized in (1) of chapter 2. Since this book is not concerned with PF, we shall say nothing systematic about this level, merely noting that (8) maintains that there is no link between it and LF, and that it is conceived of as the interface between the internalized grammar and the mechanisms of articulation and acoustic perception.

Consider first, then, Lexical Representations (LRs). In ST such representations exist and are viewed as a repository of idiosyncratic information, viz. that information about lexical items which cannot be predicted by general rule. In that account, lexical representations are related to deep structures by a rule of lexical insertion. This enters lexical items into structures which satisfy certain conditions and which are themselves independently generated by the phrase-structure rules of the base (cf. p. 35). In PPT, LRs again contain information about the idiosyncratic properties of lexical items, but in this account, there is a principled relation of *projection* between the lexicon and d-structures, with the properties of the latter being largely determined by the information contained in LRs.[5]

We shall have more to say about this projection in chapter 7, but here we can illustrate the general idea with a simple example. Consider the transitive verb *hit*. Notionally, it takes two *arguments*, an Agent who does the hitting and a Patient that receives the blow. This is clearly an idiosyncratic fact about *hit*, and therefore needs to be learned by the child. Assume, then, that the (partial) LR for *hit* is as in (9), where the arguments of the verb appear as a simple unordered list:

(9) *hit*: V; Agent, Patient

We must now specify how this representation is projected into syntax, and there are clearly two aspects to this projection. First, we need to consider what the *categorial status* of the projected arguments is. In the case of Agent and Patient, it seems that this will standardly be NP, and we can follow Grimshaw (1981), Pesetsky (1982) and Chomsky (1986a) in referring to the *Canonical Structural Realization* (CSR) of particular argument types. Thus, we might begin to define a function CSR as in (10):

(10)   CSR(Agent) = NP
       CSR(Patient) = NP

That CSR must take on values other than NP is readily seen if we consider a verb such as *put*, which may have a (partial) LR such as (11), where Theme denotes the type of argument that undergoes displacement and Goal has a transparent interpretation:

(11)   *put*: V; Agent, Theme, Goal

That *put* occurs in such sentences as (12) suggests that CSR(Theme) = NP and CSR(Goal) = PP:

(12)   The man put the book on the table

The second issue involved in elaborating the projection concerns the *configurational* status of the arguments in syntax: a specific question is whether they are projected as *external* or *internal* arguments. Internal arguments of a predicate such as a V are projected into syntax inside the maximal projection of the item in question, in this case VP; external arguments are projected outside this maximal projection. For Agent–Patient verbs such as *hit*, it appears that, for English at any rate, Agents are projected as external arguments and Patients as internal arguments (see Levin, 1984, for extensive discussion). Thus, the LR in (9), which we repeat as (13) with indexing to keep track of the arguments, projects the d-structure in (14):[6]

(13)　*hit*: V; Agent$_i$, Patient$_j$
(14)　NP$_i$ [$_{VP}$ *hit* NP$_j$]

In fact, (14) is not entirely predictable from (13) and the simple details of projection we have formulated, since it includes information about the linear order of constituents. We shall return to this in the next section.

Again, for *put*, the LR in (11), repeated with indexing in (15), is partially predictive of the d-structure in (16) on the assumption that Agents project as external arguments:

(15)　*put*: V; Agent$_i$, Theme$_j$, Goal$_k$

(16)　NP$_i$ [$_{VP}$ *put* NP$_j$ PP$_k$]

From this perspective, then, aspects of d-structure are viewed as *transparent* syntactic projections of the argument selection properties of lexical items.[7]

D-structures themselves differ in two important respects from the deep structures of ST. First, representations at this level are not independently generated by phrase-structure rules; rather, they are directly determined by the projection we have briefly considered along with other factors we shall come to presently. Second, they do not provide the input to a semantic component.

As projections of lexical properties, d-structures clearly do not provide everything we need in a theory of linguistic representation. This is because such projections can be distorted by processes which in ST were formalized as transformational rules. Consider the case of *wh*-questions in English, and again we can use the verb *hit* as illustration. Continuing to put questions of linear order to one side, the syntactic projection (d-structure) of *hit* when its internal argument is the *wh*-question word *what* is (17):

(17)　John [$_{VP}$ hit what]

Yet, the English sentence which appropriately expresses this argument structure is (18):

(18)　What did John hit?

Ignoring the auxiliary verb *do*, it appears that some operation must have been performed on (17) to yield a structure appropriate for (18). In ST, this was a transformational rule of Question Formation, which had the effect of moving the *wh*-word from its VP-internal position to some position at the front of the structure. Like other transformational rules, Question Formation was formulated in terms of a structural description and structural change (cf. p. 36), which encoded quite specific aspects of the rule's operation (see, for example, Katz and Postal, 1964; C. L. Baker, 1970). Something similar is assumed to take place in PPT with two notable differences. First, the movement process is not a customized transformational rule, but an application of the general rule, Move α, which says that *anything can be moved anywhere*. Obviously, if anything can be moved anywhere, *what* can be moved to its sentence-initial position in (18); the problem, to which we shall return in the next section, is how to prevent such a general rule from producing a wide range of ill-formed s-structures. Second, the movement leaves behind a *co-indexed empty category* (standardly represented by *e*) in the VP-internal position, indicating the original d-structure position of the moved item. Thus, the schematic s-structure for (18) is (19):

(19)   what$_i$ did [$_S$John [$_{VP}$hit e_i]]

Again, we shall return to the status of such empty categories in the next section. For now, we can simply note that if the PF processes in (8) regard the empty category as just that, there is no principled reason why (19) should not give rise to an appropriate phonological representation for the string.[8] Interfacing with phonology in this way was, of course, a property of surface structures in ST, and this is a similarity between that level of representation and s-structures. The latter, however, are 'more abstract' than surface structures by dint of containing empty categories resulting from movement.

A further distinction between surface structures and s-structures is that the former were insulated from semantic interpretation in ST, this interpretation being defined on deep structures. However, (8) shows that Logical Form (LF), the name of which suggests it is somehow related to semantic interpretation, is directly linked to s-structures. We will first offer a brief justification for LF as a further level of representation and then say something about its status *vis-à-vis* semantics.

Our justification for LF is less direct than what has gone before. Indeed, it involves the presentation of a linguistic argument, but it should be possible to follow this easily enough with the basic concepts we have introduced so far. The argument concerns a group of phenomena illustrating *Weak Crossover* (see Postal, 1974, for the original observations).

Consider the distribution of pronouns in English, and particularly the conditions under which a pronoun can be co-referential with an antecedent. The data in (20), where co-indexing indicates co-referentiality, enable us to begin thinking about the appropriate generalization:[9]

(20)   a. John$_i$ likes his$_i$ mother
       b. His$_i$ mother likes John$_i$
       c. John$_i$'s mother likes him$_i$
       d. *He$_i$ likes John$_i$'s mother

What distinguishes the well-formed examples (20a, b, c) from (20d)? Omitting irrelevant details, the s-structures for these sentences are as in (21):

(21)　a. [John$_i$ [$_{VP}$likes [$_{NP}$his$_i$ mother]]]
　　　b. [[$_{NP}$His$_i$ mother][$_{VP}$likes John$_i$]]
　　　c. [[$_{NP}$John$_i$'s mother][$_{VP}$likes him$_i$]]
　　　d. *[He$_i$ [$_{VP}$likes [$_{NP}$John$_i$'s mother]]]

In these structures, consider the c-command relationships between the pronoun and its co-indexed antecedent. In (21a), *his* does not c-command *John* because of the intervening maximal projections NP and VP. In (21b, c), the same conclusion obtains for *his* and *him* with the NP and VP respectively blocking c-command. Thus, in each of (21a, b, c), the pronoun does not c-command its antecedent. In (21d), however, *he* does c-command *John*, as its c-command domain, defined by its most immediately dominating maximal projection, extends over the entire clause. From the data in (20), then, we can formulate the generalization in (22):

(22)　A pronoun may not be co-indexed with an expression in its s-structure c-command domain.

But now consider the data in (23), which at d-structure are exactly like those in (20) except that the expression co-indexed with the pronoun is a *wh*-word:[10]

(23)　a. Who$_i$ likes his$_i$ mother?
　　　b. *Who$_i$ does his$_i$ mother like?
　　　c. Whose$_i$ mother likes him$_i$?
　　　d. *Whose$_i$ mother does he$_i$ like?

Assuming that Move α has applied in each case in the mapping between d-structure and s-structure, leaving behind a co-indexed empty category, and again ignoring many details, the s-structures for (23) are as in (24):[11]

(24)　a. Who$_i$[e_i [$_{VP}$likes [$_{NP}$his$_i$ mother]]]
　　　b. *Who$_i$ does [[$_{NP}$his$_i$ mother][$_{VP}$like e_i]]
　　　c. [Whose$_i$ mother]$_j$[e_j [$_{VP}$likes him$_i$]]
　　　d. *[Whose$_i$ mother]$_j$ does [he$_i$ [$_{VP}$like e_j]]

The generalization we have formulated in (22) does not extend to this range of data. Specifically, (24a, c) are not problematic for (22), because in each of them, the pronoun does not c-command the co-indexed *wh*-word; in (24a), c-command is blocked by the maximal projections NP and VP, and in (24c) by the maximal projection VP. It might also be maintained that (24d) can be accommodated, if *he* in subject position has a c-command domain extending over the entire clause and encompassing the *wh*-phrase in its clause-initial position, although it would involve us in too much theoretical discussion at this stage to investigate this question. The problem for (22) is obvious anyway in (24b), where c-command of anything outside its containing NP is blocked for the pronoun. Therefore, *his* does not c-command *who* and co-indexing ought to be possible by (22). It isn't, so (22) is not adequate.

　　Various attempts have been made to formulate the additional requirement necessary to rule out (24b) (see, for example, Koopman and Sportiche, 1982;

Hornstein, 1983), but we shall not pursue these here. Rather, I shall content myself with the descriptive observation that what distinguishes (24b) (and (24d)) from (24a, c) at s-structure is that in the former a *wh*-expression has 'crossed over' a pronoun with which it is co-indexed in the mapping from d-structure to s-structure; and it is this fact, which of course gives the phenomenon its name, that is vital, however we choose to explicate it theoretically.

But now consider the paradigm in (25), which simply substitutes the quantifier phrase *everyone* for *John* in (20):

(25)   a. Everyone$_i$ likes his$_i$ mother
       b. *His$_i$ mother likes everyone$_i$
       c. Everyone$_i$'s mother likes him$_i$
       d. *He$_i$ likes everyone$_i$'s mother

We can immediately see that the quantifier patterns with the *wh*-expressions and not with the name *John*, despite the fact that at s-structure it appears throughout the paradigm in exactly the same structural positions as *John*. Thus, the s-structures for the sentences in (25) are as in (26):

(26)   a. [Everyone$_i$ [$_{VP}$likes [$_{NP}$his$_i$ mother]]]
       b. *[[$_{NP}$His$_i$ mother][$_{VP}$likes everyone$_i$]]
       c. [[$_{NP}$Everyone$_i$'s mother][$_{VP}$likes him$_i$]]
       d. *[He$_i$ [$_{VP}$likes [$_{NP}$everyone$_i$'s mother]]]

The status of (26a, c and d) follows from (22); the problem is (26b), which is predicted to be well-formed by (22) and does not exhibit 'crossover', since no movement has taken place in the mapping from d-structure to s-structure here.

The way out of this dilemma is to propose a further level of linguistic representation beyond s-structure at which certain expressions, including quantifier phrases, *do* move. The standard assumption since May (1977) (see May (1985) for substantial modifications) is that quantifier phrases move to a clause-initial position at LF. This means that the crucial case of (26b) (but also (26d)) will now give rise to an LF-representation similar in the relevant respects to the s-structure representation in (24b). For (26b), this is (27):

(27)   Everyone$_i$[[$_{NP}$his$_i$ mother][$_{VP}$likes e_i]]

In (27), *everyone* has 'crossed over' a co-indexed pronoun, and the *wh*- and quantifier paradigms will now fall under the same generalization so long as this generalization is stated as holding at LF.[12] Failure to recognize such a level entails that the appropriate generalization cannot be stated. This example of *Quantifier Raising* is also seen as another instantiation of Move α, but this time it operates in the mapping from s-structure to LF.

Turning to the role of LF as a level of semantic representation, it will not have escaped the notice of readers familiar with the syntactic treatment of quantification in first-order predicate logic, that the representation in (27) is rather similar to that devised by logicians in their investigations of the scope properties of logical quantifiers. And, of course, once we adopt the assumption that quantifiers do move at LF, the way is open to see LF as a linguistic level at which standard scope ambiguities are resolved. Consider the simple example in (28):

(28)   Every boy loves a girl

It is customary to regard this sentence as ambiguous, the preferred reading being that for every boy, there is some girl or other such that he loves her, and the less obvious reading that there is some particular girl such that every boy loves her. Traditionally, in logic, these two interpretations are represented by two distinct formulae as in (29):

(29)   a. $\forall x(x$ a boy$)\exists y(y$ a girl$)(x$ loves $y)$
     b. $\exists y(y$ a girl$)\forall x(x$ a boy$)(x$ loves $y)$

Formula (29a) corresponds to the preferred interpretation and includes a *wide-scope* universal quantifier and a *narrow-scope* existential quantifier; (29b) corresponds to the alternative interpretation with the scope properties of the quantifiers reversed.

Now, given a rule which operates in the mapping from s-structure to LF and moves a quantifier to a clause-initial position, and the assumption that different tokens of this rule can apply in any order, it is easy to see how the s-structure for (28) is converted to two LFs, as in (30):

(30)   a.   [every boy]$_i$[[a girl]$_j$[e_i loves e_j]]
     b.   [a girl]$_j$[[every boy]$_i$[e_i loves e_j]]

In (30a), the rule has first moved *a girl* to clause-initial position followed by a similar movement of *every boy*. The movements have taken place in the reverse order for (30b). If we fully specify the nature of the structures produced by such movements, an exercise we are avoiding here, it is straightforward to define the *scope* of a quantifier expression in terms of its c-command domain and to conclude that (30a, b) are appropriate representations for resolving the scope ambiguity exhibited by (28). Thus, it appears that LF includes resources for approaching some issues which are standardly regarded as semantic.

It is important to be clear on the differential status of the two sets of observations we have considered in this brief discussion of LF. The Weak Crossover discussion contains an *argument* for this level, the general form of which is familiar to linguists working within this framework. The discussion of scope ambiguities noted what looks like a positive *consequence* of postulating this level of representation. In this distinction lies the key to understanding the status of LF with respect to traditional approaches to semantics. It is in fact a further level of *syntactic* representation and is justified by syntactic criteria. Particularly, it does not satisfy any a priori semantic conditions such as being the level at which natural language inferences can be formalized. Like PF, it functions as an interface between the language system and other cognitive mechanisms. If 'meaning' in a broad sense is embedded in a general conceptual system, LF can be seen as encoding the contribution of the theory of linguistic structure to the study of meaning (May, 1985). What this contribution is is an empirical question, and is not to be resolved by stipulation.

Nothing could make the status of LF clearer than May's (1985) conclusions, contrary to his own earlier views but overtly derived from *syntactic* arguments, that the standard quantifier scope ambiguities should *not* be resolved at LF. In his later work, (28) has a *single* LF representation, which is compatible with either of its interpretations, and the resolution of the ambiguity is left as a task for 'real semantics' (see also Hornstein, 1983).

This concludes our discussion of the levels of representation in PPT. Necessarily, a number of additional aspects of the theory have been raised in a preliminary way. The next section will provide a more systematic discussion of some of these.

3.3 Modules and Principles

A characteristic of PPT is its *modular* character. The idea is that a grammar, recognizing the levels of the previous section, can be decomposed into a fairly small number of simple sub-theories which can interact in complex ways to account for the properties of linguistic expressions. The theoretical statements which provide the content of each module are the *principles* which appear in the name of the approach. In addition, some principles are *parameterized* and we shall pay attention to what this means in the next section. Because we shall not be concerned with linguistic variation in this section, our discussion will be based on English. Of course, to adopt a modular perspective is no more than a research strategy, and its value must ultimately be assessed in terms of standard empirical criteria.

In this section, then, we shall introduce each of the modules with which we shall subsequently be concerned, along with an indication of the linguistic phenomena which motivate it. Additionally, we shall formulate the major principles operative within each module and provide some indication of the level or levels of representation at which these principles apply. It should be pointed out at the outset that the exact constituency of the set of modules is not fixed and is itself the subject of ongoing research. This justifies a certain amount of expository convenience in an introductory discussion.

The modules with which we shall be concerned are those listed in (31):

(31)   a. X-bar Theory
       b. The Theory of Move α
       c. Binding Theory
       d. Bounding Theory
       e. Control Theory
       f. Case Theory
       g. Θ-Theory
       h. The Theory of Empty Categories

This list is standard except for (31b) – Move α is not usually viewed as comprising a module, belonging instead to a residual 'rule component' – and (31h) – the taxonomy of empty categories and their properties emerges to a large extent in connection with other modules. Additionally, it is not uncommon to find Government Theory included in a list of modules (see, for example, Koopman, 1984, p. 2), but, given the pervasive role of this structural relation in other modules, I have chosen not to give it this status (cf. Section 3.1).

We noted in the previous section that the projection of lexical representations partially determines the nature of d-structures without the need to invoke independent phrase-structure rules. *X-bar Theory*, traditionally concerned with the configurational properties of *lexical heads* (N, V, A, P) and the phrases in which they occur, provides a further contribution to this process. Extension of the relevant concepts to non-lexical, functional heads features in a significant amount of more recent work and is something to which we shall return in chapter 10.

Chomsky (1970) noted important structural parallels between clauses and noun phrases, parallels which are readily apparent in the examples in (32):

(32)   a. The enemy destroyed the city.
       b. The enemy's destruction of the city.

Example (32a) is a clause containing a finite verb *destroyed* which occurs with a direct object *the city* and a subject *the enemy*; (32b) is a complex noun phrase, but it is plausible to suggest that the head noun *destruction* is structurally related to *the city* and *the enemy's* in much the same way as the verb is to the analogous items in (32a). Such *cross-categorial* similarities, in so far as they exist, provide one of the major motivations for the development of X-bar Theory.

Further issues arise if we consider the internal structure of a variety of constituents. The expressions in (33) provide examples of NP, VP, AP and PP:

(33)   a. the senior *author of the book* (NP)
       b. is *writing a book* (VP)
       c. very *proud of the book* (AP)
       d. right *on the nose* (PP)

Our concern in these cases is with the italicized sequences, and there is considerable evidence that these form constituents. Thus, *author of the book* in (33a) can be 'replaced' by the pronominal form *one*, as in (34):

(34)   The senior author of the book is dimmer than the junior *one*.

The possibility of being replaced in this way is a standard test used by linguists to identify constituents. *Writing a book* in (33b) can be 'moved' to clause-initial position in certain constructions such as (35):

(35)   John thought Bill was writing a book, and writing a book, he was.

Again, if a sequence can be moved, this provides prima facie evidence for its being a constituent. Similar tests can be applied to the italicized sequences in (33c, d) and the reader is referred to Radford (1988a, Sections 4.3, 5.2, 5.3 and 5.4) for very full discussion. The question that concerns us is: given that these sequences are constituents, what sort of constituent are they? *Author of the book*, containing the head noun *author*, looks like some kind of nominal constituent, but it is neither an NP (it can be preceded by determiners, unlike NPs) nor a simple N. So, perhaps it is some kind of intermediate nominal constituent. X-bar Theory is concerned with articulating this perception.

X-bar Theory consists of the principles in (36):[13]

(36) a. $X'' = (Y''), X'$
      b. $X' = Y''^*, X^0$

There are several points to make in clarifying these rather abstract expressions. First, X and Y are variables ranging over the lexical categories. Second, the superscripts on the variables indicate *level of projection*.[14] Thus, N^0 is a zero-level projection of a noun, i.e. simply a lexical noun, such as *author* (henceforth, we follow standard practice in suppressing the superscript 0); N' (read 'N-bar') is a first-level projection of a noun corresponding to the intermediate level of category introduced above and exemplified by *author of the book*; and N'' (read 'N-double-bar') is a second-level projection of a noun, such as *the senior author of the book*. In the system we are assuming, such second-level projections are *maximal* projections and correspond to what have traditionally been referred to as *phrases* of certain categories. So, N'' is equivalent to NP, V'' to VP, and so on. Most linguists continue to use the familiar phrasal symbols to designate maximal projections and we shall also adopt this practice. Thus (36) can be 'translated' into (37):

(37) a. $XP = (YP), X'$
      b. $X' = YP^*, X$

For anyone familiar with the format of phrase-structure rules, this is probably still alarmingly opaque, and there are two further pieces of notation to explain before the content of (36) becomes clear. The * is simply an abbreviation for a set of zero or more YPs. So, (37b) could be 'expanded' to a set of statements, the first three of which appear in (38):

(38) a. $X' = X$
      b. $X' = YP, X$
      c. $X' = YP, YP, X$

Finally, the comma appearing on the right-hand side of (36) indicates that the elements flanked by it are *unordered* with respect to each other. Replacing the variables in (38b) by one of their legitimate instantiations gives (39):

(39) $V' = NP, V$

The content of this is that a V' (a first-level V-projection) consists of an NP and a V, i.e a maximal N-projection and a zero-level V-projection. Order is not specified, so (39) itself is consistent with both (40a, b) where the dash signifies ordered concatenation:

(40)   a. V' = NP – V
      b. V' = V – NP

Now what we have in (40) is a pair of phrase-structure rules as this notion is understood in ST, the only novel aspect being that we employ a notation for referring to an intermediate level of projection (V'). However, these rules themselves have only a *derivative* status with respect to X-bar Theory. The latter consists entirely of the principles in (36) supplemented by any scope for parameterization that we discuss in the next section.

Returning to (36), note that the use of the variable X on the left- and right-hand sides of both statements makes a substantive claim about the *endocentricity* of lexical projections: an XP contains an X' which contains an X as its lexical head; thus noun phrases are headed by nouns, verb phrases by verbs, and so on, and the large range of structures permitted by unrestricted phrase-structure rules is severely reduced. The position occupied by the YP in (37a) is filled by the *specifier* of the head; in (37b), the YP positions contain *complements* of the head. These notions are defined on the configurations permitted by (37) and are not primitives in the theory.[15] A final point about (37) is that it maintains that expressions occupying specifier and complement positions are themselves maximal projections of a lexical head.

Consider, now, the expressions in (41):

(41)   a. the enemy's destruction of the city
      b. very proud of the book
      c. right on the nose

Example (41a) is an NP, the head of which is *destruction, the city* is a complement of this head noun and *the enemy's* is its specifier. Both of these are themselves NPs, so an appropriate d-structure for (41) is (42):[16]

(42) $[_{NP}[_{NP}$the enemy's$][_{N'}[_{N}$destruction$]$ $[_{NP}$ (of) the city$]]]$

Example (41b) is an AP, headed by the adjective *proud, the book* is a complement of this head and the adverbial *very* is its specifier. Assuming that adverbs are a special class of adjectives (see Radford, 1988a, Section 3.7 for justification for this suggestion), the structure for (41b) is (43):

(43) $[_{AP}[_{AP}$very$][_{A'}[_{A}$proud$]$ $[_{NP}$ (of) the book$]]]$

Example (41c), a PP, can be analysed along similar lines to yield (44):

(44) $[_{PP}[_{AP}$right$][_{P'}[_{P}$on$]$ $[_{NP}$ the nose$]]]$

Such phrases under these analyses suggest that (36), apart from information about linear order, accurately captures the nature of a range of lexical projections in English. Each of them can be schematically represented as (45):

(45) $[_{XP}$ Specifier $[_{X'}[_X$ Head] Complement]]

Furthermore, in principle, it appears that the system ought to be extendible to clause-structure, particularly if we take account of Chomsky's original observations on the parallels between (32a) and (32b).

Parallelism requires that *destroyed* should be treated as the lexical head of the clause taking *the city* as a complement and *the enemy* as its specifier. Indeed, ST analyses of clause-structure go some way towards this, by treating the direct object as an *internal* argument of the V and the subject as an *external* argument, the deep structure bracketing for (32a) being as in (46):

(46)   [[the enemy][[destroyed][the city]]]

Difficulties arise, however, when we consider the way in which ST attaches labels to this structure. Such a labelling appears in (47):

(47) $[_S[_{NP}$the enemy$][_{VP}[_V$destroyed$][_{NP}$the city]]]

For reasons to which we shall return in chapter 10, the proposal that clauses be analysed in a manner consistent with the X-bar framework introduced here was not adopted for a considerable time. Clauses remained a structural anomaly within the system until it was extended to embrace non-lexical heads and their projections. For now, we might simply note that if the X-bar principles are truly cross-categorial, the labelling associated with (46) ought to be not (47), but (48):

(48) $[_{VP}[_{NP}$the enemy$][_{V'}[_V$destroyed$][_{NP}$the city]]]

To illustrate the interaction of LRs and X-bar theory, consider again (41a). To produce an appropriate structure for this NP using phrase-structure rules, we might postulate the rules in (49):

(49)   a. NP → NP – N′
        b. N′ → N – NP

In the system we are now developing, there are no phrase-structure rules. What we have is the X-bar principles of (36) and an LR for *destruction*, paralleling that for *destroy*, along the lines of (50):

(50) *destruction*: N; Agent$_i$, Patient$_j$

The suggestions we have made in the previous section require the Agent and Patient arguments to be projected as NPs, with the Patient being 'internal'. Interpreting 'internal' to mean within the single bar projection, (36) determines the correct d-structure for (41a) apart from linear order.[17] No phrase-structure rules are involved in this determination.

The final issue for X-bar Theory concerns the level at which (36) holds. Uncontroversially, it holds at d-structure and it is standard to assume that it need not hold at s-structure or LF, as these levels may be the reflection of movement processes which destroy the configurations it licenses (although, see May, 1985; Radford, 1988a, Section 10.5).[18]

Move α has already been introduced in the previous section. That movement of some kind must be embraced by the theory is clear if d-structures are partially determined by projections of lexical properties. In the previous section, this was illustrated using *wh*-questions, but Passive and Raising constructions can be used to make the same point. Thus, consider the examples in (51):

(51) a. John was kissed
      b. John seems to like Mary

Kiss, like *hit* in (9), notionally takes two arguments, an Agent and a Patient. In contrast, it appears that *seem* takes a single propositional argument, which, for the sake of concreteness, we will refer to as Proposition. Thus, LRs for *kiss* and *seem* might be along the lines of (52):

(52) a. *kiss*: V; Agent, Patient
      b. *seem*: V; Proposition

If we now assume that any d-structure must contain an external argument position, irrespective of whether this is filled by an argument (see the Extended Projection Principle below), that CSR(Proposition) = S, and that Patients and Propositions must project into syntax as internal arguments, schematic d-structures for (51a, b) will be (53a, b):[19]

(53) a. [$_S$e [$_{VP}$was kissed John]]
      b. [$_S$ e [$_{VP}$ seems [$_S$John to like Mary]]]

In order to produce the correct s-structure in these examples, *John* has to move from a VP-internal position to external argument position leaving behind a co-indexed empty category:

(54) a. [$_S$John$_i$ [$_{VP}$was kissed e_i]]
      b. [$_S$ John$_i$ [$_{VP}$ seems [$_S$$e_i$ to like Mary]]]

Such movements are further tokens of Move α, differing from that described in the previous section in terms of what gets moved (*wh*-expression vs. lexical NP) and the destination of the movement. Regarding the latter, the movements in the above examples are to positions which *can* be filled by arguments at d-structure (*A-positions*), whereas in the case of *wh*-questions (and Quantifier Raising at LF), the *wh*-expression is moved to a position outside the argument structure projected by the verb (an *A'-position*).

Of course, Move α, interpreted as 'move anything anywhere', while extraordinarily simple to state, legitimizes a vast range of possibilities which would yield ill-formed s-structures. Additionally, we noted in Section 2.5 the desirability of *all* operations being optional, and this means that we cannot build into the statement of Move α that it *must* apply to (53a, b). Faced with such observations, the strategy of PPT is to have the operation of Move α constrained by requirements imposed by other modules, most notably Case Theory and Θ-Theory (see below, pp. 86, 88). These requirements are such that Move α is *prevented* from applying in a profligate manner and is *required* to apply in appropriate circumstances, thus allowing the operation itself to be simply stated and to remain optional.

It was noted at the outset of this section that it is not customary to regard Move α as an independent module. This may be because it is not entirely clear whether there are constraints on its operation which are not readily derivable from the requirements of other modules. If such constraints exist, they might be legitimately regarded as principles in the Theory of Move α. One candidate, deriving from the work of Emonds (1976), is that instances of Move α must be *structure-preserving*, and what is involved here can be appreciated by considering again (53) and (54). In these examples, Move α applied to move an NP into *another NP position*. Thus, the s-structures in (54) can be seen as preserving the essential details of the d-structures in (53).[20]

Finally, we must consider the levels of the previous section at which Move α applies. While recent work on LRs (for example, Hale and Keyser, forthcoming) has proposed a role for Move α at this level, we shall make the standard assumption, motivated by the examples above and those of the previous section, that the operation mediates two mappings: that from d-structure to s-structure and that from s-structure to LF.

Binding Theory is largely concerned with the distribution of *anaphoric* and *pronominal* NPs. Consider the English reflexive anaphor *himself* and the corresponding pronoun *him*. *Himself* is an anaphor, because it requires a co-referential antecedent to precede it in the same sentence in which it occurs; (55) illustrates this:

(55)   a. John$_i$ likes himself$_i$
       b. *Himself$_i$ likes John$_i$
       c. John$_i$ got out of bed. *Himself$_i$ got dressed.

Him, a pronoun, *can* be interpreted as co-referential with another expression in a sentence under certain conditions, as in (56):

(56)   John$_i$ wants Mary to like him$_i$

However, *him* is almost always free to refer outside its containing sentence, either to some entity identified elsewhere in the discourse or to some contextually specified individual.[21] Thus, (57), in which *John* and *him* bear distinct indices to show disjoint reference, is also well-formed in English:

(57)   John$_i$ wants Mary to like him$_j$

Inspection of a variety of contexts suggests that *himself*, co-indexed with its obligatory antecedent, and *him*, co-indexed with that same antecedent, are in complementary distribution in English. Some of these contexts appear in (58)–(61):

(58) a. John$_i$ likes himself$_i$
      b. *John$_i$ likes him$_i$

(59) a. *John$_i$ wants Mary to like himself$_i$
      b. John$_i$ wants Mary to like him$_i$

(60) a. John$_i$ likes photographs of himself$_i$
      b. *John$_i$ likes photographs of him$_i$

(61) a. *John$_i$ likes Mary's photographs of himself$_i$
      b. John$_i$ likes Mary's photographs of him$_i$

Unfortunately, there are contexts where this complementary distribution breaks down. This is illustrated by the case of the English reciprocal anaphor *each other*. This anaphor can occur as subject of a noun phrase when its antecedent lies outside this noun phrase, as in (62):[22]

(62) The men$_i$ like [each other$_i$'s pictures of Bill]

However, it is also possible for a third person plural genitive pronoun in this position to be interpreted as co-referential with the subject of the matrix clause:

(63) The men$_i$ like [their$_i$ pictures of Bill]

To take account of this adequately leads to considerable complications in the statement of the principles in the Binding Theory, and for the purposes of our present discussion, we shall assume that the complementary distribution illustrated by (58)–(61) is general.[23]

    If anaphors are characterized as those expressions which *always* lack independent reference, receiving their referential interpretation from an obligatory antecedent, and pronouns as those expressions which *sometimes* lack such reference, it is natural to consider whether there is a third class of expressions which *never* lack independent reference. Such expressions are referred to as *R-expressions* and are represented by lexical NPs such as *John*, and *the man*. Example (64) illustrates some aspects of their distribution:

(64) a. *He$_i$ likes John$_i$
      b. *Mary$_i$ likes the woman$_i$
      c. *John$_i$ believes that Mary likes the man$_i$
      d. *The boss$_i$ wants to make John$_i$ redundant
      e. *John$_i$ likes Mary's photographs of the boss$_i$
      f. His$_i$ mother likes John$_i$

The principles of the Binding Theory can now be introduced and illustrated fairly easily if we equip ourselves with the definition of *binding* in (65):

(65)   α *binds* β iff (i) α c-commands β; (ii) α and β are co-indexed.

The obvious converse notion is defined in (66):

(66) If α is not bound, it is *free*.

To illustrate these definitions, consider the examples in (67):

(67)   a. John$_i$ hates himself$_i$
        b. John$_i$'s mother likes him$_i$
        c. John$_i$ hates him$_j$

In (67a), *himself* is bound by *John*, because (i) *John* c-commands *himself*, and (ii) *John* and *himself* are co-indexed; *John* is free in this sentence. In (67b), both *John* and *him* are free, because, while the two expressions are co-indexed, neither is c-commanded by the other. Finally, in (67c), both *John* and *him* are again free – in this case, *John* does c-command *him*, but the co-indexing condition is not satisfied.

   With these definitions in place, let us now return to the data in (58) – (61), beginning with the contrast illustrated by (60) and (61). These examples all have the schematic structure illustrated in (68):

(68)   antecedent$_i$ . . . [$_{NP}$ (subject) . . . anaphor$_i$/pronoun$_i$]

The presence of a subject in the NP appears to be crucial: if it appears, the anaphor cannot be co-indexed with the matrix subject but the pronoun can (61a, b); if it is not there, the anaphor must be co-indexed with the matrix subject and the pronoun cannot be (60a, b). We can use this to formulate a hypothesis about the domain in which an anaphor must be bound and a pronoun free, subsequently testing this against additional data.

   The domain in question is referred to as the *governing category* for an anaphor/pronoun, and is defined as in (69):

(69)   The *governing category* for α is the smallest category containing α, a governor for α and a subject.

For present purposes, we can take the set of governors as the set of lexical heads {N, V, A, P}. Then, it follows that the governing category for *himself/him* in (61a, b) is the NP *Mary's photographs of himself/him*, since this NP contains the anaphor/pronoun, a governor for this item (*of*) and a subject *Mary*. On the other hand, in (60a, b), the governing category for *himself/him* is the matrix sentence – the NP *photographs of himself/him* does not contain a subject, so the search for the governing category has to proceed into the matrix sentence where a subject (*John*) is found. From these observations, we can formulate the principles of the Binding Theory in (70):

(70) A: An anaphor must be bound in its governing category
      B: A pronoun must be free in its governing category

In the light of (70), consider (58) and (59). Example (58) is very straightforward. In (58a, b), the governing category for *himself/him* is the matrix clause; *himself* is bound in this domain satisfying Principle A, so (58a) is well-formed; *him* is also bound in this domain violating Principle B, so (58b) is ill-formed with this indexing. Examples (59a, b) are similar to (61a, b) in that a subordinate subject *Mary* intervenes between the anaphor/pronoun and its potential antecedent. This means that the clause *Mary to like himself/him* constitutes the governing category for *himself/him* and the correct predictions for (59a, b) follow.

What of R-expressions? The fact that they never lack independent reference suggests that they should be accommodated in the Binding Theory by (71):

(71) C: An R-expression is free everywhere

Inspection of the examples in (64) reveals that this appears to be accurate. In (64a–e), R-expressions (*John, the woman*, etc.) are bound by the matrix subject and the sentences are ungrammatical with co-indexing; (64f) is not a counter-example to (71), since *his* does not c-command *John* in this sentence's structure, so *John* remains free.

We can now put (70) and (71) together, and formulate the full set of principles in the Binding Theory as (72):

(72) A: An anaphor must be bound in its governing category
      B: A pronoun must be free in its governing category
      C: An R-expression must be free everywhere

An intriguing and important suggestion is that the empty category which is left as a result of some applications of Move α behaves like an anaphor in satisfying Principle A of (72). Recall that above (p. 73) we have noted that the movement of lexical NPs in such constructions as Passives is to A-positions, whereas movement of *wh*-expressions in the formation of questions is to A′-positions. Correspondingly, we can refer to instances of Move α as A-movement (NP-movement) or A′-movement (*wh*-movement). It follows that the co-indexing of a moved item with an empty category in the case of A-movement is similar to the co-indexings we have considered in connection with binding in that both apply to expressions in A-positions.

Note further that the empty category resulting from A-movement must have a co-indexed antecedent which c-commands it. That it must have an antecedent follows from the fact that it only arises as a result of movement; as a consequence it will always be co-indexed with the moved element. That this antecedent must c-command the empty category is indicated by the ill-formed s-structure in (73):

(73) *[e_i [kissed John$_i$]]

In (73), we have assumed that *John* appears in external argument position at d-structure, with the internal argument position empty. Lowering of *John* to a position where it does not c-command the empty category is illegitimate. Thus, if we treat the empty category resulting from A-movement (so-called *NP-trace*) as an anaphor, an immediate consequence is that applications of Move α which lower an NP to a position from which it cannot c-command its trace are ruled out by the Binding Theory. This is our first example of Move α being constrained by a principle from a different module. The place of NP-trace in a taxonomy of empty categories will be further considered below.

Finally, consider the level at which (72) applies. This is a complex issue, which we will not pursue seriously here. We have noted, however, that the theory is intended to contribute to an account of the distribution of NP-trace, this being an empty anaphor. NP-trace only results from movement, from which it follows that (72) cannot apply comprehensively at d-structure. For concreteness, we shall assume that it is operative at s-structure, but nothing in what follows will depend upon this decision.[24]

The above discussion has drawn attention to constraints on the operation of Move α when it operates on lexical NPs. However, it has long been known that A′-movement, specifically when it involves the movement of *wh*-phrases, is not entirely free (see Ross, 1967, for the earliest systematic study of this area). Some conditions on A′-movement fall within *Bounding Theory*.

Before embarking on a brief exposition of this module, it is necessary to be more explicit than we have so far about the target of moved *wh*-expressions. Up to now, we have simply noted that such expressions end up in some sentence-initial position which is outside the argument structure projected by the verb. Originating with the work of Bresnan (1970) and informing theoretical discussion until the more recent focus on functional categories, this position was identified with that of *complementizers* and abbreviated to C or COMP. In English, overt complementizers introduce a variety of subordinate clauses, and some examples are italicized in (74):

(74)   a. John believes *that* Bill will win
       b. John wonders *whether* Bill will win
       c. John hopes *for* Bill to win

It was suggested that the structure of such clauses should be dealt with by partially assimilating S to the X-bar framework via the rule in (75):[25]

(75)   S′ → C – S

This rule is generalized to matrix clauses, despite the fact that in English, these are not introduced by overt complementizers. The d-structure C-position is thereby available as the target for moved *wh*-expressions.

Note now that, alongside such simple examples as (76), we also find (77), which exhibits long-distance *wh*-movement:

(76)   What$_i$ will John eat e_i?

(77)   What$_i$ does John believe Bill will eat e_i?

The existence of such long-distance movement suggests that Move α, applied to *wh*-expressions, might be relatively unconstrained, but if we take account of a wider range of subordinate clauses, this turns out not to be the case. For example, if the moved *wh*-expression originates in a complex NP headed by a noun such as *fact, statement* or *opinion*, what we get is considerably worse than (77):·

(78)   ??What$_i$ does John hold the opinion that Bill will eat e_i?

And if it originates in a relative clause or an interrogative clause in which a *wh*-expression has already been fronted, the outcome is total ill-formedness:

(79)   a. *What$_i$ does John know the man who$_j$ e_j will eat e_i?
        b. *Where$_i$ do you know what$_j$ John put e_j e_i?

It appears, then, that some sort of locality constraint is operative in the case of A′-movement, and, because it is A′-movement, the nature of this is not going to be derivable from the Binding Theory which is involved with relationships between expressions in A-positions (but see Hornstein, 1983; Aoun and Hornstein, 1985; Aoun, 1985, 1986).
    Assuming the rule in (75), we shall now consider these examples in a little more detail. Example (76) is straightforward, with the d-structure in (80a) and the s-structure in (80b):[26]

(80)   a. [$_{S'}$[$_C$ *e*] [$_S$ John will eat what]]

        b. [$_{S'}$[what$_i$] [will John eat e_i]]

Consider next (77). A schematic d-structure is (81):

(81)   [$_{S'}$[$_C$ *e*] [$_S$ John believes [$_{S'}$ [$_C$ *e*] [Bill will eat what]]]]

Move α applies to this structure so that *what* ends up in the matrix C- position, but if we only require *wh*-expressions always to move to C, there are two ways in which this could happen: *what* might move to the matrix C in one step or two, stopping off at the subordinate C-position in the latter case. The s-structures derived from these alternatives are (82a, b):

(82)   a. [$_{S'}$[what$_i$][does John believe [$_{S'}$[*e*] [Bill will eat e_i]]]]
        b. [$_{S'}$[what$_i$][does John believe [$_{S'}$[e_i] [Bill will eat e_i]]]]

The fact that movement of *wh*-expressions is constrained in other contexts suggests that perhaps (82b) is correct. Let us assume that it is and move to the ill-formed examples above. Consider (78) and its d-structure (83):

(83) $[_{S'}[_C e][_S$ John holds $[_{NP}$the opinion $[_{S'}[_C$ that] $[_S$ Bill will eat what]]]]]

If, in order to get to the matrix C-position, *what* first stops off at the subordinate C, the s-structure we derive is (84):

(84) $[_{S'}$[what$_i$][$_S$does John hold $[_{NP}$the opinion $[_{S'}[e_i$ that] $[_S$ Bill will eat e_i]]]]]

What is significant here is that, in taking its second step, *what* has moved out of both an NP and an S, there being no C-position in NPs where it can stop off. The result is less than fully grammatical.

   Now consider (79b) with its d-structure (85) (79a is identical in the relevant respects):

(85) $[_{S'}[_C e]$ $[_S$ you know $[_{S'}[_C e]$ $[_S$ John put what where]]]]

In the interrogative complement, *what* has to move to the subordinate C, giving the intermediate structure in (86):

(86) $[_{S'}[_C e]$ $[_S$ you know $[_{S'}$[what$_j$] $[_S$ John put e_j where]]]]

Thus, the subordinate C is already occupied by a *wh*-expression, so if *where* is to move to the matrix C, it must do so in one step. In doing this, it will have to move out of two Ss. The result is ungrammatical.[27]
   What the above analyses suggest is that there is indeed a locality constraint on the movement of *wh*-expressions and that it concerns the number and type of constituent boundaries which can be crossed. NP and S are designated *bounding nodes* and the *Subjacency Principle*, the single principle of Bounding Theory, is then formulated as in (87):

(87)   No movement can cross more than one bounding node

Thus, (78) is ungrammatical because *two* bounding nodes (NP and S) are crossed in one step of the derivation of (84); (79a, b) are ungrammatical because *two* Ss are crossed in one step of the derivation of (86).
   Having suggested that NP-trace resulting from A-movement is an empty anaphor, we might wonder about the status of *wh*-trace. Examples such as those in (88) suggest that, from the perspective of the Binding Theory, it has the properties of an R-expression:

(88)   a. *Who$_i$ did [he$_i$ see e_i]
        b. *Who$_i$ did he$_i$ say [Mary saw e_i]

In (88a), *he* binds the empty category in the latter's governing category and the result is ungrammatical with this indexing. Thus, e_i does not behave like an anaphor. In (88b), *he* binds e_i from outside e_i's governing category and again the result is ungrammatical, i.e. e_i is not pronominal. It is clear that e_i must be free of all binding by expressions in A-positions. Empty R-expressions are known as *variables*.[28]

Finally, as a condition on movement, the Subjacency Principle does not operate at a single level of representation.

Control Theory is concerned with the distribution of a third empty category, PRO (read 'big pro'). Justification for the postulation of such a category is provided by examples such as those in (89):

(89) a. John ordered Mary to work
      b. John promised Mary to work
      c. To work would be a mistake

Consider (89a). *Work* is an intransitive verb which has a single Agent argument. Thus, its (partial) LR will be as in (90):

(90) *work*: V; Agent

As it is a characteristic of Agents to project into syntax as external arguments (cf. Section 3.2), the d-structure projected by this representation is (91):

(91) [NP [$_{VP}$work]]

Now, what is in the external argument position in (89a)? It might be proposed that this is *Mary*, but consideration of the lexical structure of the matrix verb *order* argues against this. This verb has three arguments, and we might suggest (92) as its LR:

(92) *order*: V; Agent, Goal, Proposition

But then it is evident that *Mary* is the Goal argument of *order*. If it is illegitimate for an expression to fulfil two argument roles simultaneously – a principle of Θ-Theory which will be discussed presently – it follows that *Mary* cannot be in the external argument position of *work*. We propose, therefore, that this position is occupied by an empty category PRO which is *controlled* by *Mary* in the matrix clause. On this account, a schematic d-structure for (89a) is (93):

(93) [John ordered Mary$_i$ [PRO$_i$ to work]]

This is an example of *object* control, where the controller is direct object in the matrix clause. Example (89b) provides an instance of *subject* control, as (94) indicates:

(94) [John$_i$ promised Mary [PRO$_i$ to work]

An obvious question to ask is whether the empty category we are now postulating is distinct from those arising from movement processes. An immediate difference between PRO and those is that it occurs in d-structures, whereas they appear in the course of a derivation. Furthermore, while PRO has clear anaphoric properties, indicated by the co-indexing in (93) and (94), it

appears to have additional interpretive possibilities in (89c). Exactly the same
argument as we have adduced above concerning the argument structure of
work applies to this example, suggesting that it has a d-structure along the
lines of (95):

(95) [[PRO to work] would be a mistake]

But in (95), there is no potential antecedent for PRO, a fact that is related to
the observation that it has an *arbitrary* interpretation in (89c), referring to an
unspecified individual or individuals. It is customary to build this into the
representation and to replace (95) by (96):[29]

(96)   [[PRO$_{arb}$ to work] would be a mistake]

In so far as it is possible for PRO to be free from control by an antecedent, it
appears to have pronominal properties (cf. the discussion of the Binding
Theory above), leading to the rather odd conclusion that PRO is both
anaphoric and pronominal. If this characterization is correct, the central
questions in Control Theory are: (i) what is the distribution of PRO and how is
this related to its anaphoric and pronominal properties? (ii) for controlled
PRO, how do we handle the distinction between subject- and object-control?
    Control Theory is a poor relation among the modules, in that it is not
associated with any independent principles.[30] Question (ii) is usually answered
by maintaining that subject- and object-control are lexically specified properties and are simply stipulated in the LRs of the appropriate items (see
Jackendoff, 1987, for the suggestion that systematic aspects of Θ-Theory may
be involved here). Question (i) has provoked a rather more interesting answer.
Recall that it has been suggested that PRO has both anaphoric and pronominal
properties. If we represent these by features, (97) expresses the characteristics
of the empty categories we have met so far:

(97)   a. NP-trace: [+anaphoric, −pronominal]
       b. variable: [−anaphoric, −pronominal]
       c. PRO: [+anaphoric, +pronominal]

The Binding Theory (72) can then be minimally reconstrued as referring to
features, with Principle A applicable to the [+anaphoric] NP-trace and lexical
anaphors such as *himself*, and Principle C applicable to variables and lexical
R-expressions which share the featural specification [−anaphoric,
−pronominal]. What now of PRO?
    It seems that PRO should fall under both Principles A and B, but to maintain
this requires it to be simultaneously bound *and* free in its governing category.
This looks like a contradiction and would be *if PRO had a governing category*.
If, however, PRO lacks a governing category, (72A, B) will simply not apply to
it, and it will be possible to retain the analysis in (97c). We can ensure that
PRO lacks a governing category if it is ungoverned, and this claim is made by
the so-called PRO Theorem in (98):

(98)   PRO is ungoverned

On the basis of what we have introduced so far, (98) looks as if it is correct. Recall that we assumed that the class of governors included the lexical heads N, V, A and P. They govern their complements, so it ought to follow that PRO cannot appear as complement of a lexical head. The examples in (99) show that this prediction is borne out:

(99)   a.   *John kissed PRO
       b.   *John put the book on PRO
       c.   *John is proud of PRO
       d.   *John is the author of PRO

Consider now the subject of a tensed matrix or subordinate clause. Examples (100) and (101) show that, while a lexical NP can occur in this position, PRO cannot:

(100)   a.   John kissed Mary
        b.   *PRO kissed Mary

(101)   a.   John believes Bill kissed Mary
        b.   *John believes PRO kissed Mary

Such data are accounted for by (98) if this position is governed. That it is is required by Case Theory, as we shall see shortly, but we can usefully anticipate aspects of the relevant discussion here. Along with (75), a further residue of rule-based systems which persisted into PPT was the phrase-structure rule in (102):

(102)   S → NP – I – VP

I (AUX in more traditional systems of notation) is the position in which modal verbs (*will, may, can*, etc.) appear at d-structure, and it also contains features encoding agreement, finiteness and tense. Thus, a typical representation for these features in I might be (103).[31]

(103)

$$
\begin{array}{c}
\text{I} \\
\diagup \diagdown \\
\text{[+TNS]} \quad \text{[AGR]} \\
\text{[+PAST]} \quad \text{[+3SING]}
\end{array}
$$

Given (102), it is clear that I is in an appropriate structural position to govern NP (the subject), – whether S or S′ (or neither) is a maximal projection, the subject appears in the government domain of I – and now we simply add to our set of governors I[+TNS]. Thus, the governors in English are as in (104):[32]

(104)   The set of governors = {N, V, A, P, I[+TNS]}

With (104) stipulated, we can see that the subject position of a tensed clause is governed. Accordingly, by (98), PRO is excluded from this position. Furthermore, the subject of a non-finite clause is not governed and it follows that this environment accurately characterizes the distribution of PRO: PRO can occur as subject of an infinitive as in (93) – (95) or as subject of a gerund clause as in (105):[33]

(105) a. John$_i$ likes [PRO$_i$ working]
    b. [PRO$_{arb}$ working] is good for the soul

That the PRO Theorem (98) makes the correct predictions and *follows* from the independently motivated Binding Theory in this way is often offered as a paradigmatic illustration of the deductive structure of PPT.

 Case is, of course, a traditional grammatical notion and is elaborately exemplified morphologically in a range of languages including German, Latin and Finnish. *Case Theory* is concerned with the mechanisms whereby NPs receive Case, the capitalization indicating that something more abstract than morphologically marked case is involved.

 In modern English, there is somewhat attenuated overt marking of case. Personal pronouns, however, display nominative, accusative and genitive forms, as illustrated in (106):

(106)

	Nominative	accusative	genitive
1 Sing.	I	me	my/mine
2 Sing.	you	you	your(s)
3 Sing. Masc.	he	him	his
3 Sing. Fem.	she	her	her(s)
1 Pl.	we	us	our(s)
2 Pl.	you	you	your(s)
3 Pl.	they	them	their(s)

Many singular noun phrases also have a genitive form (*John's, the man's*), but there is no overt marking of other cases on lexical NPs in the language. Consideration of examples in which case is morphologically marked is sufficient to show that the case borne by an expression is related to the syntactic configuration in which it occurs. Thus, the examples in (107) are all ill-formed in most varieties of English because the pronouns are inappropriately case-marked:

(107) a. *Me like(s) he.
   b. *Our(s) like(s) they
   c. *She book is interesting
   d. *John's saw my

It follows that the theory must somehow ensure that NPs which need case get the right case in the right configuration. Generalizing, it is perhaps appropriate to assume that *all* NPs are assigned Case by whatever mechanisms are postulated, despite the fact that in English, Case-marking will not be overt in the majority of instances.

The assumption that all non-empty NPs require Case is the central principle of Case Theory, the Case Filter (108):

(108)   *NP if NP has a phonetic matrix and no Case.

How, then, do NPs receive Case so as to avoid the effects of (108)? The theory claims that designated elements have Case to assign and this assignment takes place under government. However, the class of Case-assigners is more restricted than the class of governors in (104). In particular, N and A are *not* Case-assigners, and this is the reason for their not taking bare complements. Consider the examples in (109):

(109)   a. *destruction the city
        b. *proud the book

The N′ in (109a) consists of the head N *destruction* and its complement *the city*. Clearly, the N governs its complement, and if it had Case to assign, this assignment should take place with (109a) being well-formed. That (109a) is not well-formed suggests that the N does not have Case to assign. The structure is 'saved' by the introduction of a preposition *of*, as in (110):

(110)   destruction *of* the city

Prepositions are Case-assigners, so *the city* in (110) can now escape from the Case Filter. Furthermore, this token of *of* has no semantic content (in particular, it does not signal possession), suggesting that it is discharging a purely syntactic function. Analogous remarks apply to (109b).

The lexical Case-assigners are members of V and P, with the former assigning objective (or accusative) Case to its complement and the latter oblique Case. Additionally, I[+TNS], which we have already seen to be a governor, assigns nominative Case to the subject position. Thus, the standard configurations for Case-assignment are as in (111).[34]

(111)

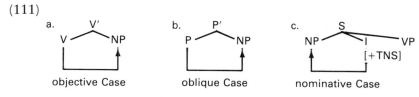

Given (108) and some additional assumptions, we can return to the Passive and illustrate another way in which Move α is constrained. Example (51a) was assigned the d-structure (53a), repeated here as (112a, b):

(112)   a. John was kissed
        b. [s e [vp was kissed John]]

Move α then moves *John* from the VP-internal position to the empty external argument position at s-structure. Why is this necessary?

Assume that the addition of passive morphology to a verb 'absorbs' the objective Case the verb normally assigns.[35] Then, *John* in its d-structure position will not be able to receive Case, so it must move to satisfy the Case Filter. The external argument position is free and nominative Case is available there from the finite I. Therefore, we have an account of why Move α is obligatory in this configuration which has not required any complications to be introduced into the operation itself. The obligatoriness arises from Case Theory.

If this treatment of Passives is along the right lines, it also shows that (108) operates at s-structure. *John*, which is Caseless in (112b), only has Case assigned at s-structure, so the well-formedness of (112a) indicates that the Case Filter is operative at this level.[36]

Much of the content of Θ-*Theory* has been presupposed in the discussion of this and the previous section. In particular, we have taken for granted a set of semantic roles such as Agent, Patient, Goal, etc. Originally studied within rather different frameworks by Gruber (1965) and Fillmore (1968), these are known as Θ-*roles*, and their status within the theory is a matter of some controversy (see, for example, Jackendoff, 1983, 1987; Hoekstra, forthcoming; Hale and Keyser, forthcoming).

Θ-Theory aims to articulate the principles determining the projection of lexical heads and their selected Θ-roles into syntax. In discussing the relationship between LRs and d-structures in the previous section, we assumed that there are principles preserving such selectional properties at the latter level. This assumption is part of one of the principles of Θ-theory, the Projection Principle, stated in (113):

(113)   Lexical properties are represented at all levels of syntactic structure (d-structure, s-structure and LF).

As well as encompassing our earlier assumptions about the nature of d-structures, (113) has as a consequence the requirement that instances of Move α leave an empty category behind. To see this, consider again the simple passive sentence (112a). Why not assume that its s-structure is (114)?

(114)   [s John [vp was kissed]]

The answer provided by the Projection Principle is that in (114) there is no representation of the internal argument which is a reflection of a lexical property of the verb *kiss*. The empty category we have assumed provides this representation, and ensures that the Projection Principle is satisfied at s-structure. Because of predicates such as *seem* and *appear* which do not select an external Θ-role as a lexical property, it is necessary to supplement the Projection Principle. These verbs require a subject as (115) indicates:

(115)   a. *Seems/*Appears that John loves Mary
        b. It seems/appears that John loves Mary

But a position for this *pleonastic* or *expletive* subject is not required by the lexical properties of the verb which only selects a propositional (internal) Θ-role. The necessary supplement is (116):

(116)   All clauses must have subjects

The statements in (113) and (116) together constitute the Extended Projection Principle, and (116) can be seen as the 'principle' corresponding to the 'rule' in (102).[37] It is also (116) that licenses the empty external argument position we have assumed in our earlier discussion of moved NPs in sentences including *seem* (cf. p. 73).

A further principle of Θ-theory is the Θ-criterion in (117):

(117)   Every argument is associated with one and only one position to which Θ-roles are assigned, and every Θ-role selected by a lexical head is associated with one and only one argument.

There is a sense in which (117) is saying something rather trite: that a head which selects n Θ-roles as a lexical property can only appear in syntactic configurations containing positions for exactly n arguments. As such, the Θ-criterion can be invoked to account for the ill-formedness of the examples in (118):[38]

(118)   a.   *John kissed
        b.   *John arrived Mary
        c.   *John put a book

Kiss selects two Θ-roles as a lexical property, but in (118a) it appears in a configuration which contains only one position with the consequence that one role remains unassigned; conversely, *arrive* selects only one Θ-role, and in (118b) there are two positions, one of which cannot be assigned a role; finally, *put* selects three Θ-roles, and (118c) contains only two positions.

The possibility of movement in the grammar introduces a layer of complication to this rather simple conception. To see this, consider the d-structure in (119):

(119)   [$_S$ *e* [$_{VP}$kissed Mary]]

There is nothing immediately wrong with this structure from the point of view of the principles we have discussed so far; it contains an empty external argument position, but we have seen the possibility of this as essential in other contexts. But now suppose Move α applies to (119) to give (120):

(120)   *[$_S$ Mary$_i$ [$_{VP}$kissed e_i]]

Such a movement would not be necessary for Case reasons, but again nothing we have seen so far rules it out. Now consider the assignment of Θ-roles to positions. The Patient role will be assigned to the VP-internal position and the

Agent role to the external position. As a consequence, the argument *Mary* will be associated with both roles, the former at d-structure and the latter at s-structure, and this is in violation of the Θ-criterion.[39] From this conclusion, a general prohibition follows: NP-movement can only be to positions to which Θ-roles are not assigned (*Θ'-positions*). Disregard for this will yield a situation in which an argument is associated with more than one Θ-role and this possibility is ruled out by the Θ-criterion.

With these ideas in mind, let us return to Passives one last time. Recall that we accounted for the obligatory movement of the internal argument in a passive by suggesting that passive morphology 'absorbs' the verb's objective Case. Burzio's Generalization (1981, 1986) states that if a verb fails to assign objective Case to its internal argument, then it has an athematic (Θ') external argument position. Assume, then, that a further effect of passive morphology is to de-thematize a verb's external argument position in line with Burzio's Generalization. Then, the movement of the internal argument into the external position that we have proposed for passives is legitimate; it is movement from a Θ-position to a Θ'-position. Jointly, Case Theory and Θ-Theory *require* and *permit* the movement we have assumed to take place in the derivation of passives.

We arrive at our final module, the *Theory of Empty Categories*. We have already met three of these (NP-trace, variable and PRO) and the feature-representation (97) we introduced in connection with these suggests that there might be a fourth, an empty pronominal specified as [−anaphoric, +prono-minal]. Such an empty category does not play a role in the grammar of English for reasons to which we shall return in chapter 4. However, *pro* (read 'little pro') exists in a range of languages with the predicted pronominal properties. So, consider (121) and (122) from Italian and Mandarin Chinese respectively (throughout, tones are omitted from Chinese examples for typographical convenience):

(121)   vado al cinema stasera
        (I) go to-the cinema tonight
        'I go to the cinema tonight'

(122)   xihuan tang-mian
        like soup-noodle
        'I/you/he/she/it/we/they like(s) noodle soup'

In both (121) and (122), there is no overt expression of a subject. Yet, in each case, a subject is understood and is interpreted as having a definite reference. In the Italian example, this has to be the speaker, because of the agreement features on the verb, but in the Chinese example, it can be any contextually determined referent since Chinese has no agreement morphology. As *pro* does not occur in the syntax of English, we shall not discuss it further here. In chapter 4, we shall see that it has played a important part in some recent acquisition studies. For now, we simply note that if there is an empty category in the subject position of (121) and (122), it cannot be a trace of movement since there is no reason to believe any movement has taken place. Nor, in the

Italian example, can it be PRO, since by the PRO Theorem PRO must be ungoverned and the subject position in Italian is presumably governed by a finite I.[40]

The existence of empty categories in the theory of grammar poses a number of profound questions. Most notably, we need to ask (i) what *licenses* the occurrence of an empty category of a particular type; and (ii) how are the referential properties of an empty category *identified* (cf. Rizzi, 1986, pp. 518–19). We can answer these questions for PRO: (i) PRO is licensed by the PRO Theorem, i.e. it can occur in ungoverned positions; (ii) controlled PRO is interpreted by the co-indexing induced by control verbs (arbitrary PRO raises issues which would take us too far afield, but see Rizzi (1986, pp. 520ff.)). Similarly, we can answer (ii) for the empty categories resulting from movement: they are interpreted via the co-indexing induced by the movement itself. But what about (i) for these empty categories? Binding Theory and Bounding Theory constrain the 'distance' a movement can cover in ways we have briefly described, but tell us nothing in detail about the sites from which an expression can be extracted. That this is a genuine issue is indicated by (123):

(123) a. ??Who$_i$ does John wonder whether Mary loves e_i?
       b. *Who$_i$ does John wonder whether e_i loves Mary?

Example (123a), which involves moving *who* from the embedded object position, is less than perfect, a fact that can be put down to its violating Subjacency. But (123b), with movement of the embedded subject, is considerably worse. Now, the important observation is that (123a, b) do not differ with respect to Subjacency, so some other factor must be contributing to produce the total ill-formedness of the latter. This is a complex area, so I shall only hint at how the phenomena are approached here.[41]

Recall that our set of governors in (104) included a finite I to ensure that the subject position was governed and Case-marked in tensed clauses. We can use this to insert a wedge between subject position and complement positions by defining a notion of *lexical government* and a class of lexical governors which excludes finite I. By this criterion, subject position is governed but not lexically governed, whereas direct object position is lexically governed. We might then try to capture the distinction between (123a, b) by (124):

(124) Empty categories resulting from movement must be lexically governed.

But (124) is too strong, since it prohibits any movement from subject position. That such movement is possible is amply illustrated by simple clauses such as (125a) with the s-structure (125b):

(125) a. Who loves Mary?
       b. [$_{S'}$[$_C$ who$_i$] [$_S$ e_i loves Mary]]

Furthermore, *wh*-expressions can be extracted from subordinate clause subject position under some circumstances. Particularly important are examples such as those in Section 2.2, repeated here as (126):

(126)   a. Who$_i$ does John believe Bill kissed e_i
        b. Who$_i$ does John believe e_i kissed Mary
        c. Who$_i$ does John believe that Bill kissed e_i
        d. *Who$_i$ does John believe that e_i kissed Mary

The well-formedness of (126a, c) is immediately accounted for by the lexical government of the empty category by *kissed,* and the presence of the complementizer *that* is irrelevant in this case. However, this is not so in (126b, d) where there is no lexical government of the subject position.

Assuming that long-distance movement goes through intermediate Cs to satisfy Subjacency, the s-structures we associate with (126b, d) are (127a, b) respectively:

(127)   a. $[_{S'}[_C$ who$_i][_S$ does John believe $[_{S'}[_C e_i][_S e_i$ kissed Mary$]]]]$
        b. $[_{S'}[_C$ who$_i][_S$ does John believe $[_{S'}[_C e_i$ that$][_S e_i$ kissed Mary$]]]]$

Ignoring various complications, let us concentrate on the embedded S′ in these representations. In (127a), this is structurally parallel to (125b), the only difference being that (125b) has *who*$_i$ where (127a) has e_i in C. Assume that C also bears an index which it inherits from an item appearing in it. Thus, the embedded S′ in (127a) is more fully represented as (128):

(128) $[_{S'}[_C e_i]_i [_S e_i$ kissed Mary$]]$

It is clear, given our definition of government, that $[_C e_i]_i$ governs e_i and it is also co-indexed with it. Refer to this relationship as *antecedent government.* Now consider the embedded S′ in (127b). Here C will not bear an index if the inheritance of indices requires *all* items in C to bear the inherited index. Thus, the structure we are concerned with is (129):

(129) $[_{S'}[_C e_i$ that$_j] [_S e_i$ kissed Mary$]]$

In (129), $[_C e_i$ that$_j]$ does not antecedent govern e_i; it does govern it, but the required co-indexing does not obtain. Furthermore, the e_i in C does not antecedent govern the empty subject, since it does not c-command it (assuming here Reinhart's 'branching node' definition of c-command). Thus, the empty subject is neither lexically nor antecedent governed in this case. These observations suggest that we can approach an analysis of these phenomena by introducing a relation of *proper government* which subsumes lexical government and antecedent government. This is defined in (130):

(130)   α properly governs β iff:
        (i) α lexically governs β; or
        (ii) α antecedent governs β.

We can then state the *Empty Category Principle* (ECP), the licensing condition for NP-trace and variables, as (131):

(131) Empty categories resulting from movement must be properly governed.

There is considerable evidence that the ECP extends to LF, but we shall not go into this here. The interested reader is referred to Kayne (1981), Rizzi (1982) and May (1985).

We have now completed our survey of the major principles which define the content of the modules in PPT. Needless to say, many details have been omitted and some of these will be considered in later chapters. Our next task is to investigate how linguistic variation is dealt with in the model.

3.4 Parameters

Of the modules introduced in the previous section, several of them have been identified as admitting *parametric variation*, this being the concept which allows PPT to begin to come to terms with the obvious differences in the world's languages. In this section, we shall perform another pass through the modules to get some idea of what this strategy involves.

First, consider again *X-bar Theory*, and recall that in the X-bar schema (37), repeated here as (132), *order* is not specified:

(132) a. $XP = (YP), X'$

b. $X' = YP^*, X$

This was reflected in our discussion of the projection of lexical representations into d-structures, when we pointed out that linear order was not determined by the conjunction of lexical properties and X-bar Principles. Of course, it is well known that word-order varies across languages, and a simple example is provided by the comparison between the English phrase in (133a) and its Japanese equivalent in (133b):

(133)   a. gave a book to Shunsuke

      b. Shunsuke ni hon o age-ta
        Shunsuke ind. obj. book dir. obj. give-past
        'gave a book to Shunsuke'

On the assumption that *give* in English and its Japanese equivalent have identical argument selection properties, both plausibly project into syntax heading a VP and taking two complements within V'. But the order in which these complements appear relative to each other and relative to the head verb is different in the two languages.

It is easy to formulate a statement of the *Head-Direction Parameter* to express variations in head–complement word-order as in (134):

(134)   The Head-Direction Parameter has two values:
         (a) $X' = YP^* - X$ (head-final);
         (b) $X' = X - YP^*$ (head-initial).

Then, on the basis of (133), we could propose that English selects value (b), whereas Japanese selects value (a). And we might be further attracted to (134) by noting that Japanese appears to have postpositions where English uses prepositions, suggesting that X might genuinely range over the full set of lexical categories. As we shall see below, this is a somewhat illusory goal, but descriptive cross-linguistic work on variations in head–complement order has discovered significant generalizations, and (134) can be viewed as expressing a particularly strong claim about these.[42]

The parameter in (134) concerns the relationship between heads and complements, and it is straightforward to formulate the *Specifier Parameter* in an identical format in (135):

(135)   The Specifier Parameter has two values:
         (a) $XP = (YP) - X'$ (specifier-initial);
         (b) $XP = X' - (YP)$ (specifier-final).

Assuming that determiners occur in the specifier position of NPs, a language such as Bulgarian, which expresses definiteness by means of nominal *suffixes*, perhaps provides evidence for value (b). Obviously, as we saw in the previous section, English appears to adopt value (a) uniformly across its lexical categories (for discussion of the Specifier Parameter relying on detailed theoretical analysis, see Georgopoulos, 1991).

Next consider *Move* α. Since its content is that anything can be moved anywhere, it might be anticipated that any parameterization affecting it will only arise from variations in other modules which constrain its operation. However, Chinese is often cited as a language which indicates the necessity to parameterize Move α itself. Specifically, the suggestion is that the range of the variable α may be parameterized in terms of the *level* at which Move α operates.

The relevant Chinese data are *wh*-questions. We have already seen that, in English, Move α applies to *wh*-phrases in the mapping from d- to s-structure, moving them to the clause-initial C-position. However, this does not happen in Chinese, and the Chinese *wh*-question corresponding to (136a) is (136b):

(136)   a. What$_i$ do you like e_i?

         b. Ni xihuan shenme?
            you like what
            'What do you like?'

In (136b) *shenme* ('what') appears at s-structure in its d-structure position, an observation that is reinforced by the fact that an appropriate answer to (136b) might be (137):

(137)   wo xihuan jidan chaofan
        I like egg fry-rice
        'I like egg and fried rice'

In (137), the NP *jidan chaofan* ('egg and fried rice') substitutes directly for the *wh*-question word, suggesting that the latter appears in s-structure in a position determined by lexical properties of *xihuan* ('like'), i.e. as a d-structure internal argument. On the basis of such data, it seems that Move α does not affect Chinese *wh*-words in the mapping from d- to s-structure.

There is evidence, however, that Chinese *wh*-words are moved to A'-positions at LF. This evidence is provided by first considering the English examples in (138):

(138)   a. Who$_i$ does John believe Mary kissed e_i?
        b. *John believes who$_i$ Mary kissed e_i
        c. John wonders who$_i$ Mary kissed e_i
        d. *Who$_i$ does John wonder Mary kissed e_i?

We have already suggested that in (138a) *who* is moved in two steps through the intermediate C. Sentence (138b) shows that if *who* remains in its intermediate position, the result is ungrammatical. If, instead of *believe*, our matrix verb is *wonder*, exactly the opposite situation obtains, as (138c, d) show – here *who* must remain in the intermediate position, and if it moves to the front of the sentence, the outcome is ungrammatical. How are we to account for this?

Plausibly, the answer lies in the lexical properties of the matrix verbs *believe* and *wonder*. Both of them take a clausal complement, but whereas in the case of *believe*, this clause is indicative, for *wonder*, it is interrogative. We can represent this in the projection of lexical representations into syntax by indicating that the internal argument of *believe* is non-interrogative and that of *wonder* is interrogative. Assume that this is achieved by marking the C-position to which *wh*-words move as [±WH], and suppose that this is always an option for matrix clauses which are not lexically selected. Then, d-structures like the following will be well-formed:

(139)   a. [$_{S'}$[$_C$+WH][$_S$ John believes[$_{S'C}$[−WH][$_S$Mary kissed who]]]]
        b. [$_{S'}$[$_C$−WH][$_S$ John wonders [$_{S'}$[$_C$+WH][$_S$Mary kissed who]]]]

Suppose further that in English, (140) holds:[43]

(140)   a [+WH] C must be occupied by a *wh*-phrase and a *wh*-phrase must occupy a [+WH] C at s-structure.

Statement (140) is a further constraint on Move α, and accounts for the data we are presently concerned with. Consider (139a). *Who* first moves to the intermediate [−WH] C. However, (140) does not allow it to stay there, so it must make a further move to the matrix [+WH] C. This gives (138a) and accounts for the ill-formedness of (138b). Now consider (139b). *Who* first moves to the intermediate [+WH] C. If it subsequently moved to the matrix [−WH] C, this would be inconsistent with (140) in two ways, since a *wh*-phrase would occupy a [−WH] C and a [+WH] C would not be occupied by a *wh*-phrase at s-structure. We thereby account for the well-formedness of (138c) and the ill-formedness of (138d).[44]

A final observation we need concerns *scope* (cf. Section 3.2). The fact that a *wh*-phrase appears in clause-initial position can be viewed as articulating the intuition that in such cases the scope of interrogation extends across the whole clause. On the other hand, when the *wh*-word appears in the intermediate position, the scope of interrogation is restricted to the subordinate clause, i.e. the whole sentence is not used to encode a question.

Now let us return to Chinese and see how the above bears on the parameterization of Move α. The relevant data appear in (141):

(141)   a. Zhang xiangxin Bi kanjian shui?
            Zhang believe Bi see who
            'Who does Zhang believe Bi saw'

        b. Zhang xiang-zhidao Bi kanjian shui
            Zhang wonder Bi see who
            'Zhang wonders who Bi saw'

Note that in both of these examples the *wh*-word *shui* ('who') appears in exactly the same position – direct object of the embedded verb *kanjian* ('see'). Yet the two examples are interpreted quite differently, with the scope of *shui* extending over the whole clause in (141a) but being restricted to the subordinate clause in (141b). How might these interpretive differences be accounted for?

It is reasonable to suggest that the Chinese verbs share their argument selection properties with the English equivalents, i.e. *xiangxin* ('believe') selects a propositional argument which is indicative and *xiang-zhidao* ('wonder') one which is interrogative. Chinese, however, does not embrace (140) as a condition on well-formed s-structures. But to leave matters there is to leave unexplained the interpretive differences in interrogative scope exhibited by (141a, b).

The solution to this difficulty is to propose that Chinese *wh*-words *do* in fact move to A'-positions, but that this movement takes place at LF, i.e. it is *covert* movement (for this proposal, partially based on examples such as those under discussion, see Huang, 1982). If we assume, then, that (140) is modified to (142), we can maintain it as a universal principle:

(142)   A [+WH] C must be occupied by a *wh*-phrase and a *wh*-phrase must occupy a [+WH] C *at LF*.

Then, (140) can be retained as a statement of an s-structure condition required by the grammar of English but not by the grammar of Chinese.

In fact, this last suggestion is not quite right, since there is evidence that English too allows for covert movement of *wh*-phrases (see, for instance, Aoun, Hornstein and Sportiche, 1981; May, 1985). Consider the examples in (143):

(143)   a. Who kissed whom?
        b. John wonders who kissed whom?

Example (143a) is a multiple question, appropriate answers to which must provide *pairs* of individuals such that the first kissed the second. This indicates that both *wh*-phrases in (143a) have scope extending over the whole clause. Similarly, in (143b), John is described as wondering about *pairs* of individuals with each *wh*-phrase having scope over the internal clause. If intuitions about scope are understood in terms of the scope-bearing expressions appearing in positions from which their scope domains can be defined, it follows that in (143a), *both wh*-phrases must appear in the appropriate position at some level of representation, and similarly for (143b). This is possible if we assume English to permit covert movement (in LF) of *wh*-phrases which have not moved to A'-positions at s-structure. Statement (140), then, must be replaced by (144) which is a condition only on *positions*, not on *wh*-phrases:

(144)   A [+WH] C must be occupied by a *wh*-phrase at s-structure.

The parameter required by the above discussion can now be formulated in (145):[45]

(145)   The Move α Parameter has two values:
        (a) +Move *wh* in syntax (i.e. the d-structure–s-structure mapping), for those grammars which include (144)
        (b) −Move *wh* in syntax for those grammars which do not include (144)

English chooses value (a) in (145) and Chinese chooses value (b). Both languages satisfy (142), a universal condition on LF.

Our next module is *Binding Theory*. Parameterization and its implications for acquisition have been extensively studied in this area, and we shall be surveying the results of this work in chapter 5. For now, though, we can simply note one set of data which constitutes an initial case for parameterization.

The paradigm in (146) is from Manzini and Wexler (1987, p. 416) and illustrates the distribution of the Italian reflexive anaphor *sè*:

(146)   a. Alice$_j$ sapeva che [Mario$_i$ aveva guardato sè$_{i/*j}$ nello specchio]
           'Alice knew that Mario had looked at himself/*herself in the mirror'

        b. Alice$_j$ pensava che [Mario$_i$ avesse guardato sè$_{i/*j}$ nello specchio]
           'Alice thought that Mario had (subjunctive) looked at himself/*herself in the mirror'

c. Alice$_j$ disse a Mario$_i$ [PRO$_i$ di guardare sè$_{i/*j}$ nello specchio]
'Alice told Mario to look at himself/*herself in the mirror'

d. Alice$_j$ vide [Mario$_i$ guardare sè$_{i/j}$ nello specchio]
'Alice saw Mario look at himself/herself in the mirror'

e. Alice$_j$ guardò [i ritratti di sè$_{i/j}$ di Mario$_i$]
'Alice looked at Mario's portraits of himself/herself'

In these examples, the bracketing indicates the governing category for *sè*, as defined in (69) from the previous section. Examples (146a, b, c) are entirely consistent with this definition; in each case it is not possible for *sè* to be bound by *Alice*, an expression which falls outside the appropriate governing category. But (146d, e) show that (69) does not account for the whole paradigm. In (146d) the governing category for *sè* is the clause containing *sè* and the subject *Mario*; and in (146e) the same elements determine the governing category for *sè* as the bracketed NP. Yet, in both cases, it is possible for *sè* to be bound outside this governing category by *Alice*.

As we shall see in chapter 5, one response to such observations is to suggest that the notion of governing category should be parameterized, allowing the actual *principles* of the Binding Theory to be fixed. Because the possibilities are considerably more complex than those considered earlier in this section, we shall put off offering a formulation of the Governing Category Parameter (and other Binding Theory parameters) until chapter 5. Our present purposes are served by simply noting that the need for parameterization infects this module.

Italian again suggests the need for parameterization in *Bounding Theory*. Rizzi (1982, p. 50) cites (147) as apparently violating Subjacency:

(147)   Tuo fratello, a cui mi domando che storie abbiano raccontato, era molto preoccupato
'Your brother, to whom I wonder which stories they have told, was very worried'

What is of interest here is the relative clause, which is shown in (148) with the moved elements and their d-structure positions co-indexed:

(148)   [$_{S'}$[$_C$a cui$_i$][$_S$ mi domando [$_{S'}$[$_C$che storie$_j$][$_S$abbiano raccontato e_j e_i]]]]

In (148), *che storie* is moved to the embedded C-position. Then *a cui* has to move from its position in the embedded S to the matrix C, since the embedded C is filled by *che storie*. But this movement takes *a cui* out of two Ss, and if S is a bounding node, this is a violation of the Subjacency Principle in (87). Rizzi's response to this, supported by examination of a complex range of Italian data, is that (87) should be retained. However, to do this it is necessary to assume that the bounding nodes in Italian are NP and S', not NP and S as in English. It is easy to see that this deals with (148), as the movement of *a cui* crosses only a single S'. Again, as with Binding Theory, the strategy is to retain the principle and parameterize one of the concepts which appears in its formulation:

governing category in the case of Binding Theory, bounding node in the case of Bounding Theory.

It appears that the parameter at issue here must have a third value. In (149) are examples from Russian, cited by Freidin and Quicoli (1989, pp. 338–9):

(149)   a. Kavo ljubit Marija
           Who-acc. loves Mary-nom.
           'who does Mary love?'

        b. *Kavo govorit Ivan čto Marija ljubit
           Who-acc. says Ivan that Mary-nom. loves
           'Who does Ivan say that Mary loves'

Example (149a) simply illustrates that a *wh*-expression is moved to sentence-initial position in Russian, just as in English and Italian. But (149b) indicates that this process is more constrained in Russian – note that the English translation of (149b) is well-formed. Consider (150), the s-structure of (149b):

(150) $[_{S'}[_C Kavo_i][_S govorit\ Ivan\ [_{S'}[_C\ e_i\ čto][_S\ Marija\ ljubit\ e_i]]]]$

So long as only one of S and S' is a bounding node, there ought to be nothing wrong with this derivation. However, (150) is not a well-formed s-structure, so to retain (87), it is necessary to propose that *both* S and S' are bounding nodes in Russian. Based on these examples, we can express the *Bounding Node Parameter* as (151):

(151)   The Bounding Node Parameter has three values:
        (a) The set of bounding nodes = {NP, S, S'}
        (b) The set of bounding nodes = {NP, S}
        (c) The set of bounding nodes = {NP, S'}

Russian selects the most restrictive value (a), English the intermediate value (b), and Italian the least restrictive value (c).

Omitting *Control Theory*, which has not participated in significant discussions of parameterization, we come to *Case Theory and Θ-Theory*. It is of interest that parameterization in these modules has been proposed as an attractive way of dealing with some word-order differences, with the consequence that the need for parameterization in X-bar Theory is reduced.

We have noted that Case-assignment takes place under government in the configurations of (111). Government, as a hierarchically defined notion, is insensitive to direction, i.e a V governs an NP in its government domain, irrespective of whether the NP precedes or follows the V (but see Kayne, 1983). We might suggest, however, that Case-assignment *is* a directionally sensitive process, with Case-assigners (we shall restrict attention here to the lexical case-assigners, V and P) assigning their Case either rightwards or leftwards. Consider, then, a language in which Case-assignment is to the right, as might be true for English. This immediately enables us to predict that verbs and adpositions *precede* their complements in such a language, i.e., in these respects, the language is head-initial. If Case is assigned to the left in Japanese, the head-final characteristic of VPs and PPs in this language is similarly accounted for.

Of course, such considerations do not address the properties of non-Case-assigning configurations, i.e. those headed by N and A. But now consider Θ-role assignment. For internal arguments, this too takes place under government by a head.[46] Thus, the N *destruction* and the A *proud* project partial d-structures along the lines of (152):

(152)   a. $[_{N'}[_N\text{destruction}]\ [_{NP}\ ]]$
      b. $[_{A'}[_A\text{proud}]\ [_{NP}\ ]]$

In both cases, the complement *NP* is governed by the head, and so it receives its Θ-role under government. So we might suppose that Θ-role assignment (or Θ-*marking*) is another directional process, and that in English it parallels Case-marking in operating rightwards. The consequence is that we can formulate two parameters, the *Direction of Case-Marking Parameter* (153) and the *Direction of Θ-Marking Parameter* (154):

(153)   The Direction of Case-Marking Parameter has two values:
      a. Right
      b. Left

(154)   The Direction of Θ-Marking Parameter has two values:
      a. Right
      b. Left

A consistently head-initial language selects (153a) and (154a); a consistently head-final language selects (153b) and (154b).

On the basis of our considerations so far, there is no reason to prefer (153) and (154) to the Head-Direction Parameter in (134). Such reasons emerge, however, if we move away from the ideal case. Huang (1982) examined the word-order of Chinese from an X-bar perspective, formulating the following conclusions (among others): (i) the Chinese NP is *strictly* head-final; (ii) in the VP, at most *one* complement can follow the head; (iii) Chinese is prepositional, i.e the language is head-initial in this respect. That such data are not easily accommodated by a simple choice between head-final and head-initial is clear, and Huang formulates a somewhat complex X-bar schema to deal with them (see chapter 8 for discussion of some of the implications of this for acquisition).

Koopman (1984, pp. 122ff.) offers an alternative account of Chinese word-order in terms of the concepts under consideration here (see also Travis, 1984). As well as predicting the existence of consistent head-final and head-initial languages, (153) and (154) predict that we should expect to find languages combining (153a) and (154b) or (153b) and (154a). Chinese, claims Koopman, illustrates the first of these possibilities. Conclusion (i) above is immediately accounted for. N Θ-marks to the left and does not assign Case;

therefore complements of N appear in d-structure preceding N and there is no need for them to move to the right of N to receive Case (typically, they will receive Case *in situ* from an inserted preposition, fulfilling a role similar to English *of*). Conclusion (ii) is accounted for by assuming that verbal complements precede the V at d-structure – they must in order to be Θ-marked. However, a V has a Case to assign, so an NP complement needing Case moves to the post-V position at s-structure where it can receive the rightward-assigned Case. If there are additional complements they must remain in pre-verbal position as the V has only a single Case to assign, and Chinese allows the insertion of a preposition *ba* to Case-mark such an unmoved complement. Finally, what of (iii)? Koopman has to assume that Chinese has Θ-marking *postpositions* at d-structure since Θ-marking is, by assumption, to the left.[47] Because the complement of such a postposition needs Case and because Case-marking is to the right, the NP must move to the right of the adposition at s-structure, thereby creating an s-structure *prepositional* phrase.

In this way, Koopman accounts for a range of observations about Chinese word-order without resort to a complex X-bar schema. Of course, there is a price to pay, as she is forced to adopt an 'abstract' view on adpositions. Our task here, however, is not to evaluate the proposal, but to use it to illustrate what is involved in incorporating directionality parameters into Case- and Θ-Theory. Issues concerning directional Case-assignment will reappear in a different context in Chapter 10.

Of course, the above does not suggest that the core principle of Case Theory, the Case Filter of (108), is parameterized; rather we have been concerned with aspects of the procedures by which NPs receive Case.[48]

A similar observation is appropriate for the principles of Θ-Theory, and little sense can be attached to the idea that the Projection Principle and the Θ-Criterion themselves might be subject to parameterization. Again, however, the details of *how* lexical properties are projected into syntactic representations clearly varies from language to language, and the suggestion that Θ-marking may itself be directional is just one example of variation of this type. We shall return to some of these issues in chapter 7.

This brings us again to the Theory of Empty Categories, and we might consider it unlikely that there will be extensive parameterization in this module, if only because the nature of the *evidence* which a child would need in order to fix the values of parameters here is extremely obscure. The clear exception to this expectation concerns the availability of *pro*, and, as we noted at the end of the previous section, there is evidence that this empty category exists in a range of languages but not English. It follows that we should be able to discover a locus of variation in the theory of grammar which will enable us to predict whether a grammar contains *pro* or not. The search for this locus has led to numerous formulations of the *pro-drop Parameter* or the *Null Subject Parameter*. Because this work will occupy us throughout chapter 4, I shall not go into further details here.

Our final task in this chapter is to consider the status of PPT as an acquisition theory in terms of our learnability framework in chapter 1.

3.5 Principles and Parameters Theory and the Theory of Language Acquisition

It is straightforward to outline a view of language acquisition which is consistent with PPT. Adopting first the instantaneous idealization of (36) in chapter 2 gives (155) as a representation of this view.

(155)

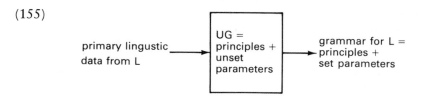

As discussed in chapter 2, the instantaneous idealization may well be appropriate for the theoretical linguist. For the developmentalist interested in the actual course of acquisition, however, it is necessary to abandon it. A non-instantaneous model is (156).

(156)

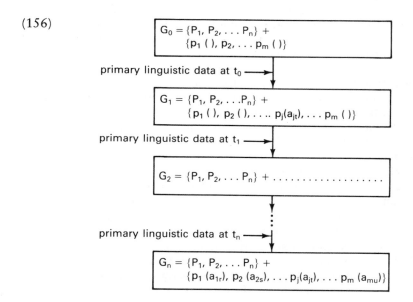

A few words of explanation are in order with respect to this. The P_i $(1 \leqslant i \leqslant n)$ refer to the UG *principles* and the p_i $(1 \leqslant i \leqslant m)$ are the UG *parameters*. Open parentheses indicate that the value of a parameter is not fixed. Thus, in G_0, the initial state, all parameter values are open; in G_1, after exposure to some data, the parameter p_j has the value a_{jt}, where this is one of its legitimate values selected from a range $\{a_{j1}, a_{j2}, \ldots a_{jt}, \ldots a_{jw}\}$ and no other parameter has been set. Parameter-setting proceeds up to G_n, the final state, where the mature grammar consists of the full set of principles along with the full set of parameters appropriately set.

Despite the fact that (156) represents a transparent translation of the framework into a schematic theory of language acquisition, it is not surprising that it leaves many questions unanswered. The remainder of this book attempts to engage some of these in considerable detail, but it will be useful to raise them here in a preliminary way, in the context of the four-component model of chapter 1.

Consider first the status of primary linguistic data. The schema in (156) says nothing about the nature of such data, but we have already seen in the previous two chapters that they are likely to be limited in certain respects.[49] Specifically, we have noted the No Negative Data Assumption and this is carried over into the majority of studies with which we shall subsequently be concerned. Additionally, we have seen that it is empirically implausible to suppose that children are exposed to arbitrarily complex data, although we also noted that the notion of complexity involved may be subject to a range of interpretations.

What this adds up to is a recognition that some empirically plausible constraints must be placed on the notion 'primary linguistic data', and Chomsky (1981, p. 9) acknowledges this when he characterizes the data available to the child as subject to a criterion of 'epistemological priority'. This issue will concern us in chapters 7 and 9.

Turning to the relationship between the data and the setting of parameters, this is acknowledged to be *causal* and, of course, it is customary to refer to it as 'parameter-setting'. But this entirely begs the question of what sort of process parameter-setting is. For example, is it a species of learning, interpreted as the selection and testing of hypotheses, or does it embody processes which are quite distinct from this? The orthodox view seems to be that it is inappropriate to identify parameter-setting with learning, and it is commonplace to find the expression 'triggering' in discussions of this notion. To assess this issue, it is necessary to try to develop a clear idea on the distinction between these processes in so far as they are understood. We shall undertake this task in chapter 8, but for now we simply note that there is an issue here.

Assuming for the sake of discussion that (156) embodies claims about a 'hypothesis space' available to a 'learner', consider next the nature of this space. The outline of a theory in (156) assumes that *all* principles and *all* parameters are constitutive of this space from the onset of acquisition, i.e. just like our ST model, it embodies the Continuity Hypothesis (Pinker, 1984). Is this a reasonable assumption?

Evidence suggesting that principles are operative fairly early in the child's development will be considered in chapter 6, but we must acknowledge at this stage that the Continuity Hypothesis could be incorrect in at least two ways. First, it is possible that the child constructs grammars which are at *variance* with the principles of UG – such grammars are perhaps what Goodluck (1986) refers to as 'wild' grammars. What might it mean for a child's grammar to have this property? This is not altogether clear, but if we take a non-parameterized principle such as the Case Filter (108), I suppose we could conceive of a child who has NPs and has a Case system but produces consistent evidence that NPs do not have to receive Case. Such a child might produce sentences like (157) with *Bill* in a non-Case-marked position:

(157)   *John promised Mary Bill to go

Alternatively, taking a parameterized principle for which UG supplies a set of values, say $\{v_1, v_2, \ldots, v_n\}$, it is conceivable that a child's grammar might be such that the principle is clearly operative but on the basis of a non-allowed value v_{n+1}. Suffice it to say that such speculations are rather fanciful, and I am familiar with no observations to suggest that we should regard them as anything other than conceivable possibilities.

The second way in which the assumption could be incorrect is perhaps more interesting. It is possible that certain principles (or, indeed, whole modules) are simply not operative at early stages of development. On this construal, a grammar would be better characterized as *incomplete* rather than illegitimate from the perspective of UG. To suppose that some principles enter children's grammars at a relatively late stage naturally raises a further issue: how are such late-attained principles acquired by the child? Are they learned, or is some other developmental mechanism in play here? Maturation has received significant attention recently in this connection, and we shall consider this in chapters 8, 10 and 11.

Another matter on which (156) is less than fully explicit concerns the parameters and their values. We have looked at a number of parameters in this chapter, but we have not attempted to articulate a theory of *possible parameters*. As it stands, (156) assumes that there are only finitely many parameters, but it is urgent to back up this view with an account of how a theory of parameters might be constrained. We shall look at some of the possibilities in chapter 9.

Regarding parameter values, (156) starts the child off at G_0 with all parameter values open. This is one option, but there are others. Some (or all) parameters could appear in G_0 set at some *unmarked* value. This would amount to equipping the child with an initial hypothesis about aspects of his or her grammar independently of any primary linguistic data. Primary linguistic data would then serve to *reset* parameters (where necessary) rather than simply set them. If such unmarked settings exist, we can go on to ask about where in the theory information about markedness occurs. For example, it is possible that UG contains full ranges of parameter values with markedness orderings defined on them. Alternatively, markedness orderings might not belong to UG but arise from the properties of acquisition mechanisms. These issues will be of central importance in chapters 4 and 5.

The final component of our learnability model is the criterion for acquisition. Since this has not played a significant role in the work we shall be going on to consider, we can safely assume here that the model requires there to be some finite time at which the full set of parameters is fixed and at no subsequent time is this modified, i.e. an informal version of identification in the limit.

Given the above discussion, it is clear that (156) does not represent a single well-defined model of first language acquisition. Because of the questions it leaves unanswered, it is better to see it as characterizing a framework of assumptions for structuring research. For purposes of explicit comparison with the ST account of language acquisition, outlined in the previous chapter, (158) is a summary of PPT in terms of our familiar four components:

(158) a. The hypothesis space is defined by a *finite* set of universal principles and a *finite* set of parameters, each with a *finite* number of values. There is an open question as to whether the constraints thus defined are operative at all stages of development.

      b. The data available to the child are restricted by the No Negative Data Assumption. Additionally, they satisfy a condition of epistemological priority, the nature of which remains to be clarified.

      c. The mechanism by which hypotheses are selected may involve 'triggering'. To the extent that it does, there is a reduced role for anything we might call 'learning'. If certain representational capacities are not initially available – a possibility left open by (a) – maturation may have a role to play as a developmental mechanism.

      d. The criterion for acquisition is an informal version of identification in the limit.

It is clear where this account differs most obviously from that offered in ST. The hypothesis space now defines only a finite number of candidate grammars and the logical aspect of the learnability problem is correspondingly simplified.[50] Non-parameterized principles have a wide range of deductive consequences, determining the properties of superficially dissimilar phenomena throughout the grammar. Similarly, the effects of parameterized principles permeate throughout the system, with different choices of parameter values having markedly divergent consequences. There is no role for an Evaluation Measure which will compare hypotheses all of which are compatible with the primary linguistic data. The process of acquisition is much more deterministic, with large chunks of the grammar falling into place on the basis of a single parametric decision. To put it crudely, a child equipped with an ST UG who has worked out how questions work in English might then entertain a range of hypotheses for coming to terms with the structure of relative clauses. In ST, the *rules* for forming questions and relative clauses, while similar in certain respects, had built into their statements construction-specific peculiarities. The PPT child has no such range of hypotheses. Indeed, questions and relative clauses as separate constructions have no status for such a child, who simply has Move α, constrained in various ways by other principles. These principles may permit some parametric variation, but once this is fixed, the role of Move α in questions and relative clauses is also fixed.

Whereas the ST account focused on a rather superficial notion of 'degeneracy' in the primary linguistic data, here we see an explicit commitment to the latter's being informationally impoverished, although the precise nature of this impoverishment remains to be elucidated. Finally, hypothesis selection and testing is now joined, or perhaps replaced, by triggering and maturation as possible developmental mechanisms.

3.6 Summary

If you have despaired of escaping from abstract linguistic analyses, you have some sympathy, and the next chapter will begin to redress the balance a little by considering some developmental phenomena. However, you do not have too much sympathy, since I firmly believe that a genuine understanding of the PPT approach to language acquisition can only be based on a grasp of the linguistic principles which it presupposes. This chapter has attempted to introduce some of these.

There are difficulties in attempting to provide an overview of this kind, and I am certain that the chapter has fallen foul of many of these. In particular, many of the notions I have introduced will strike some readers as no more than tricks to deal with a few recalcitrant data. There are many such tricks around, but I have tried to avoid them and concentrate on introducing notions which have a robustness going some way beyond what we have had time to consider here. The status of principles and the sense in which they are to be distinguished from construction-specific rules is extremely important for understanding the difference between ST and PPT, and I have tried to show how a set of principles, themselves stated in rather simple terms, can achieve the same descriptive coverage as an elaborate rule system. Complexity is achieved via the interaction of the principles and not from the statement of individual rules. If this mode of interaction is part of UG, the child's task in acquiring a grammar becomes more tractable. Fix the parameters, and let the innately supplied computational mechanisms do the rest. At this stage, this is no more than a promissory statement, and, as we saw in the last section, there is a significant number of fundamental issues to be resolved before it can be adequately assessed. We now commence discussion of some of these issues and the business of assessment.

4   Null Subjects in the Theory of Grammar and Language Acquisition

Introduction

It is probably true to say that no single topic has had a greater impact on the ideas with which this book is concerned than that of null (empty) subjects. This is partly due to the accidental fact that Hyams (1986) represents the first concerted effort to apply the concepts of PPT to first language acquisition. Her pioneering efforts have led Chomsky (1987a, p. 18) to refer to the outcome of her work as:

> . . . an example of a hypothesis about universal grammar deriving from language acquisition studies that might be tested by linguists, rather than the converse, as in the usual practice.

It seems appropriate, then, to take this area as a specimen to illustrate the sort of claims which have been made, the analyses backing up these claims, the extent to which they engage the questions raised in Section 3.5 and the difficulties which still persist. At the outset, we should be clear that the issues surrounding null subjects in the theory of grammar are far from resolved, and Hyams' claims regarding acquisition have been disputed in various ways. At the same time, it is undeniable that the questions we now ask of the early stages of acquisition, when null subjects are common, are quite different from those asked before Hyams' work.

The chapter begins by introducing a set of linguistic phenomena which tend to cluster together in a number of languages. The methodology of PPT requires investigation of the proposition that the existence of such clusters is not accidental; rather, it is diagnostic of a single dimension of grammatical variation, a parameter. Naturally, whether such a parameter exists is an empirical issue which can only be resolved by detailed grammatical investigation. So as to get some perspective on Hyams' own theoretical assumptions, the classic accounts of these phenomena, developed in the early 1980s and resulting in different formulations of the Null Subject Parameter, are briefly presented.

Exposition and discussion of Hyams' own work constitutes the bulk of the chapter, with different sections being devoted to her original (1986) analysis and to an alternative she has sketched in later work. A final section provides a

review of some of the difficulties, empirical and conceptual, which confront
Hyams' ideas. Some of these issues will reappear in chapter 10.

4.1 Phenomena and Analyses

The earliest work on null subjects concentrated on Romance and Semitic
languages. We have already noted in Section 3.3 that Chinese permits null
subjects, but for now we shall put this case to one side, returning to it in
Section 4.3.

Italian has verbal paradigms such as those in (1) (van Riemsdijk and
Williams, 1986, p. 299):

(1)   a. io parlo 'I talk'   b. parlo '(I) talk'
         tu parli 'you talk'   parli '(you) talk'
         lui parla 'he talks'   parla '(he) talks'
         noi parlamo 'we talk'   parlamo '(we) talk'
         voi parlate 'you (pl.) talk'   parlate '(you (pl.)) talk'
         loro parlano 'they talk'   parlano '(they) talk'

In the paradigm on the right, there is no overt expression of the subject
pronoun, and, in fact, such pronouns are used in Italian only for emphasis or
to signal a change in topic.

Spanish behaves similarly, as the examples in (2), cited by Jaeggli (1982, p.
128) indicate:

(2)   a. Baila bien
         '(He/she) dances well'

      b. Estamos cansadisimos
         '(We) are very tired'

Borer (1984, p. 212) illustrates the same phenomenon in Hebrew by (3):

(3)   'axalti 'et ha-tapua'x
      ate-1 Sing. acc. the-apple
      '(I) ate the apple'

In addition to allowing null subjects in tensed clauses, these three languages
share a number of further properties. In particular, in each of them it is
possible to invert subjects, placing them in sentence-final position, as the
following examples illustrate:

(4)   Italian (Rizzi, 1982, p. 117):
      verrà Gianni
      will-come Gianni
      'Gianni will come'

(5) Spanish (Jaeggli, 1982, p. 139):
     Vino Juan
     came Juan
     'Juan came'

(6) Hebrew (Borer, 1984, p. 212)
     kafcu min ha-matos Ran ve-Dan
     jumped from the-plane Ran and-Dan
     'Ran and Dan jumped from the plane'

Thus, in allowing empty subjects in tensed clauses and inverted subjects, Italian, Spanish and Hebrew contrast with English, which permits neither of these constructions. A further property shared by Italian, Spanish and Hebrew is that subjects can be extracted from tensed subordinate clauses even when these clauses contain an overt complementizer (cf. pp. 41, 90). Examples to illustrate this are (7)–(9):

(7) Italian (Rizzi, 1982, p. 117):
     Chi$_i$ credi che e_i verrà?
     Who (you) believe that will come
     'Who do you believe that will come?'

(8) Spanish (Jaeggli, 1982, p. 145):
     Quién$_i$ dijiste que e_i llego ayer?
     Who (you) said that arrived yesterday
     'Who did you say (that) arrived yesterday?'

(9) Hebrew (Borer, 1984, p. 212):
     Mi$_i$ xasavta se e_i 'exer la-mesiba?
     Who (you) thought that late-was to-the-party
     'Who did you think (that) was late to the party?'

Again, as the translations indicate, such movements are not legitimate in English.

We shall now briefly consider two attempts to uncover the nature of this variation. Recall that the Extended Projection Principle requires all clauses to have subjects. Furthermore, there is striking evidence that empty subjects are syntactically active in that they can serve as antecedents for anaphors in a manner which is entirely predictable from the Binding Theory. This is indicated by the Spanish example in (10) (Jaeggli and Safir, 1989):

(10) Juan/él/ϕ siempre habla de si mismo
      'Juan/he/ϕ always talks about himself'

In (10), the reflexive anaphor *si mismo* must be bound in its governing category, the matrix clause. Its binder can be *Juan*, *él* or the empty category in subject position.

Focusing on the simple null subject cases (1)–(3), the first question we must consider concerns the identity of the empty category. When discussing the taxonomy of empty categories in Section 3.3, we noted that this could not be PRO because the PRO Theorem requires PRO to appear only in ungoverned positions. The subject position in a tensed clause in Italian, Spanish and Hebrew is presumably governed by the finite I, thereby ruling out PRO. Despite this, one attempt to come to terms with the data assumed that the empty subject *is* PRO (Chomsky, 1981; Borer, 1984).[1] How did this work?

Recall from Section 3.3 that a small set of residual rules remains in the theory, one of which is repeated here as (11):

(11)   S → NP – I – VP

I contains Tense and Agreement features, and the presence of [+TNS] in I guarantees that the subject position is governed and can receive nominative Case. What it also guarantees, of course, is that PRO cannot appear in this position, clearly a desirable outcome for English. But now note that if no modal verb appears in I, the Tense and Agreement features in I have to be suffixed to the main verb in the VP. Consider the simple sentence in (12):

(12)   John runs

Given (11), an appropriate d-structure for (12) will be (13):

(13)   [$_{NP}$John][$_I$+TNS, −PAST, 3SING.][$_{VP}$[$_V$ run]]

Nothing happens in the mapping to s-structure, but in PF a rule, known as Rule R, suffixes the contents of I to V, yielding (14):[2]

(14)   [$_{NP}$John][$_{VP}$[$_V$run + [$_I$+TNS, −PAST, 3SING.]]]

Morphological rules then spell out the contents of the V as *runs*. Now observe that if (14) were an s-structure, i.e. if Rule R applied in the syntax rather than in PF, I would no longer govern the subject position. In (14), the government domain of I is determined by the VP maximal projection. This is the key to the analysis, since if the subject position is ungoverned, PRO is free to occur there. Accordingly, the *Null Subject Parameter* can be stated as in (15):[3]

(15)   Rule R (a) can/(b) cannot apply in syntax

Italian, Spanish and Hebrew select value (a), thereby permitting PRO in subject position in tensed clauses; English selects value (b), ensuring that PRO can never appear in this position.

The details of the other properties of Null Subject Languages can also be seen to follow from these assumptions, although some of the arguments are quite complex and will not be pursued here.[4] We might, however, note that the possibility of inverted subjects falls out of the account fairly naturally, on the assumption that such subjects are adjoined to VP. Thus, consider (4) with its s-structure in (16):

(16) e_i [$_{VP}$ [$_{VP}$ [$_V$verrà + I] Gianni$_i$]]

In (16), the option, available in Italian, of applying Rule R in syntax has been taken. The consequence is that the inverted subject *Gianni* falls within the government domain of the tensed I and so can receive nominative Case. Since this movement is not an option for English, inverted subjects are not allowed in the language.[5]

While it may be possible to produce an analysis of null subjects along these lines, whereby they are identified with tokens of PRO in simple tensed clauses, there is considerable evidence that this is not the right way to proceed. Most directly, the *interpretations* of null subjects and PRO diverge in striking ways.[6] For example, the null subject, when not co-referential with some other expression in the sentence, can be interpreted as having definite reference or as pleonastic (expletive). The Italian examples in (17) are from Rizzi (1982, p. 162):

(17)   a. Racconta la sua storia
           '(He$_i$) tells his$_j$ story'

       b. Piove
           '(It) rains'

It is possible to interpret (17a) such that the teller tells his own story, but this is not necessary as the indexing indicates. As we have seen in Section 3.3, non-controlled PRO also does not derive its interpretation from some other expression in the sentence, but its interpretation is then some *arbitrary*, non-definite individual or set of individuals. Rizzi (1982, p. 162) cites (18) as an Italian example to illustrate this:

(18)   Non è chiaro come PRO raccontare certe storie
       'It is unclear how to tell certain stories'

Here PRO has the arbitrary interpretation we have already come across.

An alternative approach to null subjects, developed by Rizzi and adopted in modified form by Hyams, locates the source of linguistic variation in substantive properties of I. The crucial idea behind this approach is that in Null Subject Languages, I can optionally be specified as [+pronominal]. If I is so specified, two consequences follow: (i) the [+pronominal] feature 'absorbs' the nominative Case normally available for the subject position in a tensed clause; (ii) I qualifies as a proper governor for purposes of the ECP, as it now has 'lexical' properties. Because of (i), the presence of a lexical subject in simple tensed clauses is no longer permitted, since such a subject would not receive Case; because of (ii), the empty category in subject position resulting from subject inversion is properly governed.[7]

Let us see how this works in a little more detail for simple tensed clauses. With optional null subjects and the option of I being [+pronominal], there are four structures to consider:

(19)   a. NP – I – VP   b. NP –   I   – VP
                                                                  [+pronominal]

       c. [$_{NP}$e] – I – VP   d. [$_{NP}$e] –   I   – VP
                                                                  [+pronominal]

Of these, (19a) is what we find in English where the [+pronominal] specification of I is not an option. Of course, we also find it in Null Subject Languages, since lexical subjects occur in such languages. The structure in (19b) is not legitimate, since nominative Case is 'absorbed' by [+pronominal] and is not available for the lexical NP in subject position. We can rule out (19c) if we assume that the proper government requirement on empty categories resulting from movement is extended to this configuration. Finally, (19d) is legitimate and represents the null subject case when the [+pronominal] option is taken.

According to this construal, then, the empty category in the subject position of tensed clauses in Null Subject Languages is not PRO and no manoeuvres are necessary to ensure that the position it occupies is ungoverned. In fact, it is governed by a [+pronominal] I, and it is this which licenses it. In subsequent literature, this empty category is referred to as *pro*.[8] The *Null Subject Parameter* derived from this approach is (20):

(20)   I (a) can/(b) cannot be specified as [+pronominal]

Null Subject Languages select value (a); non-Null Subject Languages select value (b). We now turn to an uncritical exposition of Hyams' implementation of some of these ideas in connection with language acquisition.

4.2 The AG/PRO Parameter and Early Child Grammar

Hyams (1986, p. 27) proposes that Universal Grammar contains the rules in (21) with order parameterized:

(21)   a. S → NP, I, VP
       b. I → (AG), AUX

Rule (21a) is already familiar, but a word of explanation is in order for (21b) which is not standard. AG (for agreement – AGR is more conventional, but I will follow Hyams' usage throughout for references to her work) contains features of person, number and gender (ϕ-features), and of course languages differ in which, if any, of these features they encode. The optionality of AG is necessary since there is no agreement in English infinitives, and some languages (e.g. Chinese) may not employ such features at all. AUX, contains at least Tense features and, for different languages, may contain a range of other elements. In particular, in English, modal verbs are generated under AUX and *be* and *have* may be raised into AUX at s-structure from their d-structure position inside the VP (see Emonds, 1976, for an early formulation of *have/be* raising, and chapter 10 for discussion within a contemporary framework).

An issue which is crucial for Hyams concerns the identity of the *head* of I. The X-bar notation is not extended to this constituent, and Hyams (1986, p. 28) *stipulates* the Head Assignment Principle in (22):

(22)   Where AUX contains lexical material, AUX heads I; otherwise AG heads I.

It follows that if, say, a modal appears under AUX, a possibility allowed in English, the AUX will constitute the head of I and govern other constituents within I, specifically AG. If, however, AUX contains only tense features, AG will be the head of I and will not be governed. These structural possibilities are central to Hyams' account, as will become clear.

One of the phenomena noted in the previous section as typical of Null Subject Languages was the possibility of inverted subjects. In our earlier discussion, we have assumed that a unitary account of null subjects and inverted subjects is desirable, and the two proposals we described have this characteristic. Hyams, however, chooses to treat the appearance of null subjects and inverted subjects as arising from different parameters.[9] For inverted subjects, she adopts the parameterization of Rule R we have already discussed. For null subjects, she produces a modified version of Rizzi's proposals, and it is the latter that we are principally concerned with here.

Her specific idea is that the pronominal analysis of Rizzi should be modified so that in Null Subject Languages, AG can be *identified* with PRO. Hence the claim is that the *Null Subject Parameter* can be stated as in (23):

(23)   The Null Subject Parameter has two values:
       (a) AG = PRO
       (b) AG ≠ PRO

Again, Italian and other Null Subject Languages will select value (a); English, French and other languages requiring overt subjects will select value (b). An AG identified with PRO is referred to by Hyams as AG/PRO. The presence of AG/PRO is what licenses *pro* in subject position. As Hyams (p. 32) puts it: '. . . a necessary condition on *pro* is that it be governed by AG/PRO.' According to this suggestion, then, an Italian sentence such as (24a) will have a structure along the lines of (24b):

(24)   a. Parla
          '(He) talks'

       b. [$_{NP}$*pro*][$_I$AG/PRO, AUX] [$_{VP}$. . .]

Now, the location of pronominal features in AG makes considerable sense, since the ϕ features associated with agreement (person, number and gender) are characteristically marked on pronominals. What reasons are there for wishing to say that these pronominal features can be identified with PRO?

Recall from Section 3.3 that PRO has a range of properties which collectively distinguish it from other empty categories. First, it is subject to obligatory control by subjects and objects of specific verbs; second, it admits an arbitrary interpretation when it occurs outside an obligatory control context; third, the PRO Theorem restricts its distribution to ungoverned positions. Hyams argues that these three properties can plausibly be attributed to AG in Null Subject Languages. Since it is the third of these properties which is utilized in her account of the early stages of acquisition, we shall not go into the details of her arguments regarding the first two.[10]

Focusing on the requirement that PRO be ungoverned then, we have already noted that Hyams assumes that modals are generated under AUX and that *be* and *have* may be raised to this position from the VP. This means that the structure of I in English for a sentence containing a modal before the application of Rule R is as in (25):

(25) $[_I \text{ AG } [_{AUX} \text{ M }]]$

Now recall (22). Since AUX is lexically filled in (25), it counts as the head of I and governs AG. It immediately follows that PRO cannot appear in AG, since this would violate the PRO Theorem. Thus, the fact that by assumption English is associated with value (b) of (23) immediately provides an account of why modals can be base-generated under AUX in this language and why *be* and *have* can be raised into this position: such operations are not inconsistent with the requirement that PRO be ungoverned, since there is no PRO in AG in English. What now of Italian?

There is considerable evidence that the Italian modal verbs *potere* 'can' and *dovere* 'must' are generated in the VP and are most appropriately analysed as main verbs. In particular, they take the full range of verbal inflections and, according to a number of syntactic criteria, they behave like the typical 'raising' verb *sembrare* 'seem' (see Hyams, 1986, pp. 46–7, for details). Additionally, the auxiliary verbs *essere* 'to be' and *avere* 'to have' are not raised to AUX in Italian. Whereas in English, yes–no questions are formed by moving the element in AUX to a clause-initial position, as in (26), this is not possible in Italian, as (27) shows:[11]

(26)   Has Mario agreed to help us?

(27)   a. Mario ha accettato di aiutarci
          'Mario has agreed to help us'

       b.*Ha Mario accettato di aiutarci

Now, of course, (23) provides a ready explanation for this. In Italian, AG = PRO and must remain ungoverned. Given (22), this means that lexical material can never appear in AUX, so modals cannot be base-generated in AUX and forms of *essere* and *avere* cannot be raised to AUX. Accordingly, these verbs are never in a position to be inverted with the subject in the formation of questions.[12]

Let us now consider how Hyams applies these rather abstract considerations in developing a view on the grammars of children acquiring English and other languages. First, in subscribing to a *continuous* view of development, she takes an explicit stance on one of the issues raised in Section 3.5. The child's early grammar may be *different* from the adult grammar, but any such difference will be within the bounds defined by UG. Specifically, if UG contains parameters determining the distribution of empty categories, differences between child and adult grammars with respect to empty categories will fall within the range determined by these parameters, i.e. the child may have an incorrect parameter setting, but such a setting will be permitted by UG. This is precisely what Hyams claims for children acquiring English: at the early stages, they have an incorrect setting for the AG/PRO parameter, i.e. in the relevant respects, such a child has an Italian/Spanish/Hebrew grammar. The evidence for this proposition is rather straightforward.

First, Hyams notes repeated claims in the literature that children acquiring English go through a stage during which subjects are optional. From Bloom (1970) and Bloom, Lightbown and Hood (1975), she cites data such as those in (28) (1986, pp. 63, 65ff.):

(28) a. throw away
      b. make a house
      c. helping mommy
      d. read bear book
      e. sit on piano
      f. make a choo-choo train

At the same time as they produce such utterances, children also utilize overt subjects and in this respect, early English is reminiscent of adult Italian. Furthermore, the 'missing' subjects in examples like (28) are typically interpreted by adults as having definite reference, a characteristic of the interpretation of *pro* in Null Subject Languages (cf. Section 4.1). Nor, Hyams maintains, is it plausible to suggest that these 'subjectless' utterances are indicative of some sort of performance constraint, since children's omission of subjects occurs in 'simple' as well as 'complex' utterances. The fact that subject-omission is more common than object-omission also argues against a simple performance-based account of the phenomenon. These are observations to which we shall return in Section 4.4.

As well as utterances indicating the optionality of referential subjects at this early stage, Hyams also notes examples in which adult English would require an *expletive* subject, either *it* or *there*. Such subjects are illustrated in (29):

(29) a. It seems that John likes Mary
      b. It's cold outside
      c. There's a fly in my soup

Expletive subjects are peculiar in that they do not bear any Θ-role – they are not referential – and their occurrence appears to be motivated entirely by the grammatical requirement that all sentences in English must have overt subjects. A common feature of Null Subject Languages is that they lack lexical expletives entirely, and an Italian example to illustrate this is (17b) in the previous section. It is noteworthy, then, that children acquiring English consistently omit expletive subjects in the data examined by Hyams. She cites the examples in (30) from Bloom, Lightbown and Hood (1975) (1986, p. 63):

(30)   a. Outside cold (= it's cold outside)
       b. That's cold (referring to the weather)
       c. No morning (= it's not morning)
       d. Yes, is toys in there (= yes, there are toys in there)
       e. No more cookies (= there's no more cookies)

Here, (30a, b) appear to have referential subjects where expletive subjects are required in the adult grammar; (30c–e) simply lack subjects entirely. So we have a further sense in which early English appears to behave like a Null Subject Language.

If the optionality of referential subjects and the omission of expletive subjects were the only data relevant to evaluating Hyams' hypothesis, it is unlikely that it would have influenced acquisition research in the way it undoubtedly has. It is, however, a feature of her approach that she offers a deductive account of the distribution of *pro* from which it is possible to derive further predictions. Specifically, recall that her analysis requires that modal verbs cannot occur in AUX so long as AG = PRO, since this would lead to PRO being governed. What, then, are we to make of the observation that modal verbs do not appear at all in the samples of early English she worked with?

By assumption, early English is +AG/PRO. From this it follows that the child's grammar does not allow him or her to accommodate modal verbs in AUX. But there is an alternative that we have already met: as in adult Italian, modal verbs could be analysed as main verbs and appear within VP. If Hyams is to *explain* the absence of modal verbs, she must rule out this possibility.

If a modal verb is going to head a VP, it must be analysed by the child as a verb. But modal verbs in English, unlike in Italian, have defective agreement paradigms. Morphological cues which might assist children in determining the syntactic status of lexical items (Maratsos and Chalkley, 1980; Maratsos, 1982) are lacking in this case, suggesting that it is unlikely that the English-speaking child will be tempted to assimilate modals to the class of verbs. Thus, it is plausible to suggest that neither the English nor the Italian option for categorizing modal verbs is available to the child, who has no alternative but to effectively 'ignore' them (for a somewhat more complex discussion of auxiliary *be*, see Hyams, 1986, pp. 87ff.).[13]

The suggestion that early English is +AG/PRO appears to have considerable explanatory force, but if we are to see it as part of a developmental account, one substantial issue remains outstanding: what is the process whereby this parameter is reset to −AG/PRO, clearly a necessary process for the child acquiring English? Hyams offers two possibilities for 'triggering' this resetting, and to appreciate these we must briefly consider the status of overt subject pronouns in Null Subject Languages like Italian and Spanish.

Such pronouns are only used for emphasis or to signal a change in topic. In other words, in 'unmarked' discourse situations, the native speaker of Italian or Spanish will omit pronominal subjects. This generalization is codified by Chomsky (1981) as the Avoid Pronoun Principle:

(31)   Avoid lexical pronominal if a null pronominal is possible.

Now, the status of (31) is not at all clear – it seems most natural to regard it as a pragmatic principle which can interact with the theory of grammar – but let us assume, following Hyams, that the child has access to it. If this is so, recognition of expletive subjects in the primary linguistic data will serve as a signal that the AG/PRO parameter should be reset. By definition, expletive subjects lack any referential and discourse function. Therefore, they cannot be motivated in the same way as overt subject pronouns in Italian and Spanish. They must, then, be grammatically motivated and indicative of the fact that English subjects cannot be null, i.e. English AG cannot be PRO.

The second potential trigger is the presence of unstressed subject pronouns in the input. We might suppose that circumstances which require an overt subject pronoun in Italian or Spanish (emphasis, change of topic) would require a stressed subject pronoun in English. But, then, recognition by the child of unstressed subject pronouns would indicate that subjects are necessary in English even when pragmatic and discourse factors do not require them.

In summary, Hyams maintains that the child acquiring English initially has a grammar containing the parameter setting +AG/PRO. In terms of the general framework of PPT described in Section 3.5, this means that UG supplies the parameter *and a markedness ordering on its values* such that +AG/PRO is the unmarked value. This explains (i) the optionality of referential subjects; (ii) the absence of expletive subjects; (iii) the absence of modal and auxiliary verbs. At some point, typically during the third year, the child has access to data (expletive subjects or unstressed subject pronouns) which 'trigger' a resetting of the parameter to −AG/PRO. Very soon after this resetting, the data indicate that (i) subjects become obligatory; (ii) expletive subjects appear; (iii) modal and auxiliary verbs appear.

In addition to English, Hyams assesses her hypothesis in the context of the early stages of the acquisition of Italian and German. Young speakers of Italian produce data indicating the optionality of subjects when they are at a comparable age to the English-speaking children on whom Hyams based her claims. This is not surprising, as adult Italian is +AG/PRO and the assumed unmarked value of the parameter is correct for this language. Hyams (1986, p. 111) reports data like those in (32):

(32)   a. Ha collo lungo, lungo, lungo
          has neck long, long, long
          '(It) has a long, long, long neck'

b. E mia palla
is my ball
'(It) is my ball'

In such examples, the missing subject is interpreted as having definite reference and, alongside them, there are examples in which a subject is overtly expressed. Furthermore, German-speaking children alternate between null and overt subjects in their early language, despite the fact that German, like English, is not a Null Subject Language (Roeper, 1973).[14]

What of Italian modals, which, as we have seen, are best analysed as main verbs in adult Italian? Given their categorial status, they ought not to give rise to the same acquisition difficulties as English modals. It is, therefore, important for Hyams that Italian modals are not delayed in acquisition, and she notes that the available evidence indicates that they are acquired at about the same time as the 'semi-auxiliaries' *hafta* and *gonna* by English-speaking children. Additionally, *essere* 'to be' is present from well before the second birthday, typically in its third person singular form *è*, again contrasting markedly with the typical course of acquisition in English. These observations, while not bearing directly on the AG/PRO Parameter, do make Hyams' account of the delayed acquisition of these forms in English more plausible.

A final piece of evidence cited by Hyams as supporting her account comes from additional observations on the acquisition of German. The optionality of subjects, already alluded to, is juxtaposed with large numbers of word-order errors from young German speakers. Specifically, Clahsen (1986) reports German children producing *incorrect* OV word-order in simple clauses over 50 per cent of the time during the period in which subjects are optional for them. The onset of obligatory subjects coincides with a quite dramatic shift to 90 per cent correct VO word-order. How might this be explained?

Standard accounts of the syntax of German assume that d-structure word-order is SOV, the order which appears in subordinate clauses. Hyams proposes to implement this suggestion by postulating the rules in (33):

(33)   a. S → NP – VP – I
       b. VP → NP – V

In subordinate clauses, V is raised to I to receive the verbal inflections and the correct SOV order in such clauses results. In matrix clauses, however, an additional operation is needed to move the I (along with its raised V) into the position following the subject. This process only takes place if I contains lexical material, so it is contingent on the prior raising of the verb.[15] Now, noting that I contains AG, if the initial setting of the AG/PRO parameter for German-speaking children is +AG/PRO, such V-raising is impossible, as it would lead to PRO being governed. But if V-raising is impossible, I-movement is also impossible on these assumptions and the German-speaking child has no alternative to the SOV word-order which the base rules define.

Overall, then, considerable explanatory force is claimed for the AG/PRO hypothesis: not only does it offer an account of aspects of the early stages of English grammar, but it also appears to engage interesting issues in the acquisition of Italian and German. In the next section, we shall see how Hyams has developed a rather different proposal in her more recent work.

4.3 Morphological uniformity and null subjects

One of the difficulties Hyams (1987a) perceives in the account summarized in the previous section concerns the distinction drawn in Section 3.3 between the *licensing conditions* for empty categories and their *identification conditions* (see also Jaeggli and Hyams, 1987). In the analysis of null subjects in Rizzi (1982), these are not clearly distinguished. The presence of [+pronominal] features in I licenses the null subject, and the 'spelling out' of these features as verbal inflections permits the identification of the referential properties of the null subject as, for example, Third Person Singular. Given the focus in this early work on languages with 'rich' agreement systems, it is hardly surprising that the necessity to draw the distinction was not readily appreciated.

Of course, exactly the same considerations can be applied to Hyams' analysis of early Italian: +AG/PRO licenses *pro* subjects and the identification of such subjects is ensured by the system of verbal agreement, aspects of which are in place at the stage in which Hyams is interested. However, these considerations *cannot* be extended to her treatment of early English. If the grammars of children acquiring English are also specified as +AG/PRO at this stage, *pro* subjects are licensed. But it is a common observation that verbal inflections are relatively late to develop for such children, so while *pro* may be licensed it cannot be identified, unless we wish to postulate a totally abstract system of agreement which never shows up in the speech of the child.

This difficulty can be linked to a more general one confronting those linguistic accounts of the null-subject phenomena which assume that identification is mediated by 'rich' agreement: there are languages which permit null-subjects despite the fact that their agreement systems are impoverished. Indeed, as was noted in Section 3.3, Chinese is a null-subject language, but Chinese verbs exhibit *no* agreement features whatever, as the paradigm in (34) indicates:

(34) wo gongzuo   'I work'
      ni gongzuo   'You work'
      ta gongzuo   'He/she/it works'
      women gongzuo   'We work'
      nimen gongzuo   'You (plural) work'
      tamen gongzuo   'They work'

Despite this absence of agreement, the sentence in (35) is well-formed with the range of interpretations indicated:

(35) gongzuo
      work
      'I work/you work/he, she, it works/we work/you (plural) work/they work'

This multiplicity of interpretations with the sentence taken out of context can be seen as due to the fact that there are no agreement features on the verb to permit identification of the referential properties of the subject. It follows that 'rich' agreement is not a necessary condition for the appearance of null subjects.

Nor is it a sufficient condition, as is demonstrated by the case of German. Intuitively, this language has a 'rich' agreement system, as the paradigm in (36) illustrates (Jaeggli and Hyams, 1987, p. 4):

(36) Ich arbeit-e   'I work'
      Du arbeit-est   'You (singular familiar) work'
      Er arbeit-et   'He/she/it works'
      Wir arbeit-en   'We work'
      Ihr arbeit-et   'You (singular polite, plural) work'
      Sie arbeit-en   'They work'

While there is some inflectional homonymy here, these inflections provide reasonably explicit indications of the referential features of the subject.[16] But German does not permit thematic (referential) null subjects at all, although it does allow for expletive (non-referential) null subjects in certain contexts, a point to which we shall return.[17] It seems, then, that cross-linguistically and in the grammars of children, 'rich' agreement provides neither a necessary nor a sufficient condition for the presence of null subjects. This conclusion motivates Hyams' re-analysis of null subjects to which this section is devoted. Again, evaluation of the proposal will be postponed to the next section.

The linguistic account of null subjects which Hyams adopts for this re-analysis is developed by Jaeggli and Safir (1989). This proposal draws a sharp distinction between *licensing* and *identification*.

Take a Null Subject Language such as Italian, put alongside it Chinese, and consider what distinguishes these languages from non-Null Subject Languages such as English and French. Italian and Chinese share the property of being *morphologically uniform* in their verbal paradigms, although this uniformity takes quite different forms in the two languages. In Italian, a verbal paradigm is uniform by virtue of *all* of its forms being inflected; in Chinese, uniformity is achieved by *none* of the forms in the paradigm being inflected. Contrast this with the situation in English, illustrated by the paradigm in (37):

(37) I work
      You (singular) work
      He/she/it work-s
      We work
      You (plural) work
      They work

Unlike in Italian and Chinese, what we have here is a *mixed* paradigm with all the verbal forms corresponding to the base form except for the third person singular which carries the -*s* inflection.

This correlation between uniform verbal paradigms and the presence of null subjects on the one hand and mixed verbal paradigms and their absence on the other is taken by Jaeggli and Safir (1989) as the crucial factor in the *licensing* condition for null subjects.[18] They state this as (38):

(38)   Null subjects are permitted in all and only languages with morphologically uniform inflectional paradigms.

Morphological uniformity is defined as:

(39)   An inflectional paradigm P in a language L is morphologically uniform if P has either only underived inflectional forms or only derived inflectional forms.

Of course, according to (38), German, being morphologically uniform, should permit null subjects. But (38) only establishes the *possibility* of null subjects (necessary for German anyway because it permits null expletives). In order for *referential* null subjects to appear, they must also be identified. Therefore, the way is open to suggest that, while German satisfies the licensing condition, it does not satisfy whatever additional conditions might be appropriate for the identification of referential null subjects.

Consider first the most straightforward case of Italian. Null subjects are licensed in Italian by virtue of (38). Additionally, Italian is a paradigmatic case of a language with 'rich' agreement, and it is the features in I (or AGR) which, spelled out as verbal inflections, permit identification. Null subjects are legitimate in Italian because they are licensed via (38) *and* they are identifiable by means of rich agreement.[19] This is *agreement-identification*. What then of Chinese which lacks agreement entirely? Once again, null subjects are licensed by virtue of (38), but since referential null subjects do occur in this language which lacks agreement, there must be some other mechanism of identification available. Hyams follows Jaeggli and Safir in referring to Huang's (1982, 1984) analysis of empty subjects (and objects) in Chinese.

Huang maintains that languages can be broadly characterized as either *discourse-oriented* or *sentence-oriented*. Chinese and Japanese are notable members of the former type; English, French and Italian belong to the latter. What the distinction amounts to and how it should be incorporated into a theory of UG is not clear, but for our purposes all we need to note is that in discourse-oriented languages, a notion of 'discourse-topic' appears to be able to interact with purely formal, grammatical processes (see also Xu, 1986, for the role of discourse notions in establishing an appropriate taxonomy of empty categories for Chinese). But if this is so, there is another mechanism available for the identification of empty subjects in Chinese – *topic-identification*.

Briefly, Huang maintains that an appropriate structure for the Chinese sentence in (35) is (40):

(40)   [$_{Top}$ e_i] [$_S$ e_i gongzuo]

In (40), an empty topic, the referential properties of which will be derived from discourse, indentifies the empty subject. Technically, since Top is an A'–position, the empty category in subject position is not *pro* but a *variable* (see Section 3.3) and this enables Huang to employ exactly the same concepts to account for null objects in Chinese. Thus, we have two ways in which grammars can satisfy the identification requirement on empty subjects: identification by agreement in sentence-oriented languages and identification by topic in discourse-oriented languages.[20]

What now of German? Jaeggli and Safir do not attempt to provide a definitive answer to this question, and we shall not pursue it in detail here. What is clear is that if German is sentence-oriented in terms of Huang's distinction, the only mechanism available to it for the identification of empty subjects is agreement-identification.[21] At the end of the last section, we alluded to various movement processes in the derivation of SVO order in German main clauses, and Jaeggli and Safir (p. 31) suggest that as a result of these, '. . . it may be reasonable to argue that Tense is located in [C], while agreement is located in [I]'. If the formal requirement for agreement-identification states that the identified empty category must be governed by AGR and TENSE, the separation of these elements in German s-structures may ensure that the identification condition is not satisfied. That expletive empty subjects can occur in the language is now explained by noting that, being non-referential, they do not have to be identified. They are licensed in German by (38).

In summary, then, we are contemplating two conditions on null thematic subjects, licensing and identification. Null expletive subjects need satisfy only the former of these. There is a single licensing condition stated in (38) and two types of identification conditions, one applicable in sentence-oriented languages and the other in discourse-oriented languages. With the theoretical assumptions in place, we can now turn to how Hyams applies these in her re-analysis of early child grammars.

Consider first the acquisition of a 'mixed' language such as English or French. Because children acquiring these languages omit obligatory subjects at the null subject stage, they must be treating the languages as if they were morphologically uniform, the parameter responsible for null subjects now being (41):[22]

(41) The Morphological Uniformity Parameter has two values:
       a. [+uniform]
       b. [−uniform]

From this an obvious prediction follows: at this stage, children acquiring English will systematically omit verbal inflections (Tense and Agreement). If they were to exhibit knowledge of such inflections, this would indicate that they are aware of morphologically complex verbal forms and such awareness should be sufficient to rule out null subjects. At this stage, children *do* systematically omit verbal inflections, the emergence of these more or less coinciding with the disappearance of null subjects (Guilfoyle, 1984). Thus, Hyams' re-analysis enables her to link two observations which remained unconnected in the AG/PRO framework.

Next, consider the acquisition of German. German-speaking children produce null subjects and we have seen above that such subjects are illegitimate in
adult German because they are not identified (but see note 21). As observed at
the end of the previous section, word-order errors are a concomitant of null
subjects in early German. But with the SOV word-order which is incorrect in
main clauses, the movement processes responsible for separating TENSE and
AGR do not apply, so the conditions for agreement-identification are satisfied
and null subjects are identifiable. Again, Clahsen's observation from the
previous section that the end of the null subject stage is accompanied by a
dramatic shift to (standard) SVO word-order in German-speaking children is
consistent with this account.[23]

From the different perspective of learnability, Hyams feels that (41) with the
unmarked setting [+uniform] is readily intelligible. With this initial setting, the
child will receive positive data to indicate that [−uniform] is correct. This is
irrespective of whether [+uniform] is interpreted as uniformly complex or
uniformly simple. If, on the other hand, the initial setting is [−uniform] and
this is incorrect, the child will never receive data to indicate this. A [−uniform]
setting requires only that any form be inflected or not, and exposure to only
inflected forms or only uninflected forms will not confound this hypothesis.
Hyams speculates that this brings the parameter within the domain of the
Subset Principle (see chapter 5). We shall delay discussion of this until chapter
9, where the role of the Subset Principle as a constraint on parameterization
will be discussed in some detail.

There remains one outstanding problem for the morphological uniformity
account. This concerns the notion of identification which is operative in
English-speaking children at the null-subject stage. We assume that for Italian
children, with their rapidly acquired inflectional paradigms, agreement-
identification is all that is necessary to account for their null subjects. As
agreement inflections are not present for English-speaking children, we are
forced to consider the possibility that identification is by some other mechanism and Hyams must discard her (1986) claim that small children acquiring
English have, in the relevant respects, Italian grammars. Given what has gone
before, it will come as no great surprise that such children are now regarded as
having, in the relevant respects, Chinese grammars. However, the extension of
Huang's account of empty subjects in Chinese, briefly outlined above, to early
English turns out to be not straightforward.

Recall that Huang's notion of topic-identification permits not only the
identification of null subjects but also that of null objects which occur in
Chinese. Thus, alongside (35), Chinese also has grammatical sentences like
(42):

(42)   wo xihuan
       I like
       'I like him/her/it'

For Huang, this is accounted for via a structure like (43):

(43) $[_{Top}\ e_i]\ [_S\ wo\ xihuan\ e_i]$

In (43), e_i is a *variable* and, as such, there is nothing to prevent it being bound from the Top position.

Now, if Huang's analysis were appropriate for early English, we would predict that null objects are also legitimate at this stage, just as they are in adult Chinese. But it is a foundational assumption of all Hyams' work in this area that there is an asymmetry in early child speech between the omission of subjects and of objects: the former is universal and frequent, the latter much less frequent. Assuming this is correct, the absence of null objects in early English becomes perplexing.

Hyams' response to this predicament is to suggest that UG makes available a further option of topic-identification. That is, as well as an empty topic being able to identify an empty subject which has the status of a variable, it can perform the same function for a *pro*. Thus, in early English, the structure of a null subject sentence is (44):

(44) $[_{Top} e_i]$ $[_S pro_i. . .]$

In (44), the empty topic is identified by discourse and itself identifies the *pro* subject. How does this help? To see this, we have to follow Hyams in making a further assumption: that a null pronominal (*pro*) must be identified by its closest c-commanding NP. In (44), we can take this to be the empty topic, but now consider what happens if we attempt to extend this analysis to null objects. The structure we get for (42) is (45):

(45) $[_{Top} e]$ $[_S$ wo xihuan *pro*$]$

If *pro* were identified by (and co-indexed with) its closest c-commanding NP (*wo*), this would produce (46):

(46) $[_{Top} e]$ $[_S$ wo$_i$ xihuan *pro*$_i]$

But in this configuration, a pronoun (*pro*) is bound within its governing category, i.e. (46) is in violation of Principle B of the Binding Theory (see Section 3.3). Therefore, it is not a legitimate structure in any language, and topic-identified null objects *must* be variables.

Hyams' proposal for the status of null subjects in early English can now be easily formulated. Such subjects are tokens of *pro*, licensed by morphological uniformity and topic-identified. There are no null objects in early English because these require topic-identification of variables.[24]

This concludes our presentation of Hyams' re-analysis of the linguistic basis for null subjects in the grammars of children acquiring English. Its major advantage over its predecessor is that it attempts to address seriously the question of identification and, in so doing, links the emergence of verbal inflections with the disappearance of null subjects in a theoretically satisfying way. In the next section, we take steps to evaluate the two proposals.

4.4 Null Subjects: Problems and Alternatives

Since the appearance of Hyams' seminal work, a number of reservations have been expressed about its theoretical status and its relationship to data. One of these (the failure of the initial account to link the emergence of tense inflections with the demise of null subjects) provided partial motivation for the development of the morphological uniformity alternative, but there are others. In this section, without aiming to be exhaustive, we shall briefly examine some of the most salient of these and give notice of alternative proposals for explaining features of these earliest stages of grammatical development. The majority of our observations apply to either formulation of the Null Subject Parameter; where this is not the case, the target of the criticism will be clear.

At a general conceptual level, there is a sense in which Hyams' formulations of the Null Subject Parameter are at variance with the spirit of PPT. Recall that we introduced this chapter by enumerating a set of phenomena which are highly correlated with the null subject option and by summarizing two accounts which attempt to accommodate these within a single locus of parametric variation. Neither the AG/PRO Parameter nor the Morphological Uniformity Parameter embraces this range of data. Hyams (1986) explicitly locates the possibility of inverted subjects in the parameterization of Rule R, and there is no attempt to account for this and other null subject phenomena in terms of morphological uniformity. Now, of course, an appropriate inventory of parameters is an empirical issue, and it is certainly possible that the initial recognition of a set of correlated phenomena constitutes a spurious generalization. But what Safir (1987, p. 80) refers to as 'an atomization of parameters', whereby the construction-specific rules of ST are replaced by construction-specific parameters, is a general methodological concern to which we shall return in the next chapter and in chapter 9.

A more specific theoretical concern regarding Hyams (1986) is her reliance on the Head Assignment Principle (22). As Section 4.2 made clear, this principle plays a vital role in Hyams' discussion of the differential acquisition of modals in English and Italian, as well as in her attempt to account for features of early German. However, these uses of the principle constitute its only motivation, and to that extent it is stipulative and *ad hoc* (see Aldridge, 1989, pp. 52–3). Furthermore, as a stipulation, it has a character quite unrelated to any of the major principles we have surveyed in Section 3.3. Of course, detailed linguistic analysis of different languages is always throwing up anomalies which might be resolved by the stipulation of a 'principle', but what is worrying about (22) is the extent to which the whole enterprise depends on it.

Regarding morphological uniformity, the licensing condition for null subjects (38) is extremely odd, particularly when it is set alongside something as intuitively transparent as agreement-identification. Naturally, there is no reason to believe that linguistic principles will have an immediately obvious motivation, particularly if we believe that UG constitutes an autonomous mental faculty; but the juxtaposition of uniformly complex and uniformly simple morphological paradigms to the exclusion of those which are mixed and the tentative correlation between sentence-oriented languages and agreement-identification conditions hints that some more fundamental linguistic divisions may be at work here. Jaeggli and Safir (1989, p. 41) give explicit recognition to this unease when they say:

> Unfortunately we do not have any answer to the natural question that arises; we have no explanation to offer as to why [38] should be a property of natural languages.

Furthermore, the modifications to Huang's (1984) account to allow the topic-identification of a *pro* subject are not worked out in detail and their theoretical consequences are not at all clear.

Turning to more specific difficulties, Hyams' reliance on the Avoid Pronoun Principle (31) in her earlier treatment, a reliance which presumably would carry over into the morphological uniformity approach, appears to make an incorrect prediction. Recall that subject pronouns are uncommon in Null Subject Languages, occurring only when required by the pragmatics of the discourse. Hyams' account of the resetting of the parameter depends crucially on the child taking note of expletive subject pronouns or unstressed subject pronouns which, given (31), signal that subjects are syntactically obligatory. For this to be plausible, the child has to have access to (31). But then if the child has a grammar which permits null subjects, (31) requires that pronominal subjects should be avoided. Therefore, there should be a paucity of pronominal subjects up to the point at which the parameter is reset. This prediction is not confirmed. Valian (1989, 1990a) reports a study of a group of English-speaking children, the youngest of whom produced subjects in about 70 per cent of their utterances which included verbs. It seems reasonable to suggest that subjects are optional for such children and that they therefore provide an appropriate population on which to test the prediction. Unfortunately, 77 per cent of this group's subjects were pronouns.[25]

Recall now that the analysis of early German in both frameworks was intended to account not only for the German-speaking child's use of null subjects, but also for the incorrect use of OV word-order in main clauses. This was achieved by ensuring that a rule of V-movement could not apply in the AG/PRO framework and by the separation of TENSE and AGR in the morphological uniformity account.[26] But Clahsen's (1986) original observations, which motivated Hyams' analyses, were that the incorrect OV word-order appeared something over 50 per cent of the time. The remainder of the child's simple clauses had the correct VO order, and this remainder is substantial enough to need to be accounted for. Neither approach to the parameter we have considered can offer an account. On the AG/PRO hypothesis, movement of the verb is prevented by the illegitimacy of its being first raised into I; such a raising would lead to AG = PRO being governed in violation of the PRO Theorem. From the perspective of morphological uniformity, VO order requires the separation of TENSE and AGR and, once this has occurred, empty referential subjects are no longer licensed.

A crucial concern arises in connection with Hyams' attitude towards null *objects*. Bloom (1970) provided one of the first discussions of this phenomenon, concluding that at early stages, children tend to omit one of the major constituents in an SVO string. Her data indicated that while omission of subjects was more frequent than that of objects, tokens of the latter were not insubstantial in number. Such an observation is clearly at variance with Hyams' (1987c, p. 10) remark that: 'While missing subjects are pervasive, sentences with missing objects are strikingly rare.' As we have seen earlier, the non-existence of null objects in early English is an important issue for Hyams, but numerous investigators (Aldridge, 1989; de Haan and Tuijnman, 1988; Radford, 1990a) have now produced extensive data to corroborate Bloom's original remarks, and it appears that this position can no longer be maintained. What are the implications of this?

At the very least, the existence of null objects demonstrates that the accounts in the previous two sections are incomplete. Neither of them addresses the licensing and identification conditions of null objects (see Rizzi, 1986, for lengthy discussion of these conditions in adult Italian). However, it is certainly conceivable that the proposals can be supplemented so as to permit this possibility. De Haan and Tuijnman (1988) pursue such a strategy in attempting to explain the occurrence of empty categories in early Dutch, implementing Huang's (1984) ideas on topic-identification that we have already met. Indeed, it will be recalled that Hyams' reason for modifying Huang's proposals hinged on the non-occurrence of null objects; these modifications are no longer necessary if null objects exist (see Radford, 1990a, for critical discussion of de Haan and Tuijnman's proposal).

Let us now consider parameter resetting on Hyams' account for a child acquiring English. There are at least two difficulties, one general and the other quite specific. The general difficulty will be considered more systematically in chapter 8, but it is appropriate to mention it briefly here. Hyams assumes that resetting of the AG/PRO Parameter is occasioned by expletive subjects (*it*, *there*) and unstressed pronominal subjects. But such forms are presumably present in the child's linguistic environment throughout the period during which he or she is producing null subjects; so, why do they not 'trigger' parameter resetting earlier? Hyams (1986, p. 94) acknowledges this as 'a problem with the 'expletive trigger' hypothesis', and describes it as 'one for which we have no ready solution'. She subsequently speculates about the maturation of certain representational capacities.

The specific difficulty is articulated by Lebeaux (1987). In her explanation for the non-occurrence of modals, Hyams argues that the child must be capable of recognizing that these are not typical verbs. If they were, they could appear in VP and their co-occurrence with AG = PRO would be legitimate. Lebeaux simply asks why the rather sophisticated analysis required of the child to determine that modals are not typical verbs does not justify the conclusion that they are therefore non-typical (i.e. modal) verbs, leading to a resetting of the AG/PRO Parameter. In other words, the presence of modal verbs with their defective paradigms in the child's linguistic environment could be seen as a 'trigger' for resetting the parameter. The fact that such resetting does not occur on this basis remains puzzling on Hyams' account.

Finally, it is necessary to draw attention to alternative explanations for missing subjects. In chapter 10, we shall look in some detail at proposals which make use of a rather different set of linguistic assumptions (Kazman, 1988;

Guilfoyle and Noonan, 1989; Radford, 1988b, 1990a). Here, however, we can briefly consider the suggestion that the omission of subjects, rather than being linguistically motivated, is a consequence of processing constraints.

In Section 4.2, it was pointed out that Hyams rejects a processing account of null subjects, drawing attention to the claim that the occurrence of such subjects is independent of utterance complexity. Recently, this has been explicitly disputed by P. Bloom (1990), who performed a series of analyses on the data of three children studied by Brown (1973). Most directly, he compared the average length of the VPs produced by the children in sentences containing overt subjects with those in sentences containing null subjects. His results indicated that VPs occurring with overt subjects were longer across a number of samples, and he suggests that this is consistent with a processing interpretation. It is, of course, important to be clear that demonstration of such consistency does not refute the parametric hypothesis. It does, however, present an alternative which some may find congenial.[27]

Valian (1990a) also argues for a 'performance'-based account of null subjects, but on a somewhat different basis. She suggests that if at the null subject stage both English- and Italian-speaking children have *grammars* which permit empty subjects, we might expect the extent of subject-omission to be comparable for the two groups. However, this turns out not to be the case. The 70 per cent production rate for subjects in English children referred to above compared to a 30 per cent rate in Italian children. While there may be several ways of accounting for this disparity, some of them considered by Valian, it is tempting to suggest that the grammars of the English children require subjects, but processing constraints ensure that subjects are not always produced; the grammars of the Italian children, on the other hand, license null subjects. Again, it is important to be clear on the force of Valian's observation. If her interpretation is correct, it shows that subject-omitting English children do not have incorrect parameter settings. It does not question the appropriateness of the parameter-setting approach to acquisition. Even less does it challenge the value of this approach to linguistic theory.[28]

4.5 Summary

In this chapter, we have focused attention on one rather small area of the theory of grammar, introducing the best-known views on null subject phenomena and describing how these views have been modified and applied in the acquisition sphere. The problems we have raised in the previous section almost certainly indicate that the theoretical ideas we have considered are misguided, and parts of our subsequent discussion will return to some of these issues to offer alternative analyses.

To a large extent, it is irrelevant to our present purposes whether Hyams and her colleagues are right in their insistence that early English contains grammatically licensed empty subjects. What is important is to realize how a reasonably precise grammatical hypothesis, presented within the context of a set of general principles, can generate new questions and perspectives. Starting from null subjects, we have been led to consider the nature of agreement, the status of modal verbs, etc., a consequence that we might expect if we are working within a highly connected group of theoretical concepts. While we have not been directly concerned with any of the principles from Section 3.3 in this chapter, we have invoked the PRO Theorem (derivative on the Binding Theory) and referred to the different properties of empty categories in constructing and considering arguments. In the next chapter, we shall focus directly on the Binding Theory module and its principles, showing how it is possible to derive some rather provocative conclusions about acquisition from consideration of cross-linguistic variation.

5 Parameterized Binding Theory and the Subset Principle

Introduction

In Section 3.3, we introduced the Binding Theory as principally concerned with accounting for the distribution of overt anaphors (reciprocals such as *each other* and reflexives such as *himself*) and pronominals (such as *him*). We also noted the desirable extension of the theory to embrace NP-trace. In this chapter, we shall be concerned exclusively with overt elements.

Section 3.4 indicated, with minimal justification, that some parameterization is needed in this module and we begin this chapter by briefly discussing several more examples which, at first sight, offer a bewildering variety of options. One of the major concerns of the chapter is to present in some detail the most systematic attempt to come to terms with this variation, the Parameterized Binding Theory of Wexler and Manzini (1987) and Manzini and Wexler (1987). As we shall see, this theory postulates a set of binding parameters, the values of which yield *set-theoretically nested languages*. This gives rise to a serious learnability problem which Wexler and Manzini resolve by formulating the Subset Principle as a condition on acquisition mechanisms, and the second important goal of the chapter is to convey an understanding of this crucial notion. We have already met an allusion to it in our discussion of morphological uniformity (Section 4.3) and a hint of the overgeneralizations it is designed to avoid in Section 1.3. It is probably the single most important background concept in theoretical discussions of language acquisition, so the motivation for giving it a thorough airing is clear. Indeed, it sometimes appears to have the character of a talisman, with investigators being convinced of the plausibility of their proposals because they require invocation of it. For the Subset Principle to operate appropriately, parameters have to satisfy certain conditions, and these too will be introduced in this chapter.

A range of difficulties remain with the Wexler and Manzini account, and several of these are raised. The chapter concludes with a brief presentation of some recent ideas which offer a new perspective on some of these difficulties.

The actual course of children's acquisition of anaphors and pronominals will not be of concern in this chapter. Rather, we shall be investigating how a set of assumptions, faced with a range of linguistic variation, lead to some rather clear claims about how children *must* proceed if they are to succeed. Needless to say the assumptions are not logically necessary, so the conclusions we shall reach should be viewed as embodying empirical hypotheses.

5.1 Cross-Linguistic Binding Phenomena

We begin by repeating the definition of governing category from Section 3.3 for reference:

(1) The governing category for α is the smallest category containing α, a governor for α and a subject.

Yang (1983) is one of the first systematic attempts to survey the binding properties of anaphors and pronominals in a variety of languages. In this section, we present a small sample of the examples he describes to get some idea of the variability that obtains in this area of grammar. In the next section, we will consider how such observations can be systematized.[1]

Yang notes that the cross-linguistic behaviour of reciprocals such as English *each other*, Dutch *elkaar* and Japanese *tagai* is fairly uniform; with one or two minor technical adjustments, the definition for governing category in (1) accounts for the distribution of such forms. Turning to reflexives, however, the situation is rather different. Consider the Russian examples in (2):

(2) a. Vanja$_i$ znaet [čto Volodja$_j$ očen' ljubit sebja$_{*i/j}$]
        Vanja knows that Volodja very much loves self
        'Vanja knows that Volodja loves herself very much'

     b. Professor$_i$ proposil assistenta$_j$ [PRO$_j$ čitat' svoj$_{i/j}$ doklad]
        Professor asked assistant read self's report
        'The professor asked the assistant to read his own report'

Example (2a) is unproblematic for the definition in (1). Principle A requires the anaphor *sebja* to be bound in its governing category. In this sentence, this is the bracketed clause, and it follows that the anaphor can be co-indexed with *Volodja* inside this clause, but not with *Vanja*, which occurs outside this domain. Example (2b), however, is different. Here the embedded clause is infinitival and contains a PRO subject controlled by the direct object of the matrix clause. Again, the anaphor *svoj* should be bound within the infinitival clause, but, as the indexing indicates, it is possible for it to be bound by the matrix subject. Clearly, Principle A, utilizing (1), makes the wrong prediction here.

A similar situation is found in Hindi in connection with the behaviour of the reflexive anaphor *əpne*:

(3) a. Ashok$_i$-ne kəha [kii Lalita$_j$ əpne$_{*i/j}$ liye cha kəreegi]
        Ashok−ERG said that Lalita self for tea make
        'Ashok said that Lalita would make tea for herself'
     b. Ashok$_i$-ne Lalita$_j$ se [PRO$_j$ əpne$_{i/j}$ liye cha bənane ko] kəha
        Ashok-ERG Lalita with self for tea to make asked
        'Ashok asked Lalita to make tea for self'

Once more, the governing categories defined by (1) are bracketed. Example (3a) is consistent with the theory, as *əpne* cannot be bound by *Ashok*; however (3b) is not, since it seems that the anaphor, occurring here in a non-finite clause, can be bound by the matrix subject.

Furthermore, there are languages containing anaphors which can be bound by an arbitrarily distant antecedent. The examples in (4) and (5), from Korean and Kannada respectively, illustrate this possibility:

(4) John$_i$-in [Bill$_j$-i [Mary$_k$-ka [Tom$_l$iy caki$_{i,j,k,l}$-e taehan
     John-TOP Bill-NM Mary-NM Tom's self toward

     thaeto]-lil silhəha-n-ta-ko] saengkakha-n-ta-ko]
     attitude-ACC hate-ASP-DEC-COMP think-ASP-DEC-COMP

     mit-nin-ta
     believe-ASP-DEC

     'John believes that Bill thinks that Mary hates Tom's attitude towards self'

(5) [[[taanu$_{i,j,k}$ aanayennu killidalendu] amma$_i$ magalige
     self elephant pinch-PAST-COMP mother daughter

     heelidalendu] raani$_j$ cintisidalendu] aa hengasu$_k$ nanna
     tell-PAST-COMP queen think-PAST-COMP that woman my

     hendatiyenndu nambisidalu
     wife believe-cause-PAST

     'The woman convinced my wife that the queen thought that the mother told the daughter that self pinched the elephant'

These rather complex examples deserve a little comment. Note first that Korean is a head-final language in which the basic clausal word-order is SOV. Thus, in (4), the main verb is *mit-nin-ta*, the subject is *John-in* and the remainder of the sentence is a sentential object complement of the main verb. Within that complement, the main verb is *saengkakha-n-ta* to which is cliticized the complementizer *-ko*, the subject is *Billi*, and the remainder is a sentential object complement of the verb. Within *that* complement, the main verb is *silhəha-n-ta*, again appearing with a cliticized complementizer, the subject is *Mary-ka* and the object is the nominal expression *Tom-iy caki-e taehan thaeto-lil*, which carries the accusative case marker. Within this nominal expression, the head-final characteristic of Korean is still obvious, as the head noun is *thaeto* 'attitude', its subject is *Tom-iy* which is marked genitive and its object is *caki-e* Case-marked by the postposition *taehan*. Of course, the occurrence of postpositions, as opposed to prepositions, is another symptom of the head-finalness of Korean.

With a measure of understanding of the structure of (4) in place, we can now note that the reflexive anaphor *caki* can be bound by any one of the four subjects appearing in the sentence. Our version of Principle A with the definition of governing category in (1) predicts that it can only be bound by *Tom-iy*, since this is a subject and defines the anaphor's governing category as the innermost object. In fact, *caki* can be bound outside this domain and outside the domains defined by the next two subjects up the structure *Mary-ka* and *Bill-i* – the subject-defined binding domains are indicated by the brackets in (4). Very similar considerations apply to the Kannada example, and it is left to the interested reader to check that the binding domains defined by the various subjects are as indicated.

Turning now to pronominals, Yang cites a number of examples that behave like English pronouns, their distribution being accounted for by Principle B of the Binding Theory. For instance, the Japanese pronominal *kare* exhibits the paradigm in (6):

(6) a. John$_i$-wa [kare$_i$-no shashin-o] mita
     John-TOP he-GEN picture-ACC saw
     'John saw his picture'

     b. [John$_i$-ga Tom$_j$-o kare$_{*i/*j}$-ni shokaisita]
     John-NOM Tom-ACC him-to introduced
     'John introduced Tom to him'

     c. John$_i$-wa [Tom$_j$-ga kare$_{i/*j}$-o aisite-iru-to] omotte-iru
     John-TOP Tom-NOM him-ACC love-COMP think
     'John thinks that Tom loves him'

In (6), the governing categories defined by (1) are bracketed; in (6a), we have a noun phrase with a subject (*kare* itself), in (6b) the matrix clause, and in (6c) the subordinate tensed clause. In each case, as the possible indexings indicate, *kare* must be free inside this governing category.

The distribution of the Norwegian third person plural pronoun *de* (with accusative and genitive forms *dem* and *deres*), however, is not consistent with Principle B and (1). This is indicated in (7):

(7) a. *De$_i$ liker [deres$_i$ bøker]
     'They like their books'

     b. De$_i$ leste [mine klager mot dem$_i$]
     'They read my complaints against them'

     c. *[De$_i$ leste klager mot dem$_i$]
     'They read complaints against them'

In this paradigm, (7b, c) are as expected. In (7b), the governing category for *dem* is the bracketed noun phrase which has a subject and the pronoun is free in this domain; in (7c), as the noun phrase lacks a subject, the governing category for *dem* is the matrix clause, and binding is impossible in this domain. The problematic example is (7a), where the governing category for *deres* is the noun phrase (which has a subject, *deres* itself). Accordingly, it should be possible for the pronoun to be bound outside this governing category, but (7a) indicates that this is not so in general.

Finally, the Icelandic pronominal *hann* also displays behaviour which is inconsistent with our current version of Principle B:

(8) a. Jón$_i$ retti Haraldi$_j$ [hans$_{*i/j}$ föt]
     'Jon handed Harold his clothes'

     b. *Jón$_i$ skipaði mer$_j$ að [PRO$_j$ raka hann$_i$]
     'Jon ordered me to shave him'

     c. Jón$_i$ segir að [Maria elski hann$_i$]
     'Jon says that Maria loves him'

Here, (8c) is consistent with Principle B. The governing category for *hann* is indicated by the bracketed clause, and *hann* is free in this category as required. In (8b), however, *hann* occurs in an infinitival clause with a controlled PRO subject. Equivalent English data suggest that this clause should be *hann*'s governing category, and binding of the pronoun outside this category should be legitimate. But the ill-formedness of (8b) indicates that this is not so. Example (8a) introduces a further complication. In this sentence, the governing category for *hans*, the genitive form of *hann*, is the bracketed noun phrase. It should be possible for the pronoun to be bound outside this noun phrase, and it is so long as the binder is the direct object *Haraldi*. However, the subject *Jón* cannot bind this pronoun, suggesting that in certain constructions it must be free of subject-binding. This property of *subject obviation* for pronouns is matched by a property of *subject orientation* for anaphors which is illustrated by the Norwegian example in (9):

(9) [Han$_i$ fortalte Knut$_j$ om seg-selv$_{i/*j}$]
     'Han told Knut about himself'

In (9), *seg-selv* is an anaphor and its governing category is the whole clause. It ought to follow from our version of the Binding Theory that *seg-selv* can be bound by any c-commanding antecedent in the clause. Both *Han* and *Knut* c-command *seg-selv*, but only the subject *Han* can bind the anaphor.

These few examples give some idea of the range of variation found in the binding properties of anaphors and pronominals. It seems that this variation can be of two kinds, one concerning the 'distance' over which an anaphor can be bound and a pronoun must be free, and another to do with the subject or non-subject status of antecedents. We now turn to Wexler and Manzini's attempt to produce a systematic parameter-based account of this range of variation.

5.2 Parameterized Binding Theory: The Governing Category Parameter

Wexler and Manzini have presented two accounts of their influential analysis of the variation we have sampled in the previous section. Wexler and Manzini (1987) is relatively non-technical and does not engage the full complexity of binding phenomena confronted in Manzini and Wexler (1987).[2]

The latter paper also raises residual problematic issues which do not appear in the former. This and the following two sections contain an uncritical exposition of the less technical version of their theory; for our purposes, it contains all the essential ideas of the more complex alternative. In Section 5.5, a number of difficulties will be raised for the theory. Some of these are presented as problems, along with tentative solutions, in the more technical presentation. However, recognition of their status as difficulties does not require detailed acquaintance with this version of the theory.

A paradigm which has not been mentioned in the previous section and which further illustrates the inadequacy of the English-based Binding Principles is provided by the Icelandic anaphor *sig* in (10):[3]

(10)   a. *Jón$_i$ segir að [Maria elskar sig$_i$]
           'Jon says that Maria loves (indicative) self'

       b. Jón$_i$ segir að [Maria elski sig$_i$]
           'Jon says that Maria loves (subjunctive) self'

       c. Jón$_i$ skipaði Haraldi að [PRO raka sig$_i$]
           'Jon ordered Harald to shave self'

       d. Jón$_i$ heyrdu [lysingu Maria af sér$_i$]
       'Jon heard Maria's description of self'

Sig is an anaphor and must be co-referential with some antecedent in the sentence in which it occurs, so it ought to fall under Principle A of the Binding Theory. The ill-formedness of (10a) is consistent with this, since the governing category for *sig* in this sentence is the bracketed clause. Principle A says that *sig* must be bound in this domain. But *sig* is not bound in this domain – it is bound by *Jón* outside the domain – and the fact that it is ungrammatical follows. However, each of (10b, c, d) is embarrassing for Principle A. In (10b), the governing category for *sig* is the bracketed subjunctive clause; in (10c), the infinitival clause provides the governing category, since it contains a PRO subject controlled by the direct object in the matrix clause; in (10d), the governing category is the bracketed noun phrase, since this contains *sér* (the genitive form of *sig*), a governor for *sér* (*af*) and a subject *Maria*. Unfortunately for Principle A as it is currently stated, in each of these examples, *sig* is bound outside its governing category without inducing ungrammaticality.

What responses are available to this situation? One possibility would be to abandon Principle A as a universal condition on binding and allow each language to obey its own Binding Principles. Thus, we might have Principle A (English), Principle A (Icelandic), and so on, and the child's task would be to determine which Principle A was operative in the target grammar. There is, however, another possibility. According to this, the principles of the Binding Theory are left intact as universal, and the notion of 'governing category' which appears in these principles is parameterized. Thus, we can contemplate the possibility of defining Governing Category (English), Governing Category (Icelandic), and so on. Since the latter strategy leaves intact the distinction between principles and parameters as this was introduced in chapter 3, we follow Wexler and Manzini in adopting it.

With this option in mind, consider again the paradigm in (10). Examples (10b, c, d) show that the definition of governing category which includes a reference to *subject* is not appropriate for this Icelandic anaphor. What distinguishes (10a) from the other sentences in the paradigm is that the bracketed expression appearing in it contains an *indicative tense* − (10b) contains a subjunctive tense, (10c), being infinitival, no tense at all (but see Stowell, 1982), and (10d), being nominal, not even an I constituent (but see Abney, 1987; Milsark, 1987; Ouhalla, 1988). The obvious move, then, is to replace the reference to subject in the definition of governing category with a reference to indicative tense. This yields the definition in (11):

(11) α is a governing category for β iff α is the minimal category containing β, a governor for β and an indicative tense.

It is immediately clear that this definition, working in tandem with an unmodified Principle A, is consistent with (10). In (10a), the bracketed clause contains an indicative tense, so *sig* should be bound within it. This is not the case, so (10a) is ungrammatical. In none of (10b, c, d) does the bracketed expression contain an indicative tense; in each case the minimal category containing the anaphor, its governor and an indicative tense is the matrix clause. Therefore, Principle A requires that the anaphor be bound within this clause. In each case, it is so bound, and the grammaticality of (10b, c, d) follows.

Of course, (11) is not appropriate for English, and in order to accommodate both English and Icelandic in the Binding Theory, we have to embrace a disjunctive (i.e. parameterized) definition of governing category, as in (12):

(12) α is a governing category for β iff α is the minimal category containing β, a governor for β and
        (i) a subject OR
        (ii) an indicative tense

The first disjunct in (12) provides the appropriate definition for English, and the second disjunct is appropriate for Icelandic *sig*.

Consideration of the behaviour of anaphors from further languages indicates that the two definitions of governing category that we have considered so far do not exhaust the possibilities.

To see this, recall (146) from Section 3.4, the paradigm displaying the distribution of the Italian anaphor *sè*, repeated here as (13):

(13) a. Alice$_j$ sapeva che [Mario$_i$ aveva guardato sè$_{i/*j}$ nello specchio]
       'Alice knew that Mario had looked at self in the mirror'

     b. Alice$_j$ pensava che [Mario$_i$ avesse guardato sè$_{i/*j}$ nello specchio]
       'Alice thought that Mario had (subjunctive) looked at self in the mirror'

     c. Alice$_j$ disse a Mario$_i$ [PRO$_i$ di guardare sè$_{i/*j}$ nello specchio]
       'Alice told Mario to look at self in the mirror'

     d. Alice$_j$ vide [Mario$_i$ guardare sè$_{i/j}$ nello specchio
       'Alice saw Mario look at self in the mirror'

     e. Alice$_j$ guardò [i ritratti di sè$_{i/j}$ di Mario$_i$]
       'Alice looked at Mario's portraits of self'

In this paradigm, (13a, b, c) are consistent with Principle A if governing category is defined as in (12i). In each case, *sè* must be bound within the domain of its closest subject. This breaks down, however, in (13d, e). In the former, *sè* occurs in a constituent known as a Small Clause which has a subject *Mario*. We would expect this Small Clause to define the governing category for *sè*, but the anaphor can be bound outside this domain. By the same token, we might anticipate that the bracketed noun phrase is the governing category for *sè* in (13e); again, however, binding of *sè* from outside this domain is possible. Note further that the value for governing category introduced for Icelandic *sig* will not serve for *sè*. Neither of the bracketed expressions in (13b) and (13c) contains an indicative tense, so if *sè* had the same governing category as *sig*, we would expect both of these examples to allow the anaphor to be bound by the matrix subject. This indicates that a third value for governing category is necessary.

To see what this should be, consider what distinguishes the structures containing *sè* in (13d, e) from those in (13a, b, c). The tensed indicative clause of (13a), the tensed subjunctive clause of (13b) and the infinitival clause of (13c) all contain an I constituent. This is not so for Small Clauses (see Radford, 1988a, Section 6.8, for extensive justification) nor for noun phrases. The Italian data, then, are accommodated by the definition of governing category in (14):

(14) α is a governing category for β iff α is the minimal category containing
     β, a governor for β and an I.

Consider next the Icelandic pronominal *hann*, part of the paradigm for which appeared as (8) in the previous section. Alongside (8a, b, c) we need to take account of (15):

(15) Jón$_i$ segir að [Maria elski hann$_i$]
     'Jon says that Maria loves (subjunctive) him'

Example (15), like (8c), is consistent with Principle B if governing category is defined as in (12i). However, this is not the case for (8a, b). Setting aside for later discussion the subject obviation property of *hann* revealed by (8a), it seems that *hann* must be free in the domain of a tense (indicative or subjunctive). If *hann* occurs in an infinitival (8b), nothing in the infinitival clause serves to define a binding domain; and if *hann* occurs in a noun phrase, nothing occurring in the noun phrase has this property either. What infinitival clauses and noun phrases lack, when compared to indicative and subjunctive clauses, is Tense, so the distribution of *hann* will be accounted for by the definition of governing category in (16):

(16) α is a governing category for β iff α is the minimal category containing β, a governor for β and a Tense.

Finally, the Korean and Kannada examples cited in the previous section show that for the anaphors *caki* (Korean) and *taanu* (Kannada), none of the definitions we have formulated so far is appropriate. These anaphors must be bound, but it appears that their binder can be an arbitrary distance away. It must, of course, occur in the sentence in which the anaphor occurs, and Wexler and Manzini identify this binding domain with the presence of a 'root' tense, i.e. a tense occurring in a main clause. The last definition for governing category we shall consider, then, is given in (17):

(17) α is a governing category for β iff α is the minimal category containing β, a governor for β and a 'root' Tense.

Putting all of the above observations together, we can see that we must contemplate a five-valued parameter for governing category if we are to account for the behaviour of anaphors and pronouns cross-linguistically:[4]

(18) The Governing Category Parameter (GCP) has five values defined as follows:
α is a governing category for β iff α is the minimal category which contains β, a governor for β and
(a) a subject
(b) an I
(c) a TENSE
(d) an indicative TENSE
(e) a root TENSE

English anaphors and pronouns provide the evidence for value (a), Italian *sè* behaves in accordance with value (b), the Icelandic pronoun *hann* motivates value (c), the anaphor *sig* from the same language has its distribution determined by (d), and the Korean anaphor *caki* and Kannada anaphor *taanu* show that it is necessary also to include value (e). If we accept that (18) offers an accurate picture of the range of linguistic variation in this module of grammar, we must now contemplate how, in principle, a child might come to terms with the properties of anaphors and pronouns in the target grammar.

5.3 The Subset Principle

To begin with, let us be as concrete as possible, by considering the English anaphor *himself*, associated with value (a) in (18), and the Korean 'long-distance' anaphor *caki*, associated with value (e). Consider the English-speaking child who has somehow worked out that *himself* is an anaphor.[5] Such a child grows into an adult who knows that the sentence in (19) is ill-formed in English:

(19)   *John asked the men to look after himself

On the No Negative Data Assumption, we must ask where this knowledge comes from, and the theory of UG, as an account of the child's initial state, provides a ready answer to this, *so long as the Binding Theory is not parameterized*. Given access to such a theory, the child can construct the following deduction:

(20)   *Premise 1*: *himself* is an anaphor (derived from primary linguistic data)
       Premise 2: an anaphor is bound in its governing category (supplied by UG)
       Premise 3: the governing category for α is the minimal category containing α, a governor for α and a subject (supplied by UG)
       Premise 4: in *John asked the men to look after himself* the governing category for *himself* is [PRO to look after himself] (supplied by an interaction of primary linguistic data and principles of UG not relevant to the Binding Theory)
       Premise 5: *himself* is not bound in this category (the only potential binder is PRO and, because this is controlled by *the men*, it is not an appropriate antecedent for *himself*)

       Conclusion: *John asked the men to look after himself* is ill-formed.

As an account of how the child might acquire knowledge of the grammatical properties of strings of words to which he or she has not been exposed, this is fine and nicely illustrates the deductive structure of PPT. Unfortunately, in relying on *Premise 3*, it makes use of a universal definition of governing category, a definition the discussion of the previous section has shown to be inappropriate. Instead, what we are now contemplating is that UG supplies the child with a set of options, and (20) completely ignores the question of how the child selects the correct option.

Suppose, then, that children acquiring English have access to these options, but are not disposed to prefer any one of them to the others. This means that our English-speaking children may select value (e), which only requires an anaphor to be bound in a root sentence. But then, taking due account of the fact that they are not provided with systematic negative evidence, they should grow up to accept (19) as well-formed. No English speaker does this, so something has gone wrong.

Now consider Korean-speaking children attempting to work out the properties of *caki*. They too may make an incorrect selection of the GCP for this anaphor, say value (a), but in this case, they will subsequently be presented with data which indicate their incorrectness, viz. data in which *caki* occurs bound outside the domain defined by a subject. Such children will be able to reset their parameter value, but this procedure will not be available to English-speaking children who have taken the incorrect step described above.

This specific example illustrates a general point which emerged in chapter 1: with the No Negative Data Assumption, adoption of a hypothesis which is 'too general' will never be correctable. Treating English *himself* as if it had the properties of Korean *caki* constitutes just such a too general hypothesis and the problem arises. The alternative of adopting a hypothesis which is 'too narrow' does not give rise to the same difficulties, since, in this case, positive evidence, not accounted for by the narrow hypothesis, will always reveal the error. In short, in circumstances such as these, we need to constrain children to be 'conservative' in the sense that they will always select the most restrictive hypothesis compatible with the data.

That these considerations are relevant to the GCP formulated in (18) will come as no surprise, given the use which has been made of *himself* and *caki* in our concrete illustration. In fact, Wexler and Manzini are able to prove that if we consider the GCP for anaphors, and designate the 'language' associated with each of the values as $L(a)$, $L(b)$, $L(c)$, $L(d)$ and $L(e)$, then the following strict set-theoretic inclusions obtain:[6]

(21) $L(a) \subset L(b) \subset L(c) \subset L(d) \subset L(e)$

$L(a)$, of course, is just the language associated with the setting for English *himself* and $L(e)$ is the language associated with the setting for Korean *caki*, so we have already informally exploited part of the information in (21) in the above example.

The formal proof of (21) is rather lengthy and will not be reproduced in full here. However, it is fairly straightforward to give an indication of how it proceeds. So consider $L(a)$ and $L(b)$. $L(a)$ will contain all of those sentences in which an anaphor is bound in a domain defined by a subject. If such a domain is itself a clause, it will have an I, and the anaphor will be bound in the domain of the I. Therefore, sentences in $L(a)$ which have this characteristic will also be in $L(b)$. Alternatively, the domain of a subject may be an NP as in (22):

(22)   John admired [Mary$_i$'s photographs of herself$_i$]

Such an NP must be contained in a clause which will have an I, the domain of this I will be the containing clause, and it follows that any anaphor bound within a subject-defined NP-domain will also be bound within an I-defined domain. Thus, sentences of this type too which belong to $L(a)$ also belong to $L(b)$. This shows that $L(a)$ is included in $L(b)$, and, in order to strengthen this to proper inclusion, all we need to do is exhibit sentences in $L(b)$ which are not in $L(a)$. This is easy to do. Such sentences are simply those in which an anaphor occurring inside an NP with a subject is bound outside that NP. We have already met such examples in (13e), repeated here as (23):

(23)   Alice$_j$ guardò [i ritratti di sè$_{i/j}$ di Mario$_i$]
       'Alice looked at Mario's portraits of self'

The fact that *sè* in (23) can be bound outside its containing noun phrase shows that there are sentences in $L(b)$ which are not contained in $L(a)$. We can thus conclude that $L(a)$ is properly included in $L(b)$.

Similar reasoning can be applied to the other proper inclusions in (21) with the fundamental observations being that any category containing a TENSE contains an I but not vice versa (infinitivals), any category that contains an indicative TENSE contains a TENSE but not vice versa (subjunctives), and any category that contains a root TENSE contains an indicative TENSE but not vice versa (subordinate indicative tensed clauses).

Putting (21) alongside our discussion of *himself* and *caki*, it should now be clear that the difficulty posed by adopting a 'too general' hypothesis arises throughout the Parameterized Binding Theory for anaphors. Quite simply, if for any x and y such that $L(x)$ properly contains $L(y)$, a child selects value x for the governing category value when y is correct, he or she will never receive evidence to overthrow this hypothesis. How is this to be avoided?

At this stage, there are two possibilities to consider. The first holds that the ordering of parameter values inherent in (21) is specified in UG. Recalling the discussion in Section 3.5, this amounts to UG containing a *markedness hierarchy* for values of the GCP, such that (a) is unmarked and adopted by the child until evidence which shows that it is incorrect is provided, and in Section 4.2 we have seen that Hyams adopts something along these lines for her AG/PRO analysis. The alternative is to locate the solution not in UG, but in the *learning* procedure itself, constraining this so that it will always select the smallest language compatible with the data. Wexler and Manzini favour this second alternative, and to see why we have briefly to consider pronouns.

Using similar considerations to those employed above, it is fairly easy to see that the governing category values for pronouns also define a nested set of languages. Take values (a) and (b) again. Value (b) requires a pronoun to be free in the domain of an I. I-defined domains are clauses, finite or non-finite, and form a proper subset of subject-defined domains. Therefore, any sentence which contains a pronoun free in the domain of an I can also be described as containing a pronoun free in the domain of a subject, i.e. $L(b)$ is included in $L(a)$. Again, to strengthen this to proper inclusion, we need to exhibit sentences which contain pronouns free in the domain of a subject but not free in the domain of an I; (24) from English is such an example:

(24)   John$_i$ admired [Mary's photographs of him$_i$]

Example (24) is grammatical in a language like English which associates its pronominals with value (a), but (7a), repeated here as (25), is ungrammatical in Norwegian, thereby showing that there are sentences in $L(a)$ which do not belong to $L(b)$:

(25)   *De$_i$ liker deres$_i$ bøker
       'They like their books'

Extending this line of reasoning in obvious ways, we derive the set-theoretic relations between the languages associated with different values of the GCP for pronouns as in (26):

(26) $L(e) \subset L(d) \subset L(c) \subset L(b) \subset L(a)$

Now, it is noteworthy that (26) is the exact opposite of (21), so the option of stating a single markedness hierarchy for the GCP in UG is not available. Indeed, Wexler and Manzini (1987, p. 58) propose that such set-theoretic relations are no business of UG:

> . . . as the theory now stands, no reason exists for the facts that $L(a)$, $L(b)$, $L(c)$, $L(d)$ and $L(e)$ are a subset one of another, but more generally the formal properties and relations of the languages defined by different values of a parameter seem to be no concern of the theory at all.

The principle that ensures learnability of the GCP for anaphors and pronouns, then, will be a principle of the *learning module*, a cognitive system probably specific to the acquisition of language, which interacts with UG but must be distinguished from it. This principle is the *Subset Principle* and is stated by Wexler and Manzini (1987, p. 61) as (27) (see also Berwick, 1986):

(27)   The learning function maps the input data to that value of a parameter which generates a language:
       (a) compatible with the input data; and
       (b) smallest among the languages compatible with the input data.

There are presuppositions in this formulation, most notably that this is a constraint on *the* learning function. These presuppositions are investigated by Wexler and Manzini in a discussion of something they call the *Subset Condition*, which must be clearly distinguished from (27). Because I believe that there are some fundamental problems surrounding this matter, I shall postpone discussion of it until Section 5.5, simply noting for now that *a* learning procedure constrained along the lines of (27) will have the desired

effects for the acquisition of parameter values for both anaphors and pronouns; (27) prevents the child from hypothesizing a value which is 'too
general'.

The Subset Principle is a fundamental part of Wexler and Manzini's
theoretical framework. However, there are others, and we shall consider some
of these in the next section.

5.4 The Lexical Parameterization Hypothesis and the Independence Principle

In the previous section, we have implicitly assumed that values of the GCP are
associated with *grammars*, and for the grammar of English, there is no reason
to believe that this is incorrect. But now consider again (8), (10) and (15),
which illustrated the distribution of the Icelandic anaphor *sig* and the pronoun
hann from the same language. These data suggested that *sig* has to be
associated with value (d) of the GCP and *hann* with value (c). This sort of
intra-language variability appears to be quite common and suggests that the
familiar situation we find in English might be quite unusual. Whether this is so
or not, the Icelandic case indicates that in general it must be possible for
individual lexical items in the same language to be associated with different
values of the same parameter. This is a situation Wexler and Manzini are
happy to accept, and to accommodate it they propose the *Lexical Parameterization Hypothesis* (1987, p. 55):

(28)   Values of a parameter are associated not with particular languages, but
        with particular lexical items in a language.

We shall return to this hypothesis several times in what follows and again in
chapter 9. For now, we simply note that it is clearly motivated by the data
under consideration.

A further important issue arises once we acknowledge that the acquisition of
a language involves the setting of more than one parameter, and the possibility
that parameter settings may interact in complex ways. This is sometimes
known as the *many parameters problem*. The Subset Principle relies upon the
learning mechanism being able to compute the set-theoretic relationships
between languages. Clearly, if we restrict attention to a single parameter, there
is no problem of principle here, but it is conceivable that once we take account
of more than one parameter, the procedure becomes quite unworkable.

To see this in the abstract, consider two parameters p_1 and p_2; p_1 has a range
of values $\{a, b\}$ and p_2 a range of values $\{c, d\}$. Suppose that we consider the
languages resulting from all possible settings of these parameters and discover
that the set-theoretic inclusions in (29) obtain:

(29)   a. $L(a, c) \subset L(b, c)$
        b. $L(b, d) \subset L(a, d)$

A learning procedure relying on the Subset Principle and attempting to determine the correct value for p_1 is at a loss here. With p_2 set at c, (29a) tells the learning procedure to select a as its first guess for p_1; however, with p_2 set at d, it is b which must be tried first.

To rule out this possibility, Wexler and Manzini formulate a condition on parameter values which they call the Independence Principle (1987, p. 65):[7]

(30)   The subset relations between languages generated under different values of a parameter remain constant whatever the values of the other parameters are taken to be.

Thus, applied to the hypothetical case above, if, say, $L(a, c)$ is properly contained in $L(b, c)$, then it will also be the case that $L(a, d)$ is properly contained in $L(b, d)$, i.e. the situation depicted in (29) can never arise. While it is one thing to appreciate the need for a principle such as (30) in the abstract, it would be comforting if this need could be concretely illustrated. Wexler and Manzini believe that it can in the Binding Theory itself.

At the end of Section 5.1, we noted that (8a) from Icelandic and (9) from Norwegian illustrated *subject obviation* for pronouns and *subject orientation* for anaphors. Thus, some pronouns in some languages must only be free of *subjects* in a specified domain, whereas some anaphors can only be bound by *subjects*. Again, this variability does not infect English. Pronouns in English must be free of all antecedents inside, and may be bound by all antecedents outside their governing category; anaphors may be bound by all antecedents inside their governing category. This is illustrated in (31) (for pronouns) and (32) (for anaphors):

(31)   a. John$_i$ told Bill$_j$ about him$_{*i/*j}$
       b. John$_i$ told Bill$_j$ that Mary didn't care about him$_{i/j}$

(32)   John$_i$ told Bill$_j$ about himself$_{i/j}$

Recognition of this sort of variability leads to the formulation of a second parameter in the Binding Theory, known as the Proper Antecedent Parameter. Assume that Principles A and B of the Binding Theory are modified as in (33):[8]

(33)   A: An anaphor must be bound in its governing category by a proper antecedent.
       B: A pronoun must be free of proper antecedents in its governing category.

Then, the *Proper Antecedent Parameter* (PAP) can be stated as in (34):

(34)   A proper antecedent for α is:
       (a) a subject
       (b) any element

English *himself* selects value (b); Icelandic *hann* and Norwegian *seg-selv* select value (a).

Now, defining $L(a)$ and $L(b)$ according to the convention introduced in connection with the GCP, it is easy to see that for anaphors $L(a)$ is properly included in $L(b)$, and that the converse obtains for pronouns. For anaphors, assume the binding domain is fixed at *some* value of the GCP. $L(a)$ will contain all sentences in which an anaphor is bound in that domain by a subject and all such sentences will also belong to $L(b)$. Additionally, however, $L(b)$ will contain those sentences in which an anaphor is bound in its binding domain by non-subjects and these sentences will not belong to $L(a)$. Thus $L(a)$ is properly contained in $L(b)$, and reasoning to the converse conclusion for pronouns is equally direct. Again, we have a situation where the Subset Principle will do its work, leading the child to select value (a) for an anaphor and value (b) for a pronoun unless there is evidence to require a more inclusive setting.

Note further, however, that the Independence Principle is also satisfied by the GCP and the PAP. In the previous paragraph, we assumed that the former was fixed and demonstrated that $L(a)$ was properly contained in $L(b)$ for anaphors. Crucially, we did not assume that it was fixed at a *specific* value, and it follows that the demonstrated inclusion obtains whatever value is assumed for the GCP, i.e. the inclusions in (35) are all true for anaphors, where $L(x, y)$ is the language obtained by setting the GCP at x and the PAP at y:

(35)   a. $L(a, a) \subset L(a, b)$
       b. $L(b, a) \subset L(b, b)$
       c. $L(c, a) \subset L(c, b)$
       d. $L(d, a) \subset L(d, b)$
       e. $L(e, a) \subset L(e, b)$

It is equally easy to see that the converse inclusions hold for pronouns, and (35) with its pronoun analogue summarize the results of the effects of different values of the GCP on the subset relations induced by the PAP – there are no such effects. Nor are there effects on the subset relations induced by the GCP from variations in the values of the PAP, i.e. (36) also holds for anaphors, and its converse obtains for pronouns:

(36)   a. $L(a, a) \subset L(b, a) \subset L(c, a) \subset L(d, a) \subset L(e, a)$
       b. $L(a, b) \subset L(b, b) \subset L(c, b) \subset L(d, b) \subset L(e, b)$

To find empirical support for the Independence Principle is encouraging – a principle motivated on completely abstract learning-theoretic grounds is satisfied by attested parameters.

At this stage, it is necessary to raise a query in connection with the above. Is it necessary to postulate *two* distinct parameters in the Binding Theory? It is surely conceivable that we could formulate a single parameter, the values of which would simultaneously determine a binding domain and a value for proper antecedents, thereby simplifying the theory and perhaps also the task confronting the child. But consider what this would mean in terms of the Subset Principle. In particular, consider the relationship between the languages $L(a, b)$ and $L(b, a)$ for anaphors. $L(a, b)$ has a smaller binding domain than $L(b, a)$ and there will therefore be sentences in $L(b, a)$ which are not in $L(a, b)$. However, $L(a, b)$ allows anything to be a proper antecedent, while $L(b, a)$

restricts this property to subjects. Thus, within the smaller binding domain of $L(a, b)$, there will be anaphor–antecedent relations which are not legitimate in $L(b, a)$. Equivalently, there will be sentences in $L(a, b)$ which are not in $L(b, a)$. Thus, $L(a, b)$ and $L(b, a)$ will intersect in the manner schematized in (37).

(37)

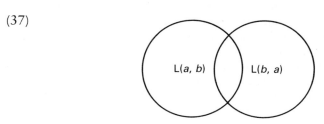

It follows that the Subset Principle is not applicable to these circumstances and Wexler and Manzini (1987, p. 68), assigning a regulative role to satisfaction of the Subset Principle, conclude that: 'the governing category and proper antecedent parameters must indeed be two separate parameters'. We shall return to this conclusion in the next section.

5.5 Parameterized Binding: Further Issues

So far, we have avoided taking a critical view of the Wexler and Manzini framework. Indeed, if we accept the formulation of the Binding Theory they present and adopt the No Negative Data Assumption, there is an air of inevitability to their major conclusions. In this section, introducing where appropriate some of the observations in Manzini and Wexler (1987), we shall be a little more searching.

One issue concerns the status of the *Subset Condition*, briefly mentioned at the end of Section 5.3. This is introduced in the following terms (Wexler and Manzini, 1987, p. 45):

> In order for the Subset Principle to determine a strictly ordered learning hierarchy . . . it is necessary that two values of a parameter in fact yield languages which are in a subset relation to each other. This requirement we will call the 'Subset Condition'. It is necessary for the Subset Condition to hold in order for the Subset Principle to apply.

This statement is entirely innocent. It is simply saying that there is a condition which the values of individual parameters *may* satisfy, and that it is necessary for this condition to be satisfied in order for the Subset Principle to apply and determine a markedness hierarchy. It is *not* a universal condition on parameters and their values, since it leaves open the possibility that there may be parameters with values determined by a mechanism distinct from the Subset Principle.

Somewhat later in the same paper, Manzini and Wexler adopt a different emphasis (p. 60):

What the governing category parameter . . . suggests is that . . . in fact the theory of learnability requires that for *every* given parameter and every two given values of it, the languages defined by the two values of the parameter are one a subset of another. (my emphasis – MA)

This is followed by a formal statement of the Subset Condition as in (38):[9]

(38)   For every parameter p and every two values i, j of p, the languages generated under the two values of the parameter are one a subset of the other, that is $L(p(i)) \subset L(p(j))$ or $L(p(j)) \subset L(p(i))$.

What are the issues here? Given a parameter p with values i and j, there are three relevantly different set-theoretic relations between $L(p(i))$ and $L(p(j))$. First, these languages could be disjoint as in (39).

(39)

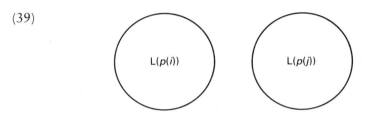

In such circumstances, there is no serious learnability problem. In principle, learners can initially adopt either value of p in their grammar. If the value is correct, they will never receive data to change this hypothesis; if the value is incorrect, any relevant datum will be sufficient to indicate this. Naturally, there remain questions as to whether one of the values is adopted as the default value and if so, which one; and what the *actual* relationship between confounding data and hypothesis change is, but these are not questions of *principle* for the abstract theory of learnability.

Exactly the same conclusion holds for the second possibility where the two languages have a non-empty intersection which does not extend to one being included in the other. This situation is represented in (40).

(40)

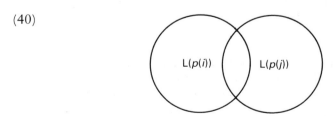

Again, here the theory of learnability can allow the learner to select $p(i)$ or $p(j)$ as the initial hypothesis. If this is correct, it will be retained; if not, there will be positive data from $L(p(i)) - L(p(j))$ or from $L(p(j)) - L(p(i))$ to indicate this.

The third possibility is the one *required* by the formulation of the Subset Condition in (38) and is represented in (41).

(41)

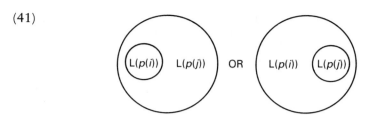

Why should Wexler and Manzini wish to impose this requirement? At one point, they appear to believe that the correctness of the Subset Condition provides some sort of foundation for the Subset Principle, saying (ibid.):

> For such a requirement [the Subset Condition] forces the languages defined by the values of the governing category parameter . . . to be one a subset of another; hence *explains* the fact that they are. (my emphasis – MA)

The notion of explanation here is elusive. If we were in the business of designing languages so as to minimize learnability problems, it would be sensible to regard the situation in (41) as the one to avoid, and we might be tempted by the suggestion that so long as this situation does *not* arise, we could explain *this* on learnability grounds. However, Wexler and Manzini are suggesting that it *does* arise *and* is explicable on the basis of learnability considerations.[10]

The puzzlement is deepened by recalling the first passage cited in this section, a passage which does not impose the Subset Condition on all parameter values. Later, Wexler and Manzini revert to this emphasis (1987, p. 61):

> What do we mean when we say that the Subset Condition is necessary? We say that it is necessary in order for the Subset Principle to be *always* applicable. In other words, *if* the values that the learning function selects on the basis of data are determined by the Subset Principle and by nothing else, then the values of a parameter must determine languages which form a strict hierarchy of subsets. . . (my emphases – MA)

And a few lines later:

> It is important to note that the basis for the derivation of the Subset Condition is the assumption that the Subset Principle determines *every* value of the learning function. Thus we cannot allow two values of a parameter to yield languages which are disjoint, or intersecting, and not in a subset relation to each other. Of course, this assumption is itself *not necessary*. If two values of a parameter yield languages which are not in a subset relation, then we can arbitrarily order the two values, it would seem, in terms of the learning function. Then the Subset Principle would *only* have to apply to the cases of parameter values where a subset relation did hold between the languages. To repeat, the Subset Condition

is necessary *only in the special case* where the Subset Principle is the *only* determinant of learning (or of markedness). (my emphases – MA)

This is a bit tortuous, but contains an explicit acknowledgement that not all parameters have to satisfy the Subset Condition, and an indication that those which do not will not give rise to learnability problems. What are the implications of this for the status of (38)?

Statement (38) is universally quantified and makes a strong and extremely interesting claim about possible parameters (cf. Section 9.2). But the above passage suggests that (38) might be too strong and proposes weakening it so that it should apply only to those parameters for which the Subset Principle is the 'only determinant of learning'. It seems, though, that such a weakening runs the risk of voiding (38) of any content, since the Subset Principle includes reference to 'smallest among the languages compatible with the input data'. Now, 'smallest' here could simply refer to cardinality, but there is no motivation for this interpretation, since if two languages were intersecting or disjoint and one happened to be of smaller cardinality than the other, there would be no learning-theoretic grounds for adopting the parameter value giving rise to it as an initial assumption. If 'smallest' has to be interpreted in terms of nested sets, the formulation of the Subset Principle presupposes its application to languages entering into such relations. But then the required weakening of (38) limits its application to those parameter values which give rise to nested sets of languages. The reformulation of the Subset Condition we end up with is (42):

(42) For every parameter p and every two values i, j of p *such that i and j give rise to set-theoretically nested languages*, the languages generated under the two values of the parameter are one a subset of the other, that is, $L(p(i)) \subset L(p(j))$ or $L(p(j)) \subset L(p(i))$.

But this is devoid of content, and any suggestion that it may serve as an explanatory basis for why parameters have the properties they do must be dismissed.

We have two interpretations of the Subset Condition. One is contentful and interesting, the other is not; and Wexler and Manzini appear to adopt both in different parts of their discussion. The fact that they flirt with the empty version suggests that they believe that the stronger version cannot be maintained, but I shall put off systematic discussion of this until chapter 9. For now, it will be sufficient to have persuaded the reader that the weaker, relativized version of the Subset Condition is of no interest. Naturally, the status of the Subset Principle as a principle of the learning module is not prejudiced at all by this conclusion.

A second issue, which bears some relationship to the foregoing, is raised by Safir (1987) in his commentary on Wexler and Manzini (1987). Safir is concerned with various aspects of the 'undergeneralization problem' that he sees arising in connection with the Lexical Parameterization Hypothesis and we shall return to his worries in this regard shortly. One of them, however, can be linked to the above discussion.

Recall Wexler and Manzini's argument (pp. 143–4 above) that the GCP and the PAP have to be distinct parameters; if they were not, the resulting languages would not be nested and the Subset Principle would not apply. But we have seen now that Wexler and Manzini are ready to acknowledge the existence of parameters giving rise to such languages, the price they have to pay for this being the content of the Subset Condition. Safir points out that there appear to be non-trivial correlations cross-linguistically between the values selected for the two parameters in question. Thus, an anaphor which allows unrestricted antecedents is unlikely to be 'long-distance', English *himself* being an obvious example. Equally, an anaphor which is subject-oriented, such as Japanese *zibun*, will probably also be 'long-distance'. If this correlation is strong, it is unlikely to be accidental, and the natural way to approach this would be to suggest that there is a single parameter which determines both the domain properties and the antecedent properties of anaphors and pronouns, the approach Wexler and Manzini have rejected.

We have seen though that such a rejection can no longer be regarded as principled, unless the strong form of the Subset Condition in (38) is maintained. If it is not, there is no reason why we should not contemplate a parameter along the lines suggested by Safir's discussion. Since it will give rise to intersecting languages, there will be no profound learnability problems.[11]

Manzini and Wexler (1987) recognize the existence of correlations like those indicated by Safir. To appreciate the response they choose to adopt, consider the data in (43) where each item is paired with its values for the GCP and the PAP:

(43)
	Governing Category	Proper Antecedent
himself (English)	(a)	(b)
he (English)	(a)	(b)
hann (Icelandic)	(c)	(a)
zibun (Japanese)	(e)	(a)

What is noteworthy about (43) is that each of the expressions is associated with value (a) for one of the parameters but not the other. If this simple generalization extends to a large number of expressions, it needs to be accounted for, but, as noted, one obvious way of doing this by formulating a 'super-parameter' is not open to Wexler and Manzini. In confronting this difficulty, they consider the following Icelandic data:

(44)   a. Jón$_i$ elskar sig$_i$
              'Jon loves himself'

          b. Ég sendi Jóni$_i$ föt a sig$_i$
              'I sent Jon clothes for himself'

(45)   a. Jón$_i$ segir að Maria elski sig$_i$
              'Jon says that Maria loves (subjunctive) himself'

b. *Ég sagði Jóni$_i$ að Maria hefði boðið sér$_i$
   'I told Jon that Maria had (subjunctive) invited himself'

As we have already seen, Icelandic *sig* is associated with value (d) of the GCP, according to which governing categories are defined by indicative Tense. Consider first (44a) and (45a). These are quite unproblematic: for each of them, the governing category for *sig* is the matrix clause, *sig* is bound by a subject in this matrix clause, and, as expected, the examples are well-formed. In (44b), the governing category for *sig* is again the matrix clause, and on this occasion *sig* is bound by an object in this domain. Given that *sig* can be bound by subjects in (44a) and (45a) and by an object in (44b), it appears that *sig* must be associated with value (b) of the PAP. If it is, the generalization suggested by (43) is counter-exemplified, as *sig* would not be associated with value (a) for either parameter. And if the generalization is spurious, it does not need to be explained – an attractive outcome for Manzini and Wexler, since they have no means of explaining it!

As the reader will have noted, (45b) immediately creates a difficulty for this line of argument. Again, the governing category for *sér* is the matrix clause and *sér* is bound in this matrix clause by an object. Unfortunately, this sentence is ill-formed, suggesting that the value of the PAP for *sig* is value (a) after all. It is clear that something must be done, since *sig* cannot simultaneously have values (a) and (b) of the PAP, and logically there are two ways to proceed: assume the appropriate value is (a) and somehow account for the well-formedness of (44b); assume that the appropriate value is (b) and somehow account for the ill-formedness of (45b). For reasons which should be clear, Manzini and Wexler adopt the second strategy.

What they propose is that the unmarked Binding Theory parameter values retain a special status *even for expressions which are associated with marked alternatives*. Specifically, if, say, an anaphor is associated with value (c) of the GCP, Manzini and Wexler maintain that value (a) still plays a role in determining the distribution of the anaphor. They formulate the proposition in (46), along with an analogous statement for pronouns which we will not discuss here:

(46)   An anaphor must be bound either in its unmarked governing category or by its unmarked antecedent (or both).

Consider what (46) says about an anaphor associated with value (c) of the GCP and value (b) of the PAP. Particular tokens of the anaphor will be bound outside the unmarked governing category (defined by value (a)) and other tokens will be bound inside this unmarked domain. For these latter, (46) is silent; such a token of the anaphor may be bound by a subject or an object. But, when binding extends beyond the unmarked governing category, (46) says this binding must be by the unmarked antecedent, i.e. a subject.

Statement (46) accommodates the data in (44) and (45). In (44b), *sig* is bound in the unmarked governing category. Of course, it *can* be bound outside this domain, but *on this occasion*, it is not. Therefore (46) imposes no conditions on the markedness status of the antecedent. In particular, if *sig* is associated with value (b) of the PAP, the antecedent can be an object. By contrast, in (45b), *sér* is bound outside the unmarked governing category (although still within its own governing category). Now (46) requires the antecedent of *sér* to be unmarked, i.e. a subject. *Jóni* is not a subject in (45b) and ill-formedness results. In this manner, Manzini and Wexler are able to conclude that *sig* is in fact associated with value (d) of the GCP and value (b) of the PAP. Thus, the generalization suggested by (43) is indeed spurious.

What remains as questionable is the status of (46) (and its pronoun analogue). Manzini and Wexler are attracted by the possibility that it may reflect a much more general phenomenon. They say (1987. p. 439):

> . . . [46] can naturally be extended from the case of the binding theory parameters to the general case of lexical items associated with the marked value of two or more parameters. The idea is that nothing prevents a lexical item from being associated with n marked values of parameters; but only one is realizable at each instantiation of the lexical item, the other values being realized as the unmarked values.

This is a provocative suggestion, but it must be noted that no extensions of (46) are presented. As things stand, it is a manoeuvre which enables the disarming of an objection. Whether it has a more substantial status is unknown.

Consideration of the relationship between the binding domains of pronouns and anaphors gives rise to two further, closely related problems. Many languages have pronoun–anaphor pairs which are morphologically related, like *him/himself* in English. For such pairs, it seems that the governing category for the pronominal never properly includes that of the anaphor.

To see what this means, consider the abstract schematizations in (47), where α is either an anaphor or a pronoun, β, γ and δ are potential binders of α, $GC(A)$ is the governing category for α when it is an anaphor and $GC(P)$ is the governing category for α when it is a pronominal:

(47)   a. . . . β . . . $[_{GC(A) = GC(P)}$ . . . γ . . . α . . .] . . .
       b. . . . δ . . . $[_{GC(A)}$ . . . β . . . $[_{GC(P)}$ . . . γ . . . α . . .] . . .] . . .
       c. . . . δ . . . $[_{GC(P)}$ . . . β . . . $[_{GC(A)}$ . . . γ . . . α . . .] . . .] . . .

Take (47a). In this representation, if α is an anaphor, it must be bound inside $GC(A)$, for example, by γ. If α is a pronoun, it may be bound outside $GC(P)$, for example, by β. Thus, in (47a), there is no domain which excludes the possibility of an antecedent occurring in it. The same goes for (47b). If α is an anaphor, it can be bound by either β or γ; if it is a pronoun, it can be bound by either β or δ. The structure in (47c) is different, however. If α is an anaphor, it must be bound inside $GC(A)$, perhaps by γ. If α is a pronoun, it may be bound outside $GC(P)$, for example, by δ. But, *under no conditions*, can it be bound by β, i.e. the part of the structure between $GC(P)$ and $GC(A)$ constitutes a domain in which an antecedent cannot appear under any circumstances.

If, as seems to be the case, grammars do not allow the situation represented in (47c), this needs to be accounted for. To this end, Manzini and Wexler (1987, p. 440) formulate the *Spanning Hypothesis*:[12]

(48)   Any given grammar contains at least an anaphor and a pronominal that have complementary or overlapping distribution.

The content of (48) is not as clear as it might be, but the intention is transparent enough in the light of (47).[13] In (47a), the pronoun and anaphor will be in complementary distribution; in (47b), they will have overlapping distributions, since both of them can be bound from β. Thus, (48) is intended to rule out (47c), a move which, as we have noted, is empirically desirable.

Once more, the outstanding question concerns the status of the Spanning Hypothesis, an issue of which Manzini and Wexler are keenly aware. They say (ibid.):

> . . . it seems plausible that [48] expresses a proposition that happens to be true of natural languages as they have actually evolved, but has no psychological necessity, either as part of the theory of learnability or as part of the theory of grammar.

This is an odd statement for at least two reasons. First, it relies on dubious intuitions about what is and is not psychologically necessary. Second, and more importantly, in so far as such intuitions are available, it is far from clear that they give the answer Manzini and Wexler prefer. Certainly, there do not appear to be any learnability considerations which would provide a foundation for the Spanning Hypothesis, but there is no immediate reason why a constraint ruling out domains on which binding relations cannot be defined should not be part of UG.

The second problem in this area actually provided the initial motivation for the Spanning Hypothesis. It would obviously be pleasing if the markedness orderings defined by the parameters of the Binding Theory bore some relationship to traditional notions of markedness in terms of frequency of distribution in the world's languages. For anaphors, this seems to work out fairly well, with the majority of anaphors studied by Manzini and Wexler and others being associated with value (a), i.e. the unmarked value for anaphors. For pronouns, however, exactly the opposite occurs; the vast majority of pronouns which have been examined within this framework are also associated with value (a), and for them, this is the *most marked* value.

Now, there is no a priori necessity for the notion of markedness induced by set-theoretic inclusion to coincide with the traditional notion. But a massive non-correspondence, which is what we appear to have in the case of pronouns, is worrying.

Returning to (47), it is easy to see that in the two attested configurations (47a, b), pronominal governing categories are always the same size as or smaller than anaphoric governing categories. Now, the majority of anaphoric governing categories are defined by value (a) and are of minimal size (which is unmarked for anaphors). If pronominal governing categories are either identical in size to their anaphoric counterparts or smaller, they will tend to be defined by value (a), despite the fact that this is the most marked value for them in terms of set-theoretic inclusion. So the Spanning Hypothesis, which excludes (47c), can also be invoked to account for the peculiar (from the learnability perspective) properties of pronouns. Whether this hypothesis is capable of discharging this explanatory burden is not clear, and we shall briefly consider an alternative in the next section.

Finally, we can return to Safir's (1987) concerns surrounding *undergeneralization problems*. The Subset Principle is designed to prevent the child indulging in overgeneralizations from which he or she cannot recover in the absence of negative data. For the Subset Principle to function, the Independence Principle is a necessary constraint on parameters, and we have seen above that this prevents the expression of generalizations linking domain properties and antecedent properties. We have also seen that Manzini and Wexler respond to this difficulty by denying the generalization, this denial being underwritten by their (46).

A different species of undergeneralization arises in connection with the Lexical Parameterization Hypothesis. This will be discussed more fully in chapter 9, but it is appropriate to draw attention to some of Safir's concerns here. First, he notes a tendency for subject-oriented anaphors and subject-obviative pronouns to occur in the same languages. Second, he draws attention to the tendency for the binding domains for anaphors and pronouns to coincide within a language. Regarding the latter, it is of course exceptions to this tendency which motivate the Lexical Parameterization Hypothesis in the first place, but adopting a traditional view of markedness, it is attractive to contemplate that non-identity in this regard is exceptional rather than accidental. As Safir puts it (p. 89):

> Within the Wexler and Manzini theory, it is always a coincidence if the domains for anaphors and the domains for pronouns should coincide . . . any tendency for even close coincidence of domains should be accidental.

Again, in the next section, proposals providing a basis for accounting for this coincidence will be introduced.[14]

5.6 Deductively Linked Parameters in the Binding Theory

One elegant way of dealing with some of the problems raised in the previous section has recently been developed by Newson (1990a, 1990b). Central to his account is a notion of *lexical dependency*, and this section will briefly outline his approach.

Accepting the Lexical Parameterization Hypothesis, Newson defines a lexical dependency as a deductive relationship, stipulated in UG to hold between pairs of parameter values associated with specific lexical items. At first sight, it might appear that the existence of such relationships would prejudice the Independence Principle, but this turns out not to be so. However, they do prevent the Subset Principle from doing its job, and this shows that the Independence Principle, even in conjunction with the Subset Condition, is not a sufficient condition for the functioning of the Subset Principle.

Recall that the Independence Principle is introduced to ensure that the operation of the Subset Principle is not disturbed in a situation where more than one parameter is to be set. Given a parameter p_1 with values $\{a, b, c\}$ such that $L(a) \subset L(b) \subset L(c)$, the Independence Principle requires that these inclusion relations continue to obtain even when other parameters are taken into account. Thus, if there is a second parameter p_2 with values $\{d, e\}$, the Principle requires that (49) holds:

(49)   a. $L(a, d) \subset L(b, d) \subset L(c, d)$
       b. $L(a, e) \subset L(b, e) \subset L(c, e)$

Now, let us complicate the situation by assuming that there is a deductive relationship between values of p_1 and p_2, as indicated by the arrows in (50).

(50)

What (50) says is that if a language has value a for p_1, then it has value e for p_2, and if it has value b for p_1, then it has value d for p_2. Effectively, the languages $L(a, d)$ and $L(b, e)$ are 'impossible' languages according to UG. What follows from this? Clearly, the subset relations in (49) are not affected by the stipulation in (50), so deductive links of this kind are not inconsistent with the Independence Principle. However, in order for the Subset Principle to apply, the learning module would need to have access to 'impossible' languages. To show this, (51) repeats (49) with the 'impossible' languages prefixed by *:

(51)   *$L(a, d) \subset L(b, d) \subset L(c, d)$
       $L(a, e) \subset$ *$L(b, e) \subset L(c, e)$

The Subset Principle requires children to compute set-theoretic relations in their learning module so as to determine a markedness ordering for the values of p_1. If now the learning module does not have access to $L(a, d)$ and $L(b, e)$, a child will only be able to compute the relations in (52):

(52) $L(b, d) \subset L(c, d)$
       $L(a, e) \subset L(c, e)$

This is sufficient for the child to treat the values *a* and *b* as unmarked relative to *c*, but he or she will not be in a position to order *a* and *b* relative to each other. The Subset Principle will not be able to function as intended in these circumstances.

There are various responses that could be contemplated to this analysis, which locates the difficulty created by linked parameters in the computations of the learning module. For example, some have seen this reliance on extensional computations as implausible anyway (Safir, 1987), and certainly it is not immediately consistent with an emphasis on I-languages (cf. Section 1.5).[15] Alternatively, we could allow the learning module access to 'impossible' languages, but only for the purposes of its computations, i.e. such a language could never be a hypothesis emerging from the operation of the learning module. A third possibility is to revert to the position rejected by Wexler and Manzini, which holds that markedness orderings are specified in UG, and live with the implication of this that there cannot be a single such ordering for governing category. Obviously, this third possibility is not threatened in any way by deductive links between parameter values, so let us adopt it and turn attention to the Spanning Hypothesis.[16]

Newson notes that the impossibility of domains in which binding relations cannot be defined is assured if we assume that UG contains the information in (53).

(53)

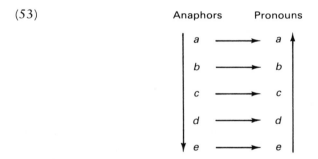

The schema in (53) is to be interpreted as follows. The vertical arrows indicate the markedness orderings for the governing category parameter for anaphors and pronouns. The horizontal arrows indicate deductive links between parameter values for anaphor–pronoun pairs; they are lexical dependencies. Their interpretation is that if an anaphor is associated with value *x* on the basis of primary linguistic data, then the child's default assumption is that the 'paired' pronoun will also be associated with value *x*. Of course, given that the direction of markedness proceeds upwards towards value (a) for pronouns, primary linguistic data may cause this setting to be revised in that direction.

It should be reasonably clear how this deals with the facts motivating the Spanning Hypothesis. The governing category for a pronominal is always going to be at most as big as the governing category for the paired anaphor – recall that governing categories increase in size as we move from value (a) to value (e) for both anaphors and pronouns. If, say, the governing category for a specific anaphor is set at value (c), then the only possible values for the governing category of its paired pronoun are (c), (b) and (a). The child will first select (c) as the default assumption in the light of (53), but primary linguistic data in the form of grammatical sentences may force this value to be changed to (b) or (a). What *cannot* happen is that this value will be reset to (d) or (e), since such resettings would require access to negative data.

Now consider the paucity of pronouns which are associated with unmarked values of their governing category parameter, another motivation for the Spanning Hypothesis. On Newson's account, this is exactly what we should expect. Cross-linguistically, most anaphors are unmarked, selecting value (a). Given (53), this means that their paired pronominals are also initially associated with value (a). Furthermore, once a pronominal is associated with value (a), there are no primary linguistic data which will occasion parameter resetting. It follows that most pronouns will have (a) as their governing category parameter value. Additionally, if a pronoun were associated with a value other than (a) by virtue of its paired anaphor having a marked (for anaphors) value, there is scope for its value moving up towards (a) on the basis of primary linguistic data.

Finally, recall Safir's observation that the binding domains for anaphors and pronouns tend to coincide within a language. Again, this is largely what we expect on the basis of (53) which severely reduces the options for these being distinct.

By offering a more structured proposal concerning the information supplied by UG, Newson is thus able to deal with some of the phenomena which cause difficulties for Wexler and Manzini's account. Of course, as it requires the acquisition process to be 'driven' by anaphors, it makes predictions about the order of acquisition of anaphors and pronouns and about the distribution of these elements in the world's languages. Newson (1990a) investigates these predictions with some encouraging results, and the acquisition studies he cites will be of central importance in the next chapter.

5.7 Summary

This chapter has provided a rather detailed account of parametric variation in the Binding Theory. The justification for this is twofold. First, cross-linguistic variation with respect to binding has probably given rise to more systematic investigation than has variation in other modules. As a consequence, it provides an appropriate illustration of the methods of PPT. Second, it has enabled us to introduce the interplay between linguistic theory and learning-theoretic questions in a particularly explicit way. Most notably, we have met the Subset Principle, which with its partner, the Subset Condition, will be of considerable importance in chapter 9. The chapter has contrasted with the previous one, where work on null subjects, while motivated by sophisticated linguistic analyses, made substantial, if inconclusive, contact with acquisition data.

Such acquisition data have been notable by their absence throughout this chapter, although, as we noted in our discussion of Newson's ideas, it is possible to begin to formulate predictions about the course of acquisition on the basis of theoretical speculations. Of course, the same is true in principle of Wexler and Manzini's work and there is an increasing amount of cross-linguistic research into Binding Theory phenomena, paying particular attention to 'long-distance' anaphors (see, for example, Hyams and Sigurjonsdottir, 1990). However, a more pressing issue than parametric variation has been the developmental status of the Binding Principles themselves. Our next chapter is devoted to experimental investigations of some of the theoretical concepts we have introduced, and once more the Binding Theory will be a major focus of our attention.

6 The Child's Knowledge of Principles of Grammar

Introduction

With the exception of part of the discussion in chapter 4, empirical work with children has not played a large role in our deliberations to date. Such work is central to this chapter.

The schematic theory of language acquisition formulated in Section 3.5 suggests that at the outset of acquisition the child is equipped with UG, where this comprises a system of principles and open parameters. To date, in Chapter 4, we have met the suggestion that one such parameter, the Null Subject Parameter, is indeed in place very early (although incorrectly set for English-speaking children). Furthermore, if the AG/PRO account is correct, the Binding Theory, at least in so far as it determines the distribution of PRO, must also be operative at this stage. Chapter 5, on the other hand, was concerned with rather abstract issues in the theory of learnability, and did not contribute to assessing the questions of whether and when the binding principles for anaphors and pronominals are operative in children's grammars. On the other modules introduced in chapter 3, we have so far been silent, and this silence will be maintained for Θ-Theory until the next chapter and for Case Theory until chapter 10.

One issue should be clarified at the outset. Evidence as to whether or not a child's grammar contains certain principles clearly depends on the acquisition of the lexical items and complexity of representations to which the principles are relevant; there is little point in investigating whether the child's grammar contains Principle A of the Binding Theory before he or she has anaphors. Equally, there is little point in investigating Subjacency at the two-word stage. Accordingly, when we maintain that a principle is operative at the outset of development, this must be understood as a claim that the principle is operative *as soon as there is evidence which enables us to investigate its role.*

What we shall do in what follows is look at some of the evidence which a developmentalist would find of interest in assessing whether children's grammars at particular stages do or do not contain the principles from some of the modules. One of the difficulties confronting this exercise is, of course, methodological. We are committed to the study of the emergence of internalized systems of grammatical representation, and the evidence we have available in such study is rather indirect — tokens of children's speech and understanding. Such behaviour has a complex aetiology, crucially involving the system of grammatical representation but also a variety of other cognitive systems. We have already seen that this difficulty can infect naturalistic studies in the case of P. Bloom's (1990) and Valian's (1990a) suggestion that processing constraints may account for missing subjects in early English, but task demands can also ensure that the interpretation of results of experimental studies is riddled with indeterminacy. In my view, this is an important issue, and it will be a recurrent theme throughout the chapter. Because of this emphasis, the chapter does not attempt a systematic survey of all the relevant work which has been conducted through the 1980s. Rather, we shall focus on those developments which illustrate this methodological dilemma and provide some hints as to how it can sometimes be resolved. As a consequence, the bulk of the chapter is devoted to Binding Theory, X-bar Theory and the Empty Category Principle. Bounding Theory and Control Theory will receive only brief discussion at the end.

6.1 An Experiment with Reciprocals

We begin with a concrete illustration of the issues referred to above. Matthei (1981) is one of the earliest experimental studies of the Binding Theory, although, for historical reasons, it is presented as an investigation of the Tensed S Condition and the Specified Subject Condition from Chomsky (1973). The descriptive coverage of these conditions has been largely taken over by the Binding Theory, and, in discussing Matthei's experiment, we shall adopt the more recent terminology.

One expression to which Principle A of the Binding Theory applies in English is the reciprocal anaphor *each other*, and the experiment concerns children's interpretation of sentences containing this item. Matthei utilized a task which has enjoyed considerable popularity in experimental studies of language comprehension, the act-out task. In such tasks the child is supplied with a set of props, usually in the form of toy animals, and is asked to make these act out an event corresponding to the content of the whole or part of an utterance produced by the experimenter or a toy puppet.

Each other displays the standard behaviour of an English anaphor, i.e. it must be bound within the domain defined by its closest subject, selecting value (a) of the GCP from Section 5.2. This can be seen in the examples in (1), where *each other* appears as direct object in a variety of complements:

(1)   a. The horses$_i$ said that [the cows$_j$ jumped over each other$_{*i/j}$]
       b. The pigs$_i$ said [the chickens$_j$ tickled each other$_{*i/j}$]
       c. The cows$_i$ want [the lambs$_j$ to kiss each other$_{*i/j}$]
       d. The pigs$_i$ noticed [the boys$_j$ kissing each other$_{*i/j}$]

In (1a), *each other* occurs in a tensed complement with an overt complementizer, in (1b) in a tensed complement without overt complementizer, in (1c) in an infinitival complement, and in (1d) in a gerundive complement. In each case, it is impossible for *each other* to be bound by the matrix subject, since its governing category is defined by the subordinate subject. Sentences like those in (1) were employed by Matthei in the experiment.

The procedure involved the experimenter producing an utterance, and the instruction to the children was that they should show the experimenter 'what happened' by 'making them do it.' Pre-tests familiarized the children with the animal props (there were two of each animal) and tested their comprehension of *each other* in simple sentences by the use of examples such as (2):

(2) a. The cows were kicking each other
     b. The pig and the lamb were kissing each other

Children who failed to act out such sentences appropriately were not used in the experiment. A total of 17 children, aged between 4:2 and 6:6 were tested in the experiment proper on 34 sentences of the types represented in (1) using a variety of complement-taking verbs. A further variable was introduced into the experiment by manipulating the syntactic characteristics of the noun phrases appearing in the matrix and subordinate subject positions. The matrix subject could be singular (*the cow*), plural (*the cows*) or conjoined (*the cow and the pig*); the subordinate subject could be plural or conjoined.

Of the 17 children tested, four made no errors at all across the sentence types. The remaining 13, however, made large numbers of errors which Matthei (1981, p. 107) describes in the following way:[1]

> 64.4 per cent of the total number of responses were ones in which the children chose the matrix clause subject as the referent of *each other*. That is, they would interpret a sentence like [*the chickens said that the pigs tickled each other*] as meaning that the pigs tickled the chickens and vice versa.

He concludes (p. 111):

> There appears to be evidence that the constraints the experiment was designed to test are *learned*. (my emphasis – MA)

Is this conclusion justified?

Accepting for the sake of argument that the results show that the children were not applying Principle A to *each other*, the answer must be negative. First, *learning* is a developmental mechanism which may or may not be involved in the subsequent appearance of Principle A. All the results indicate is that Principle A is not operative at this stage in the children's development; they do not address the nature of the mechanism by which it becomes available. As we shall see in chapter 8, there are alternatives to learning, and in general the move from a claim that some representational capacity is not present at an early stage to the conclusion that it is learned requires justification. Second, Matthei's experiment is concerned exclusively with *each other*. Presumably, children do have to learn that *each other* is an anaphor, and such learning is a prerequisite for the applicability of Principle A to its distribution. If the 13 children who produced the errors had not learned that *each other* is an anaphor, there is no sense in which the experiment is testing the presence of Principle A. In other words, there are at least two candidate explanations for why the children made errors: they knew that *each other* is an anaphor but did not know Principle A, or they did not know that *each other* is an anaphor.

This second possibility might be seen as ruled out by Matthei's pre-tests using sentences like (2). But it would be premature to adopt this conclusion, since there is evidence that children will try to interpret *pronouns* as having discourse-specified antecedents, rather than as referring to some entity which is present in the situation but is not mentioned in the discourse (see Section 6.3 below). Conceivably, then, the children in Matthei's study were treating *each other* as a reciprocal pronominal, a suggestion he himself tentatively considers. If this is so, however, Principle A is not at issue, and the experiment would be more properly interpreted as a study of Principle B.

The above reservations are based on the assumption that *each other* was not subject to Principle A for Matthei's subjects. Should we accept this assumption? Consider the sentence to which Matthei refers in the passage cited above:

(3)   The chickens said that the pigs tickled each other

A Principle A violation in this sentence would allow *each other* to be bound outside the subordinate clause, and there is only one candidate for the binder, *the chickens*, i.e. if the child is violating Principle A in the most straightforward way, (4) should be well-formed:

(4)   The chickens$_i$ said that the pigs$_j$ tickled each other$_i$

If the child construed (4) in this way, what we would expect is that he or she would make the pigs tickle the chickens. But note that this is *not* what Matthei found. Although he does not provide a detailed breakdown of the children's errors, he suggests that these errors typically involved *symmetrical* actions between the referents of the matrix and subordinate subjects, as the passage cited above makes clear. But this interpretation suggests that the child has misanalysed the sentence or, perhaps, re-analysed it to make it more readily intelligible in terms of the task demands.

Consider misanalysis first (cf. White, 1981). Sentences like (3) are moderately complex syntactically, and it is conceivable that they approach the limits of the child's parsing abilities. If this is so, it might be the case that on a significant number of occasions (and note that the children who produced errors did not do so for all test sentences), the child's parser would misrepresent (3) as (5):

(5)   The chickens and the pigs tickled each other

But (5) contains a single clause with a conjoined subject. Principle A requires the indexing in (6) and this would lead to the symmetrical tickling observed by Matthei:

(6)   [The chickens and the pigs]$_i$ tickled each other$_i$

Alternatively, the child's parser may function effectively and produce a structure containing a subordinate clause. But now the child is confronted with the potentially puzzling task of 'making them do it'. The problem is that *the chickens* is assigned the Agent Θ-role in the main clause, but 'saying' is hardly something they can be made to do. It is not implausible that this constitutes a difficult situation for children to resolve, and that they respond to this by re-analysing (3) along the lines of (6). The children's preference, noted by Matthei, to associate *each other* with a conjoined antecedent could also contribute to this process (cf. note 1).[2]

The above discussion is not intended as an exhaustive dissection of the experiment, but to emphasize the need for care in the design of experiments and caution in the interpretation of their results. Obviously, it is important to attempt to minimize the role of extra-linguistic cognitive factors in an experimental situation, and to try to ensure that the tasks we set children do not encourage the development of strategies which will by-pass linguistic capacities. As we shall see in the sections that follow, these are no small requirements. Awareness of them should be sufficient to persuade us that a child producing or comprehending language tokens in naturalistic or experimental environments is just *one* source of evidence bearing on the nature of the internalized grammar. There is no reason in principle why it should be more compelling than the abstract speculations described in the previous chapter (cf. Chomsky, 1980, pp. 106ff., on the types of evidence for 'psychological reality').[3]

6.2 The Binding Theory: Principle C

The experiment reported in the previous section is intended to engage Principle A of the Binding Theory. We shall return to the interplay between Principle A and Principle B in the next section, but here we briefly consider experimental work aimed at determining whether children's grammars contain Principle C. This principle concerns the distribution of R-expressions ('names' and variables) and is repeated in (7):

(7)   An R-expression must be free everywhere

One phenomenon which has been widely used to investigate children's control of this principle is *backward anaphora*. Consider the examples in (8):

(8)   a. John$_i$ saw Mary while he$_i$ was shopping
       b. While he$_i$ was shopping, John$_i$ saw Mary
       c. *He$_i$ saw Mary while John$_i$ was shopping

These examples are readily accounted for by Principle C. In (8a), the R-expression *John*, while co-indexed with *he*, is not c-commanded by the pronominal. Accordingly, it is not bound by it either, i.e. it is free as required by Principle C. Exactly the same situation obtains in (8b), despite the fact that the pronoun precedes the R-expression; *he*, as subject of the subordinate clause, does not c-command *John*, so the latter is once again free. Example (8b), then, illustrates the possibility of backward anaphora in English. Finally, in (8c), *he* is subject of the main clause, a position from which it c-commands *John*. As it is also co-indexed with *John*, *John* is bound by *he*, yielding a Principle C violation.

The first experimental study of backward anaphora was reported by Tavakolian (1978). She used sentences like those in (9), requiring children, aged 3–5, to act out the content of the sentences with toy animals:

(9)   a. For him to kiss the lion would make the duck happy
      b. That he kissed the lion made the duck happy

Such sentences allow backward anaphora, so one way in which the children could respond correctly would be to make the duck kiss the lion. As it is not obligatory for these pronouns to co-refer with some other expression in the sentences, another way would be to make some third, unmentioned animal kiss the lion. Tavakolian discovered that a large majority of the children's responses were of this latter type and that a substantial number of children produced only this type of response. Such behaviour is consistent with the children adopting a *linear strategy* for pronoun interpretation which rules out backward anaphora, rather than the structural condition expressed by Principle C (see also Lust, 1981; Solan, 1983).

However, the conclusion that the children in Tavakolian's study did not have Principle C in their grammars would be premature. First, a significant number of the responses did manifest backward anaphora, a fact which is inexplicable on the linear strategy hypothesis. Second, since an exophoric interpretation of the pronouns in (9) is entirely compatible with Principle C, a preference for this interpretation can hardly be seen as casting doubt on the status of the principle (see Lasnik and Crain, 1985).

More directly, Crain and McKee (1985) conducted an experiment on the comprehension of backward anaphora which introduced important modifications to Tavakolian's methodology. In this experiment, the *experimenter* first acted out an event and then the child was presented with a sentence credited to a puppet figure. The task for the child was to reward or punish the puppet, depending on whether the produced sentence was true or false of the preceding event. Sentences tested included those in (10):

(10)   a. When he ate the hamburger, the Smurf was in the box
       b. He ate the hamburger when the Smurf was in the box

In both of these sentences, the pronoun precedes the R-expression *the Smurf*. By virtue of Principle C, backward anaphora is possible only for (10a). Crain and McKee found that children, aged 2–5, accepted sentences like (10a), when they followed an event requiring the backward anaphoric reading, as true about two-thirds of the time, i.e. there was overwhelming evidence that these children were not relying on a linear strategy to interpret the pronoun. Furthermore, sentences like (10b) were consistently rejected by the children, when their interpretation in the light of the preceding event required the pronoun and the R-expression to be co-referential. It therefore appears that the earlier results of Tavakolian and others were indicative of a *preference* to avoid backward anaphora. When the experimental design prevents the exercising of this preference, children's behaviour is consistent with their grammars containing Principle C.

Principle C also applies to variables (traces of moved *wh*-expressions), and Crain and Thornton (1990) (see also Crain, in press) used Strong Crossover sentences to investigate whether children's grammars obey the adult constraints. Strong Crossover is illustrated in (11):[4]

(11)   a. *Who$_i$ does he$_i$ believe loves Mary?
       b. Who$_i$ believes he$_i$ loves Mary?

Example (11a) cannot be interpreted as 'who is the x such that x believes x loves Mary', whereas this interpretation is readily available for (11b). The theoretical account of this distinction can be readily appreciated by considering the schematic s-structures in (12):

(12)   a. *Who$_i$ [does he$_i$ believe e_i loves Mary]
       b. Who$_i$ [e_i believes he$_i$ loves Mary]

In (12a), the pronoun c-commands the *wh*-trace, and co-indexing of the pronoun and the trace produces a Principle C violation. In (12b), however, the *wh*-trace is not bound by any expression in an A-position, and the structure is consistent with the Binding Theory.

The procedure adopted in the experiment was a variant on the grammaticality judgement technique of Crain and McKee (1985) briefly described above. Children, aged 3:7–4:8, were told stories involving five characters. Some misfortune, e.g. mosquito bites, afflicts the characters in the story, and they respond to this in different ways. One of them is 'helpless' and requires assistance, two are 'self-reliant' and look after themselves, and two are unaffected and go to the aid of the 'helpless' one. The experimenter reads the story, and, at its conclusion, a puppet produces an utterance like those in (13):

(13)   a. I know who they scratched/washed/dressed. X and Y.
       b. I know who they scratched/washed/dressed. Z.

The choice of verb is determined by the misfortune in the story (*scratched* goes with the mosquito bite story). In (13a), X and Y name the two characters who are self-reliant and scratched/washed/dressed themselves; in (13b), Z names the 'helpless' character who is scratched/watched/dressed. Consider (13a). The *story* supplies the child with the information that *they* = X and Y; the *puppet* tells the child that *who* = X and Y. Therefore (13a) is an instance of Strong Crossover with *who* and *they* co-indexed as in (14):

(14)   I know [who$_i$ [they$_i$ scratched e_i]]

Crain and Thornton found that examples modelled on (13a) were rejected by the children over 95 per cent of the time. This suggests, then, that well before they are 5, children implicitly recognize the status of the trace of *wh*-phrases as variables and treat these variables as R-expressions subject to Principle C.

6.3 The Binding Theory: Principles A and B

A fairly robust finding over a number of experimental paradigms is that children acquiring English experience more difficulties with pronominals than with anaphors. It would be natural to suggest that these difficulties arise because Principle B is somehow less available to children early in their grammatical development than is Principle A. We shall first briefly consider some of the evidence for the ontogenetic primacy of anaphors, and then look at the consequences of this evidence for Principles A and B.

Jakubowicz (1984) tested children's comprehension of anaphors and pronominals using an act-out task. Children (aged 3–5) were presented with sentences like those in (15) and were instructed to act out the content of what John said:

(15)   a. John said that Peter washed him
       b. John said that Peter washed himself

The majority of errors that appeared in this task were on sentences containing pronouns and typically consisted of the child treating the pronoun as if it were an anaphor, i.e. assigning it an antecedent inside its governing category.[5]

Chien and Wexler (1985) also used an act-out task (based on the Simon Says game), presenting children (2:6–6:6) with sentences like those in (16):

(16)   a. (Puppet name) says that (child name) should point to herself/her
       b. (Puppet name) wants (child name) to point to herself/her

Their findings were strikingly consistent across a number of conditions.[6] First, for reflexive anaphors, there was a steady increase in the level of performance across the age range; the youngest group of children were correct on reflexives only 13 per cent of the time, but the 6-year-olds achieved 90 per cent accuracy. Second, the profile on pronouns was quite different. Even the oldest children in the sample achieved a modest 64 per cent correct, and this represented little or no improvement on the very youngest children. Faced with this outcome, one of the options considered by Chien and Wexler is that by the age of 6, Principle A is in place but Principle B must still be acquired (but see below).[7]

There are several ways in which this apparent difficulty children have with Principle B has been responded to. First, Newson (1990a) has suggested that his notion of lexical dependency, discussed in Section 5.6, could provide some leverage on the findings. Recall that he maintains that the governing categories for pronouns depend on those for corresponding anaphors. Accordingly, he could maintain that until the child has sorted out the appropriate governing categories for anaphors, pronouns lack governing categories entirely. In such a scenario, Principle B would be 'latently' present, but effectively inoperative since one of the primitives which provides its content would not be defined.

A difficulty with this suggestion and for any other which ascribes no role to Principle B is that in the Chien and Wexler study, even the youngest children were already performing at a level approaching 70 per cent correct on the pronoun sentences. This seems to suggest that their behaviour was governed by Principle B to some extent, and the truly puzzling aspect of the results is the lack of improvement with age, particularly when this is put alongside the dramatic development with respect to anaphors.

This and several similar points have been raised in a recent study by Grimshaw and Rosen (1990), which argues that there is ample evidence that Principle B is *not* delayed relative to Principle A, and also offers a range of suggestions as to why experimental studies lead to the conclusion that it is. The crucial distinction they draw is between *knowledge* of Principle B and *obedience* of it, and they argue that earlier studies have succeeded only in showing that young children do not reliably obey this principle.

Grimshaw and Rosen report a simple experiment of their own to give initial support to the claim that children do know Principle B from an early age. The logic they employ is summarized as follows (1990, p. 189):

> To the hypothetical child who does not know the principles, a violation is no different from a non-violation. Thus a subject who does not know the principles should accept all sentences (regardless of whether they are grammatical or ungrammatical according to the adult grammar). Suppose, then, that the subject systematically treats [Binding Theory]-ungrammatical sentences differently from [Binding Theory]-grammatical ones. The only possible explanation is that the subject does in fact know the Binding Theory. A key feature of this design is that subjects do not have to be particularly successful in their treatment of [Binding Theory]-ungrammatical sentences − to demonstrate knowledge on their part, it is only necessary for them to treat the two classes in a systematically different way.

The study which implements this logic is a grammaticality judgement experiment which involves a puppet learning to speak English. The child watches a short video including characters from the television programme 'Sesame Street'. Subsequently, the English-learning puppet produces two sentences, the first of which includes potential antecedents and the second either a pronoun or an anaphor. The context provided by the video can be seen as imposing an indexing on the second sentence, which is either grammatical or ungrammatical according to the Binding Theory on this indexing. For example, given a video in which Big Bird pats Ernie, the puppet may produce (17):

(17)   I saw Big Bird doing something with Ernie. Big Bird$_i$ patted him$_j$

Here, the second sentence is grammatical according to the Binding Theory. Alternatively, the video might show Big Bird hitting himself and be followed by:

(18)   Big Bird was standing with Ernie. Big Bird$_i$ hit him$_{*i}$

The children, aged 4–5, are told that the puppet is trying to learn how to use *him/himself* and are to reward or punish him according to their judgements of the grammaticality of his sentences.

The result of concern to us is the children's level of acceptance of grammatical and ungrammatical sentences containing pronouns; the former were accepted 83 per cent of the time and the latter 42 per cent of the time. Now, a figure of 42 per cent suggests that the children are performing rather poorly on the Principle B violations, but, according to the logic of the passage cited above, this is not the point. The important observation is that there is a very significant difference between the children's treatment of sentences which are consistent with Principle B and those which violate it, a difference which can only be accounted for by the assumption that the children *know* Principle B. For some reason, particularly when confronted with violations of the principle, children do not *obey* it.

What might such reasons be? In this experiment, a range of response biases is the obvious suggestion to explore. Thus, it is likely that children are more inclined to accept what the puppet says rather than reject it, as they know that the utterance originates with the authority figure of an adult. Additionally, the ungrammatical sentences *are* always grammatical on an indexing which ignores the constraints imposed by the video, and this too could be seen as contributing to false positives.

Grimshaw and Rosen proceed to a detailed examination of factors in other experiments which might be responsible for leading the child who knows Principle B to disobey it. These fall into two categories: the design of the experiments which suggest less than perfect knowledge of Principle B, and the properties of emphatic pronouns. Here we shall concentrate briefly on the most important aspects of the former.

First, they note that a *pragmatic* constraint on the use of third person pronouns (when used non-contrastively and non-deictically) is that they should have an antecedent within the discourse. Thus, as a discourse, (19) is distinctly odd, unless we assume that *her* is contrastively stressed or identified deictically. Even in the latter case, *her* will typically bear some non-neutral stress:

(19)   John$_i$ got on the train. He$_i$ saw her$_j$.

If a child knows Principle B and is also familiar with this pragmatic constraint, it is easy to see that experimental designs which do not supply potential discourse antecedents for pronouns will create a conflict: the child must either disobey Principle B and make sense of the sentence he or she is presented with, or obey Principle B and fail to assign a referent to the pronoun. Such conflict could readily lead to the chance level of performance on sentences including pronouns which has often been reported. Furthermore, it provides a ready explanation of the fact that when a design provides the child with a choice between a previously mentioned entity and an entity outside the discourse as referents for a pronoun, the previously mentioned entity is overwhelmingly preferred.[8]

A second design problem arises in connection with the use of possessive subjects, as in studies by Wexler and Chien (1985) and Deutsch, Koster and Koster (1986). Wexler and Chien used sentences like those in (20) in a task in which the child has to choose one of two pictures which is correctly depicted by the sentence:

(20)   a. Cinderella's sister pointed to her
       b. Cinderella's sister pointed to herself

These sentences can be indexed as in (21) so as to be consistent with Principles A and B of the Binding Theory:

(21)   a. $[_S[_{NP} [_{NP}Cinderella's]_i$ sister] pointed to her$_i]$
       b. $[_S[_{NP}Cinderella's$ sister$]_i$ pointed to herself$_i]$

For both *her* and *herself*, the governing category is the matrix clause. By Principle B, *her* must be free in this domain. If it is co-indexed with the NP Cinderella, this condition is satisfied, since this NP does not c-command *her* and so cannot bind it. However, if it were co-indexed with the containing NP *Cinderella's sister*, a Principle B violation would result. By Principle A, *herself* must be bound in the matrix clause. This is the case if it is co-indexed with *Cinderella's sister*, but not if it is co-indexed with *Cinderella*. Hence, the indexings in (21) are the only legitimate ones so long as the pronoun has its antecedent in the sentence.

Using sentences like these, Wexler and Chien report chance level performance on pronoun sentences until children are about 5:6 with performance on anaphor sentences being much better. Now, Grimshaw and Rosen suggest that the use of possessive subjects is a complicating factor here. In particular, consider what would happen if the child misanalysed the subject NP in (21) so that *Cinderella* was its head rather than *sister*, i.e. rather than the subject in (21a), the child has something along the lines of (22):

(22) $[_{NP}Cinderella's [_{NP}sister]]$

If this were the case, Principle B would allow *her* to be co-indexed with *sister* in (20a) and Principle A would allow *herself* to be co-indexed with *Cinderella* in (20b). Thus, what were interpreted by Wexler and Chien as Binding Theory errors might in fact reflect misanalysis of a possessive subject.

Wexler and Chien's study does not allow these two possibilities to be disentangled, since they presented children with only two pictures, one in which the sister points at Cinderella and the other in which the sister points at herself. Both of these presuppose a *correct* analysis of the subject. But suppose that the child has misanalysed the subject. What is he or she likely to do? It is impossible to predict, but what is clear is that the principles of the Binding Theory will be irrelevant to the decision. The importance of the possibility of misanalysis is emphasized by the results of Deutsch, Koster and Koster (1986). They gave children *four* pictures to choose from, including a pair that was consistent with a misanalysis of the structure of the subject. Incorrect choice of one of these pictures was by far the most common error in this study.[9]

We see, then, that methodological reflections can be utilized to confound the proposal that Principle B is not present in early grammars. An alternative suggestion, leading to the same conclusion, has been developed by Chien and Wexler (1990). Since this relies on taking a stance on some rather fundamental questions in the Binding Theory, it will not be possible to pursue the details of this here. However, it is reasonably straightforward to convey the general idea. Consider (23):

(23)   He$_i$ is wearing John$_j$'s coat

Principle C requires the indicated indexing, but now we ask how this indexing is to be *interpreted*. The natural suggestion is that NPs bearing distinct indices must denote *distinct* individuals, but as has been pointed out by Evans (1980) and Higginbotham (1980), this is not correct. Example (24) is a case where differentially indexed NPs must be interpreted as *co-referential*:

(24)   He$_i$ is wearing John$_j$'s coat. Therefore he must be John

The upshot of this is that the Binding Theory itself as a determinant of well-formed indexings does not require distinct indices to be interpreted in terms of disjoint reference. This is the task of some other, pragmatic (or possibly semantic) theory.

If the above is correct, a child who interprets (15a) by making Peter wash himself does not necessarily reveal ignorance of Principle B. This principle requires the *indexing* in (25):

(25)   John said that Peter$_i$ washed him$_j$

But this indexing does not itself require that *Peter* and *him* be disjoint in reference. Rather, this requirement emanates from a to-be-articulated pragmatic principle, P. And perhaps the child does not know P.

Interestingly, Chien and Wexler perceive the possibility of directly assessing the role of Principle B in children's grammars via the properties of examples like (26):

(26)   Every politician thinks he's smart

The indexings permitted by Principle B appear in (27):

(27)   a. Every politician$_i$ thinks he$_i$'s smart
       b. Every politician$_i$ thinks he$_j$'s smart

Examples (27a, b) correspond to the two interpretations of the sentence. In (27a) we have an example of *bound variable anaphora* which informally has the interpretation in (28):

(28) For every x, x a politician, x thinks x is smart

By contrast, (27b) has the interpretation where every politician thinks that some discourse-identified individual is smart, and if we identify occurrences of co-indexed expressions with tokens of the *same* variable in quasi-logical formulae such as (28), it is clear that the bound variable reading *requires* co-indexing.

Given this, consider (29):

(29) Every bear touched her

If a child did not know Principle B, co-indexing would be possible here, as in (30):

(30) Every bear$_i$ touched her$_i$

But then (30) satisfies the conditions for a bound variable interpretation along the lines of (31):

(31) For every x, x a bear, x touched x

Accordingly, the crucial test is how children perform on Principle B sentences like (29) with quantified NP subjects; if they do not have Principle B, bound variable interpretations like (31) should be available to them. Chien and Wexler report the results of an experiment showing that 5- to 6-year-olds are 90 per cent correct on such sentences, i.e. they do *not* give bound variable interpretations.

Overall, then, we can see that, while the issue is far from settled, there is no reason to be pessimistic about the presence of Principle B in children's grammars.

6.4 X-Bar Theory

The principles of X-bar Theory, along with the thematic properties of lexical items, determine the class of possible d-structures in a grammar once the parameter or parameters governing directionality are fixed. We might expect X-bar principles to constrain the child's grammatical system from a very early age, and in this section we shall consider some of the evidence which suggests that this is so.

In the case of this module, there is a source of evidence distinct from the results of experimentation which we can consult: a naturalistic corpus collected from a sample of children. Radford (1990a) contains a detailed analysis of such a corpus, and we begin with an examination of his claims. Before embarking on this, it is necessary to introduce a further layer of structure into the X-bar principles, that of *adjuncts*, which necessitates a modification in the system we outlined in Section 3.3.

We have seen that according to the X-bar principles, the addition of a complement to a head (X) yields an X'. Thus, for the major lexical categories, we have the structures in (32):

(32)   a. [$_{N'}$[$_N$ picture] of Mary]
      b. [$_{V'}$[$_V$ destroy] the city]
      c. [$_{A'}$[$_A$ proud] of the book]
      d. [$_{P'}$[$_P$ off] the wall]

Each of these can be expanded to a maximal projection by the addition of a specifier, and in Section 3.3, we used (33) to exemplify this:

(33)   a. [$_{NP}$[$_{NP}$ the enemy's][$_{N'}$[$_N$ destruction][$_{NP}$ (of) the city]]]
      b. [$_{AP}$[$_{AP}$ very][$_{A'}$[$_A$proud][$_{NP}$ (of) the book]]]
      c. [$_{PP}$[$_{AP}$ right][$_{P'}$[$_P$ on][$_{NP}$ the nose]]]

However, a moment's reflection should persuade us that these examples have rather different properties. In particular, it makes intuitive sense to regard *the enemy's* as a subject of the NP in (33a), whereas the suggestion that *very* and *right* are subjects of the AP and PP in (33b, c) is rather strange. This observation correlates with the fact that we cannot iterate expressions like *the enemy's* in (33a):

(34)   *the enemy's the barbarian's destruction of the city

In contrast, degree modifiers like *very* and *right* can appear in sequence:

(35)   a. really very very proud of the book
      b. right smack on the nose

This suggests that we might be justified in extending our intuitive notion of 'subject' to the specifier position cross-categorially, using the examples in (36) to illustrate the X-bar schema:[10]

(36)   a. [$_{NP}$ John's [$_{N'}$[$_N$ picture] of Mary]]
      b. [$_{VP}$ John [$_{V'}$[$_V$ destroy] the city]]
      c. [$_{AP}$ John [$_{A'}$[$_A$ proud] of the book]]
      d. [$_{PP}$ John [$_{P'}$[$_P$ off] the wall]]

Of course, (36b, c, d) do not immediately strike us as well-formed maximal projections, but they do occur as *Small Clause* complements of a restricted class of verbs:

(37)   a. I saw [$_{VP}$ John destroy the city]
       b. I consider [$_{AP}$ John proud of the book]
       c. I consider [$_{PP}$ John off the wall]

Now, if we reserve the specifier position for 'subjects' in this way, we must reconsider the X-bar status of such expressions as *very*, *right*, etc. in (35).[11]

The proposal we adopt is that these constituents are *X′−adjuncts*, which may be recursively added to an X′ to yield another X′. That they may be recursively added is illustrated above, and obviously this characterization extends to prenominal attributive adjectives, as in (38):

(38)   John's *beautiful, old, flattering* picture of Mary

According to this proposal, (38) will have the structure in (39):

(39)   [$_{NP}$ John's [$_{N′}$ beautiful [$_{N′}$ old [$_{N′}$ flattering [$_{N′}$ picture of Mary]]]]]

To accommodate adjuncts, the X-bar principles must be extended to (40):

(40)   a. XP = (YP), X′
       b. X′ = (YP), X′
       c. X′ = YP*, X

The schemas in (40a, c) are familiar from Section 3.3; (40b) says that an X′ can project into another X′ by the addition of an adjunct, and of course the possibility of iterated adjuncts is guaranteed by the appearance of X′ on both sides of the schema.

Let us now turn to the relevance of Radford's findings to (40). Here we shall restrict attention to the N-system, and merely note that most of the observations carry over into the other lexical projection systems.

The first question is whether there is evidence that English-speaking children project N into N′ by the addition of a complement at an early age. That they do is suggested by such examples as those in (41) produced by children under 2 years of age:[12]

(41)   a. cup tea (= 'cup of tea')
       b. picture Gia (= 'picture of Gia')

Commenting on the relative scarcity of these, Radford says (p. 62):

> Although such structures are by no means common at this stage, I assume that this is an 'accidental' lexical gap attributable to the fact that most of the Nouns in the child's early vocabulary are concrete Nouns which do not take complements.

He suggests that they are appropriately analysed as in (42), a view which is consistent with the claim that the child's grammar already contains (40c):

(42)   [$_{N'N}$[cup] $_{NP}$[tea]]

Turning now to (40b), is there evidence that the child is aware that prenominal adjectives can be attached to an N'-constituent to yield a further N'? Once more, Radford feels that this can be answered affirmatively, citing such data as those in (43) from the same stage:

(43)   a. nice book
      b. good girl
      c. blue ball wool

Example (43c) suggests that the adjunct (*blue*) is indeed in construction with an N' (and not just an N) as *ball wool* ('ball of wool') is a head-complement structure. Furthermore, there is evidence that children of this age already know that adjuncts can be iterated, as they produce sequences of prenominal adjectives as in (44):

(44)   a. big heavy book
      b. nice yellow pen

Finally, adopting the view that possessor expressions are correctly analysed as 'subjects' (and therefore specifiers) of NPs, Radford cites data such as those in (45), which are interpreted as possessives, in support of the claim that the child's grammar at this stage also contains (40a):

(45)   a. mummy car
      b. daddy shoe
      c. Claire pencil

Now, while Radford's observations are clearly consistent with the data he cites, we might legitimately ask whether certain alternative analyses can be discounted. For example, given a child's utterance containing a sequence of prenominal adjectives, such as *big heavy book*, Radford analyses its structure as (46):

(46)   [$_{N'}$big [$_{N'}$heavy [$_{N'}$[$_{N}$ book]]]]

This analysis imposes hierarchical structure on the prenominal adjuncts, but it is certainly open to someone antagonistic to this proposal to suggest that it is incorrect. Perhaps, the 'flat' structure in (47) is more appropriate:

(47)   [$_{N'}$ [big] [heavy] [book]]

Or, again, in connection with possessor subjects, the analysis of *mummy car* favoured by Radford is (48):

(48)   [$_{NP}$ [mummy] [$_{N'}$[$_{N}$ car]]]

But what justification is there for this structure rather than an alternative where *mummy* is a prenominal adjunct?

Consider first utterances containing sequences of prenominal adjectives. It is customary to regard the English pro-form *one* as a pro-N' and not a pro-N:

(49) a. John is an avid *reader of books* and Mary is an unenthusiastic *one*.
      b. *John is an avid *reader* of books and Mary is an unenthusiastic *one* of magazines.

In (49a), *one* replaces *reader of books*, which is an N', and the result is grammatical. When *one* replaces the simple N *reader* in (49b), the sentence is ill-formed (see Hornstein and Lightfoot, 1981; Radford, 1988a; Lightfoot, 1989, for extensive discussion).

Given this property of *one*, it is of interest that it occurs commonly in Radford's corpus preceded by an adjective, e.g. *yellow one*, *fat one*. More significant, however, are examples like (50), produced by a child of 23 months:

(50) Nice yellow pen, nice one

The most natural interpretation of (50) is that *one* replaces *yellow pen* (it may of course replace only *pen*, but there is no way of deciding this in a naturalistic study). If it does replace *yellow pen*, this is strong evidence that the adjective–noun sequence forms a constituent. However, on a 'flat' analysis of *nice yellow pen*, *yellow pen* would not be a constituent. The occurrence of such examples as (50) thus provides support for the hierarchical analysis proposed by Radford and required by adherence to the X-bar principles.

Consider now the claim that possessors are NP subjects. Evidence for the appropriateness of this can be seen in utterances which include both a possessor and a prenominal adjective, e.g. *mummy blue dress*. If we adopted an analysis of such structures in which *mummy* and *blue* were both prenominal adjuncts, there would be no obvious reason to expect this word-order as opposed to *blue mummy dress*. However, while the former order is frequently present in Radford's corpus, the latter is non-existent. The attested order is, of course, predicted by the hierarchical analysis.

Carefully conducted analyses of naturalistic data, then, reveal that the system of N-projections (and those of other lexical categories) is typically in place before the age of 2. Furthermore, whatever parameters are responsible for fixing d-structure order (see Section 3.4) also appear to be fixed very early, as Radford echoes the traditional finding that word-order errors were strikingly rare in his corpus (see chapter 11 for discussion of word-order at the earliest stages of word-combination).

In the light of the preceding discussion, it is of some interest that experimental work with considerably older children has been interpreted as leading to different conclusions.

Matthei (1982) investigated children's comprehension of such phrases as *the second striped ball*. The children studied ranged in age from 3:9 to 6:3, and they were to identify the referent of the phrase with respect to an array such as that in (51).

(51)

Pre-testing established that the children knew the meanings of the words in the phrases and pre-training ensured that their counting took place from left to right. Diagram (51) is an example of a *biased* array in that the ball which is second from the left is also striped. It is to be contrasted with the *unbiased* array in (52).

(52)

Matthei found that for biased conditions, there was a strong tendency for the children to select the ball which satisfied each of the prenominal modifiers individually, i.e. in the case we are considering, the ball which is second *and* striped. He refers to this as the Intersective interpretation and, of course, from the adult perspective, it constitutes an error. For unbiased conditions, a common response was for the child to exhibit confusion and often to attempt to modify the structure of the array. This would be consistent with the child interpreting the expression intersectively, but not being able to identify an object in the array which satisfied this interpretation.

The relevance of this to our discussion of X-bar principles can now be addressed. Given the status of prenominal adjectives as N'-adjuncts, the structure of *the second striped ball* is (53):

(53)   [NP the [N' second [N' striped [N'[N ball]]]]]

Employing some informal semantics on (53), we might suggest that the 'meaning' of *striped ball* is here modified by the meaning of *second* which yields the correct interpretation, i.e the striped ball which is second among striped balls.

Alternatively, if the prenominal adjectives appear in a 'flat' structure, this is (54):

(54)   [NP the [N'[second][striped][ball]]]

Here, informal semantic considerations suggest the interpretation 'ball which is striped and second among balls', which is just the Intersective interpretation. That children acted in accordance with this interpretation in the biased condition and were confused in the unbiased condition, which did not accord with this interpretation, convinced Matthei that they were operating with structures like (54) rather than (53). Such a conclusion is clearly at variance with the view that even much younger children appear to control the X-bar principles, so something would appear to be seriously amiss.

Hamburger and Crain (1984) approach this dilemma by noting that Matthei's design requires much more of a child than simply comprehension of the relevant phrase. Specifically, they draw attention to the fact that, having comprehended the phrase, the child must formulate a *plan* for identifying the referent of the phrase in the array. It would take us too far afield here to go into the details of the embryonic theory of plans they set out, but it should come as no surprise that the structure of the plan to identify the referent of *the second striped ball* is rather complex. Given this, the authors reason that if children's planning could be somehow facilitated, the implications of their behaviour for the properties of their grammatical system in this sort of experiment could be more confidently assessed. One way in which this could be achieved is by giving the child practice at executing a similar plan, and Hamburger and Crain demonstrate a dramatic improvement in ability to identify the referent of *the second striped ball* correctly if children have first been asked to identify the referent of *the first striped ball*. Identification of this latter is seen as integral to identification of the former, so prior experience with a sub-part of the plan leads to a marked improvement on the execution of the whole plan. The upshot is that there is no reason to doubt that the X-bar principles are determining the child's linguistic representations. Thus, again, we can see the importance of the methodological issues with which we opened this chapter.

Finally, to close this section, I would like to draw attention to the very extensive, cross-linguistic experimental studies of Lust and her colleagues (see, for example, Lust and Mangione, 1983; Lust and Chien, 1984; Lust, 1986a; Lust and Mazuka, 1989). The guiding principle of this work is the *Principle Branching Direction Parameter*, which concerns the unmarked positioning of a range of subordinate clauses. For example, English is deemed to be Right-Branching because relative clauses follow the head and the unmarked position for temporal adverbial clauses and sentential complements is sentence-final. These constructions are illustrated by Lust and Mangione (1983, p. 149) as in (55):

(55)   a. The child [who is eating rice] is crying
       b. The child drank the milk [after he ate the rice]
       c. It is good [that Tatsuko went to the village]

By contrast, Chinese is Left-Branching (Lust and Mangione, 1983, p. 151):

(56)   a. Zhen du-le [Mali xie de] shu
          Jan read-ASP Mary write DE book
          'Jan read the book that Mary wrote'

       b. [Dang Mali dasao fangzi de shihou] mama huilai-le
          While Mary clean house DE time mother return-ASP
          'While Mary was cleaning the house, mother returned'

       c. [Women nenggou anquan de huidao jiali] zhen hao
          We can safe DE arrive home really good
          'It's really good that we could arrive home safely'

Now Principle Branching Direction clearly bears some relationship to Head Direction, and Lust and her colleagues have shown that children's performance on a range of tasks involving the direction of anaphora is predicted by this parameter. Specifically, they have shown that for a right-branching language, such as English, children perform better with forward anaphora, whereas the converse obtains for a left-branching language like Chinese. The conclusion is that the setting of the parameter is a prerequisite for dealing with a variety of anaphoric processes, and the cross-linguistic differences in children's behaviour suggests that this parameter is set early.[13]

6.5 The Empty Category Principle

In Section 3.3, we sketched a formulation of the ECP which requires that the traces of moved expressions should be properly governed, and we illustrated how this principle could be invoked to account for subject–object asymmetries in examples like (57):

(57)   a. *Who$_i$ does John believe that e_i loves Mary
       b. Who$_i$ does John believe that Bill loves e_i

In (57b), e_i is properly governed by virtue of being lexically governed by *loves*; in (57a), e_i is not properly governed, as it has no lexical governor and antecedent government is blocked by the complementizer *that*.

As well as explaining subject–object asymmetries, the ECP has been viewed as the appropriate mechanism for understanding another set of asymmetries obtaining between complements and adjuncts. (See Rizzi (1990) for very clear discussion of the issue and of competing analyses.) Consider the contrast in (58):

(58)   a. ?Who$_i$ do you wonder [whether Bill married e_i last week]
       b. *When$_i$ do you wonder [whether Bill married Mary e_i]

Example (58a) is perhaps not perfectly well-formed, but it is considerably better than (58b). What differentiates the two examples is that *who* is moved from an A-position in (58a), a position which is projected into the syntax by the argument-selection properties of the transitive verb *marry*, whereas *when* is extracted from an adjunct position in (58b) – there is nothing about the argument-selection properties of *marry* which requires the projection of an argument denoting the time of marrying. Suppose, then, that the definition of proper government is adjusted so that adjunct NPs are not properly governed by verbs.[14] Then, (58b) can be accounted for as an ECP violation.

This complement–adjunct asymmetry has been used to investigate the role of the ECP in early grammar by de Villiers, Roeper and Vainikka (1990). The outcome of this study is far from clear-cut, and the authors pursue a range of complex and interesting issues which will not be raised here. We shall simply offer a description of their experiment and draw attention to one feature of their results which is consistent with the claim that the ECP is in place in the grammars of the children they studied.

Consider the sentences in (59):

(59) a. Who did Big Bird ask how to paint?
      b. How did Kermit ask who to help?

These sentences are distinguished in the following ways: (i) in (59a), the *wh*-expression *who* is related to a complement position, whereas in (59b), *how* is related to an adjunct position; (ii) (59a) has an adjunct *wh*-expression (*how*) in the lower C, whereas (59b) has a complement *wh*-expression (*who*) in this position; (iii) (59a) is ambiguous, with *who* being interpreted as complement of *ask* or complement of *paint*, whereas (59b) only allows the interpretation in which *how* relates to *ask*. Let us see how this is accounted for by the ECP.

For (59a), there are two legitimate s-structures corresponding to the two interpretations:

(60) a. Who$_i$ did Big Bird ask e_i [how$_j$ to paint e_j]
      b. Who$_i$ did Big Bird ask [how$_j$ to paint e_i e_j]

In (60a), *who* moves from the position of e_i and this empty category is properly governed by the verb *ask*; e_j, the trace of *how*, is properly governed by this item in the subordinate C.[15] Again, in (60b), e_i is properly governed but this time by *paint*, and the structural relationship between *how* and e_j is as in (60a). So both s-structures are well-formed.

Now consider (59b). If we again construct two s-structures, these are as in (61):

(61) a. How$_i$ did Kermit ask e_i [who$_j$ to help e_j]
      b. How$_i$ did Kermit ask [who$_j$ to help e_j e_i]

The structure in (61a) is fine, with e_j properly governed by *help* and e_i by the co-indexed *how* in the matrix C; however, e_i in (61b) is not properly governed. Being the trace of an adjunct, it is not governed by the verb, and *how* in the matrix C is too remote to govern it. So (61b) includes an ECP violation, and (59b) is unambiguous.

De Villiers et al. presented children (3:7–6:11) with short stories accompanied by pictures which were followed by questions of several types including those exemplified by (59). The stories and pictures provided the children with information which enabled them to answer the questions by relating the *wh*-expression to the matrix or subordinate clause, and a further aspect of their design was intended to bias the children towards subordinate clause answers. The point is, of course, that whatever the contextual support, a subordinate clause answer is not appropriate for (59b). The only finding which I shall mention here is that children were significantly more likely to give subordinate clause answers to (59a) than to (59b), a result which is consistent with these children's grammars containing the ECP.[16]

6.6 Other Modules

The development of control has been thoroughly investigated by a number of investigators (see, for example, Tavakolian, 1978; Goodluck, 1981; Hsu, Cairns, Eisenberg and Schlisselberg, 1989; Goodluck and Behne, in press). A consistent finding in this work is that controlled PRO in infinitival complements selected by a verb is correctly interpreted by the age of about 4 years. Thus, children of this age will exhibit understanding of sentences such as those in (62), where the obligatory controller of PRO in the matrix clause bears the Θ−role of Goal, and its surface grammatical function (object or subject) is irrelevant:

(62)   a. John told Mary$_i$ [PRO$_i$ to leave]
       b. Mary$_i$ was told by John [PRO$_i$ to leave]

This contrasts with the situation in temporal adverbials such as (63):

(63)   a. John$_i$ kissed Mary [before PRO$_i$ leaving]
       b. Mary$_i$ was kissed by John [before PRO$_i$ leaving]

In such constructions, the surface grammatical function appears to be the factor determining the identity of the controller, and children experience more difficulty in interpreting such sentences.

A different finding is that controlled PRO in sentential subjects appears to provide special difficulties for children. Thus, Tavakolian (1978) used sentences like (64) in an act-out task, and found that children tended to interpret PRO as having some extra-sentential reference:

(64)   PRO to kiss the lion would make the duck happy

It is not clear what to make of such observations in the context of this chapter, since principles and parameters do not appear to be crucially involved. Of course, this may well be a reflex of a lack of theoretical understanding in this area.[17]

Finally, there have been relatively few investigations which can be interpreted as direct tests of Subjacency in the Bounding Theory. Truscott (1984) is an examination of the theoretical learnability problems in this domain, and Otsu (1981) contains some relevant experimental studies (but see O'Grady, 1987, for alternative interpretations). Reasons for this relative neglect are not difficult to find. First, the materials necessary to test a child's knowledge of Subjacency are necessarily complex and the ruling out of alternative interpretations correspondingly difficult. Second, Subjacency violations alone often produce quite weak effects, and this factor multiplies the methodological difficulties.

6.7 Summary

This chapter has had two themes. The first has been methodological, stressing the difficulties associated with the interpretation of experimental results. The second has been that when we can be reasonably confident that design problems have been tamed, there is evidence that children have access to some remarkably abstract principles from an early age. It would be foolhardy to suggest that the issues are settled, but if we are prepared to accept that children's grammars contain the Binding Principles, X-bar Principles and the Empty Category Principle, we must concede that there is no ready inductive basis for these principles in the child's linguistic environment, i.e. the proposal that they are part of UG and are innately supplied to the child receives a measure of support (for a particularly optimistic view of the state of the evidence on this, see Crain, in press).

This positive view must be tempered, however, by the fact that up to now, we have ignored a very serious issue. The principles we have discussed are stated in terms of formal grammatical categories, and, if they are to be engaged and do their deductive work, they must be presented with data in an appropriate format. But it is transparent that the child's primary linguistic data do not come pre-packaged and labelled in a form to interact with the principles we have considered here. Of course, this is just the 'epistemological priority' issue that was mentioned in Section 3.5, and the next chapter takes up this matter and related questions.

7 Epistemological Priority and Argument Structure

Introduction

Let us begin by restating our assumptions. These are that the child comes to language acquisition equipped with a universal set of abstract grammatical principles and a set of parameters which are set on the basis of interactions with a linguistic environment. The principles and parameters are stated in terms of formal syntactic categories and configurational properties of structures (c-command, government, etc.) in which these categories occur.

To be specific, consider again the X-bar principles discussed in Section 6.4. There we argued that there is evidence, naturalistic and experimental, to suggest that young children's grammars contain these principles and that the directionality parameters which characterize this module are appropriately set by the second birthday. But how are they set? Simplifying for the sake of exposition, suppose that the child is being exposed to a language which is uniformly head-initial, and is presented with the datum in (1), where the partial structure indicated is all that concerns us:

(1) .... $[_{V'}[_V \, \alpha \,] \, [_{NP} \, \beta \,]]$ ....

This is presumably an appropriate representation for engaging the X-bar principles and constitutes evidence that the child's language is head-initial. At this point, then, the child might take (1) as an instantiation of the X-bar schema in (2a) and see it as a reason for defining order in this schema as in (2b), immediately generalizing the head-initial property to all lexical categories:

(2)   a. $X' = X, \, YP^*$
      b. $X' = X - YP^*$

Such a child now knows that his or her language is prepositional, that noun complements follow nouns, etc. without having to be exposed to tokens of these constructions. What is implausible about this account?

Setting aside the fact that languages are not usually as well-behaved as this, the most blatantly uncomfortable aspect of the proposal is that the child's data have the form schematized in (1). Children are exposed to *utterances* and if we are optimistic about their perceptual abilities, we may be persuaded that these utterances contain cues which enable children to impose *some* provisional structure on them (cf. the Bracketed Input Hypothesis in Section 2.4), i.e. we may be prepared to accept that the child's representation of (1) is (3):

(3) .... [[α][β]] .....

But this structure, lacking category labels, falls some way short of what appears in (1), and cannot be viewed as instantiating the X-bar principles at any level. The difficulty, of course, is that tokens of grammatical categories do not appear in the stream of speech with labels which unequivocally determine their identity; there is no universal system of morphologically marking nouns as nouns and verbs as verbs, nor is there any position in an utterance which is universally reserved for noun phrases or verb phrases. Of course, once the X-bar principles have come into play and the relevant parameters have been set, the categorial identity of an unknown expression can be determined by consulting these principles. But this is a quite different issue from that of how the principles are engaged in the first place.

What we are raising here as a specific problem for the X-bar principles obviously generalizes to the other modules. As we have seen, notions like c-command and government play a vital role in these modules, but these are definable only on configurations constructed in accordance with the X-bar principles. Until these configurations are represented by the child, the Binding Principles, the Empty Category Principle, and so on are effectively inert.

In contemplating this issue, we confront the question of epistemological priority, this being a condition which primary linguistic data must satisfy in PPT (see Section 3.5). This chapter is concerned with attempts to come to terms with this extremely difficult problem. What properties do primary linguistic data have which enable them to satisfy the epistemological priority condition, and how do data with these properties lead the child into the grammatical system? Before turning to these questions, it is appropriate to say a little about the developmental status of one of the principles from Section 3.3 which has escaped our attention to date, the Projection Principle from Θ-Theory. This will play a significant role in our subsequent discussion.

7.1 The Projection Principle and Early Grammars

The Projection Principle is repeated here as (4):

(4) Lexical properties are represented at all levels of syntactic structure (d-structure, s-structure and LF).

In this section, we are not concerned with the different levels of syntactic representation, but merely with the relationship between specific lexical properties (argument-selection properties), and their structural projections.

It is of interest that the content of something like (4) was recognized in the earliest attempts to write children's grammars utilizing the ST. Thus, Bloom (1970) and Bowerman (1973) both grappled with the observation that children passed through a stage (the 'two-word stage'), during which few of their utterances were more than two words long. At the same time, these included a sample of transitive and di-transitive verbs such as *kiss, throw, put,* and *give* which in adult English require the overt expression of two or three arguments. Specifically, Bloom (1970) noted that during the period when SV, VO and SO strings were common, SVO strings (and anything more complex) were extremely scarce. Relying on the method of 'rich interpretation' to determine the child's intended meaning and a variety of other criteria, she was persuaded that the missing elements were present in deep structure and were deleted by a transformational rule (the notorious Reduction Transformation) which had the effect of deleting any major constituent in a structure.[1]

It should be clear that this amounts to a claim that *all* the arguments of a predicate are represented at deep structure, thereby satisfying (4), and had Bloom been in a position to utilize empty categories for the deleted constituents, this would also have been the case for her surface structures.

Furthermore, as we have seen in chapter 4 within a more modern framework, Hyams' analyses of null subjects is entirely consistent with the requirements of the Projection Principle. Unlike Bloom, of course, she does not have to postulate full lexical NPs appearing in subject position to be subsequently deleted. Instead, subject position is filled by the empty category *pro*, motivated partly by the contextual interpretation of this as having definite reference. In Hyams' account no deletions take place between d-structure and s-structure, so it is appropriate to see (4) as satisfied at both levels in her theory.

Criticisms of Hyams, considered in Section 4.4, included discussion of the claims in de Haan and Tuijnman (1988) and Radford (1990a) that her arguments for empty subjects in early English can and should be extended to other positions, most notably that of the direct object. Their observations are that Hyams' arguments for recognizing a non-overt subject can be equally applied to tokens of transitive verbs lacking phonetically realized objects. The conclusion they draw from this is not that Hyams is incorrect to postulate an empty subject in the contexts in which she does (although, as we shall see in chapter 10, Radford maintains that it cannot be a *pro* licensed by some element in I), but rather that her reasoning must be extended to other argument positions. Again, of course, to accept this is to accept a version of (4), where a child's utterance such as that in (5) would have a syntactic representation along the lines of (6) (we use *ec* here to stand for *some* empty category without committing ourselves on its identity):

(5)   throw

(6)   [*ec*][throw *ec*]

Now, given that *throw* is a transitive verb, its LR will include the information that it selects two arguments, and may be schematized as in (7):

(7)   *throw*: V; Agent, Patient

But then (6) clearly satisfies the requirement that this argument structure be represented in syntax.[2]

It appears, therefore, that there has been a consensus among theorists working within a variety of theoretical assumptions that the Projection Principle is operative in the very earliest grammars of young children.[3]

We shall now see how this conclusion may help children find their way into syntax.

7.2 Semantic Bootstrapping

The Projection Principle as stated in (4) is somewhat programmatic. It establishes the general outlines of a constraint on the representations associated with a sentence at the various levels, but it says nothing about how satisfaction of this constraint is achieved. As far as s-structure and LF are concerned, the requirement that tokens of Move α leave behind an empty category ensures that if the principle is satisfied at d-structure, it is also satisfied at these levels; but what mechanisms ensure that it *is* satisfied at d-structure? The answer to this demands an account of how LRs are projected into d-structures (cf. Section 3.2), and the central idea of this section is that such an account may also provide us with the tools we need for understanding how the child breaks into a syntactic system. We shall now present a rough sketch of how this might work.

The child is presented with utterances (complete and partial) in context and may be capable of imposing a minimal amount of structure on some of these by virtue of prosodic information (cf. Wanner and Gleitman, 1982). Perhaps he or she can also determine the semantic properties of some utterances and the expressions they contain, utilizing the context in which they occur. Certainly, in an intuitively clear sense, much of the speech directed to children is firmly anchored in the here-and-now (Snow, 1977) and is referentially and semantically transparent (Slobin, 1977). Suppose that the child can, on this basis, come to understand the semantic properties of action predicates such as *kiss* and simple nominal expressions such as *mummy* and *daddy*.

Consider *kiss*. Here we indulge in some rather notional semantics, but the general idea behind the argument is more important than any details. *Kiss* will be interpreted by the child as an action with a range of more specific properties. Assume that this interpretation is represented along the lines of (8):

(8)   *kiss*: Action [. . .]

The unfilled bracket in (8) merely acknowledges that the meaning of *kiss* extends beyond its denoting an action, but the notation is intended to suggest that denoting an action is the most general aspect of the meaning of *kiss*.

In addition to the action itself, kissing involves agents and patients, and we might further assume that the child's representation of kissing situations includes recognition of this. But this recognition amounts to precisely what we have referred to previously as the argument-selection properties of a predicate. So, we might conclude that on the basis of exposure to primary linguistic data, the child can establish representations like (9):

(9)   *kiss*: Action [. . .]; Agent, Patient

Now suppose that the proposition in (10) is part of UG, specifically a substantive component of the projection of LRs into syntax. Recall that CSR stands for 'Canonical Structural Realization':

(10) CSR(Action) = V

From Section 3.2, we can supplement (10) with (11) and the stipulation that Agents always project as external arguments and Patients as internal arguments, these being further details of the projection mapping:

(11)   a. CSR(Agent) = NP
       b. CSR(Patient) = NP

So now consider a child who has access to (10) and (11), confronted with an utterance of (12) in a semantically transparent situation:

(12)   mummy kisses daddy

As the situation is semantically transparent and the child understands the individual words, he can elaborate (12) as in (13).

(13)

Then, he can immediately employ (10) and (11) to map (13) into (14).

(14)

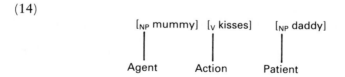

Next, he can invoke the X-bar principles, taking note of the fact that lexical heads are required to project into maximal projections. Setting aside the intermediate level of projection, this means that the V in (14) must project into a VP. Given (14), there are four possible ways in which this might be achieved:

(15) a. [$_{NP}$ mummy][$_{VP}$[$_V$kisses][$_{NP}$daddy]]
   b. [$_{VP}$[$_{NP}$mummy][$_V$kisses]][$_{NP}$daddy]
   c. [$_{NP}$mummy][$_{VP}$[$_V$kisses]][$_{NP}$daddy]
   d. [$_{VP}$[$_{NP}$mummy][$_V$kisses][$_{NP}$daddy]]

But it is easy to see that none of (15b, c, d) is consistent with the requirement that Agents be external arguments and Patients internal arguments: (15b) has the Agent as internal argument (within the V-projection) and Patient as external argument; (15c) has the Patient as external argument; and (15d) has the Agent as internal argument. Accordingly, only (15a) is consistent with UG and the primary linguistic data, and on this basis the child can set the Head Direction Parameter at head-initial.

What has appeared above is an example of a *semantic bootstrapping* approach to the question of how the child manages to engage formally specified principles and parameters when his or her primary linguistic data do not contain items from the appropriate formal vocabulary. Essentially, the method involves extending the principles of UG to include a range of semantic–syntactic correspondences which underwrite the mapping from LRs to d-structures. The semantic end of these correspondences satisfies the condition of epistemological priority, and the link to formal syntactic categories and positions enables the child to make contact with the system of formal principles.

The best-known account of this type is Pinker (1982, 1984, 1987) (see also Grimshaw, 1981 and Macnamara, 1982 for similar, but much less explicit, claims). Because Pinker's work from that period relies on Lexical Functional Grammar (Bresnan, 1982) for its linguistic concepts and is also extremely broad in scope, I shall not attempt a detailed summary and evaluation of it here. I believe that the simple example described above is in the spirit of his proposals if these are translated into the PPT framework. It is, however, appropriate to raise some general points to which Pinker draws attention.

First, he argues convincingly against alternative accounts of how the child comes to terms with the categories and structures of formal grammar. Of these, we have already come across the Bracketed Input Hypothesis (Section 2.4) and noted that even if the child can use prosodic information to impose a phrasal bracketing on a string, this is not sufficient for the purposes we are currently considering.[4] This proposal is referred to by Pinker as *prosodic bootstrapping*.

A substantial alternative, developed largely by Maratsos (1979, 1982), and Maratsos and Chalkley (1980), equips the child with the basic tools for doing distributional analysis. According to this approach, the child traces the contexts in which specific expressions occur and assigns items to the same grammatical category on the basis of co-occurrences which pass some threshold value. These co-occurrence classes are then generalized to other contexts in which only a subset of the items in question have appeared, thereby guaranteeing that the child will be able to produce and understand utterances to which he or she has not been exposed. This approach carries the mark of American structuralism (Wanner and Gleitman, 1982), and confronts familiar problems. For example, if the child (linguist) is examining the contexts in which expressions occur, what counts as a legitimate context? 'Immediately following *the*' will be useful for nouns which have no premodifiers, but 'three words from the end of the sentence' will not be useful for anything. To ensure that this process considers only appropriate contexts will arguably amount to providing it with access to UG (see Pinker, 1984, 1987; Elliott and Wexler, 1987, for much more extensive discussion).

Second, despite the reliance on semantic properties, semantic bootstrapping does not require Pinker to maintain that early grammars *are* semantic. This suggestion was popular in the 1970s, largely because of the difficulties met in applying ST to developmental data. For example, Bowerman (1973), having despaired of producing adequate ST grammars for the Finnish children she was studying, developed alternatives which were stated in terms of such notions as Agent, Patient and Location (see also Schlesinger, 1971, 1977; Brown, 1973; Bowerman, 1976; Braine, 1976). A difficulty with this emphasis is that it leaves unanswered the question of when and how the child develops a system of formal grammar, a difficulty which led Gleitman (1981) to propose that children's development displayed a radical discontinuity, with a shift from semantic to syntactic primitives being mediated by a maturational process (see Levy, 1983, and Hyams, 1986 for arguments against Gleitman's position). Semantic bootstrapping requires none of this, since it offers an account of how the child comes to manipulate *formal* categories at the earliest stages.[5]

Third, related to the previous point, the reliance on semantic criteria to get the process started does not extend to later stages of development. The use of semantic criteria rests centrally on there being a transparent interpretation of an utterance in a context, and obviously this condition is not satisfied by a large number of utterances which the child subsequently meets and understands. But this is not a problem of principle for the semantic bootstrapping approach, which merely serves to activate the grammatical principles so that parameters can be appropriately set. Once these are set, the grammar is in place and can be recruited in the interpretation of those utterances which do not concern the here-and-now, those which contain expressions referring to abstract entities, etc.

The remainder of this chapter considers a number of difficult issues which arise within the semantic bootstrapping perspective. The simple example with which we opened this section (pp. 183–5) serves to sharpen up some of these issues. That example relied on two crucial assumptions. First, we maintained that arguments of predicates bearing specific Θ-roles were projected into syntax in a rather simple and uniform manner. Second, we assumed that the semantic properties of simple expressions could be deduced by the child from the context of utterance. These assumptions are contentious and quite possibly false, although many of the issues are poorly understood and the subject of ongoing research. In the next two sections, we shall concentrate on argument projection and some of the difficulties it gives rise to; in the final section, we shall consider the extraction of verb meanings from context.[6]

7.3 The Non-Transparency of Argument Projection

A situation which would be unproblematic for an account which assumes that d-structures are transparently projected from lexical representations is described by the following propositions: (i) there is a coherent set of Θ-roles which can plausibly be regarded as satisfying the condition of epistemological priority; (ii) there is a universal specification of the function CSR which maps Θ-roles into syntactic categories, e.g. CSR(Agent) = NP, CSR(Location) = PP; (iii) there is a universal specification of the configurational properties of each Θ-role projection, e.g. whether it is an external or internal argument. It is difficult to be confident about the correctness of any of these; here we shall focus on (iii).[7]

An area where (iii) is not immediately falsified, at least for English and related languages, is in the domain of verbs which select an Agent and either a Theme or a Patient. For such verbs, the projection pattern is uniform, with the Agent being projected as an external argument and the Theme or Patient as internal argument. Verbs selecting Agent and Theme which illustrate this pattern include the causative verbs of change of position (*slide, roll, float*) and causative verbs of change of state (*melt, redden, soften*). Verbs of 'affect' such as *cut, smash* and *crash*, exemplify the phenomenon for Agent–Patient verbs (see Levin, 1984, for further discussion). Against this, however, we must set a number of observations which put (iii) under considerable pressure. Here, we consider a small group of these.

First, the Agent–Theme and Agent–Patient pattern is preserved in a sense in the Australian language Warlpiri, which is unlike English in allowing great flexibility of word-order. However, it is preserved not via a distinction between external and internal arguments, but rather via the case-marking system in the language. Thus, Agents appear with the ergative case marker for both Agent–Theme and Agent–Patient verbs, and Themes/Patients appear with the absolute case marker in these constructions. It thus appears that a certain amount of 'parameterization' may be necessary in specifying the mapping from LRs to d-structures. But, of course, as soon as this is conceded, the mapping is no longer transparent and its usefulness in guiding the child into syntax becomes less obvious (see Pinker, 1984, pp. 83ff. for how his bootstrapping account might work for Warlpiri, and Lebeaux, 1988, for further discussion. Pye, 1990, is a recent study of the acquisition of ergative languages).

A more 'local' challenge to the transparency required by (iii) occurs within English. This is provided by *argument alternations*, and we opened this book with an example of this phenomenon. Consider a verb such as *give*. Putting its external argument aside, it is reasonable to suggest that it selects a Theme (the object given) and a Goal (the person to whom it is given). The difficulty now is that these internal arguments can be projected into syntax in two different ways, as illustrated in (16):

(16)   a. John gave a book to Mary
      b. John gave Mary a book

Of course, there is no immediate problem of principle here, since we could maintain that *give* projects a single d-structure (say, similar to (16a)) based on a transparent mapping, and the structure appropriate for (16b) is derived in the syntax via Move α. But now recall that this Dative Alternation has lexical exceptions, as illustrated in (17):

(17)   a. John donated his writings to the library
       b. *John donated the library his writings

In ST, this was accommodated by building rule features into the statements of particular rules, but that option is not available in PPT. So, it is not clear that a syntactic treatment for this alternation is available (but see Larson, 1988).

   Alongside the Dative Alternation there are others which, again, admit lexical exceptions. One such is the Causative Alternation in (18) and (19):

(18)   a. The baby burped
       b. John burped the baby

(19)   a. The baby laughed
       b. *John laughed the baby

Presumably, the Θ-role of *the baby* is identical (Experiencer, perhaps) in (18a, b). Yet, in one case the argument is projected externally and in the other internally. Furthermore, with *laugh*, internal projection of the Θ-role along with an externally projected Agent is impossible. Why is this, and how does the child come to recognize (19b) as ill-formed given the No Negative Data Assumption?

   There is a range of additional argument alternations which are exhaustively dissected by Pinker (1989). Since we shall be devoting the next section to a brief discussion of his ideas, we shall simply point out the obvious difficulty their existence creates for transparent projection and say no more about them now.

   A third source of difficulty for transparency is provided by the class of *psych-verbs*. The problem is illustrated in (20):

(20)   a. This frightens John
       b. John fears this

Intuitively, we feel that *frighten* and *fear* both select an Experiencer (*John*) and a Theme (*this*).[8] Yet, these two arguments are projected into syntax quite differently depending on the choice of verb. In (20a), the Theme appears as external argument and the Experiencer as internal argument, while exactly the converse obtains in (20b). Of course, to see this as problematic requires adopting the naive view that the d-structures for (20a, b) are similar to their s-structures, a view which is elegantly disputed for similar verbs in Italian by Belletti and Rizzi (1988).

   Finally, if we turn our attention to intransitive verbs, they appear to fall into at least two classes from the point of view of their argument-selection properties. One class, exemplified by *shout, talk, wave* and *work*, selects a single Agent; the other class, illustrated by *die, occur* and *thrive* selects a single Patient or Theme. Both, however, appear in s-structures with a single external argument. Now, this is precisely what we would expect for Agents, but if Themes have a position into which they are transparently projected, consideration of transitive verbs suggests that this should be an internal argument position.

It is of considerable interest that syntactic evidence exists to show that at d-structure, Themes and Patients do indeed occur as internal arguments, only moving to external argument position at s-structure via Move α. That is to say, the d-structure of a sentence like (21a) is (21b), and its s-structure is (21c):

(21) a. John died
     b. [$_S$ e [$_{VP}$ died John]]
     c. [$_S$ John$_i$ [$_{VP}$ died e_i]]

The evidence for this analysis is rather complex and unfortunately there is not space to go into it here.[9] For reasons which are fairly obvious, intransitive verbs which project a single internal argument are known as *unaccusative* and those which project a single external argument as *unergative* (we shall return to this distinction in Section 8.4).

Now, with this analysis, transparency does not appear to be threatened – Themes project uniformly to internal argument. Unfortunately, the class of intransitive verbs of motion which obviously select a Theme does not pattern consistently with respect to the unaccusative/unergative distinction. Common sense suggests that they should be uniformly unaccusative, but Rosen (1984) has argued persuasively that this is not the case cross-linguistically. Accordingly, a transparent mapping of Theme to internal argument position is again under pressure.[10]

In this section, we have raised a sample of the difficulties which must be faced if a semantic bootstrapping account is going to meet with general success. Some of these difficulties suggest that the construal of a verb's argument-selection properties in terms of a list of Θ-roles may be inappropriate. In the next section, we shall explore what this might mean in a little more detail.

7.4 Argument Alternations

Examples (16)–(19) in the previous section provided instances of alternations in the argument structure of specific verbs. In this section, we shall consider Pinker's (1989) proposals (developing and refining ideas from his earlier work) for accounting for how these alternations and the restrictions on them are acquired. Necessarily, we shall be somewhat superficial, but the intention is to convey the central aspects of the account and understand what issues it raises. His proposals embrace the Dative and Causative Alternations, Passives, and the Locative Alternation exemplified in (22):

(22)   a. John loaded the wagon with hay
       b. John loaded hay onto the wagon

I shall restrict discussion to the Dative Alternation (for experimental investigations of the alternation in (22), see Gropen, Pinker, Hollander and Goldberg, 1991).

The starting point for Pinker's deliberations is what he refers to as *Baker's Paradox*, following the clear formulation of the problem in C. L. Baker (1979). Note first that the Dative Alternation extends across a wide class of verbs (*give, send, post, tell*, etc.)[11] This suggests that it is productive and reflects the operation of a rule of some kind, a conclusion that may be reinforced by the observation that when new de-nominal verbs such as *e-mail* are coined, they enter into the alternation (see Gropen, Pinker, Hollander, Goldberg and Wilson, 1989, for experimental demonstrations of this productivity):

(23)   a. John e-mailed the invitation to Mary
       b. John e-mailed Mary the invitation

Additionally, however, there are numerous verbs which do not permit the alternation (*donate, say, report*), suggesting that whatever rule is involved cannot be completely general. Furthermore, the constraints on the alternation do not appear to be semantically motivated in any obvious way, since *give* and *donate* are rather similar in meaning as are *tell* and *report*. Juxtaposing productivity and arbitrariness with the No Negative Data Assumption yields Baker's paradox. How are children to know that (17b) is ill-formed, given that primary linguistic data provide them with evidence for the productivity of the alternation and that they receive no negative data?

In fact, as observed by Mazurkewich and White (1984), children do produce examples of inappropriate double-object datives, thereby offering further evidence of the productivity of the alternation. However, this does not affect the logic of the learnability situation. Now the question becomes: in the absence of negative evidence, how does such a child come to retreat to a grammar which does not allow the inappropriate forms?

In terms of the framework we are assuming in this book, a 'logical space' for thinking about the Dative Alternation can be represented as in (24).

(24)

This schema in (24a) assumes that there are two distinct, unrelated LRs (LR_1 and LR_2) associated with verbs taking part in the alternation and these project into two distinct d-structures. It can be rejected because it fails to account for the noted productivity. In (24b), there is a single LR which projects into distinct d-structures. Its failing, as well as posing a problem for the transparency of projection, is that it provides no way of accounting for the restrictions on the alternation. The horizontal arrow in (24c) indicates a rule operating on LR_1 to produce LR_2, with these LRs projecting into distinct d-structures. The productivity of the alternation is accounted for by the rule, and the restrictions on it must somehow be built into its formulation. As we shall see, it is a variant of this which Pinker favours. Finally, (24d) has a single LR projecting to a single d-structure which is then mapped into distinct s-structures in the syntax. Productivity is guaranteed by the alternation being viewed as syntactic, but the restrictions must also be accounted for in a syntactic manner.

Pinker argues convincingly against accounts which adopt (24d). For example, Larson (1988) suggests that the reason for *give* taking part in the Dative Alternation whereas *donate* does not is that only *give* assigns the Goal Θ-role to its indirect object. This renders the role of *to* (also standardly an assigner of Goal) redundant, allowing its deletion in the formation of a double-object dative.[12] With *donate*, the preposition has a non-redundant role and so cannot be deleted. Pinker points out that this suggestion, whatever its technical merits, fails to address Baker's Paradox, since it is not clear how the child could come to know this difference between the Θ-role assignment properties of *give* and *donate*, given their semantic similarities and the absence of negative evidence.

The proposal schematized in (24c) claims that the productivity underlying the Dative Alternation resides in a rule operating directly on LRs. As LRs contain semantic information, we can ask whether the restrictions on the Dative Alternation are sensitive to the semantic properties of verbs. Above we have noted that any semantic motivation for a verb undergoing the alternation or not is unlikely to be very obvious. Even so, if appropriate semantic properties can be identified, the rule we are looking for might somehow refer to these.

It appears that for verbs which undergo the Dative Alternation, the Goal in the prepositional form must be capable of being construed as a possessor or potential possessor of the direct object. Thus, consider the examples in (25) and (26) (cf. Pinker, 1989, pp. 69–70):

(25)   a. John sent a book to the boarder
       b. John sent the boarder a book

(26)   a. John sent a book to the border
       b. *John sent the border a book

In (25a), as a consequence of John's action, the boarder possesses the book and (25b) is well-formed. However, it is in the nature of borders that they cannot possess material objects, so (26b) is ruled out. Furthermore, this criterion extends into the field of communication verbs which can be metaphorically interpreted as involving possession (cf. Jackendoff, 1983, for extensive exploitation of parallelisms between different semantic fields):

(27)   a. John told a story to Mary
       b. John told Mary a story

It does not stretch credulity too much to suggest that as a consequence of
John's telling it, Mary comes to have the story. How might this generalization
be stated? The rule in (28) is a rough attempt at this:[13]

(28)   X CAUSE Y GO TO Z → X CAUSE Z HAVE Y

There are several points to make about (28). First, the expressions flanking the
arrow are intended to be part of the LR of verbs such as *give*, *tell*, etc. They
replace the list of Θ-roles that we have assumed up to now, although it could
be maintained that the familiar Θ-roles can be 'read off' such representations.
For example, Agent could be identified with the first argument of CAUSE,
Theme with the second argument of CAUSE, etc.

Second, the argument positions in these representations are projected into
syntax by means of *Linking Rules*. Thus the proposal that Agents are projected
into external (subject) position is replaced by a Linking Rule which says that
the first argument of CAUSE is projected into the external position; the
suggestion that Themes are projected into internal argument position is
replaced by a Linking Rule which says that the second argument of CAUSE is
projected into internal argument position; and so on. Thus, Linking Rules
provide the machinery which ensures that the Projection Principle is satisfied at
d-structure.

Third, (28), as a rule that operates directly on semantic representations,
induces changes in syntactic argument structure in conjunction with the
Linking Rules. That is, appropriately formulated Linking Rules operating on
the left- and right-hand sides of (28) will project appropriate d-structures for
the prepositional dative and the double-object dative respectively.

Fourth, the semantic representation on the right-hand side of (28) is needed
independently to project the double-object d-structure for verbs which do not
appear in the prepositional form. Consider (29):

(29)   a. John bet Mary £5 that it would rain
       b. *John bet £5 to Mary that it would rain

Example (29a) satisfies our informal gloss of the semantic representation
appearing on the right-hand side of (28): as a consequence of John's action,
Mary is a potential possessor of £5.

Now, suppose a child hears a token of a verb in circumstances where he or
she can associate the left-hand side of (28) with that verb as its semantic
representation, i.e. suppose that semantic bootstrapping can plausibly be
invoked. Then, the child can apply (28) with two outcomes: the right-hand
side is intelligible, in which case he or she has the resources to project a
double-object d-structure; or the right-hand side is unintelligible semantically.
To see the latter, consider again (26a). If (28) is applied with these arguments,
the child derives:

(30)   John CAUSE the border HAVE a book

But this is conceptually nonsensical since borders cannot possess material objects. Accordingly, the child will not need negative evidence to know that (26b) is ill-formed.

All of this is fine, but there remains a significant problem. The rule in (28) can only be seen as providing necessary conditions for a verb to undergo the Dative Alternation: if the prepositional object is not a potential possessor, i.e. first argument of HAVE, a verb will not alternate. Unfortunately, it does not provide a sufficient condition, and recognition of this means that Baker's Paradox re-emerges with exactly the same logical force.

If (28) comprised a sufficient condition for alternation, any verb the prepositional object of which was a potential possessor ought to alternate. However, (31) and (32) show that this is not the case:

(31) a. John threw the ball to Mary
      b. John threw Mary the ball

(32) a. John pushed the cart to Mary
      b. *John pushed Mary the cart

It is clear that Mary is neither more nor less of a potential possessor in (31a) than she is in (32a); yet *throw* undergoes the Dative Alternation while *push* does not. In fact, (31) and (32) illustrate a sub-generalization. In English, verbs which encode the sudden imparting of force (*throw, kick, toss, flick*, etc.) alternate; verbs which encode the continuous imparting of force (*push, pull, ease, lift*) do not. Such sub-generalizations lead Pinker to a distinction between *broad-range rules* exemplified by (28), which provide necessary conditions for an alternation, and *narrow-range rules,* which strengthen these to sufficient conditions. Essentially, the narrow-range rules introduce additional requirements into broad-range rules. For example, the narrow range rule needed to deal with (31) and (32) will be (28) with the left-hand side elaborated to include information about the aspectual properties of the action denoted by the verb (cf. Pinker, 1989, p. 218 for details).

At this point, an obvious question to ask is whether the inclusion of a set of narrow-range rules removes the necessity for broad-range rules like (28). After all, the conjunction of a set of adequately formulated narrow-range rules will achieve exactly what we want. Pinker goes to considerable lengths in arguing for the continued importance of broad-range rules, but we shall not be able to pursue these details here. We might, however, note that violations of broad-range rules such as (26b) sound considerably worse than violations of narrow-range rules such as (32b), suggesting that the wider generalization does play a role in the organization of mature speakers' lexical knowledge.

What have we got, then, up to this point? The child is assumed to associate semantic representations with verbs on the basis of hearing tokens of these verbs in appropriate contexts. Linking Rules which are assumed not to be learned will project these semantic representations into syntactic representations.[14] The broad- and narrow-range rules, however, must be learned and a considerable part of Pinker's text is devoted to considering ways in which this might be done. Since much of this depends on rather detailed aspects of his system which I have not introduced here, I shall not pursue these issues. Suffice it to say that the resolution of Baker's Paradox emerges from the claim (substantiated by data) that children's profligate use of alternations is typically subject to the appropriate broad-range rules and that their approximation to the adult system can be located in their acquisition of narrow-range rules.

Overall, Pinker offers a provocative and detailed account of the acquisition of argument alternations which seeks to preserve (in the form of universal Linking Rules) the transparency of syntactic projection. To achieve this, however, he has to articulate a theory of lexical (semantic) representations which is considerably more elaborate than a list of Θ-roles. It is of interest that linguists working on a range of independent problems are converging on a view of LRs which resembles that of Pinker in a number of ways (see, for example, Jackendoff, 1983, 1987, 1989; Levin and Rappaport Hovav, forthcoming; Hale and Keyser, forthcoming). From the perspective of this book, the postulation and manipulation of elaborate semantic representations on which are defined rather specific lexical rules is not entirely comfortable. It seems inevitable, however, that these issues must be faced if we are to take the criterion of epistemological priority seriously.[15]

7.5 Syntactic Bootstrapping

Any semantic bootstrapping account relies crucially on the child being able to extract an appropriate semantic representation for a verb from a situation. As Pinker (1989, pp 253–4) puts it:

> The simplest possible assumption about how verbs are learned is that verb meanings correspond to concepts given by the child's perceptual and cognitive mechanisms, and that to acquire them, the child simply has to map a sound uttered in the presence of an exemplar of a concept onto the mental representation of that concept. For some verbs this is probably correct. Children must carve the flux of unique situations into recurring event types, and it is not unreasonable to expect that among them are ones that can be defined by chunks of semantic structure corresponding to the definitions of some common verbs.

This process is referred to by Pinker as *Event-Category Labelling* and in our simple illustration of semantic bootstrapping in Section 7.2, we obviously presupposed it. However, it is not clear that it is an innocent presupposition, and it is forcibly challenged by Landau and Gleitman (1985) and Gleitman (1989). In the face of this challenge, these authors have been led to develop an alternative account of how the meanings of verbs are acquired, one they refer to as *syntactic bootstrapping*. In this section, we shall consider the grounds on which they develop their challenge and the implications of their alternative for the topic of this chapter.

Landau and Gleitman (1985) offer a fascinating discussion of the early linguistic development of blind children. I shall not attempt here to survey their findings, but concentrate on those which lead directly to their syntactic bootstrapping proposal. A series of experimental studies leads them to the conclusion that the vision-related verbs *look* and *see*, when used and understood by a blind three-year-old in connection with her own perceptions, mean 'explore haptically' and 'perceive haptically'. Thus, when told to look behind her, this child would explore the space behind her own body with her hands. The question Landau and Gleitman ask is: how did these verbs come to be associated with these meanings for the child?

The most straightforward answer to this, which must be correct for some verbs if semantic bootstrapping is to be maintained, is that the verbs are used by the child's mother in circumstances which can be transparently interpreted and represented by the child, these representations providing the desired meanings for the verbs. Landau and Gleitman test this by carefully examining the circumstances in which the child's mother used a range of verbs during the period before the child exhibited mastery of *look* and *see*. They were specifically concerned with whether these circumstances contained features which were unique to these verbs and which would therefore be candidates for providing the basis for the child's understanding.

Pursuit of this question involved the use of a coding procedure for situations of utterance, and Landau and Gleitman fastened onto the proximity to the child of a relevant object as a variable worth investigating. An object within reach of the child led to an utterance concerning that object being coded as *In hand or near*, an object present but not within reach produced the coding *Far*, and a non-present object the coding *No object*.[16] Along with *look* and *see*, the authors used the same coding scheme to analyse the occurrences of other verbs which were common in the speech of the child's mother during this period. A portion of their results appears in (33) (adapted from Landau and Gleitman, 1985, p.105).

(33)

| Verb | Proportion used in contexts | | | Total number considered |
	In hand or near	Far	No object	
Look	0.73	0.09	0.18	34
See	0.39	0.56	0.05	18
Get	0.50	0.25	0.25	27
Give	0.97	0.03	0.00	21
Have	0.53	0.47	0.00	11
Hold	1.00	0.00	0.00	10
Play	0.70	0.00	0.30	10
Put	0.97	0.00	0.03	61

The important aspect of these results for Landau and Gleitman is that they do not immediately confirm the hypothesis that the haptic perception/ exploration sense of *see* and *look* could be derived from the circumstances in which the child's mother used these verbs. Haptic perception and exploration require nearness, and while occurrences of *look* are reasonably correlated with this situational feature, this is not so for *see*. Furthermore, there are other verbs (*give, hold, put*) commonly used by the child's mother, which are more highly correlated with nearness than is *look*. Now, of course, one response to this finding is to maintain that the situational coding scheme chosen by Landau and Gleitman is too crude or, perhaps, just wrong, but then the onus is on someone adopting this position to propose and evaluate an alternative.

Landau and Gleitman pursue a different strategy which results in the notion of syntactic bootstrapping. For the blind child's acquisition of *look* and *see*, they examine the *syntactic* contexts in which the mother used these and the other verbs in (33). The outcome of this analysis is a range of such contexts which are unique to *look* and *see*, another range which excludes these verbs and a third range where tokens of *look* and *see* appear in contexts which also admit other verbs. For example, only *look* among the mother's common verbs appeared as a bare imperative and only *see* appeared as a bare interrogative sometimes followed by a clause, e.g. *See? That's a circle*. Armed with these distributional differences, Landau and Gleitman then re-examine the situational variable of proximity to the child for 'canonical sentence frames and deictic uses' of *look* and *see*.[17]

The results of this analysis are that *all* occurrences of *look* in this restricted set of frames are accompanied by the relevant object being in hand or near. For *see*, the figure for which this is true goes up from the 39 per cent of (33) to 72 per cent. The tentative conclusion derived from this is that if the child restricts attention to a subset of syntactic environments, uses of *look* and *see* in these environments have the contextual support which might enable the child to determine that nearness is an essential part of their meaning. But restricting attention to a subset of syntactic environments presupposes access to those environments on the part of the child. Hence if this account can be sustained, we have a situation in which the child is using syntax to determine verb meanings, and this is what is understood by syntactic bootstrapping. Gleitman (1989, p. 22) contrasts this with semantic bootstrapping in the following terms:

> The difference between semantic bootstrapping and syntactic bootstrapping, then, is that the former procedure deduces the structures from the word meanings that are antecedently acquired from real-world observation; while the latter procedure deduces the word meanings from the semantically relevant syntactic structures associated with a verb in input sentences.

To evaluate the plausibility of syntactic bootstrapping, it is necessary to move towards an important distinction. Gleitman (1989) summarizes a number of experimental studies which indicate that children are capable of using syntactic properties of utterances to deduce the semantic properties of verbs (see also Naigles, 1990). For example, children aged 3 and 4 were shown a video in which a rabbit appears, looks to the left and then disappears to the right. This is followed by a skunk moving across the screen from left to right. The child is subsequently presented with one of the sentences in (34) which is produced by a puppet who talks puppet-talk, and the child's task is to help the experimenter understand what the puppet means:

(34)   a. The rabbit is gorping the skunk
      b. The skunk is gorping the rabbit

Asked what *gorping* means, children who have heard (34a) will say something like 'running away' and those who have heard (34b) will say 'chasing'. Thus, syntactic structure (in this case, the relative positions of Agent and Patient) enables the child to deduce the meaning of an unknown verb. But, of course, such children already *have* a syntax and while it is intriguing to ask about the extent to which they can recruit this to help them make semantic decisions, this does not bear on how the child gets into syntax in the first place. This latter is the problem that semantic bootstrapping is designed to solve, and by definition a child cannot use syntax to bootstrap *syntax*.

The distinction we need to be clear about, then, is one that recognizes two issues which pertain to different stages of development. The first is where the burden of utilizing semantics–syntax correspondences (Linking Rules in Pinker's system) falls for a child who has a syntax. Gleitman believes that a substantial part of this burden may fall on the syntax with the child using this to determine the semantic properties of unknown expressions. Pinker, according to Gleitman, adopts the opposite perspective.[18] There are important matters of fact to be resolved in this connection, but these are distinct from the issue of how the child engages a system of principles and parameters in the first place.

Of course, Gleitman is well aware of this and suggests that the way into syntax is via the use of prosodic cues, a proposal we have already come across in Section 2.4 and expressed reservations about in Section 7.2 above (see also Gleitman, Gleitman, Landau and Wanner, 1988). The important issue to be clear about is that syntactic bootstrapping is not, and cannot be, an alternative to semantic bootstrapping for the child's initial steps in acquiring syntax. Prosodic bootstrapping may be, but at the moment there is no reason to believe that the information derivable by this route is sufficiently rich to get the child started.[19]

7.6 Summary

In this chapter, we have raised some of the most difficult problems facing any account of language acquisition. Obviously, a satisfactory theory which fully recognizes the epistemological priority condition on primary linguistic data is currently a rather distant prospect. The majority of people working in the field believe that a measure of semantic bootstrapping is necessary to enable the child to gain access to the system of principles and parameters. Accordingly, the bulk of the chapter has been concerned with presenting some of the issues which arise from this perspective.

We began with a simple outline of what the semantic bootstrapping approach involves and went on to sketch some of the difficulties which must be confronted by a satisfactory theory. As things stand, we do not have, and desperately need, a theory of lexical/semantic representation which is explicit enough to be submitted to the sort of learnability considerations to which this book is largely devoted. Fortunately, progress in understanding the development of the syntactic modules themselves need not await the arrival of such a theory, and in this respect we are in the same position as Wexler and Culicover (1980) who felt justified in taking for granted a 'preanalysis' of primary linguistic data into the syntactic vocabulary required by their theory. But it must be recognized that the absence of a theory of this type is a substantial weakness at the foundations of PPT. An optimistic note can be sounded by observing the convergence between acquisition-driven work, such as that of Pinker, and theoretical speculations on the nature of LRs.

Finally, we briefly examined the notion of syntactic bootstrapping, concluding that it does not provide an alternative to semantic bootstrapping in the face of the epistemological priority problem. On the other hand, it does offer an interesting perspective on the utilization of semantics–syntax correspondences once the child has a syntax.

We shall now turn our attention to another set of intriguing and difficult questions concerning the nature of developmental mechanisms.

8   Developmental Mechanisms

Introduction

Up to now, we have used such expressions as *learning, acquisition* and *development* unreflectively and, to a large extent, interchangeably. Of these expressions, the last two carry no particular connotations regarding the mechanisms by which the child moves from one grammar to another.

'Learning' is different, however, since it is a specific type of process, and to say that the developmental mechanism employed in some domain is a learning process is to make a substantive claim. In first language acquisition, it is not only a substantive but also a controversial claim, and in our schematic representation of PPT as an account of acquisition in Section 3.5, we noted that 'triggering' is often adopted as a more appropriate label for this process. Indeed, Chomsky himself throughout his writings has consistently sought to minimize the part that learning has to play in language acquisition, seeing any emphasis on this notion as the legacy of the largely discredited behaviourist tradition in psychology. For example, he says (1987a, p. 9):

> The term 'learning' is, in fact, a very misleading one, and one that is probably best abandoned as a relic of an earlier age, and earlier misunderstandings. Knowledge of language grows in the mind/brain of a child placed in a certain speech community.

A similarly negative tone is adopted by Piattelli-Palmarini (1989) in a discussion where he opposes *instructive* to *selective* accounts of development, linking views on these notions in language acquisition to ideas in developmental biology and immunology. Instructive theories are identified with learning-theoretic proposals, regarding which Piattelli-Palmarini (p. 2) says:

> I, for one, see no advantage in the preservation of the term 'learning.' I agree with those who maintain that we would gain in clarity if the *scientific* use of the term were simply discontinued.

If we are to follow the advice of Chomsky and Piattelli-Palmarini, it is an urgent task to clarify the nature of alternatives to learning. 'Triggering' is one such, and it is interesting to note the common reliance on this concept in the sort of account of language acquisition we are concerned with in this book. For example, in chapter 4 in our discussion of Hyams (1986), we noted her suggestion that the resetting of the AG/PRO parameter is *triggered* by the child's recognition of the presence of expletive subjects. Here, triggering is a relationship between primary linguistic data and their consequences, and a somewhat different usage can be identified when Roeper (1988, p. 39), in the context of an overview of PPT, says:

> The child would, on the basis of particular data, set the values for particular parameters. The setting of a value for one module triggers a series of obligatory consequences in other modules.

In this statement, it appears that consequences of parameter-setting can trigger other consequences, a rather different notion from that contemplated by Hyams.

Alongside such emphases, we also find prominent examples where the advice of Chomsky and Piattelli-Palmarini is apparently unheeded. Recall Wexler and Manzini's account of the GCP in chapter 5 and their insistence that markedness orderings were derivative on the operation of a *learning* module.

And, of course, there is 'growth', mentioned by Chomsky in the passage cited above. Is this to be identified with triggering as an alternative to learning, or does it label a further option? Is such a further option maturation perhaps?

It seems to me that it is worth trying to sort all of this out, and the aim of this chapter is to do just that. In particular, I believe it will be useful to try to get a clear idea on where parameter-setting is best located in a taxonomy of developmental mechanisms, and the bulk of the chapter is devoted to this. We shall also consider the plausibility of maturational accounts of development and look at the sort of evidence which might motivate such an account.

8.1 Learning and Triggering: General Considerations

Fodor (1978, 1981) has considered the distinction between learning and triggering in detail, and this section summarizes his deliberations (see Atkinson, 1987, 1990, for related discussion).

An attempt to articulate a definition of learning appears in Fodor (1978). At the outset, we should be clear that this takes place within a cognitive framework. Thus, successful learning does not need to be signalled by any overt behaviour (although such behaviour may be necessary for a psychologist or any observer to know that it has occurred) and is not identified with an establishment of links between stimulus parameters and response parameters such that the former control the latter. Rather, learning is initially defined as an *externally occasioned change in epistemic state*. The reference to epistemic state here simply makes clear the cognitive emphasis of Fodor's definition, and the requirement that this change in state be externally occasioned reflects the need to distinguish learning from any endogenously determined cognitive change.

Paradigmatic cases of learning appear to fall under this definition. So, consider coming to believe that London buses are red by observing tokens of red London buses; or coming to believe that London buses are red by being told that they are; or coming to believe that London buses are red by being told that they are the same colour as ripe tomatoes and already believing that ripe tomatoes are red; and so on. In all of these cases, there are external events which have as a consequence a change in the learner's epistemic state.

While the above definition plausibly provides a necessary condition on learning, Fodor is convinced that it is not sufficient, since there are conceivable externally occasioned changes in epistemic state which would not intuitively count as learning. What Fodor has in mind here are philosophers' favourites such as the blow on the head which turns someone who is ignorant of London bus colours into someone who firmly believes that London buses are red; or the Chinese pill, ingestion of which turns the ingester into someone who knows Chinese. The interesting question, then, is: what distinguishes these non-learning cases from the earlier examples?

It seems clear that some notion of *content* is what underlies the distinction. If I perceive a red London bus, take it to be a red London bus, and as a consequence come to believe that London buses are red, there is a non-arbitrary relationship between the content of my perception ('That is a London bus and it is red') and the content of my resultant belief ('London buses are red'). Similarly, if I am presented with the Chinese sentence in (1), take it to be a sentence displaying SVO word-order, and as a consequence come to believe that Chinese is an SVO language, the relationship in question is non-arbitrary:[1]

(1) Lao Wang xihuan xiao Gao
     old Wang like little Gao
     'Old Wang likes young Gao'

Now contrast this with the blow-on-the-head and pill-swallowing scenarios. In these cases, if the representations of the external events have content at all, the relationship between this content and the consequent change of state is quite arbitrary.

The above shows that it is necessary to modify the definition of learning along the following lines if it is to approach sufficiency: learning is an externally occasioned change in epistemic state *where there is an appropriate relation of content* between the learner's representation of the externally occasioning event(s) and the consequent change in epistemic state. This definition enables us, then, to partition externally induced cognitive changes into those which instantiate learning and those which instantiate something else. We can provisionally label this second possibility *triggering*, its defining characteristic being an *arbitrary* relationship of content between the representation of the external event(s) (if they have such content at all) and the change in epistemic state.

This discussion can be extended in ways which will be useful in the next section by considering Fodor's (1981) views on concept acquisition. These ideas are presented in the course of an evaluation of the plausibility of empiricism and nativism in this domain, and Fodor begins by drawing a distinction between *lexical* and *phrasal* concepts. As these labels suggest, this involves relativizing the discussion to the way in which concepts are expressed in a particular language (English in what follows), and this is seen as a strategic rather than a principled move. We shall come back to this issue, but for now we can simply regard it as a way to get started.

According to this distinction, then, those concepts which are expressed at all in English can be partitioned into those which are expressed by single morphemes (RED, COW, TABLE, HYACINTH, etc.) and those which require phrases or morphologically complex words for their expression ((IS) MARRIED TO ELIZABETH WINDSOR, LIVES IN A FLAT, (IS) UNHAPPY, etc.). Empiricists and rationalists (nativists) agree about how the semantic properties of phrasal concepts are fixed. These are derived from the semantic properties of their component concepts by means of some sort of combinatorial apparatus. If we consider UNHAPPY, this is morphologically complex *qua* linguistic expression, and its semantic properties are derived from those of UN- and those of HAPPY. The manner of the derivation need not concern us here; all we need to be clear on is that *some* combinatorial machinery is assumed by both approaches.[2]

Turning now to lexical concepts, an empiricist theme is that these do not comprise a homogeneous set. Some of them are *complex* and reducible to others; those which cannot be reduced are *primitive*. Thus, to take a familiar example, it might be maintained that the lexical concept BACHELOR is complex, being reducible to some combination of UN-, MARRIED and MALE. These also, with the exception of UN-, might be complex, permitting further reductions until eventually we are left with only primitive, i.e. non-reducible, concepts. An attractive feature of such an account is that the same combinatorial apparatus is operative in the decomposition of complex concepts into primitive concepts as in the analysis of phrasal concepts. Thus, the synonymy of *bachelor* and *unmarried man* can be straightforwardly accounted for: they both express the concept UNMARRIED MAN.

What candidates are there for membership in the set of primitive concepts? If conceptual reduction is to be of any theoretical value, it is important that the number of primitive, non-reducible concepts should be relatively small when compared to the number of reducible concepts. This can be achieved by proposing that the contrast between primitive and complex concepts is *principled* by virtue of the primitive concepts being identified with *sensory* concepts. Then RED is a primitive concept but BACHELOR is not. That we find it difficult to conceive of reducing sensory concepts adds an air of plausibility to this view.

So we now have three types of empiricist concepts in place – phrasal, complex lexical and primitive lexical. How are these acquired? For phrasal and complex lexical concepts, the empiricist tells the same story: acquisition proceeds by formulating hypotheses and testing them against further experience. These hypotheses will be ultimately formulable in terms of just the primitive lexical concepts and whatever combinatorial apparatus is assumed in the account. For example, in acquiring the concept BACHELOR, the child will be confronted with a token of the concept and will formulate a hypothesis along the lines of (2):

(2) $\forall\, x\ \text{BACHELOR}(x) = P_1(x)\ \&\ P_2(x)\ \&\ \ldots\ \&\ P_n(x)$

In (2), the P_i $(1 \leqslant i \leqslant n)$ are intended to designate primitive (sensory) concepts and the only combinatorial apparatus used is logical conjunction, symbolized by '&'. Subsequently confronted bachelors will no doubt confound aspects of this hypothesis, leading to modifications within the prescribed constraints.[3]

Recall, now, our brief discussion of a concept learning experiment in Section 1.1. It is apparent that what is described above is simply a naturalized version of this. In the experiment, the experimenter determines the concept to be acquired and fixes the parameters of stimulus variation; in the present account, the child's social/linguistic environment determines the nature of the to-be-acquired concepts and the sensory/non-sensory distinction fixes the terms in which stimuli can vary. Furthermore, it is apparent that there is a sense in which this is not an account of the acquisition of concepts at all. In chapter 1, we pointed out that the story told there presupposed a source of hypotheses – a hypothesis space – and exactly the same situation obtains in the naturalized setting, i.e. in order to so much as entertain the hypothesis in (2), the child must already *have* the concept on the right-hand side available in his or her hypothesis space. What acquisition amounts to, then, is coming to believe that instances of this concept should or may evoke behaviour of certain kinds, e.g. referring to them using *bachelor*, trying to marry them off, trying to persuade them to propose to eligible females, etc. (for extensive discussion of this and related issues, see Fodor, 1975; Piattelli-Palmarini, 1980).

Putting this concern to one side, it is clear that the hypothesis formulation and testing account is a *learning* account: the external events which occasion the belief that BACHELORs are P_1, P_2, and so on, are events which are taken to be BACHELOR-events, P_1-events, P_2-events, and so on. Such learning is also in an intuitive sense a *rational* process, and formalizations of it typically employ an inductive logic. Fodor concludes that the empiricist account of the acquisition of phrasal and complex lexical concepts views this as a *rational causal* process, i.e. it is a learning account.

Turning now to primitive lexical concepts, empiricism tells a very different story. As these concepts are primitive, there is no question of their being acquired via the projection of hypotheses which are themselves the result of applying the combinatorial apparatus to the primitive vocabulary. Rather, they must be a direct product of the organism's *sensorium* or sensory apparatus. This latter can thus be construed as a device which maps the flux of sensory input into a discrete set of sensory concepts. As such, there is nothing *rational* about its operation and the causal relation between occasioning stimuli, tokens of RED say, and the entertaining of the concept RED is not grounded in any kind of intelligence – it is a *brute causal* relationship, and the rationality embodied in learning's need for content-relatedness is not in play. As Fodor puts it (1981, p. 273): 'The structure of the sensorium is such that certain inputs trigger the availability of certain concepts. Punkt'. On this account, sensory concepts are *innate* in the sense that they are not *learned* on the basis of experience. This is not to say, however, that they are acquired in the absence of experience; relevant experience is necessary to *trigger* the concepts.

The picture of concept acquisition that emerges from the above discussion is as schematized in (3) (based on Fodor, 1981, p. 264).

(3)

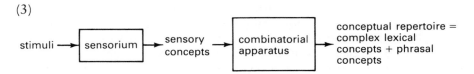

The sensorium, mediating between stimuli and sensory concepts, embodies triggering mechanisms; the combinatorial apparatus, mediating between sensory concepts and the remainder of the organism's conceptual repertoire, embodies learning mechanisms.

One final observation should be made before turning to nativism. Just as the primitive concepts must be innate for the empiricist, so must the combinatorial apparatus. This latter is necessary for the learning part of the account to work; the combinatorial apparatus, necessary for learning to work at all, cannot be an *outcome* of learning.

The major difference between nativism and empiricism can now be easily stated. Whereas for the latter, only a small number of epistemologically privileged (sensory) concepts are innate and triggered, for the former this is a property of most (perhaps all) lexical concepts, i.e. for the nativist, concept acquisition is schematized as in (4).[4]

(4)

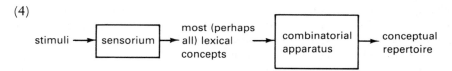

With the distinction set up in this way, Fodor believes that available evidence strongly favours the nativist account. He offers a number of observations to substantiate this view, but here we focus on just one of these.[5]

If empiricism were correct, a natural prediction would be that most lexical concepts (and therefore the lexical items which express them) should be *definable*. Ideally, such definitions should be in terms of the primitive sensory basis. But, Fodor maintains, this is not so, as witnessed by several centuries of effort to produce adequate definitions. Indeed, this observation remains true even if the restriction to terms expressing sensory concepts is removed. It seems to be almost always possible to produce counter-examples to purported definitions, showing that while they may encapsulate necessary conditions for the instantiation of a concept, such conditions are rarely sufficient; and, of course, a *definition* must provide necessary and sufficient conditions. Nativism, which releases lexical concepts from the need to be defined, is consistent with this failure.

For the sake of argument, then, let us accept Fodorian nativism for lexical concepts and consider a problem it gives rise to, which will provide further useful perspective for when we return to the acquisition of grammar. The problem is this: all the evidence we have suggests that the child's lexical concepts are acquired in some sort of order. There is no reason to believe that what is at issue here is a total ordering, i.e. we are not committed to the view that all children acquire, say, COW before HORSE or vice versa. But that a fairly robust partial ordering is definable on the set of acquired lexical concepts appears to be incontestable. For ATOM to appear in a child's conceptual repertoire before COW and concepts corresponding to other categories of middle-sized objects is surely just not on.

Now, the empiricist, equipped with the view that most concepts are definable in terms of a primitive basis, has *some* story to tell here: the concepts in the primitive basis must be acquired before other concepts since these latter are actually defined in terms of them. But certainly if 'primitive' is identified with 'sensory', this story appears to be empirically falsified: the order which children actually manifest in concept acquisition is not one in which they get the sensory concepts first. Whether a false story is better than no story at all is not something on which I have a view, but what is plain is that up to now, the nativist cannot meaningfully address the order question at all. According to the nativist, most lexical concepts are not acquired via construction out of a primitive vocabulary; they are triggered by appropriate encounters with the environment, and, in the absence of any demonstration that the environment is so structured that for all children triggering stimuli for late-acquired concepts are withheld until early-acquired concepts are in place, this looks like a real dilemma.

Fodor's speculative response to this is to suggest that the innate structure of the mind (specifically, the sensorium in (4)) is functionally *layered*, with those concepts which are acquired early appearing in a 'basic' layer, interfacing directly with the environment. Beyond this 'basic' layer, there are further layers and the concepts which reside in these have more basic concepts as *causal* antecedents. To exemplify, ATOM on the empiricist account will be reducible to primitive concepts, via a series of definitions, and this is why it is relatively late to be acquired. For Fodor, this relative lateness is accounted for by locating ATOM in an appropriately deep layer in the innate structure of the mind. In its position here, its acquisition is determined by a set of causal antecedents, some of which may be external stimuli but others of which may be other concepts. This situation is represented in (5).

(5)

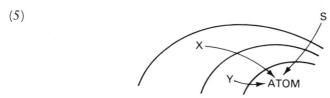

In (5), it is assumed that the acquisition of ATOM does in fact require an encounter with a stimulus of type S. This, in itself, is not sufficient for acquisition, however, since ATOM also requires, as causal antecedents, acquisition of the concepts X and Y. It is vital for Fodor's position that ATOM should not be seen as somehow composed out of X and Y – this is the definitional view – but instead, the content relation between X, Y and ATOM is an arbitrary one, just as it is in cases of triggering where the process is induced solely by external stimulation. Thus, the causal relationship between X, Y and ATOM is *brute-causal* as opposed to *rational-causal*, with triggering mediating not only world-concept relations but also concept-concept relations.

Finally, it is appropriate to say a few words about the properties concepts should have if they are to belong to the basic layer. Not surprisingly, Fodor does not have a comprehensive account of these, but he does offer some preliminary remarks. What these amount to is that such concepts (i) should be ontogenetically basic – this just recapitulates the observation that led to the recognition of the problem, viz. that there is an order defined on the acquisition of lexical concepts; (ii) should be ostensively definable, and here Fodor adverts to the well-known work of Rosch and her colleagues on 'basic objects' (Rosch, Mervis, Gray, Johnson and Boyes-Braem, 1976. See also, in this connection, Berlin, Breedlove and Raven, 1973; Berlin, 1978). A reason for this speculation being of importance is that it may provide a foundation for the claim that the lexical/phrasal distinction, which Fodor initially takes as a strategic step, is in fact principled, with 'basic' layer concepts attracting simple lexical labels cross-linguistically.

We shall now take advantage of the ideas and distinctions arising in this presentation of Fodor's views to examine the developmental mechanisms assumed by accounts of syntactic development offered within PPT.

8.2 The Nature of Parameter-Setting

Should parameter-setting, as introduced in Section 3.4 and illustrated in a developmental context in chapters 4 and 5, be identified with learning, triggering or neither? What, if anything, makes parameter-setting a distinctive developmental mechanism? These are the questions with which this and the next section are concerned.

It is a common theme in Chomsky's reflections on acquisition to stress the *deterministic* nature of the process. Thus, he says (1987a, p. 8):

> It is fairly clear that the process of maturation to the steady state is deterministic. Language learning is not really something that the child does; it is something that happens to the child placed in an appropriate environment, much as the child's body grows and matures in a predetermined way when provided with appropriate nutrition and environmental stimulation.

It is clear that hypothesis selection and testing is not deterministic in this sense, so again it appears appropriate to see Chomsky as rejecting a learning-based account. Before turning to content-relatedness of occasioning stimulus and change in cognitive state as diagnostic of learning, let us briefly consider this issue of determinism.

On a strict reading, determinism is incompatible with the notion of *parameter-resetting*, so the fact that the best-known accounts of development presented within this paradigm readily adopt this latter notion suggests that strict determinism is not correct.[6]

Recall that in chapter 4, we considered two developmental accounts of null subject phenomena. Both of these had the English-speaking child starting with the *wrong* setting for a parameter and subsequently having to reset it. Furthermore, the motivation for the Subset Principle in chapter 5 was precisely to allow the child to mis-set the Binding Theory parameters and to ensure recovery from such mis-settings.

A further example to illustrate the same point is Huang's (1982) discussion of the X-bar structure of Chinese, mentioned briefly in Section 3.4. Having introduced the X-bar principles with head direction parameterized and suggested that they offer a better explanation of word-order properties than Greenberg's (1963) implicational universals, Huang notes that complications must be introduced into the principles to deal with the fact that Chinese is not *strictly* head-final. The unmodified X-bar principles are offered as presenting unmarked hypotheses, which need to be refined by the child acquiring Chinese. The assumption, then, is that parameter-setting in this module too is not a once-and-for-all deterministic affair, but is subject to amendment in the light of subsequent experience.[7]

Once we accept this conclusion, it is tempting to view parameter values as constituting a restricted hypothesis space through which the child must search, adopting and rejecting hypotheses in a process rather similar to that envisaged in the concept *learning* experiment. But if this is so, it is not clear that parameter-setting is a process distinct from learning. Given this, it is somewhat puzzling that Borer and Wexler (1987, p. 131), in a statement summarizing the claim that 'Learning [sic] is deterministic', say:

> This means that the child's options in constructing a grammar are so restricted that there are not many options from which the child can choose . . . *Determinism is to be contrasted with hypothesis-testing, in which there are many possible choices of hypotheses, and correction (back-up) when an error is made.* (my emphasis – MA)

A purely *quantitative* criterion, while of considerable importance, is surely not sufficient to underwrite the distinction between hypothesis-testing and a deterministic process. Strict determinism rules out options entirely, and while it may present an accurate picture of visual development, as Borer and Wexler claim, the variety of grammars itself guarantees that it is not appropriate for language acquisition. The small number of options, which Borer and Wexler are happy to accept, is quite compatible with a hypothesis-testing account.[8]

So far, we have not paid attention to the relationship between the primary linguistic data which are responsible for setting a parameter and the resultant cognitive state in which the parameter is set. As we have seen, for Fodor this relationship holds the key to distinguishing learning from triggering.

Note first that the notion of 'growth', alluded to by Chomsky in the passage cited at the beginning of this section, is probably not very useful in understanding parameter-setting. Indeed, Fodor (1983) is categorical in seeing an attempt to assimilate the acquisition of language to the growth of physical organs as quite misleading. This is because any notion of content is out of place in accounts of organic growth. If we contemplate the growth of, say, a limb or an internal organ such as the heart, it is perfectly proper to emphasize the need for appropriate external conditions in the form of nutrients, etc. But the suggestion that changes in the organ which are consequent on these conditions have a 'content' which can be linked to the 'content' of the conditions is bizarre. By contrast, for Fodor, the development of a system of linguistic representation relies crucially on such content relations. He says (1983, p. 5):

> . . . Chomsky's account of language learning is the story of how innate endowment and perceptual experience interact *in virtue of their respective contents*. (Fodor's emphasis)

When we turn to specific cases of parameter-setting, the correctness of Fodor's position is usually rather clear.

Consider again Huang's account of the setting of word-order parameters. Although he does not give a detailed portrayal of how this is supposed to work, it is reasonably clear that he has something along the following lines in mind. The child is exposed to a datum including a head and a complement and represents it as such (see chapter 7 for how this might be achieved). This representation, by virtue of its content, engages the appropriate X-bar principle and serves to fix the Head Direction Parameter. Unmarked hypotheses for Huang are those where the parameter is uniformly set for all categories, so we assume that at this point the child can make predictions about head–complement order for lexical categories to which he or she has not yet been exposed. These predictions can be confounded, as they are for Chinese, and the child has to adopt a different (marked) hypothesis to accommodate the recalcitrant data. And so on and so on, with resettings of the parameter being occasioned by encounters with data, the content of which is non-arbitrarily related to that of the reset parameter.

Next, consider Wexler and Manzini's GCP from chapter 5, and recall that this comes pre-set at unmarked values (value (a) for anaphors and value (e) for pronouns). Effectively, this requires the child to assume that when he or she identifies an expression as an anaphor or a pronoun, the distribution of this expression is (partially) determined by the unmarked GCP values. What will cause an Italian-speaking child to reset such a value for the anaphor *sè*? The most natural suggestion is exposure to a sentence such as (6) in which *sè* is not bound in the domain of a subject:

(6)   Alice$_i$ guardò i ritratti di sè$_i$ di Mario
      'Alice looked at Mario's portraits of herself'

In order for resetting to take place, (6) must be represented by the child so as to counter-exemplify the hypothesis that value (a) of the GCP is appropriate for *sè*. But the very notion of counter-exemplification presupposes that the child's representation of (6) is such that he or she can deduce from it that *sè* is not bound in the domain of a subject, so value (a) of the GCP is not correct.

Finally, consider null subjects and the two accounts of these offered by Hyams (1986, 1987a). The later proposal is very straightforward from the current perspective. It assumes that the child's initial setting of the relevant parameter is [+uniform] and that this licenses empty subjects in all languages. When the child begins to produce obligatory subjects, this is a reflex of the resetting of the parameter to [−uniform], so the question is: what occasions this resetting? As we have seen, Hyams notes that morphological marking of tense and agreement is conspicuously absent in early English and, of course, it is largely in marking these features that English displays morphologically complex verbal forms. Her suggestion is that at the null subject stage, the child represents all English verbal forms as morphologically simple, i.e. the child treats English as if it were Chinese. Then, at some point, the child is able to recognize and represent morphological endings and this leads to the resetting of the parameter to [−uniform].

A moment's reflection should persuade us that this account is identical in the relevant respects to those we have already considered. The child operates with a generalization that all verbal forms in English are uninflected. He or she is then presented with evidence that this generalization is not appropriate, this evidence being transparently related, in terms of content, to the correct parameter-setting. In familiar terms, there are two hypotheses populating the relevant part of the hypothesis space. All children start with [+uniform] for reasons briefly discussed in chapter 4 (see also chapter 9). Chinese and Italian children are never presented with evidence leading them to discard this hypothesis; English children are, and the evidence forms part of a *rational* causal (i.e. learning) process.

The data 'triggering' parameter-resetting in Hyams (1986) are overt expletive subjects; it is the recognition of such subjects which leads the child to reset the relevant parameter from + AG/PRO to −AG/PRO.[9] The lack of expletive subjects in Null Subject Languages is deduced from the conjunction of +AG/PRO, licensing null subjects, and the Avoid Pronoun Principle (cf. Section 4.2). Thus, a sentence containing an expletive subject and represented as such by the child, while not transparently related in content to the AG/PRO parameter itself, counter-exemplifies a consequence of the +AG/PRO value of the parameter. Schematically, this is analogous to coming to believe that not-*P* on the basis of being told that not-*Q* and already believing that if *P*, then *Q*, and this is an indirect but perfectly intelligible mode of *learning*.[10]

The conclusion of the above is that the relationship between occasioning stimuli and the setting of parameters gives us no reason to doubt that anything other than learning, as a rational hypothesis-testing process, is involved. We have also seen that its characterization as strictly deterministic and unrevisable cannot be maintained. Is there any other route down which we could seek its distinctive character?

Some of the best-known accounts of parameter-setting assume that parameter values are *ordered*, so that it makes sense to talk of them as forming a markedness hierarchy. This is true both of Hyams' theories of null subjects and of Wexler and Manzini's proposals for the Binding Theory parameters. Conceivably, this notion of order gives parameter-setting its special characteristics in comparison with other forms of learning.

Two different motivations have been offered for ordered parameter values. The first is straightforwardly empirical, and appears in Hyams (1986). Her claim there that the initial setting of the AG/PRO parameter is +AG/PRO is simply based on the observation that children initially omit subjects cross-linguistically. On this construal, 'unmarked' is identified with whatever children do first. By way of contrast, Wexler and Manzini (1987) and Hyams (1987a) ground their markedness claims in learnability considerations, with the Subset Principle governing the order in which hypotheses are selected.

Now the issue of ordering in itself does not seem to be diagnostic of procedures which are distinct from learning. Returning to the concept *learning* experiment, Fodor (1975) notes that the extensive literature devoted to this paradigm has repeatedly demonstrated that certain hypotheses appear to be more readily available to the learner than others. This would seem to require that candidate hypotheses are ordered for the learner before the learning commences (cf. Section 1.1).

However, the detailed structure of the ordering favoured in the linguistic accounts is not characteristic of what is found in the concept learning literature in two senses. First, for linguistic parameters, there appears to be a *single* ordering such that if value i precedes value j, then any language learner must consider value i before value j. This degree of determinism is not characteristic of the concept learning accounts (cf. note 8). Second, the ordering is itself sometimes determined by a specific set-theoretic relationship between the languages characterized by the parameter values. This is to be contrasted with rather general claims about the relative availability of conjunctive, disjunctive and negative concepts in the concept learning literature.

We can conclude, then, that while the notion of ordered hypotheses is not itself sufficient to guarantee a special status for parameter-setting as a developmental mechanism, details of how such orderings are defined may be unique to the language faculty. Note, however, that even this rather weak claim must be tempered by the observation that the Subset Condition, defining an ordering on parameter values, appears to be too strong, and that for many parameters falling outside its scope, there are no grounds for suggesting that their values are ordered (see chapter 9 for more detailed discussion).

In summary, we have struggled to find a distinctive role for parameter-setting as a developmental mechanism. Significant constraints on the learner's hypothesis space may well be a feature of this model, and these may be sufficient to ensure determinism in the sense of note 8. However, the relationship between primary linguistic data and parameter-setting is such that the latter is not *qualitatively* distinct from learning. No niche has been found for triggering, unless this term is used simply to refer to a developmental process whereby exposure to data has non-trivial consequences. Clearly, this is true of parameter-setting via its embedding in the principles of UG, but it is also true of inductive learning. In the next section, we shall briefly consider whether a role might be found for triggering beyond the relationship between primary linguistic data and initial parameter settings.

8.3 Deductive Structure and 'Remote' Triggering

Our discussion of Fodor's views on the acquisition of concepts in Section 8.1 identified two species of triggering. The first embodied a relationship between stimuli and concepts, and the second, a relationship between one or more attained concepts and other concepts. What might correspond to this latter in the parameter-setting account of acquisition?

Most obviously, we could maintain that the setting of one parameter via a rational causal interaction with primary linguistic data might be a brute causal antecedent for the setting of another parameter. Let us illustrate what this could amount to with an implausible example. Earlier in this book, we have drawn attention to two of the differences between English and Chinese. First, Chinese permits null subjects in tensed clauses; second, Chinese does not require a [+WH] C to be filled by a *wh*-expression at s-structure. We shall refer to the parameter determining whether null subjects are permitted as p_1 (with values p_1(Chinese) and p_1(English)) and the parameter governing the s-structure distribution of *wh*-expressions as p_2 (with values p_2(Chinese) and p_2(English)).

Now, it is conceivable that UG contains statements linking these two parameters and their values along the lines of (7):

(7)   a. p_1(Chinese) $\rightarrow$ p_2(Chinese)

   b. p_1(English) $\rightarrow$ p_2(English)

In (7), the arrow is to be read causally, so what we are envisaging is that the setting of p_1 is causally sufficient for the appropriate setting of p_2, i.e. once Chinese children have come to realize that their language permits null subjects, they can invoke (7a) to conclude that it also allows *wh*-in-situ constructions, and the child acquiring English can rely on (7b) in a similar way. In these circumstances, there is no readily discerned relationship of content between the parameters concerned, and it would be appropriate to talk about the setting of p_2 being *triggered* by the setting of p_1.[11] Such a situation would also clearly represent parameter-setting in one module having consequences in another module, a possibility which, as we have seen, Roeper (1988) seems happy to embrace.

The difficulty with this perspective is that it does not correspond to what linguists typically have in mind when they refer to the rich deductive structure of PPT. The *consequences* determined by this structure are standardly not parameter settings in other modules but the possibility or impossibility of a range of *structures* to which the child does not have access as primary linguistic data. To take an obvious case, Rizzi's (1982) original formulation of the parameter licensing null subjects in tensed clauses also accounted for inverted subjects and apparent extractions from the subject position of subordinate clauses introduced by overt complementizers in Italian (see Section 4.1). It is therefore appropriate to see the setting of this parameter as having a set of consequences, and for these consequences to rely on interactions of the content

of other modules, but they do not extend to fixing further parameter values in
these modules.

Returning to the fanciful example illustrated in (7), one of the reasons it is
fanciful is that it picks on two arbitrary properties of English and Chinese and
suggests that they are linked via a statement in UG. Suppose that cross-
linguistic research persuaded us that in fact the possibility of null subjects and
wh-in-situ s-structures are correlated across a range of languages. The
orthodox response to this would not be to subscribe to (7), but to search for a
single parameter from which the null subject phenomena and the *wh*-
phenomena could be seen to follow. I conclude, then, that while 'remote'
triggering of parameter values is not conceptually incoherent, current linguistic
practice is not disposed to regard it as a live possibility.[12]

8.4 Maturation as a Developmental Mechanism

In the previous two sections, we have seen that it is difficult to see parameter-
setting as a process qualitatively distinct from learning. As the very notion of
parameter-setting involves alternatives, this should not be seen as particularly
surprising, but it does mean that we have so far failed to identify clearly unique
features in the *process* of first language acquisition.

If we turn our attention to principles, by definition these are universal, so it
may be that we can locate a role for a developmental process other than
learning in connection with them. That there should be such a role is far from
clear, particularly when account is taken of the fact that most theorists adopt a
version of the *Continuity Hypothesis* (see Section 3.5). In my own earlier work
(Atkinson, 1982), I saw fit to elevate this to a condition on the adequacy of
theories of language development, and others who have been persuaded of its
attractions are Pinker (1984) and Hyams (1986). In recent work, Crain (in
press) sees adherence to it as the most restrictive, and therefore most desirable,
hypothesis to adopt until it is shown to be false.

The Continuity Hypothesis, however, faces a serious conceptual problem
which is strikingly similar to that discussed in Section 8.1 for Fodor's views on
the ontogenesis of concepts. If all principles are in place from the outset, how is
it that language acquisition appears to be rather protracted and to follow a
reasonably uniform course?

A number of answers to this question can be contemplated. First, it could be
maintained that while all principles are available, they need to be 'activated' by
data and these data come in some kind of ordered sequence. We have already
seen in chapter 1 that ordered data can significantly affect learnability
problems, but we also concluded that the evidence for the existence of such
data in the first language acquisition situation is not compelling. Alternatively,
we might maintain that, while the utterances produced by adults in the
presence of children do not display any relevant ordering characteristics, the
use which children can make of these data is subject to general cognitive
constraints; perhaps data are sufficient to 'activate' principles only when these
constraints are relaxed. Or, again, it is conceivable that some kind of ordering

could be defined over principles in terms of the primitives they employ, so that there would be some 'logical' sense in which the child's system must manifest one principle before another. Borer and Wexler (1987) consider the above suggestions among others and find them all unappealing. Accepting this conclusion leaves us with the original conceptual problem.

In this book, we are obviously committed to the view that the child is innately endowed with rich and specific information about the general form of grammar. Once we accept this, an alternative response to the problem raised above suggests itself, one which involves rejection of the Continuity Hypothesis. This response simply notes the biologically uncontroversial fact that to say that some aspect of development is genetically programmed is not equivalent to saying that the relevant capacities are present at birth. It is customary to cite secondary sexual characteristics in this regard, pointing out that while their appearance is genetically determined, this appearance does not take place until puberty. There is no reason in principle why something similar should not obtain for UG, i.e. while the various principles are genetically supplied, they do not come 'on-line' until some point specified in the genetic programme. Borer and Wexler's is probably the best-known study which adopts this stance. They say (p. 124):

> The purpose of this paper is to challenge the continuity hypothesis. . . . the assumption is that certain principles mature. The principles are not available at certain stages of a child's development, and they are available at a later stage. We definitely and clearly hypothesize that the principles are *not* learned.

In this section, I shall discuss the evidence Borer and Wexler present for this perspective.[13]

Borer and Wexler are mainly concerned with the development of passives in English-speaking children. They also discuss Hebrew in the same connection as well as the development of causatives in the two languages, and I shall briefly come back to what they have to say about these topics later.

We must first distinguish two types of passive in English: adjectival and verbal passives. Many examples of participial forms can fulfil either function, and their status is only made clear in context. Thus, in (8a), *closed* is adjectival and in (8b) it is verbal:

(8) a. The door was closed when John arrived
     b. The door was closed by John

Intuitively, (8a) is used to refer to a *state* with no implicit reference to an external agent who brings that state about; (8b) is used to refer to an *action* which has an overtly expressed external agent, *John*. Clearly, if we remove the temporal adjunct or the agentive *by*-phrase, the result is ambiguous between these two interpretations:

(9) The door was closed

As well as examples like *closed*, there are participial forms which only admit the adjectival interpretation. One such, standardly cited, is *uninhabited*, and its non-verbal status is indicated by the fact that it is extremely marginal with an agentive *by*-phrase:

(10)   ??This village was uninhabited by the peasants last year

Equally, there are participles such as *seen* which do not readily have an adjectival interpretation, the evidence for this being that if such a form, somewhat uncomfortably, occurs in a short passive such as (11), the involvement of someone who was seeing appears to be strongly implied:

(11)   ?John was seen

Furthermore, while *uninhabited* and *closed* can appear in standard adjectival environments, *seen* cannot, as is indicated by the examples in (12) and (13) (for more details, see Borer and Wexler, 1987; Wasow, 1977; Williams, 1981a):

(12)   a. an uninhabited house
       b. a closed door
       c. *a seen rabbit

(13)   a. The house appears uninhabited
       b. The door appears closed
       c. *The rabbit appears seen

How is this difference between verbal and adjectival passives to be accommodated in the grammar? We have already discussed the derivation of verbal passives in some detail in Section 3.3. Recall that what this analysis requires is that a short verbal passive such as (14a) has d- and s-structures as in (14b) and (14c) respectively:

(14)   a. John was kissed
       b. *e* was kissed John
       c. John$_i$ was kissed e_i

An application of Move α, required by Case Theory, is involved in the mapping between (14b) and (14c), moving *John* from its position of internal argument of *kissed*, a Θ-position, to the external argument position, a Θ'-position for passive participles. The important observation is that verbal passives engage A-movement, a syntactic process, and lead to the formation of A-chains, exemplified by (John$_i$, e_i) in (14c).

What, then, of adjectival passives? There are a number of reasons why it seems inappropriate to derive these syntactically, despite the fact that the morphological processes involved in these and verbal passives are identical. Borer and Wexler offer a systematic account of these, but we can simply note: (i) adjectival passive participles appear to *be* adjectives; therefore, the morphological process involved has the effect of changing grammatical category and this is traditionally seen as diagnostic of a *lexical* rule operating on LRs; (ii) unlike in verbal passives, where the Θ-role associated with the external argument remains implicit when unexpressed in a *by*-phrase, this Θ-role appears to vanish entirely in adjectival passives, as witnessed by the contrasts in (15):

(15)   a. The boat was sunk [PRO to collect the reward]
       b. *The village was uninhabited [PRO to keep it clean]
       c. The door was closed by Bill₁ [PRO₁ to keep the room tidy]
       d. ?The door was closed when John arrived [PRO to keep the room tidy]

If adjectival passives were the product of syntactic rule applications, such a disappearing Θ-role would constitute a Projection Principle violation, but, again, it is a property of lexical rules that they can perform certain operations on argument structure (Williams, 1981a. See Levin and Rappaport, 1986, for a detailed discussion of adjectival passives).

The upshot of all this is that we envisage two distinct derivations for the ambiguous *the door was closed*. For the verbal passive, *close* is specified in the lexicon as a verb which assigns two Θ-roles, and the effect of passive morphology in the syntax is to 'absorb' the Θ-role associated with the external argument position and the objective Case-assigning properties of the verb. Then, the internal argument has to move to subject position to get Case from the finite I as outlined in Section 3.3. For the adjectival passive, passive morphology is applied to the base verb in the lexicon, thereby creating an adjective and entirely eliminating the Θ-role which the verb would assign to the subject position. The verb's Patient Θ-role is externalized, and the adjective then projects into syntax in a standard way. On this account, the d- and s-structures for the adjectival reading of *the door was closed* are identically represented as in (16):

(16)   [$_{NP}$the door] I [$_{VP}$was [$_{AP}$closed]]

The importance of this distinction between verbal and adjectival passives is that there is evidence that children acquiring English produce tokens of the latter considerably earlier than they produce tokens of the former. Thus, Maratsos (1983) notes that the children he studied produced and understood 'actional' passives before 'non-actional' passives. But it is a feature of 'actional' verbs that their passive participles much more readily function as adjectives than is the case for 'non-actional' verbs. This correspondence is not exact by any means in the adult grammar, but Borer and Wexler note that certain inappropriate forms produced by children, as in (17) from Horgan (1975), suggest that for them it may be fundamental:

(17)   a ball be kicked

In (17), an 'actional' verb which does not readily admit a 'state' interpretation (?*the ball is kicked*, ?*the kicked ball*) appears without an explicit agent and is most appropriately interpreted as denoting a state. Accordingly, there is evidence to suggest that Maratsos' 'actional'/'non-actional' distinction is really an adjectival/verbal distinction.

Furthermore, it is a common observation that 'long' passives, including an explicit *by*-phrase, follow 'short' passives in acquisition. Long passives are, of course, unambiguously verbal passives, whereas short passives often admit an adjectival interpretation. This, then, is at least consistent with the view that early passives are adjectival.

If we accept this proposal, we must confront the following question: why is it that verbal passives are later to develop than adjectival passives? Note first that there is no clear way to distinguish them in terms of the complexity of the morphological operations involved or the effects of these on Θ-role assignment. For the former, the addition of the passive morpheme to the stem is all that is involved in each case; for the latter, the lexical process eliminating the external Θ-role and externalizing the internal Θ-role is arguably more complex than the syntactic process which only involves absorption of the external Θ-role. Nor is there any reason to have confidence in the suggestion that the child is simply not exposed to verbal passives until relatively late in development.

What we are left with is the fact that adjectival passives are formed in the lexicon and do not involve movement and chain formation, whereas verbal passives, formed in the syntax, do involve these processes. So, let us assume that this is the crucial difference.[14] Then our original question becomes: why is access to A-chains and Θ-role assignment to such chains relatively late to develop? Borer and Wexler's answer to this is that A-chain formation *matures* and this has the consequence that at early stages of development, children are simply incapable of manipulating the structures involved in the formation of verbal passives because they lack the appropriate representational resources.

Since the child is producing ample evidence for controlling A'-movement at this stage in the form of *wh*-movement, the reference to *A-chains* in this proposal is important. It seems that A'-movement precedes A-movement in development, and it is traditional in developmental studies to ask *why* some phenomena precede or follow others and to look for an answer to this question in the nature of the phenomena themselves. Thus, returning to definitional accounts of concepts considered in Section 8.1, if concept B were acquired later than concept A and *if* concept B were defined in terms of concept A, the answer to the 'why' question would fall out of this definitional relationship. For maturational accounts, however, there is a sense in which the 'why' question is improper, at least for the psychologist and linguist if not for the biologist; there is no point in looking at the internal structure of A-movement and A'-movement and trying to develop some analytical story in terms of relationships between these structures. Rather, the reason A'-movement precedes A-movement is simply that the human mind (specifically, the language faculty) is genetically programmed to produce this order; there is nothing else to say.

If Borer and Wexler's position rested on one set of observations, the temptation to accept it might not be overwhelming. However, A-movement is a general operation involved in the derivation of a range of structures in English and other languages, so it ought to follow that there are additional reflexes of its delayed emergence.

In English, Raising constructions, illustrated by (18), involve A-movement in their derivation:

(18)   a. John seems to be happy
      b. *e* seems [John to be happy]
      c. John$_i$ seems [e_i to be happy]

At d-structure, *seem* selects a clausal complement in which the adjective *happy* assigns a Θ-role to its external argument, *John*. In this position, however, *John* cannot receive Case, since an infinitival I is not a Case-assigner, so *John* has to move to the matrix subject position, required by the Extended Projection Principle, to get nominative Case from the matrix tensed I. This movement is A-movement since the matrix subject occupies an A-position, and (*John$_i$, e$_i$*) forms an A-chain to which the adjective's Θ-role is assigned. Borer and Wexler have to predict that the child exhibits no knowledge of Raising during the period in which he or she has no verbal passives. They say (p. 150): '. . . to the best of our knowledge, this is correct.'

The distinction between adjectival and verbal passives also exists in Hebrew where it is clearly marked morphologically. However, there are no clear complexity differences between the morphological processes involved which could be invoked to account for the fact that Hebrew-speaking children also produce adjectival passives long before they produce verbal passives. Again, it is possible to argue that Hebrew verbal passives, unlike their adjectival counterparts, are syntactically derived via A-movement, and this allows us to assimilate the Hebrew facts to the same explanation.

Finally, Borer and Wexler consider the well-known observation that English-speaking children overgeneralize their use of lexical causative verbs (Bowerman, 1982). Alongside such well-formed causatives as those in (19), overgeneralized instances like (20) are found:

(19)   a. John moved the doll (= John caused the doll to move)
      b. John dropped the doll (= John caused the doll to drop)

(20)   a. John giggled the doll (= John caused the doll to giggle)
      b. John snored the doll (= John caused the doll to snore)

Borer and Wexler's account of this phenomenon relies on the distinction between unergative and unaccusative intransitive verbs introduced in Section 7.3. In terms of this distinction, *move* is unaccusative projecting the d-structure in (21), whereas *giggle* is unergative, with the d-structure in (22):

(21)   *e* [moved John]

(22)   John [giggled]

Borer and Wexler assume that causativization is a lexical process which, *in the unmarked case*, adds an external argument to a verb's LR. For adult English, this is possible in (21), since the LR projecting into this d-structure does not already contain a designated external argument. Example (22) is different, however, as the LR of *giggle* does contain such an argument, ensuring that unmarked causativization cannot operate on this representation.

Now, the derivation of *John moved* from (21) requires an application of A-movement to move *John* from its internal argument position to the external argument position. By hypothesis, the child without access to A-movement cannot derive *John moved* in this way; therefore *all* intransitive verbs at this stage must be treated as if they were unergative and appear in d-structures such as (22), their LRs being such as to make this possible. It follows that unmarked causativization cannot apply to such LRs, so in taking due account of the presence of lexical causatives in his or her primary linguistic data, the child must formulate a *marked* causativization rule which not only introduces a new external argument but also internalizes the original external argument to make room for it. But, with this account of how causativization works, the child has no basis for not extending it to *all* intransitive verbs; hence, the overgeneralizations.

What happens when the overgeneralizations cease? At some point, A-chains become available to the child and this immediately enables him or her to *represent* the unergative/unaccusative distinction.[15] With the distinction available, the child will be free to abandon the marked causativization rule and restrict the formation of lexical causatives to unaccusative verbs.

In Hebrew, overgeneralizations of this type do not disappear, persisting into the adult language as a source of neologisms. Why is this? Because, say Borer and Wexler, causativization in Hebrew is less restricted than in English and the marked alternative, adopted by the child as a matter of necessity before he or she has A-chains, is in fact a feature of the adult grammar. Therefore, the Hebrew-speaking child continues to get evidence which leads to the retention of the marked causativization rule, despite now having the representational resources to restrict it.

I have gone into considerable detail in connection with Borer and Wexler's study but not because their detailed conclusions are particularly compelling. Indeed, a number of difficulties for their account are raised in Weinberg's (1987) commentary on their paper, and Demuth (1989, 1990a), studying the acquisition of passives in Sesotho, has cast doubt on the cross-linguistic generality of their claims (see also Hoekstra, 1990, for an alternative construal of the phenomena). However, their discussion does raise a novel perspective on the notion of UG-guided language acquisition. In particular, it is clear that there is nothing *unintelligible* about the proposition that certain grammatical capacities mature. However, if a claim of this nature is to be sustained, it is necessary to identify a *range* of phenomena, the onset of which can be reliably attributed to the newly emerging capacities. A different case which plausibly satisfies this requirement will be discussed in chapter 10.

8.5 Summary

This chapter has tried to reach some conclusions on the nature of the developmental mechanisms subscribed to by proponents of PPT. It was necessary first to attempt to get a grasp of the distinction between learning and triggering as different kinds of organism–environment interactions. With this in place, we were able to conclude that the most natural construal of parameter-setting treats it as a learning process. Most fundamentally, the very notion of a parameter implies alternatives, so talk of parameter-setting as being deterministic (in the sense of unrevisable) is out of place. The position we have sought to clarify in Section 8.2 is encapsulated in a statement from Jaeggli and Safir (1989, p. 8):

> . . . if rules are constructed rather than selected from an inventory, then formulating a rule has something of the character of hypothesis testing, whereas in the parameters approach, one might conceive of the setting of parameters as more automatic and uncreative (i.e. triggers).

We have found nothing to suggest that the *qualitative* difference suggested by these remarks is sustainable. There may well be a significant *quantitative* difference, with the rule-based format making available for selection a much wider range of options, the majority of them quite implausible, but this does not detract from the qualitative similarities in the processes.

Fodor's framework also opens up the possibility that the notion of triggering may be applied 'remotely' with parameter settings being brute-causally linked in UG. However, we saw that exploitations of the 'rich deductive structure' of UG do not typically involve such linkings, and we noted that there is an incompatibility between such linkings and the methodology of PPT.

Finally, we turned our attention to principles and, more generally, representational capacities. Here, the suggestion that maturation may have a developmental role was introduced and its plausibility illustrated in connection with the acquisition of passives. Our conclusion was that there is no reason in principle to rule out maturational accounts within this framework and that, in so far as such accounts can be sustained, they do offer a non-learning perspective on the acquisition of grammar.

We thus end up with a mixed view of the developmental processes assumed by the model. Learning has a role in the setting of the parameters; but as far as principles are concerned, the options appear to be that they are available from the start or they mature. It is important that such a conclusion should not be seen as undermining in any way the substance of the PPT position. Everything we have said in this chapter is consistent with the child approaching language acquisition with a rich fund of genetically supplied information which guides his or her course. However, when this rich fund of information is confronted with a linguistic environment, there seems to be no reason to withhold the term 'learning' from what transpires. 'Triggering' is perhaps part of the rhetoric that was necessary in a climate where empiricist and behaviourist ideas were dominant. That climate is no more, so the need for the rhetoric has disappeared.

In the next chapter, we shall focus on the 'quantitative' aspects of the model, examining ways in which an inventory of parameters might be constrained.

9 Constraining Parameters

Introduction

A recurrent theme of our discussion up to now has been the desirability of somehow constraining the space of hypotheses through which children have to search in acquiring the grammar of their native language. Chapter 1 showed that the imposition of such constraints can yield positive learnability results, and the shift from the rule-based format of ST in chapter 2 to the PPT framework of chapter 3 was partially motivated by the relatively unconstrained nature of the former. Indeed, Section 3.5 included the claim that UG contains a finite set of parameters, each with a finite number of values, but we did not elaborate on this claim. From chapter 3 onwards, we have immersed ourselves in the framework, concentrating on some of the results which have been obtained and raising some of the difficulties which have emerged within this set of assumptions. It is now time to return to this question of restrictiveness, and to see what possibilities for constraining parameters are worth exploring.

A danger we must be aware of is that the postulation of parameters to account for some aspect of linguistic variation is too easy, and could readily collapse into a mere catalogue of translations of observed differences into a more fashionable mode. To be able to assess candidate parameters from some metatheoretical perspective, while not completely removing this danger, may offer a measure of protection against descriptive excess. In broad terms, we clearly expect our parameters to have a certain explanatory depth and we should be rightly suspicious of a parameter which is proposed on the basis of the properties of one construction in a single language. Jaeggli and Safir (1989, p. 39) draw attention to the risks here:

> Some accounts of preposition-stranding treat it as determined by a specific parameter with no other effects, e.g. by making P[P] a bounding node for subjacency or claiming that P is not a proper governor. Such proposals may be too descriptive if the same parameter does not also derive a number of other effects.

In what follows, I shall survey a number of possibilities for imposing overt constraints on possible parameters. Some of these have already been introduced. Thus, the Subset Condition from Section 5.5 is a condition on parameters inspired by learnability considerations, and we shall consider this and further perspectives of this type. The Lexical Parameterization Hypothesis from Section 5.4 is an attempt to fix the locus of parametric variation in one part of the grammar, and we shall see that there is more than one way of interpreting this. Before turning to these more interesting possibilities, we shall briefly discuss the prospects for constraining the *form* of parameters.

9.1 Constraining the Form of Parameters

Without committing ourselves to the need for, or appropriateness of, all of them, we list in (1) the major parameters which we have met so far:

(1)   *Parameter*   *Module*

Parameter	Module
a. Head-Direction	X-bar Theory
b. Specifier	X-bar Theory
c. Adjunct	X-bar Theory
d. [+WH] C	Move α
e. Governing Category	Binding Theory
f. Proper Antecedent	Binding Theory
g. Bounding Node	Bounding Theory
h. Direction of Case-assignment	Case Theory
i. Direction of Θ-role assignment	Θ-Theory
j. Rule R in Syntax	Theory of Empty Categories
k. AG/PRO	Theory of Empty Categories
l. Morphological Uniformity	Theory of Empty Categories

A feature of this list is that a significant number of its members are *binary*, admitting only two values. Thus all the directionality parameters (1a, b, c, h and i) are binary by virtue of the fact that linear organization allows only two directions, and (1d, j, k and l) are binary as they are concerned with the existence or non-existence of a process or property; whether a grammar requires its [+WH] Cs to be filled with *wh*-expressions at s-structure allows for only two possibilities: yes or no. The parameter in (1f) is also binary, but, in this case, there is nothing in the parameter itself which forces this requirement. Recall that the values for a proper antecedent can be either a subject or anything at all. Clearly, there is no reason in principle why there should not be a third value, according to which an anaphor can only be bound by objects and a pronoun must be free of objects. There is a sense, then, in which the binarity of (1f), if correct, is empirical when compared to the other two-valued parameters.

Binarity is what is suggested by the switch-setting analogy popularized by Chomsky, and, of course, it can be linked to the general attractiveness of binarism in the development of featural systems in phonology, syntax and semantics. At a deeper level, one could seek additional support for such a proposal by alluding to the on-off characteristics which underlie the functioning of the nervous system, a strategy explicitly adopted by Jakobson in some of his early work on distinctive features in phonetics and phonology (e.g. Jakobson, Fant and Halle, 1952).

Piattelli-Palmarini is one commentator on PPT who appears to be attracted by a fairly literal interpretation of switch-setting. He says (1989, p. 3):

> What now replaces learning everywhere in biology has nothing to do with a transfer of structure and everything to do with mechanisms of internal selection and filtering affecting a pre-programmed chain of multiple internal recombinations and internal 'switches.' As we shall see, the basic model of acquisition [of language] is best captured by the notion of a hierarchical fixation of internal parameters. Since there are many such parameters and each can be 'set' on only one of a small number of admissible values (for many linguistic parameters there seem to be just two such possible values), the final outcome of the process is not pre-determined.

Unfortunately, there are obvious exceptions to binarity in our list. These are (1e) and (1g). So, in Section 5.2, we saw that there is considerable justification for suggesting that the GCP is five-valued, and in Section 3.4, we briefly illustrated that the parameterization of Bounding Node appears to require at least three values: {NP, S, S′}, {NP, S} and {NP, S′}. Going beyond the parameters we have considered, M. Baker (1988a), in his lengthy discussion of the Case-assigning properties of verbs in a range of Bantu languages, raises the possibility that the normal situation of verbs assigning a single structural objective Case must be supplemented by verbs in some languages which assign *two* such structural Cases and by verbs in other languages which assign one structural Case *and* one inherent Case. If the Case-assignment properties of verbs are an appropriate locus of parameterization, this suggests the need for a three-valued parameter here.

Overall, then, it seems that there is little prospect of being able to *require* that parameters be binary. It may be that those which are share a cluster of other properties, an issue that will be alluded to again below (see Atkinson, 1990, for more discussion).

9.2 Learning-Theoretic Constraints: The Subset Condition

It is natural to assume that the theory of parameters should be constrained to ensure that all parameters are learnable, in the sense that empirically plausible exposure to primary linguistic data should be sufficient to fix their appropriate values (although see Chomsky's views on this, chapter 3, note 50). In this and the next section, we shall consider ways in which this requirement might be imposed on the set of parameters.

Recall that in Section 5.5, we introduced Wexler and Manzini's (1987) Subset Condition, which is repeated here as (2):

(2)   For every parameter p and every two values i, j of p, the languages generated under the two values of the parameter are one a subset of the other, that is $L(p(i)) \subset L(p(j))$ or $L(p(j)) \subset L(p(i))$.

In our earlier discussion, we spent some time attempting to understand Wexler and Manzini's interpretation of (2), concluding that as it stands, (2) constitutes an extremely strong condition on possible parameters. But we also noted that Wexler and Manzini appear to acknowledge that it cannot be maintained in this form, and that once it is relativized, it ceases to have any interesting content. Our task in this section is to explore the issue of whether it can be maintained.

Before embarking on this, it is appropriate to provide a word of clarification regarding the status of (2) from the perspective of learnability. Clearly, (2) as a constraint on parameters and their values does not guarantee learnability. In fact, as pointed out in Section 5.5, (2) is a counter-intuitive requirement from this point of view. What (2) does, if it is correct, is necessitate the Subset Principle as a feature of the learning module. So (2) does not derive its status directly from learnability considerations. Rather, it emerges as a correct or incorrect generalization on the basis of consideration of attested parameters. If some parameters give rise to set-theoretically nested languages, the Subset Condition is the empirical hypothesis that all do.

It is also important to note that the plausibility of the Subset Condition (and the Subset Principle), like conditions we shall attend to in the next section, is crucially related to assumptions about the data available to the child. Our old friend, the No Negative Data Assumption, provides this initial plausibility. Without this assumption, set-theoretically nested languages would not produce principled learnability problems, the Subset Principle would not be a necessary component of the learning module and the Subset Condition would not embody a motivated empirical hypothesis. What, then, is the state of the evidence with respect to the Subset Condition? We can consider this in the light of our list of parameters in (1).

First, we have seen in chapter 5 that (1e) and (1f), the Binding Theory parameters, satisfy (2). Second, (1g), the parameter fixing the set of bounding nodes in a grammar, appears to produce values satisfying (2). The three values we introduced for this parameter in Section 3.4 are reproduced in (3):

(3)   a. {NP, S, S'} − Russian
      b. {NP, S}   − English
      c. {NP, S'}   − Italian

A moment's reflection and consultation of the examples provided in Section 3.4 should be sufficient to convince the reader that the proper inclusions in (4) obtain:

(4) $L(a) \subset L(b) \subset L(c)$

The Morphological Uniformity Parameter (1l) is a slightly more complex case. Recall that Hyams (1987a) and Jaeggli and Hyams (1987) suggest that an initial setting at [+uniform] can be justified on learnability grounds, since positive data will always be available to show that [−uniform] is the required setting. This is uncontentious, but whether it is appropriate to see [±uniform] as satisfying the Subset Condition is not absolutely clear. To see this, note first that the Subset Condition requires subset relations to obtain between *languages*, where this notion is understood in an abstract, but intelligible, way for the Binding Theory parameters (cf. chapter 5, note 6). The [±uniform] parameter applies first and foremost to *forms* in verbal paradigms, and it is probably necessary to extend the scope of (2) to include such sets of forms if the condition is to be satisfied. Let us see why this is so.

There are two ways in which a paradigm can be morphologically uniform, which we shall refer to as the Chinese way and the Italian way. Assume a child is being exposed to a [−uniform] language in which the correct paradigm contains the set of forms in (5):

(5)   {STEM, STEM + AFFIX$_1$, . . ., STEM + AFFIX$_n$}

Since morphological uniformity is simply concerned with the presence or absence of inflections, this can be reduced to (6):

(6)   {STEM, STEM + AFFIX}

If the child adopts the setting [+uniform] in the Chinese way, he or she has the set of forms in (7):

(7)   {STEM}

The set in (7) is a subset of the set in (6), so the Subset Condition is satisfied by sets of forms. Alternatively, if the initial setting is in the Italian way, the child has the set of forms in (8):

(8)   {STEM + AFFIX}

Again, (8) is a subset of (6) and the Subset Condition is satisfied. What happens if we attempt to extend this sort of reasoning to the sentences in which forms from the paradigm occur?

The answer to this depends on the level of abstraction we choose for representing these sentences. To see this, consider again the child who starts off in the Chinese way. If we suppress *all* reference to material other than the members of the paradigm in our characterization of sentences, again the Subset Condition is satisfied. The child has the sentences in (9) and the target language has the sentences in (10):

(9)   {. . . STEM . . .}

(10)   {. . . STEM . . ., . . . STEM + AFFIX . . .}

Of course, these are no more than notational variants on (7) and (6). If, however, we contemplate the subset computations being performed on less skeletal sentence representations, we get different outcomes depending on just what we decide to include. So, assume that we decide to include a subject NP with no differentiation of its grammatical features. We get (11) and (12) and again the Subset Condition is satisfied on sets of sentences (recall that these representations might also abstract away from linear order if this is necessary):

(11)   {NP – STEM . . .}

(12)   {NP – STEM . . ., NP – STEM + AFFIX . . .}

Alternatively, suppose that the mixed target language exhibits agreement with a Third Person Singular subject, and we decide to include this information in our representation of sentences for the purposes of assessing whether the Subset Condition is satisfied. In this case, the child's [+uniform] setting in the Chinese way ensures that the relevant set of sentences includes (13):

(13)   NP[Third Person Singular] – STEM . . .

The target grammar, on the other hand, does *not* permit (13), but *does* allow (14) which is not in the relevant set of sentences for the child:

(14)   NP[Third Person Singular] – STEM + AFFIX . . .

In this situation, then, the sets of sentences are *disjoint* and the Subset Condition is not satisfied, and it is easy to see how to construct similar scenarios for the child who sets off with the Italian way.

This shows that the choice of the level of abstraction adopted in our representation of sentences can affect the satisfaction of the Subset Condition. On the assumption that no independent motivation can be readily adduced for favouring one or other such level, I conclude that the most natural way to link the condition to the morphological uniformity parameter is to extend it to include reference to sets of forms.

Consider next other formulations of the parameter determining the distribution of null subjects, in particular the AG/PRO parameter of Hyams (1986, 1987c).[1] Recall that a setting of +AG/PRO licenses *pro* subjects, and it immediately follows that the set of sentences in a +AG/PRO grammar is a superset of those in a –AG/PRO grammar. Once again the Subset Condition is satisfied. There are, however, complications raised in this case by the interaction of the Subset Condition and the Subset Principle.

As the Subset Condition is satisfied by the AG/PRO parameter, the Subset Principle requires the child initially to adopt the unmarked, most restrictive value. This is –AG/PRO, the correct setting for English. Hyams, however, maintains that the initial setting is the Italian value of +AG/PRO, i.e. the child begins with a superset language. Her response to this dilemma is to withdraw from the position that the AG/PRO parameter satisfies the Subset Condition.

First, it is clear that a +AG/PRO language like Italian contains sentences which are not well-formed in English, viz. those with *pro* subjects in tensed clauses. However, English also contains sentences which do not occur in Italian, notably those including preposed auxiliary verbs in questions and those containing expletive subjects. Arguably, then, +AG/PRO does *not* satisfy the Subset Condition, since the languages determined by the two values of the parameter are intersecting.[2]

Turning now to the remaining parameters in (1), the prospects for a general restrictive role for the Subset Condition look rather bleak.

This pessimism is most obviously justified in the case of the directionality parameters (1a, b, c, h, i). Consider the Head-Direction Parameter and, for the sake of simplicity, assume that it is set once and for all for a language at either left or right. The languages which result from these settings are obviously not in a nested subset relationship; indeed, under our simplifying assumption, they are disjoint. If we drop the simplifying assumption and suppose that the parameter has to be set several times, perhaps in different ways for different categories, nothing crucial is affected, since the sets of structures (the languages) relevant to the set-theoretic computations will be correspondingly restricted and again disjointness will be the outcome. Obviously, this consideration extends to all the directionality parameters in (1).

Another example leading to the same conclusion is (1d), the parameterization of Move α. A set of s-structures in which [+WH] C positions are required to be filled by *wh*-expressions is neither a subset nor a superset of one which lacks this requirement. English and Chinese have s-structures of these types, and it follows that in the relevant respects the two settings of (1d) give rise to disjoint languages.

Overall, then, it seems that we are not justified in imposing (2) as a condition on possible parameters, a conclusion which is almost certainly responsible for Wexler and Manzini's somewhat ambivalent attitude to (2) discussed in Section 5.5. In the next section, we shall consider whether rather different procedural considerations might serve to constrain parametric theory.[3]

9.3 Learning-Theoretic Constraints: Degree-*n* Learnability

In Section 2.3, we discussed the degree-2 learnability proof of Wexler and Culicover (1980), and in Section 2.4, we outlined how by enriching assumptions about the data available to the learner, Morgan (1986) was able to strengthen this to a degree-1 proof. While we have subsequently argued that the grammatical assumptions within which these proofs were constructed were inadequately constrained, the idea that grammars should be attainable on the basis of relatively simple data remains an attractive one, and in this section we shall consider how this might be pursued and what its implications are for the theory of parameters.

It seems initially plausible to suggest that if the different values of a parameter have detectable effects only on extremely complex data, the assumption that the child does not have access to such data forces the conclusion that these values could never be fixed. Accordingly, we can define a condition, the Degree-*n* Condition, on parameters and their values, as in (15):

(15)   There is an n ($n \geq 0$) such that for any parameter p and any values i, j of p, there is a primary linguistic datum d of degree less than or equal to n such that d does not belong to $L(p(i)) \cap L(p(j))$.

This condition is independent of the Subset Condition in the sense that it is operative when the latter is not satisfied and imposes additional restrictions on parameter values when it is.

To see this, consider again the relevantly different set-theoretic relations which can obtain between languages characterized by a pair of parameter values. The diagram in (16) represents the situation when the languages are disjoint.

(16)

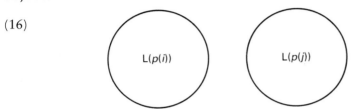

In these circumstances, the Subset Condition is not satisfied and the Degree-n Condition is satisfied vacuously for any n. Any datum from $L(p(i))$ or $L(p(j))$ can fulfil the role of d in (15). In particular, assuming that $L(p(i))$ and $L(p(j))$ contain degree-0 data, (15) will be satisfied with $n = 0$.

The second possibility, with intersecting languages, is represented in (17).

(17)

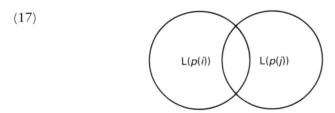

Again, the Subset Condition is not applicable, but the Degree-n Condition is. Its effect is to rule out the possibility of (17) when *all* data of degree less than or equal to n are contained in $L(p(i)) \cap L(p(j))$. In these circumstances, the only data which would serve to inform the child that his or her parameter-setting was incorrect would be of degree greater than n and the Degree-n Condition would not be satisfied.

Finally, we have the circumstances in which the Subset Condition is satisfied in (18).

(18)

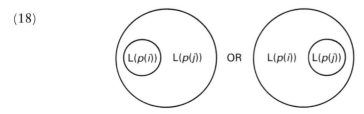

The Degree-n Condition also applies to this situation, requiring that if, say, $L(p(i)) \subset L(p(j))$, then there is a datum of degree less than or equal to n which belongs to $L(p(j))$ but not to $L(p(i))$, i.e. $L(p(i))$ does not include *all* the 'simple' data from $L(p(j))$.

Of course, the Degree-n Condition is not a single condition, since we can set n at any value we please and have a perfectly coherent constraint. It is therefore an interesting empirical issue as to whether n can be fixed at some plausibly small value when we take account of a range of parameters. For example, if we return to the list in (1), it is clear that the majority of these can be straightforwardly set on the basis of degree-0 data, i.e. simple, non-embedded clauses. The only apparent exceptions to this are the Binding Theory Parameters and the Bounding Theory Parameter.[4]

Lightfoot (1989) discusses whether *all* parameters might be set on the basis of degree-0 data, and the remainder of this section is devoted to the form of his speculations.

Before embarking on this, it is important to distinguish the enterprise from the learnability *proofs* sketched in chapter 2. As Williams (1989, p. 363) puts it:

> Wexler and Culicover proved a theorem about a general rule writing system, whereas Lightfoot has defended an empirical speculation about a system whose general properties are not known. So Lightfoot's results should not be seen as an 'improvement' on Wexler and Culicover's theorem, but rather a different kind of contribution.

Lightfoot considers three cases of parameter-setting which would initially appear to require access to complex data. Since the third of these requires acquaintance with complexities in the Binding Theory we have avoided here, I shall restrict myself to what he has to say about the first two. We shall have occasion to mention the general characteristics of the third parameter informally in the next chapter.

It was suggested above that parameterization of the set of bounding nodes in the Subjacency Principle appears likely to be problematic for the proposal that parameters can be set on the basis of degree-0 data. Recall that in Section 3.4, we introduced this topic, citing an example from Rizzi (1982), repeated here as (19):

(19)   Tuo fratello, a cui mi domando che storie abbiano raccontato, era molto preoccupato
       'Your brother, to whom I wonder which stories they have told, was very worried'

In (19), *a cui* has been moved over two S-boundaries, violating Subjacency so long as S is a bounding node in Italian. Rizzi's suggestion is that Subjacency should be saved by postulating that S' rather than S is a bounding node in this language.

As noted in the previous section, the Subset Condition appears to be satisfied by this parameter, therefore the logic of learnability requires the Subset Principle to apply, with the child's first hypothesis identifying the set of bounding nodes with {NP, S}.[5] English-speaking children will never receive data leading them to modify this hypothesis, but Italian-speaking children will eventually be exposed to such examples as (19), leading them to replace S by S' in the set of bounding nodes. But (19) is not a degree-0 datum and if exposure to examples of this type is necessary, degree-0 learnability cannot be sustained.

In response to this situation, Lightfoot considers French, which is like Italian in allowing movement of a *wh*-expression out of an indirect question.[6] Sportiche (1981) illustrates this with (20):

(20)   Voila une liste des gens a qui on n'a pas encore trouvé quoi envoyer
        'Here's a list of the people to whom we've not yet found what to send'

The s-structure of the relative clause in (20) is as in (21):

(21)   [a qui$_i$][$_S$on n'a pas encore trouvé [$_S$·[quoi$_j$][$_S$envoyer e_j e_i]]]

In order for *a qui* to get to the matrix C-position, it must traverse two S-boundaries, thereby violating Subjacency on the English setting for bounding nodes. If, however, French follows Italian in having the {NP, S'} setting for bounding nodes, no violation results, as the movement in question crosses only one S'.

The question Lightfoot poses is: assuming that {NP, S} is the child's initial hypothesis for the set of bounding nodes, are there degree-0 data which will occasion resetting of the parameter for the French child? He believes that this question can be answered affirmatively. Consider (22) with its s-structure in (23):

(22)   Combien as-tu vu de personnes
        'How many people did you see?'

(23)   combien$_i$[$_S$as-tu vu [$_{NP}$ e_i [$_{N'}$de personnes]]]

In (23), *combien* originates as specifier of the NP *combien de personnes* and must traverse NP and S boundaries to get to the clause-initial C- position. But if the bounding node parameter is set at {NP, S}, this ought not to be possible. It is possible; therefore the parameter is wrongly set at {NP, S}. If the next less restrictive option is {NP, S'}, the child adopts it, and the bounding node parameter is successfully set on the basis of a degree-0 datum.[7]

Lightfoot's second example concerns differences between English and Dutch with respect to extraction from the subject position of sentential complements. Consider the following data:

(24)   Who do you think had read the book?

(25)   *Who do you think that had read the book?

(26)   Wie denk je dat het boek gelesen had?
       who think you that the book read had
       'Who do you think that had read the book?'

Examples (24) and (25) illustrate something we have already seen: that
extraction of a *wh*-expression from this position is possible in English just so
long as there is no overt complementizer introducing the embedded clause.
Example (26) shows that in Dutch, despite the fact that such a complementizer
must be present, its presence does not prevent the movement taking place.

In Section 3.3, we introduced the Empty Category Principle and gave an
outline of how it accounted for the English contrast. To reiterate, we assume
that (24) and (25) have s-structures along the lines of (27) and (28):

(27)   [who$_i$][$_S$do you think [$_{S'}$[e$_i$]$_i$ [$_S$ e$_i$ had read the book]]]

(28)   [who$_i$][$_S$do you think [$_{S'}$[that$_j$ e$_i$] [$_S$ e$_i$ had read the book]]]

In (27), the e_i in embedded subject position is properly governed by the
immediately preceding C by virtue of co-indexing; in (28), this same e_i is not
properly governed since the C immediately preceding it lacks an index as it
contains differently indexed items. Thus, (28) contains a violation of the ECP
and (25) is ill-formed.

Now consider the Dutch example in (26). We can account for this if we
assume that the mechanism by which complementizers receive their indices is
parameterized. Specifically, we can suggest that in Dutch the index of an empty
category can percolate upwards to the C containing it irrespective of the
presence of an overt complementizer bearing a different index, whereas this is
not so in English. Adopting this proposal, the s-structure of (26) is (29):

(29)   [wie$_i$][$_S$denk je [$_{S'}$[e$_i$ dat$_j$]$_i$ [$_S$ e$_i$ het boek gelesen had]]]

In (29), the e_i in embedded subject position is properly governed by virtue of
the immediately preceding position bearing the index *i*.

Now, whether this proposal is correct or not, the relevant distinction
between English and Dutch has only been revealed so far on degree-1 data,
viz. (25) vs (26). Is it also signalled by degree-0 data?

Lightfoot maintains that it is, citing the claim of Koopman (1983) that in
Dutch *wh*-questions, the finite verb moves along with the *wh*-phrase into the
clause-initial C-position. Recall that in chapter 4, we briefly alluded to
standard accounts of the syntax of German, which assume that in d-structure
the verb appears in final position. Dutch is similar to German in the relevant
respects, so we have a contrast between the English sentence (30a), with its
s-structure (30b), and the Dutch (31a, b):

(30)   a. Who has read the book?
       b. [who$_i$] [e$_i$ has read the book]

(31)   a. Wie heeft het boek gelesen?
            who has the book read
            'Who has read the book?'

       b. [wie$_i$ heeft$_j$]$_i$ [e$_i$ het boek gelesen e$_j$]

If e_i in (31b) is to satisfy the ECP, it must be properly governed from C. This is only possible if C is co-indexed with it. But if this is so, the index of *wie* must be able to percolate upwards despite the presence of additional material (*heeft*) bearing a different index in C. Example (31a) is a degree-0 datum, and if the child knows that the d-structure order of Dutch clauses is verb-final, it must have the analysis in (31b). But then satisfaction of the ECP, a universal principle, requires indexing of C in Dutch to have the described properties, i.e. the parameter can be fixed on the basis of a degree-0 datum.

Having developed the case for degree-0 parameter-setting, Lightfoot in fact retreats from it in the face of certain cross-linguistic contrasts which appear to require that the child be exposed to degree-1 data. For example, English is unusual in allowing a phenomenon of Exceptional Case Marking, whereby certain verbs can assign objective Case to an embedded subject. This is illustrated by (32):

(32)   John expects [him to arrive on time]

As the embedded clause is non-finite, *him* cannot receive Case from a finite I (if it could, this Case would be nominative). But *expects* does not govern *him* since a maximal projection boundary (S′) intervenes between these two items. Since Case-assignment takes place under government (see Section 3.3), it follows that *him* ought to fail to satisfy the Case Filter and (32) should be ill-formed. Whatever technical devices are invoked to deal with this difficulty, PPT would require the postulation of a parameter distinguishing English from languages which lack Exceptional Case Marking. But this parameter would require access to data like (32) in order to be correctly set for English. Lightfoot says (pp. 330–1):

> Such phenomena require that children have access to at least the front of an embedded clause in order to set some parameters. This would suggest that the notion of degree-0 needs to be amended to 0-plus-a-little . . .

Much of his subsequent discussion is devoted to recasting this notion of '0-plus-a-little' as an unembedded binding domain, but it would take us too far afield to pursue this here.[8]

How are we to evaluate Lightfoot's proposals? There is a sense in which he is surely on the right track. Morgan (1989) presents a statistical analysis of the speech used by mothers when addressing the children studied by Brown (1973). The broad outlines of this are that about 90 per cent of the mothers' utterances are degree-0 and less than 1 per cent degree-2 or more. On this basis, it seems reasonable to conclude that the setting of parameters does not require degree-2 data. However, a number of commentators have suggested that Lightfoot's requirement of 'degree-0-plus-a-little' is too severe (C. L. Baker, 1989; Wasow, 1989; Wilkins, 1989). Once the 'front' of an embedded clause has been acknowledged as relevant, there appears to be no strong conceptual reason to exclude the 'back', and as Morgan's figures suggest that degree-1 data are far from scarce in the child's linguistic experience, it is not clear that anything substantial is lost by suggesting that n in (15) should be fixed at 1.[9]

There is a sense in which, from our point of view, whether n is fixed at 0 or 1 is incidental. The logic of the move remains intact and the empirical issues to be resolved remain the same: do findings on the nature of primary linguistic data mesh with the value assumed; and can any postulated parameter be set on the basis of the assumption?

In the final section of this chapter, we shall consider whether it is possible to restrict the *locus* of parametric variation to specific points in the theory of grammar. Specifically, we shall examine a proposal which, if correct, ensures the finiteness of the class of possible grammars. It is important to be clear that the issues we have discussed in this section are independent of those that follow; even if we find that grammars do vary only at certain loci, it will still be necessary to take account of procedural considerations in considering how parameters are set.

9.4 The Lexical Parameterization Hypothesis

In Section 3.4 we discussed evidence indicating that some parameterization is necessary in most of the modules familiarly recognized in PPT, and a summary of the major parameters introduced there and subsequently in this book appeared as (1) in this chapter. From this perspective, there is no reason to be optimistic that parameterization can be restricted to a designated subset of modules. Indeed, the whole ethos of the theory would suggest that the opposite is the case. However, there is an alternative way in which parameterization may be localized, and to see this we have to return to our discussion of Binding Theory parameters in chapter 5.

Recall that having initially assumed that values of the GCP were associated with *languages*, we noted that within a single language individual anaphors and pronouns seemed to require *different* values of this parameter. Particularly, we observed that the Icelandic anaphor *sig* is associated with value (d), while the pronoun *hann* from the same language is associated with value (c). Such observations led Wexler and Manzini (1987) and Manzini and Wexler (1987), developing suggestions which were originally made by Borer (1984), to propose the Lexical Parameterization Hypothesis (LPH), repeated here as (33):

(33)   Values of a parameter are associated not with particular languages but with particular lexical items in a language.

According to (33), then, the (partial) LRs of *himself*, *him*, *sig* and *hann* will be along the lines of (34):

(34) a. *himself*: N; [+anaphor, −pronominal, Governing Category (a), . .]
     b. *him*: N; [−anaphor, +pronominal, Governing Category (a), . .]
     c.*sig*: N; [+anaphor, −pronominal], Governing Category (d), . .]
     d. *hann*: N; [−anaphor, +pronominal, Governing Category (c), . .]

The attractiveness of this proposal, beyond the fact that it appears to be necessary for the Binding Theory parameters, is not difficult to discern. Everyone agrees that lexical items and their properties have to be learned. If learning is identified with fixing parameter values (cf. Section 8.2), it follows that locating the source of parametric variation in the properties of lexical items puts the *need* for learning exactly where we know learning to be required on independent grounds. Furthermore, since there is only a finite number of lexical items in any language, and making the reasonable assumption that each of these is associated with only a finite number of parameter values, it follows that the scope for grammatical variation is fixed within finite limits.

To the extent that (33) can be maintained, we have a situation which is described by Chomsky (1989, p. 44) in the following terms:

> We distinguish the lexicon from the computational system of the language . . . It has been suggested that parameters of UG do not relate to the computational system but only to the lexicon. . . . If this proposal can be maintained in a natural form, there is only one human language, apart from the lexicon, and language acquisition is in essence a matter of determining lexical idiosyncrasies.

Of course, in this passage, 'language' has to be understood as I-language in the sense of Section 1.5. At the very least, this is a provocative suggestion. Can it be maintained?

To approach this question, let us return to our set of parameters in (1). Obviously (1e) and (1f) fall under (33), as they provided Wexler and Manzini with the initial motivation for lexical parameterization. Parameters (1j, k, l) are also accommodated by this restriction if we assume, as we must, that inflectional morphemes have lexical entries. It is then natural to suggest that the content of (1j) can be captured by including in the lexical entry of a verbal inflection an indication of whether or not it can undergo Rule R in syntax; for (1k), each agreement morpheme will be specified as to whether or not it is to be identified with PRO; for (1l), each inflectional morpheme will include in its lexical entry an indication of whether or not it is realized in a uniform paradigm.

Parameter (1d) is less straightforward, since we interpreted it as a condition on C-positions (whether or not they must be filled by *wh*-expressions at s-structure) rather than as a condition on *wh*-expressions themselves. From the latter perspective, (1d) would not be a problem for (33), since we could suppose that the lexical entries for *wh*-expressions could contain (parameterizable) information about their s-structure positions, so we might maintain that the difficulty here is one of detail and not of principle.

Obviously, the directionality parameters (1a, b, c, h, i) are consistent with (33), since there is no inherent reason why the lexical entry for, say, a verb or a preposition should not contain information about whether it precedes or follows its complements or whether it assigns Case and Θ-role(s) to left or right. This leaves (1g), the parameter determining the language-specific effects of the Subjacency Principle, and it is not clear that this can be accommodated under (33). But, despite the fact that Subjacency has had a significant role to play in the development of PPT and has been alluded to several times in this book, recent work has suggested that it has some peculiar properties. It may be that these will eventually lead to its eclipse, so for the sake of argument, I shall assume that an initial survey of the evidence regarding (33) is encouraging, and go on to discuss some of the difficulties it must confront.[10]

Safir (1987), commenting on Wexler and Manzini (1987), notes that the Subset Principle is designed to prevent the child from adopting an overgeneral hypothesis from which he or she is subsequently incapable of retreating. The Independence Principle, necessary for the Subset Principle to work, and the LPH, motivated by empirical observations, are additional components of the Wexler and Manzini theory, and Safir is concerned that both of these run the risk of leading the child to *undergeneralize*. We have already dealt with the problems raised by the Independence Principle in Section 5.5, and here we are concerned only with lexical parameterization.

Above, we noted that the majority of parameters from (1) appeared to be compatible with (33). However, we did not draw attention to one uncomfortable aspect of this compatibility. To appreciate this clearly, consider again (1i), the parameter determining direction of Θ-role assignment. While there is nothing incoherent in assuming that the value of this parameter is specified in the lexical entry for each Θ-role assigner in the language, suggesting that language acquisition proceeds on an item-by-item basis in this area looks profoundly unattractive. Consider the case of verbs in English. Uniformly, they assign their internal Θ-role to the right. Furthermore, so long as they have objective Case to assign (recall that not all verbs do, e.g. passives and unaccusatives), this is also assigned to the right. Clearly, to suggest that the child must learn these properties of each verb individually is totally at odds with the PPT framework, which assumes that exposure to a small amount of primary linguistic data can have far-reaching consequences. The LPH appears to deprive the child access to some of the most robust generalizations in the theory.[11]

What are we to make of this? One possibility, briefly discussed by Safir, is to propose that there may be two distinct types of parameter. He notes that parameters for which the LPH appears to be correct (specifically, those of the Binding Theory) are also those which motivate the Subset Principle. Other parameters, most notably those determining directionality, do not characterize nested languages (cf. Section 9.2), nor does it seem appropriate to regard them as involving lexical parameterization. Conceivably, these properties could be further correlated with binarity/non-binarity, and obviously consistent correlations of this kind across a wide range of parameters would be of considerable interest and would call for explanation. For now, however, it remains a speculative suggestion.

An alternative is to weaken the LPH so as to allow lexical *categories* as well as lexical items themselves to be parameterized. That Wexler supports something along these lines is clear from Chien and Wexler (1990, p. 227, note 1): 'It is quite likely that properties of lexical *categories* can also vary and must be learned.' If this is what we understand by lexical parameterization, the directionality parameters cease to be a problem, since a statement like (35) now falls under LPH:

(35)   Members of the category V assign Case/Θ-role to the left/right

But it is important to be clear that with this move the conceptual underpinnings of lexical parameterization are severely weakened. There *is* now learning going on beyond lexical items and their properties, so the original manoeuvre of restricting learning to where it is independently known to be needed cannot be sustained. Of course, the LPH, extended to include lexical categories, might still impose substantial constraints on the locus of language variation. We shall return to this in the next chapter when we consider an alternative method for developing a constrained theory of parameters.

9.5 Summary

In this chapter we have considered three ways in which a theory of parameters might be constrained. In pursuing this, we have been trying to take seriously Safir's (1987, p. 77) concern that 'our assumptions about what counts as a 'possible parameter' or a 'learnable parameter' remain very weak'.

Three types of constraint were considered, and while each of them led us to consider novel issues, it is probably true to say that none of them can be accepted without rather extensive reservations. There is no reason to believe at the moment that the formal properties of parameters will be a fertile source of constraints. The Subset Condition has numerous exceptions, and these, coupled with the difficulties raised in chapter 5, suggest that as a UG constraint it has no future.[12] The Degree-*n* Condition, on the other hand, looks as if it has to be correct for some fairly small *n* if parameters are to be learnable. Whether *n* should be fixed at 0 or 1 or whether the appropriate restriction should be stated in terms of a structural notion like government domain rather than degree of embedding is a question which cannot be answered at present.

Finally, the conceptual attractiveness of restricting parameterization to the properties of lexical items is clear. However, this idea appears to give rise to a number of undergeneralization problems. Modification of the hypothesis to take account of these involves a reduction in conceptual attractiveness. Conceptual attractiveness of a rather different kind is enjoyed by the Functional Parameterization Hypothesis. To introduce this, it will be necessary to cash in some of the promissory notes which have appeared throughout this book. We shall do this in the next chapter.

10   Functional Categories and the Functional Parameterization Hypothesis

Introduction

An issue which has appeared implicitly on a number of occasions in earlier chapters is the importance in the theory of language acquisition of grammatical entities such as Inflection, Agreement, Tense and Complementizer. For example, our discussion of null subjects in chapter 4 centred around properties of I in different languages, and we have several times adverted to the complexities surrounding the suggestion that moved *wh*-expressions have the clause-initial C-position as their target. In recent syntactic research, considerable emphasis has been placed on understanding the properties of these and other items, which are collectively referred to as *functional categories*. If this work had stayed within the confines of grammatical theory, it would be of marginal interest to this book. But some current speculations suggest that it may be of fundamental importance in understanding the early stages of language acquisition, so it seems appropriate to attempt to come to terms with it here.

A suggestion which links this chapter to the previous one appears in Chomsky (1989). Having formulated a version of the LPH cited earlier (p. 233), he goes on in the following terms (p. 44):

> Properties of the lexicon too are sharply constrained, by UG or other systems of the mind/brain. If substantive elements (verbs, nouns, etc.) are drawn from an invariant universal vocabulary, then *only functional elements will be parameterized.* (my emphasis – MA)

What we have here is a statement of the Functional Parameterization Hypothesis (FPH).

A second suggestion has emerged in the first language acquisition literature and finds its most complete and well-argued statement in Radford (1990a) (see also Lebeaux, 1988; Kazman, 1988; Guilfoyle and Noonan, 1989; Radford, 1988b, 1990b; Platzack, 1990). This is that at a certain (early) stage of development, children's linguistic systems show no evidence of such functional categories, i.e. there is a pre-functional stage in acquisition. There is a sense in which such an observation is not new, and it can be linked to Brown and Fraser's (1963) characterization of early child speech as 'telegraphic'. However, it is distinguished from this traditional claim by being embedded in a sophisticated theory of grammatical structure, and as such, it is possible to pursue its consequences in a novel way.

This chapter considers the above suggestions and issues arising from them. Before this, however, it is necessary to provide a little background on the status of functional categories in linguistic theory and this is where we begin.

10.1 Functional Categories in the Theory of Grammar

In Section 3.3, when introducing the Projection Principle, we noted in passing certain anomalies which ensured that the nature of d-structures could not be entirely explicated in terms of the projection of lexical properties and parameterized X-bar principles. Specifically, we drew attention to the structure of clauses, noting that standard formulations of PPT supplement these notions with the *rule* in (1):

(1)   S → NP – I – VP

Furthermore, consideration of where moved *wh*-expressions end up at s-structure led to the postulation of a further *rule*:

(2)   S′ → C – S

According to (1) and (2), then, the bracketed embedded clause in (3) is assigned the structure in (4):

(3)   John believes [that Mary will kiss Bill]

(4)   [$_{S'}$[$_C$ that][$_S$ [$_{NP}$Mary] [$_I$will] [$_{VP}$kiss Bill]]]

From the point of view of the X-bar principles, (4) is quite anomalous. Recall that these principles require constructions to be *endocentric* and this is achieved by stipulating that members of a category X project into X′ by the addition of one or more complements, which in turn projects into X″ by the addition of a specifier (we omit discussion of adjuncts here). But in (4), S is not a projection of any of its contained expressions, i.e. it is an *exocentric* construction, nor does I project to any higher level. Additionally, it is a feature of the X-bar system that complements and specifiers are themselves maximal projections. However, in (4), C is like I in not projecting to a higher bar-level. Furthermore, S, while partly assimilated to the X-bar system by projecting to S′, is also eccentric in that other categories project to the double-bar level, i.e. in (4), there is no provision for a specifier as a sister of S′. Finally, whereas there is ample evidence that English is head-initial with members of V, N, A and P taking complements on their right, S appears to be head-final in (4) with its 'complement' C occurring on its left. Of course, these anomalies are a direct reflection of the fact that a residue of rules (1) and (2) was retained for articulating clausal structure.

Chomsky (1986b), developing earlier work of Stowell (1981), addressed these anomalies surrounding I and C, and the ideas he proposed in this regard are now generally accepted by those working in PPT. He suggested that the principles of X-bar Theory should be straightforwardly extended to these functional categories, i.e. I and C should both project single-bar and maximal projections exactly like the familiar lexical categories. The problematic S should be replaced by IP, representing the maximal projection of I, and S′ should be similarly replaced by CP, representing the maximal projection of C. The schematic picture of clause structure which these suggestions require is as in (5).[1]

(5)

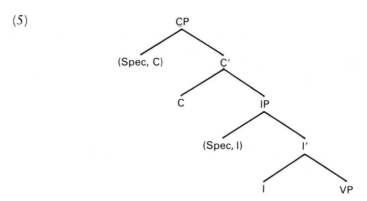

In (5), the labels (Spec, C) and (Spec, I) are simply used for clarity, as these notations have no formal status in grammatical representations. Now, (5) obviously solves our conceptual problems. I and C are both assimilated to the X-bar principles. In particular, both now project appropriate phrasal expansions (I′, IP, C′, CP), both select a complement to the right (I selects a VP, C selects an IP), this complement is itself a maximal projection (VP, IP), and both are associated with a specifier position. We shall return to (Spec, C) presently, but as far as (Spec, I) is concerned, the obvious suggestion is that this should be the position of the subject and filled by a maximal projection. Thus, ignoring C and its projections, the d-structure for a simple clause like that in (6) will be (7):

(6)   John will kiss Mary

(7) $[_{IP} [_{NP}$John$] [_{I'} [_{I}$will$][_{VP}$kiss Mary$]]]$

The question we must now ask is whether there is any empirical justification for the structure outlined in (5). In particular, we might feel that unless some justification can be provided for the extended set of positions made available in (5), it remains little more than an aesthetically pleasing manoeuvre.

A variety of arguments can be recruited for (5), but it would be inappropriate to attempt to review these in detail here (see Radford, 1988a, chapter 9, for extensive introductory discussion and Chomsky, 1986b, for technical motivation). We can, however, briefly consider one of the advantages that accrues from having both a (Spec, C)- and a C-position on the periphery of a clause. These advantages become obvious if we consider English questions such as (8):

(8)   Will John kiss Mary?

With the rules in (1) and (2), the d-structure for (8) is (9):

(9) $[_{S'}[_C \ e \ ][_S \ [_{NP}John][_I will][_{VP}kiss \ Mary]]]$

Recall that Move α simply states that anything can be moved anywhere, so it is plausible to suppose that it applies to the I, *will*, and substitutes it for the empty category e in C, yielding the s-structure in (10):[2]

(10) $[_{S'}[_C will_i][_S \ [_{NP}John][e_i][_{VP}kiss \ Mary]]]$

This is unobjectionable, but difficulties arise if we also try to take account of *wh*-questions such as (11) within this set of assumptions:

(11)   Who will John kiss?

The d-structure for this sentence projected from the lexicon will be (12):

(12) $[_{S'}[_C \ e \ ][_S \ [_{NP}John][_I will][_{VP}kiss \ who]]]$

If we suppose that *will* moves to C by Move α as in (10), an intermediate point in the derivation will be (13):

(13) $[_{S'}[_C will_i][_S[_{NP}John][_I \ e_i \ ][_{VP}kiss \ who]]]$

In this structure, *who* still has to be moved by Move α to a clause-initial position, and of course, to date we have assumed that this is also movement to C. But we must now seriously consider just what the structure resulting from such a movement looks like. As things stand in (13), the most obvious possibility is that the *wh*-phrase must adjoin to the left of C. Pursuing this, we derive an s-structure for (11) as in (14):

(14) $[_{S'}[_C who_j \ [_C will_i]][_S[_{NP}John][_I \ e_i][_{VP}kiss \ e_j]]]$

What problems arise for this analysis? There are several, some technical and others descriptive. One of the technical difficulties is that the proposed movement violates a condition on applications of Move α. This is that only adjunction of a maximal projection to another maximal projection is legitimate (see Chomsky, 1986b, p. 6 for details). Now, *who* is a maximal projection in (14) (it is an NP), but C is a zero-level category, and therefore the proposed movement violates this constraint on adjunction.

A descriptive problem arises when we note that the proposal that *wh*-expressions are moved to C makes an interesting prediction: the s-structure positions of overt Cs and moved *wh*-expressions should coincide. If there are languages in which moved *wh*-expressions occur clause-initially but overt Cs occur clause-finally, they would provide prima facie evidence against the movement-to-C analysis.[3]

Koopman (1984) claims that Vata, a West African language, is of this type. In fact, Vata has a range of complementizers, some of which occur clause-initially and others clause-finally, but Koopman argues convincingly that these are all clause-final at d-structure. A relevant Vata example from Koopman (1984, p. 35) appears in (15) (tones are omitted and Koopman's conventions for indicating vowel quality are followed):

(15)   alO$_i$ Kofi yE *e*$_i$ ye la?
       who Kofi saw particle [+WH] C
       'Who did Kofi see?'

In (15), the *wh*-phrase *alO* is moved to a clause-initial position, but, like all interrogative clauses in Vata, (15) also includes a clause-final complementizer *la*. If this is the canonical position for complementizers in this language, the *wh*-phrase cannot be moved to C at s-structure.

Let us now consider how the analysis of clause structure in (5) can handle these two problems. For English *wh*-questions, note that there is now an additional clause-initial position available, the specifier of C. Suppose, then, that the auxiliary verb moves to C as already described and the *wh*-phrase moves to (Spec, C). This gives the s-structure in (16):

(16)   [$_{CP}$who$_j$ [$_{C'}$[$_C$will$_i$] [$_{IP}$John [$_{I'}e_i$ [$_{VP}$kiss e_j]]]]]

This is now unproblematic from a technical point of view. *Will*, a member of a zero-level category, moves into C, a zero-level category. *Who*, a maximal projection, moves into (Spec, C), but recall that the X-bar principles require specifiers and complements to be maximal projections. Therefore, this movement is of a maximal projection into a maximal projection position, and the constraints on Move α are not jeopardized.

What about the situation in Vata? There is no difficulty, so long as we can maintain that the structure of the Vata clause is as schematized in (17):

(17)   [$_{CP}$ (Spec, C) [$_{C'}$ [$_{IP}$ . . .] C]

The structure in (17) has C in clause-final position as Koopman requires, and the (Spec, C) position – the target for moved *wh*-phrases – is clause-initial. This is entirely consistent with the X-bar principles which allow order to be parameterized. We thus see that, although we have only had space to consider a small proportion of the relevant arguments here, there is a measure of support for the proposal that I and C should be fully integrated into the X-bar system.

A further difficulty for the X-bar schema arises in connection with NPs. Specifically, consider the syntactic role of the determiner *the* in such expressions as (18):

(18)   the destruction of the city

The standard view on this has been that it is a specifier of the N′ *destruction of the city*, yielding a structure along the lines of (19):

(19)   [$_{NP}$ [$_D$the] [$_{N'}$[$_N$destruction] (of) [$_{NP}$ the city]]]

This is fine as far as N and its projections go, but note that D does not project to higher levels; nor is it a maximal projection despite the X-bar claim that expressions appearing in specifier position should have this property, i.e. again, D appears to be an anomalous category.

Abney (1987) develops a case for the analysis of NPs such as *the destruction of the city* as DPs, that is as maximal projections of the functional category D (see Fukui, 1986, for a similar proposal). While this has probably not been as comprehensively accepted as the IP/CP analysis of clauses, it has given rise to a good deal of discussion. More importantly from our point of view, it has been applied to the analysis of early stages of acquisition.

According to this proposal, the expression in (18) is analysed as in (20):

(20)   [$_{DP}$ [$_D$ the] [$_{NP}$ [$_{N'}$[$_N$destruction] (of) [$_{DP}$ the city]]]]

In (20), the head determiner *the* selects an NP complement (a maximal projection). The specifier positions in the DP and the NP are optionally unfilled – a general characteristic of such positions.[4] Once more, (20) addresses the conceptual problems surrounding the status of D in the X-bar system, but again we must consider whether this innovation is empirically justified.

Abney offers a number of arguments to support his claim that D heads a DP, this latter being identified with the traditional notion of noun phrase, and here we shall just mention a sample of these.

First, there are English expressions such as *that*, traditionally treated as determiners, which can appear alone. When they do so, they have the distributional properties of noun phrases. The examples in (21) and (22) show that noun phrases and single determiners cannot appear in typical prenominal modifier environments:

(21)   a. John seems pleasant
       b. *John seems the man
       c. *John seems that/this

(22)   a. Pleasant though John was, . . .
       b. *The man though John was, . . .
       c. *That/this though John was, . . .

The examples in (23) show that bare determiners, unlike prenominal modifiers, can appear in environments appropriate for full noun phrases:

(23)   a. The man is a success
       b. This/that is a success
       c. *Pleasant is a success

This sort of distributional criterion is the standard technique used by linguists attempting to determine the categorial status of expressions, and the above paradigms are at least consistent with the claim that *the man* and *this/that* belong to the same category, DP.[5]

Second, it can be argued that pronouns are members of the category D. As it is difficult to make a case for their being included in projections which contain empty heads, we are forced to the conclusion that they head their own projections, i.e. they head DPs. That pronouns are best analysed as nouns is unlikely, as they do not co-occur with a variety of items which enter into the nominal system, e.g. determiners, possessives and adjectives:

(24)   *the you, *John's we, *pleasant they/them

Further, there are constructions in which pronouns *do* share the distribution of determiners:

(25)   we strugglers, you scientists

Interestingly, in such constructions it is the ϕ-features of the pronoun which determine the form of a co-referential reflexive. For example, in (26a), the only legitimate reflexive is the first person plural which agrees with *we* and not with *strugglers* (cf. (26b)):

(26)   a. We strugglers can look after ourselves/*themselves
       b. Strugglers can look after themselves/*ourselves

Furthermore, pronouns share with determiners the property of cross-linguistically being the locus of ϕ-features in the noun phrase, i.e. it is common in languages for person, number and gender features to be encoded in determiners to a greater extent than in nouns or prenominal modifiers. This extent is often matched by the pronominal system, which suggests that these features of arguments are typically realized on the head of the expression realizing the argument, i.e. the D or a pronoun, which is itself a D.

Finally, determiners share a range of characteristics with other functional categories such as C and I. Most importantly, they lack 'descriptive content'. As Abney (1987, p. 65) puts it:[6]

> Their semantic contribution is second-order, regulating or contributing to the interpretation of their complement. They mark grammatical or relational features, rather than picking out a class of objects.

On the basis of this 'semantic similarity', Abney concludes that if C and I head their own functional projections, it is not unreasonable to suppose that the same situation obtains for D.

This small set of observations is certainly not intended to be conclusive, but merely to establish that the proposition that noun phrases, like clauses, have a functional head is not without some support. Armed with D, I and C as an initial set of functional categories, we shall now turn to the proposal that all linguistic variation can be located in properties of such categories.

10.2 The Functional Parameterization Hypothesis

In the previous section, we introduced some recent views which suggest that the functional categories D, I and C play an important role in grammatical structure. The statement from Chomsky with which we opened this chapter proposes that *all* linguistic variation (parameterization) might be reducible to the properties of such categories.

At first sight, this appears to be an extraordinary claim, and it would be misleading to suggest that it enjoys an overwhelming amount of support. However, if we have access to a universal inventory of functional categories and their properties, it does answer the challenge of the previous chapter in an interesting way. Furthermore, since there is no reason to believe that the set of functional categories will be large, the amount of learning required of the child on this view will not be extensive (see Lebeaux, 1988, for discussion of how a proposal close to the FPH underwrites the case for UG making available only a finite number of grammars in a particularly clear way). More interestingly, perhaps, in the light of one account of early language development to be considered in the next section, it raises a number of provocative questions.

In this section, my goal is restricted to establishing that the FPH is not as implausible as it might first appear. To achieve this, I shall first describe a recent influential study of syntactic differences between English and French which is consistent with the hypothesis. Then I shall briefly allude to a range of further phenomena which provide additional support.

Pollock (1989) seeks to account for a range of well-known differences concerning the positioning of various items in simple clauses in English and French. Consider the following examples:[7]

(27) a. *John likes not Mary
      b. Jean n'aime pas Marie

(28) a. *Likes he Mary?
      b. Aime-t-il Marie?

(29) a. *John kisses often Mary
      b. Jean embrasse souvent Marie
      c. John often kisses Mary
      d. *Jean souvent embrasse Marie

Example (27) shows that the negative morpheme cannot intervene between a verb and its complement in English, whereas it can in French.[8] Example (28) indicates that verbs cannot invert with pronominal subjects in English interrogatives, whereas they can in French. And (29) illustrates that certain adverbs cannot intervene between a verb and its complement in English, whereas this is their only legitimate position in French.

These data can be readily described, if we assume that the d-structure of clauses in both languages is as schematized in (30):

(30)　$[_{IP}$ NP I (*Neg*) $[_{VP}$ (*Adv*) V . . .]]

The schema in (30) is just the orthodox d-structure produced by (1) from the previous section with additional optional positions for negatives and adverbs and IP substituted for S. In such a d-structure, the verbal inflectional elements in I are separated from the verb, a situation which has to be remedied at s-structure or PF. Clearly, there are three logically possible ways to achieve this: (i) V can raise to I; (ii) I can lower to V; (iii) I and V can come together in some third position. Discounting (iii) as unnecessarily complex, it has been customary to regard French as a language which selects option (i) and English as a language which selects option (ii) (cf. our discussion of Rule R in Section 4.2). Consider how the data in (27)–(29) are thus accounted for.

For (27), the French verb raises to I crossing the negative and appears in a pre-*Neg* s-structure position. English I lowers to V, ensuring that the inflected verb remains in a post-*Neg* position. In (28), assuming that the derivation of questions involves I-to-C movement (see previous section), the French verb, having been raised to I, is in a position to be further raised to C; the English verb is unable to undergo I-to-C movement since it has not been raised to I (see below). The optional VP-initial adverb position in (30) makes the account of (29) transparent, with the logic being exactly the same as for negation.

It is important now to note that the English examples in (27)–(29) all include lexical main verbs. If, instead of such verbs, we consider auxiliary *have* and *be*, or, indeed, *have* and *be* as main verbs, a very different picture emerges:

(31)　a. John hasn't kissed Mary
　　　b. John isn't kissing Mary
　　　c. John hasn't a job
　　　d. John isn't a fool

(32)　a. Has John kissed Mary?
　　　b. Is John kissing Mary?
　　　c. Has John a job?
　　　d. Is John a fool?

(33)　a. John has often kissed Mary
　　　b. John is often kissing Mary (these days)
　　　c. ?John has often a job
　　　d. John is often a fool

Examples (31)–(33) show that English *have* and *be* behave like French main verbs in the relevant respects and suggest that the proposal that French verbs move to I should be extended to *have* and *be* in English, a suggestion which has been implemented in earlier theories of grammar by the postulation of a transformational rule of *have/be* raising (Jackendoff, 1972; Emonds, 1976).

Within PPT, of course, such rule stipulations, referring to specific lexical items, are unavailable. With Move α the only movement process available, Pollock has to confront the questions in (34):

(34)   a. Why do verbs in English not undergo V-to-I movement when this movement is an option made available by UG (as indicated by French verbs)?
        b. Why do *have* and *be*, exceptionally in English, undergo this process?

The examples cited so far have all involved finite clauses. The enquiry is deepened by considering what happens in non-finite clauses. Consider French first. A small sample of the data presented by Pollock appears in (35) and (36):

(35)   a. Ne pas être heureux est une condition pour écrire des romans
            'To not be happy is a prerequisite for writing novels'
        b. N'être pas heureux est une condition pour écrire des romans
            'To be not happy is a prerequisite for writing novels'
        c. Ne pas avoir eu d'enfance heureuse . . .
            'To not have had a happy childhood . . .'
        d. N'avoir pas eu d'enfance heureuse . . .
            'To have not had a happy childhood . . .'

(36)   a. Ne pas sembler heureux est une condition . . .
            'To not seem happy is a prerequisite . . .'
        b. *Ne sembler pas heureux est une condition . . .
            'To seem not happy is a prerequisite . . .'
        c. Ne pas posséder de voiture . . .
            'To not own a car . . .'
        d. *Ne posséder pas de voiture . . .
            'To own not a car . . .'

Assuming that the d-structure sketched in (30) is also appropriate for non-finite clauses, these examples suggest: (i) V-to-I movement is optional for *être* and *avoir* in French infinitives, with the option being exercised to move the verb over *pas* in (35b, d) and not taken in (35a, c); (ii) V-to-I movement is not possible for other verbs in French infinitives. As Pollock notes, this restriction on the class of verbs that can move into I (only *être* and *avoir* in French non-finite clauses, only *be* and *have* in English finite clauses) is unlikely to be accidental. As the English translations of the French sentences indicate, a similar restriction appears to be operative in English infinitives.

Now, linear position with respect to negation was only one of the criteria invoked above as diagnostic of V-to-I movement. What happens if we consider adverbs in infinitival constructions? First, since V-to-I movement is impossible for lexical verbs in infinitives, on the basis of (30), we should expect to find examples where the adverb precedes the lexical verb. This is the case, and Pollock cites the following:

(37)   a. A peine comprendre l'italien . . .
          'To hardly understand Italian . . .'
       b. Souvent paraître triste . . .
          'To often look sad . . .'

In (37), the non-finite verbs *comprendre* and *paraître* are preceded by the adverbs *à peine* and *souvent*. This is consistent with the claim that these non-finite verbs have not undergone V-to-I movement.

However, such non-finite verbs should also not be able to *precede* adverbs at s-structure. But this prediction is not confirmed, and alongside (37), we find examples like (38):

(38)   a. Comprendre à peine l'italien . . .
          'To understand hardly Italian . . .'
       b. Paraître souvent triste . . .
          'To look often sad . . .'

Such structures suggest that in fact lexical verbs in French infinitives *can* move out of their d-structure position to a position which precedes VP-initial adverbs. However, (36b, d) indicate that this position *cannot* be the pre-*Neg* site that we are identifying with I.

Now consider the position of adverbs in English infinitives. As the ill-formedness of the translations in (38) suggests, it appears that lexical verbs in English cannot move to the intermediate position we have been led to propose for French. However, (39) shows that this restriction does not apply to *be* and *have*:

(39)   a. John believes Bill to often be misleading
       b. John believes Bill to be often misleading
       c. John believes Bill to often have kissed Mary
       d. John believes Bill to have often kissed Mary

Summing up the differences between the two languages, we have the following: (i) in finite clauses, French has unrestricted V-to-I movement, but English has V-to-I movement only for *be* and *have*; (ii) in non-finite clauses, French has optional V-to-I movement for *être* and *avoir* and optional movement of lexical verbs to an intermediate site, but English allows optional V-to-I movement only for *be* and *have*, as well as permitting these verbs to move to the intermediate pre-adverbial position.

These observations would look more systematic if V-to-I movement were not a unitary process, but instead were composed of two movements, V-to-X movement and X-to-I movement, where X is the intermediate site. Then, we could maintain the propositions in (40):

(40) a. In French, V-to-X movement is unrestricted.
 b. In English, V-to-X movement is restricted to *be* and *have*.
 c. In French, X-to-I movement is unrestricted if I is [+finite].
 d. In French, X-to-I movement is restricted to *être* and *avoir* if I is [−finite].

These propositions do not directly address the properties of English X-to-I movement, but if V, X and I constitute a series of *heads*, movement of verbs from V directly to I will be ruled out by the *Head Movement Constraint* (Travis, 1984; Chomsky, 1986b; M. Baker, 1988a). We will not pursue a formal statement of this constraint here. Suffice it to say that it is a constraint on movement of zero-level categories which ensures that such movement cannot skip intermediate heads in a series. In our earlier discussion of questions in English and French we took it for granted when noting that English lexical verbs cannot move to C because they have not previously moved to I.[9] As a consequence of the Head Movement Constraint, the only items eligible for X-to-I movement will be those which can be moved into X, and for English these are *be* and *have*.

The obvious question raised by (40) is the identity of X, and in offering a view on this, Pollock addresses a further difficulty with the X-bar framework. We have seen in the previous section how I can be integrated with this framework, but what of the *contents* of I? Earlier, we have supposed that I contains TNS and AGR features and its internal structure is often represented as in (41).

(41)

$$
\begin{array}{c}
\text{I} \\
\diagup \; \diagdown \\
\text{TNS} \qquad \text{AGR}
\end{array}
$$

If a clear distinction is maintained between categories and features, this is merely inexplicit and not particularly disturbing. But an assumption of PPT we have not so far introduced is that category labels (N, V, etc.) are abbreviations for sets of features. According to this view, the major lexical categories are defined in terms of two binary features $[\pm \text{N}]$ and $[\pm \text{V}]$ as in (42):

(42) Noun: $[+\text{N}, -\text{V}]$
 Verb: $[-\text{N}, +\text{V}]$
 Adjective: $[+\text{N}, +\text{V}]$
 Preposition: $[-\text{N}, -\text{V}]$

Then, the X-bar principles do not apply to atomic labels, but to feature complexes with a $[+\text{N}, -\text{V}]^0$ projecting to a $[+\text{N}, -\text{V}]'$, etc.[10]

Returning now to (41), it can be seen as embodying the empirical claim that there is a syntactic category I which is an abbreviation for a feature complex containing Tense and Agreement features. However, perhaps this is mistaken, as an alternative way to approach Tense and Agreement features is to see each of them as autonomous syntactic entities, projecting their own expansions in accordance with the X-bar principles. Such an *articulated* theory of I is developed by Pollock in his search for the identity of X in (40).

According to Pollock's proposals, the structure of a clause (or Tense Phrase – TP) is as in (43) (we omit single-bar projections and specifier positions as they do not bear on the general point; the negative system has been included since this is necessary for Pollock's account to work – it is not possible to go into his treatment of negation here).

(43)

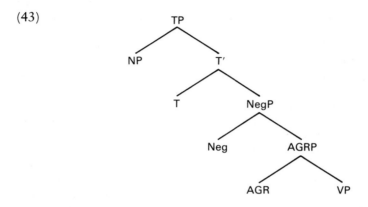

Now, a V, originating as head of VP, can move to AGR without violating the Head Movement Constraint. This is a position preceding the VP and following *Neg*, and it is the X Pollock's data require. Then, ignoring the status of *Neg*, this V + AGR complex can move to T. If both of these movements take place, the resulting schematic s-structure is (44):

(44) $[_{TP}$ NP $[[V_i + AGR_j]_j + T] \ldots (Neg) \ldots [_{AGRP} \ldots e_j \ldots [_{VP} \ldots e_i \ldots]]]$

In (44), e_i represents the original d-structure position òf the verb and e_j the original position of AGR.

With these concepts, we can now rephrase the relevant questions about English and French, as in (45):

(45)   a. Why does French but not English allow lexical Vs to move to AGR?
       b. Why does French not allow V + AGR to move to T, if T is [−finite] and V is lexical?
       c. Why are English *be* and *have* and French *être* and *avoir* excepted from these restrictions?

Pollock's answers to these questions refer to the properties of AGR and T in the two languages. AGR and T, of course, have emerged from I, one of our functional categories, and it is appropriate to regard them as functional categories too. What are these properties? Here, we can offer only a brief sketch.

If V raises to AGR, this produces the partial structure in (46):

(46)   . . .[$_{AGRP}$ [$_{AGR}$ V$_i$ + AGR] [$_{VP}$ e$_i$ – NP . . .]]

The Θ-Criterion requires the direct object NP to be assigned a Θ-role in this structure and the source of this Θ-role is the V. This V has been raised to AGR, but can transmit its Θ-role to the NP through its trace e$_i$ *so long as nothing blocks this transmission.* Pollock claims that French AGR is transparent to Θ-role transmission, but English AGR is not, and he tentatively relates this to the fact that agreement inflections are 'richer' in French than in English (cf. also Chomsky, 1989). Thus, the two languages are differentiated as indicated in (47).

(47)   a. French: . . . .

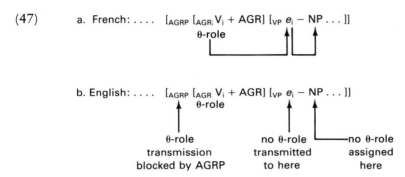

If English lexical verbs raised to AGR, the result would be a violation of the Θ-Criterion.

Of course, English agreement inflections do appear on the verb, and this is achieved by lowering AGR to V as indicated in (48):

(48)   . . .[$_{AGRP}$ e$_i$ [$_{VP}$ [V + AGR$_i$] – NP . . .]]

In (48), the V can assign its internal Θ-role to the direct object NP in its usual way since it has not moved.[11] We now have an answer to (45a): the reason lexical verbs in French, but not in English, can be raised to AGR is that French AGR is 'transparent' to Θ-role transmission, whereas English AGR is 'opaque' in this regard.

Question (45b) receives a similar answer. Obviously, if verbs can be raised to AGR as in French, they can also be raised to T so long as T is [+finite]. This is accounted for if [+finite] T, in contrast with [−finite] T, is 'transparent' to Θ-role transmission.

Finally, for (45c), the exceptional behaviour of *be/have* and *être/avoir* is explained if these verbs are not Θ-role assigners. If they have no Θ-role to assign, the Θ-Criterion will not prevent them from moving into a position which blocks Θ-role transmission. That these verbs in their auxiliary role are not Θ-role assigners is uncontroversial. When they are used as main verbs, the issues are less clear-cut, but Pollock develops a rather abstract analysis of structures of this type which has the desired consequences. I will not go into this here (see Pollock, 1989, pp. 386ff.).

To sum up, what the above argument suggests is that a range of well-known differences between English and French can be understood if we assume that AGR, a functional head, has a property which is parameterized. The property in question is whether it is opaque or transparent to Θ-role transmission. The possibility is also raised that there may be further parameterization affecting Tense, another functional head. In French, [−finite] T is opaque to Θ-role transmission, but there is no reason to believe that this is a universal property, and in principle grammars could permit movement of θ-role-assigning heads into [−finite] T.[12]

As a second example of functional parameterization, we can consider the assignment of nominative Case and its interaction with word-order. Recall that we have so far assumed that nominative Case is assigned to subject NPs by a [+finite] I, and that in Section 3.4 we briefly considered Koopman's (1984) suggestion that direction of Case-assignment should be parameterized. There we were concerned with Case-assignment by V and P, but there is no reason why similar considerations should not be extended to I. Consider the contrast in the English and Arabic examples in (49) from Fassi-Fehri (1989):

(49)   a. The enemy bombed the city
       b. qasafa lᶜaduww-u l-madi:nat-a
          bombed the-enemy-nom the-city-obj
          'The enemy bombed the city'

Fassi-Fehri suggests that the d-structure for (49b) is (50) (we follow Fassi-Fehri in omitting irrelevant structural details).

(50)

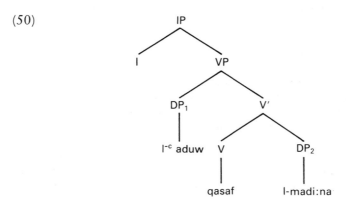

This structure differs in one obvious way from what we have assumed to date in that the subject *lᶜaduw* appears within the VP at d-structure. This analysis, advocated by Fukui (1986), Koopman and Sportiche (1988) and Sportiche (1988) among others, will be of some importance in the next section, but for now we might simply note that it removes an uncomfortable asymmetry between nominal and clausal structure hinted at in Section 3.3 (p. 72).

Subjects of both nominal and clausal constituents now both originate within a lexical maximal projection at d-structure and Θ-role assignment can be viewed as uniformly taking place inside the maximal projection of the Θ-role-assigning head.

Given (50), Fassi-Fehri notes that at s-structure, V must be raised to I to support the inflection. Objective Case is assigned to *l-madi:na* by *qasaf* via its trace and nominative Case is assigned to *lʿaduw* from I, both of these Case-assignments are to the right, and the VSO word-order characteristic of Arabic is well-formed.[13]

What now of the English example (49a)? Assume that its d-structure is analogous to that for (49b) and that again the V raises to I to receive the verbal inflection.[14] In English, the subject cannot remain within the VP, but must also be raised to the (Spec, I) position, giving the s-structure in (51).

(51)

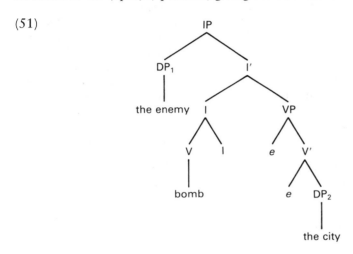

This obviously gets the SVO word-order right, but the question is raised as to why English subjects apparently *must* be raised into (Spec, I). Fassi-Fehri's answer is that direction of Case-assignment for I is parameterized and is specified as *left* for English and *right* for Arabic. If this is correct, English subjects must move to a position left of I in order to receive nominative Case and avoid violating the Case Filter. Thus, again, we have parameterization of a property of a functional category, direction of Case-assignment by I.[15]

To close this section, we can briefly return to the parameters listed in (1) of chapter 9, and note that those concerned with the distribution of null subjects clearly fall under the umbrella of functional parameterization. Thus, both of Hyams' formulations of the relevant parameter are in terms of properties of I: whether or not AG(R) = PRO and whether or not I-paradigms are morphologically uniform. Furthermore, with a little massage, the bounding nodes parameter in the Subjacency Principle can be assimilated to this view. Recall that this is a three-valued parameter, defined on subsets of {NP, S, S′}. But this set now 'translates' to {DP, IP, CP}, so we can reasonably claim that whether or not their maximal projections are bounding nodes is a parameterized property of D, I and C.[16] We shall return to some further consequences of this 'translation' in Section 10.4.

The discussion in this section might be properly considered as belonging to the more rarified reaches of syntactic research were it not for the fact that functional categories appear to be non-existent in the earliest grammars of children. In the next section, we shall look at the justification for this claim, before going on to examine some of its implications.

10.3 Pre-Functional Child Syntax

We have already met, in Section 6.4, some of Radford's (1990a) observations concerning *lexical* categories and their phrasal projections. To reiterate, he believes that there is ample evidence that typically before the age of 2 years, children have acquired the categories N, V, A and P, and manipulate them and their phrasal projections in their syntax in a manner consistent with the X-bar principles. The arguments advanced in this connection are for a *lexical* stage which, as well as being characterized positively as just described, is also remarkable for not producing any evidence for the child controlling functional category systems. Radford considers the functional categories D, I and C in turn. Here I shall summarize a sample of his observations arguing for the absence of D- and I-systems (for the absence of a C-system, see Radford, 1980a, chapter 5).

Consider, then, the D-system. The most obvious fact to note is that at early stages of development, children systematically omit determiners where adults would require them. Radford cites such examples as those in (52):

(52) a. where helicopter?
      b. got bee
      c. open door

Furthermore, children's answers to *what* questions reveal a similar pattern, typical dialogues having the form of (53):

(53) a. ADULT: What's this? CHILD: Telephone
      b. ADULT: What do we need for the diaper? CHILD: Pin

And the same situation is revealed by children's partial repetitions of adult utterances, as in (54):

(54) a. ADULT: Did you drop your tea? CHILD: Drop tea
      b. ADULT: You were playing in the water. CHILD: In water

A second source of evidence for the lack of a D-system at this stage can be linked to our discussion in the previous section of word-order differences between Arabic and English. Consider English expressions such as (55):

(55) The man's picture of Mary

Fukui (1986) has suggested that the possessive morpheme -'s is the head D of this DP and that the subject *the man* appears at d-structure within the maximal projection of the head noun *picture* as in (56):

(56)   [$_{DP}$ *e* [$_{D'}$[$_D$'s] [$_{NP}$ the man [$_{N'}$picture (of) Mary]]]]

The DP *the man* cannot receive Case in this position since nouns are not Case-assigners; therefore it must move to the empty (Spec, D) position, where it can be Case-marked by -'s. This movement yields the s-structure in (57):

(57)   [$_{DP}$ the man$_i$ [$_{D'}$[$_D$'s][e_i [$_{N'}$picture (of) Mary]]]]

Assume, for the sake of argument, that this analysis, identifying the genitive -'s as a D, is correct. What follows from this for Radford's position? Obviously, if children are at a pre-functional stage, it is predicted that they do not yet have genitive -'s in their grammar, and this turns out to be the case. Typical utterances which receive a possessive interpretation are those in (58):

(58)   a. mummy car
       b. big teddy bear supper
       c. Claire pencil

Of course, if there is no D-system, expressions like those in (58) will not have structures analogous to (56) in the child's grammar. Rather, they will be *lexical* projections, illustrated for *mummy car* in (59):

(59)   [$_{NP}$ mummy [$_{N'}$[$_N$car]]]

If this proposal is adopted, more general suggestions can also be pursued concerning the module to which we have so far not devoted any systematic attention, Case Theory. The reason offered for *the man* having to move in (56) is that it needs Case. The original version of the Case Filter, introduced in Section 3.3, stated that a *noun phrase* with a phonetic matrix had to receive Case, but, under the DP-analysis, noun phrases are in fact DPs. Accordingly, the Case Filter must be rephrased to impose a Case requirement on DPs. But, Radford's position is that as there are no Ds, *there are no DPs* either at the pre-functional stage, from which it follows that Case Theory has no role to play in the pre-functional child's grammar.[17]

Is there further evidence that nominal expressions at this stage are not subject to the Case Filter? Indeed there is, since children before the age of 2 do not use *of* to Case-mark nominal complements (recall that head nouns and adjectives are not themselves Case-assigners, therefore *of* is introduced to serve this purely grammatical function). Radford cites such examples as those in (60) in support of this claim:

(60)   a. cup tea
       b. picture Gia
       c. blue ball wool

Recall, now, Abney's (1987) suggestion that what are traditionally called pronouns are in fact Ds. Since, by hypothesis, the pre-functional child has no determiner system, it ought to follow that such a child lacks pronouns. The facts here are a little less straightforward, but we might first note that a traditional observation in child language studies has been that some young children adopt a nominal style, eschewing the use of personal pronouns in favour of proper names (Bloom, Lightbown and Hood, 1978). Such a child will use his or her own name rather than a first person pronoun and the name of others rather than a second person pronoun.

But what of children who do use pronouns? Radford argues at length that such usage is not characterized by systematic Case-marking, i.e. although some children use *forms* which are pronominal DPs in the adult grammar, they are used in a way which suggests that they are not subject to Case-marking. If they are not subject to Case-marking, they are not functioning as DPs, and Radford suggests that they should be analysed as pronominal NPs, i.e. the child has effectively misanalysed them as members of a *lexical* category, which is not subject to Case requirements.[18]

Now, let us consider the I-system. Once again, the most direct evidence that the average child lacks such a system before the age of 2 years is provided by the absence of overt lexical realizations of head Is. In adult English, there are two ways in which an I can be lexically filled, depending on whether the IP of which it is the head is finite or non-finite. In the latter case, I is realized as *to* and in the former case, it can be realized as a modal auxiliary, *can, could, may, might*, etc.

The evidence on *to* is clear. At the appropriate stage, children's clauses which would require a *to* in the adult system lack this element. Radford cites examples such as those in (61):

(61)   a. want teddy drink
       b. want do it

As far as modals are concerned, in Section 4.2, we have already met Hyams' (1986) claim that these are late to emerge in children acquiring English. Radford confirms this finding on the basis of his corpus of data, and simultaneously provides an alternative explanation for this non-appearance. Modals fill the I-position in adult grammars; if there is no such position in the child's grammar at this stage, there is nowhere for modals to be accommodated (see also Aldridge, 1989, and, again, Valian, 1990a, for a dissenting view).

What other elements occupy the I-position? As we have seen in the previous section, it has been customary to view Tense and Agreement morphemes as appearing there at d-structure. We have also seen how Pollock (1989) revises this proposal, allowing each of Tense and Agreement to head their own maximal projection, but from the point of view of the current discussion we can abstract away from these differences. The important thing for us to note is that Tense and Agreement morphemes are inflectional and must attach to a verbal stem at s-structure (or PF), if they are to avoid being 'stranded'. There are various ways in which this can be achieved.

Most straightforwardly, if we have a modal generated in I, the inflections can attach to it directly. However, we have already seen that at the relevant stage there are no modals in the child's system, so we cannot pursue the presence of these inflections by examining these elements.

An alternative is for *be* or *have*, generated inside the VP, to raise to I so as to support the inflectional morphemes, this being a possibility because these verbs have no Θ-role to assign (cf. previous section). But, again, in Radford's corpus, there are no instances of auxiliary *be* and *have*; progressive and perfect participles occur appropriately inflected, but the forms of auxiliary verbs which obligatorily co-occur with them in adult English are missing, yielding such utterances as those in (62):

(62)   a. baby talking
       b. her going on walk
       c. daddy gone
       d. teddy fallen over

Now, the fact that such forms do not occur at all is clearly consistent with there being no I-position to receive them – logically, the observation has the same status as that noting the absence of modals – but, of course, it means that we cannot investigate such forms to see whether agreement features are realized on them or not.

A third possibility for the realization of agreement features is as attached to the 'dummy' auxiliary verb *do*. One context in which this is necessary is before negatives. Thus, we have the contrast between (63a) and (63b):

(63)   a. John doesn't/does not like Mary
       b. *John not likes Mary

It seems that in English the presence of a negative precludes the possibility of the tense and agreement features being realized on the main verb – a possibility we turn to presently. In the absence of an appropriate auxiliary verb in the VP to raise to I to support these features, English resorts to the dummy verb *do* to fulfil this function. It is noteworthy, therefore, that at the stage in question children do not produce tokens of *do* in this context; their negative utterances have the general form exemplified in (64):

(64)   a. man no go in there
       b. Wayne not eating it

Once more, the hypothesis that the child has no I-position is compatible with this absence of dummy *do*. Again, however, this very absence of *do* means that we cannot independently assess whether Tense and Agreement are present in the system.

The last possibility for the realization of these features fortunately provides the independent corroboration we need. If there is no modal verb in I, no *be* or *have* to be raised from the VP, and no negative to prevent Tense and Agreement being realized on the main verb, in English these features are lowered into the VP and attached to the main verb (cf. Pollock's analysis in the previous section). Thus, we find such sentences as (65):

(65)   a. John loves Mary
       b. John loved Mary

If there is no I-position, there is no site for Tense and Agreement to appear in the child's grammar and Radford's proposal predicts that there will be no marking of Tense and Agreement in the child's equivalent of sentences like (65). This is exactly what he reports, as illustrated by such examples as (66):

(66)   a. Hayley draw it
       b. Daddy want golf ball

It appears, then, that there is a variety of evidence to support the claim that early grammars lack functional categories entirely.

Before turning to a discussion of some of the consequences of this conclusion, it is appropriate to raise a few further issues in connection with Radford's analysis of the earliest syntactic stages. The first concerns the structure that he assigns to examples like those in (66). Intuitively, these are *clauses*, but Section 10.1 has argued that 'ordinary clauses' are CPs. As the children lack C and its projections, this cannot be appropriate for these examples. Furthermore, they cannot be IPs, since the child also lacks I and its projections at this stage. The alternative is that they are *Small Clauses* analysed as in (67):

(67)   [$_{VP}$Hayley [$_{V'}$ draw it]]

The structure in (67) is appropriate for a *verbal* Small Clause which occurs in adult English in such examples as (68):

(68)   John let *Hayley draw it*

Alongside such examples, Radford cites numerous instances of children's Small Clauses headed by the other lexical categories (see also Radford, 1988b). Now, the important point to note about a structure like (67) is that both arguments of the verb (*Hayley* and *it*) appear within the verb's maximal projection and Θ-role assignment to these arguments can take place within this domain. We have seen above that recent work (Fukui, 1986; Sportiche, 1988) has argued that such an analysis is also appropriate for the adult grammar. However, the adult grammar differs from the child's grammar in containing Case requirements, and these force *Hayley* to be raised out of its non-Case-marked position in the VP to (Spec, I), where it can receive Case from the [+finite] I. In the child's grammar, there are no Case requirements since there are no DPs; nor is there an I to assign Case. Accordingly, no movement is required and (67) is well-formed. From this perspective, we can view development as a grafting of a system of functional categories and their projections on to a lexical system. The functional systems bring with them Case-theoretic requirements, and these necessitate movement (cf. Lebeaux, 1988, for a similar developmental perspective).

A second point requires that we return again to Hyams' two analyses of missing subjects. Both of these identified the licensing of such subjects as properties of I, but if Radford is right and there is no I in the child's grammar at this early stage, Hyams' speculations must be incorrect. In fact, there is an additional reason for suspecting that her theories must be abandoned if there is a pre-functional stage. This is that she seeks conditions which license and identify *pro*, a null pronominal. But if overt pronominals are Ds, presumably the same goes for empty pronominals including *pro*. Accordingly, if there are no Ds pre-functionally, there is no *pro*, so the search for its licensing and identification conditions is doomed to failure.

This conclusion raises two further issues. The first concerns the identity of null arguments in a pre-functional grammar. As noted in the discussion of Hyams' work, these are not restricted to subject position (Aldridge, 1989; Kazman, 1988; Radford, 1990a, 1990b), and Radford cites a large number of examples such as those in (69) to illustrate this:

(69) a. Man taking *ec*
      b. Wayne got *ec*
      c. Paula put them *ec*
      d. Crayon under *ec*

In (69a, b), the direct object argument is unexpressed; in (69c), there is no overt realization of the Location argument required by *put*; in (69d) the prepositional object of *under* is missing. What this range of occurrences suggests is that there are probably *no* grammatically motivated licensing conditions on null arguments at this stage, i.e. *any* argument position can remain null for the child. Radford speculates that there may be *pragmatically* motivated identification conditions on such arguments (cf. Greenfield and Smith, 1976 for a similar suggestion within a very different set of assumptions).[19]

The second issue concerns the fate of the parameter determining the distribution of *pro*. It is important to be clear that the above discussion does not prejudice the importance of this matter, since it is undoubtedly the case that adult English differs from adult Italian in not licensing *pro* subjects. If Radford is correct in his conclusion that null arguments in early English are not to be identified with *pro*, then Hyams' claims that universally the child's initial grammar is one that licenses *pro* is no longer sustainable. As Cinque (1989) points out, there is no reason now to rule out the possibility that the initial setting of the relevant parameter is the English value with *pro* not licensed anywhere. Then the Italian child can develop a set of licensing conditions for *pro* on the basis of positive evidence, i.e. hearing tokens of Italian sentences with null arguments, a position which is more readily consistent with the learnability perspective we have adopted throughout this book (see Section 9.2). Crucially, however, this process can get under way only when the child has developed a set of functional categories.[20]

Finally, Radford's position demands that he takes a stand on the mechanism responsible for the emergence of functional category systems. After surveying a number of possibilities, he is ultimately attracted to a maturational account, and we shall accept this in our subsequent discussion.

10.4 Some Consequences

In the previous two sections, we have introduced two hypotheses. The first, originating in linguistic research and partially motivated by the need to constrain a theory of possible parameters, is the FPH, which maintains that all linguistic variation can ultimately be traced to the properties of functional categories (including, perhaps, whether they exist in particular grammars). The second, relying heavily on linguistic theory, but squarely based on evidence concerning the utterances English-speaking children produce and understand early in their development, is Radford's hypothesis that the earliest stages of word-combination are pre-functional. The purpose of this section is to juxtapose these two ideas and consider some of their implications.

At the outset, it is important to be clear that the two proposals have rather different levels of support as things stand. We have presented some examples as illustrating functional parameterization, but have not sought to persuade the reader that the FPH can readily be extended to the full range of attested linguistic variation. Vital to such an extension is a firmer grasp of the criteria categories must satisfy in order to be functional, and it would be misleading to suggest that such criteria are currently available.[21] Radford's hypothesis, on the other hand, is rather solidly supported by data from English, and in so far as it has weaknesses, these involve inheritance of the looseness in our understanding of functional categories and its extension to children acquiring other languages (but see Parodi, 1989; Platzack, 1990).[22]

Cautiously accepting, then, the plausibility of the two hypotheses, let us proceed to juxtapose them. There are two consequences of this which I wish to pursue briefly here.

The first arises naturally from Radford's suggestion that at the pre-functional stage there are no Case-theoretic requirements on the distribution of DPs, for the simple reason that there are no DPs. As we noted, the Case Filter needs to be reformulated once the existence of DPs is acknowledged, but such a reformulation entails that it is not operative at the pre-functional stage.[23] Can this reasoning be extended to any of the other modules from Section 3.3? It is significant that once functional categories are given the role adumbrated in Section 10.1, a number of these must also be seen as non-operative pre-functionally. Let us take those for which this is true in turn.

Consider Move α and its two major manifestations, Move NP and Move *wh*. The former remains a legitimate option even when noun phrases are identified with DPs, since there are no restrictions on Move α to prevent it operating on NPs. But recall that Move NP was *required* for Case-theoretic reasons. In a system in which noun phrases are DPs and the Case Filter applies to DPs, Move NP will not be motivated in this way. Furthermore, Move NP was *permitted* for Θ−theoretic reasons, the Θ-Criterion requiring that movement could only be to a Θ'-position. Failure to observe this restriction would result in a chain consisting of the moved NP and its trace being assigned two Θ-roles. But if all categories are lexical, there are no non-thematic argument positions in the child's grammar. Therefore, there is no position to which an NP *could* move. The upshot of this is that Move NP will not be operative in a grammar lacking functional categories.

The same conclusion follows for Move *wh*. In our original discussions of this movement, we assumed it was movement to C, and in Section 10.1 we modified this to movement to (Spec, C). But C is a functional category which is absent from pre-functional grammars, so the target for Move *wh* is not available and tokens of such movement do not occur. It appears that we are justified in concluding that the Theory of Move α is not operative in early grammars.

Consider next Binding Theory. As noted in Section 3.3, this is principally concerned with the distribution of pronouns and anaphors. But these are members of the functional category D according to Abney, therefore the principles of the Binding Theory are not directed at NP-distributions but at DP-distributions. Radford (1990a, b) cites examples such as (70) (from Bowerman, 1973) to suggest that in fact these principles are not operative at this stage:

(70)   Kendall see Kendall (= I can see myself)

One way to see (70) is that it involves a Principle C violation with the R-expression *Kendall* being bound, i.e. Principle C does not constrain the child's grammatical representations at this stage (although see discussion of Chien and Wexler, 1990, in Section 6.3 for an alternative). The extension of the Binding Theory to contribute to an account of the distribution of traces of movement is clearly not operative if there is no movement.

What of Bounding Theory? Since this is invoked to account for the properties of rather complex sentences, it is apparent that direct evidence for its operational status at the pre-functional stage will not be available. However, recall from Section 10.2 that we noted that the set of bounding nodes for the Subjacency Principle will consist of maximal projections of functional categories {DP, IP, CP}. If there are no functional categories, there are no maximal projections for functional categories, and there is a *principled* reason for saying that Bounding Theory is not operative pre-functionally.

Control Theory is concerned with the distribution of the empty category PRO. Traditionally, this is viewed as an empty NP, and its distribution follows from the PRO Theorem which, in turn, follows from the Binding Theory. But on our current assumptions, there is no Binding Theory operative pre-functionally, so the PRO Theorem is not derivable in a grammar at this stage. This might be seen as predicting that PRO would appear in unlicensed (governed) positions in pre-functional grammars, but note that PRO will now be reconstrued as an empty DP. Like *pro*, it will not be available at all in a pre-functional grammar, so Control Theory too will not be operative at this stage.

Case Theory has already been dealt with in some detail in the previous section, so now consider the Theory of Empty Categories. The discussion above has indicated that this theory should have no role pre-functionally. There are no traces of movement because there is no movement; there is no *pro* and no PRO because these are empty DPs. The empty categories we find are empty NPs, and we shall turn to their licensing conditions in a moment.

What we are left with, then, is the X-bar principles (obviously restricted to lexical categories and their projections) and Θ-Theory. It is clearly to Θ-Theory, specifically the Projection Principle, that we must look for the licensing of pre-functional empty categories. Recalling our discussion in Section 7.1, we might assume that a child who has been exposed to tokens of *throw* in contextually appropriate circumstances is capable of establishing a lexical entry along the lines of (71):

(71)   *throw*: V; Agent, Patient

The Projection Principle then requires that the arguments of *throw* should be represented in its syntactic projections, and there seems to be no prima facie reason why these arguments should not be non-functional NPs. Furthermore, if there are pragmatic criteria governing the identification of such empty NPs, there is no prima facie reason why they should not be null.

To contemplate an early linguistic system which is lexical and 'thematic' in this way calls to mind remarks of Chomsky (1980, pp. 54–5):

> Suppose that what we call 'knowing a language' is not a unitary phenomenon, but must be resolved into several interacting but distinct components. One involves the 'computational' aspects of language . . . A second component involves the system of object-reference and also such relations as 'agent,' 'goal,' 'instrument,' and the like; what are sometimes called 'thematic relations' . . . For want of a better term, let us call the latter a 'conceptual system.' We might discover that the computational aspect of language and the conceptual system are quite differently represented in the mind and brain, and perhaps that the latter should not strictly speaking be assigned to the language faculty at all . . .

If we identify the functional category systems and their properties with the 'computational' aspects of language in this passage, it is clear that the position we are contemplating is not dissimilar from that considered by Chomsky. Interestingly, in the same discussion, he considers the status of work on the earliest stages of language acquisition, suggesting that (p. 264, note 11):

> . . . the bulk [of this work], which is limited to very early stages, is not really studying language at all, in a serious sense of the term.

The position we have arrived at places an interesting perspective on this assertion. If the system of lexical categories and projections is in place at an early stage, it is not appropriate to regard study of this stage as 'not really studying language at all', particularly as this system continues to function in an important way when it is embedded within a set of principles formulated in terms of functional categories. However, the onset of functional category systems marks a clear discontinuity in development, since it is only at this point that the full range of UG principles becomes operative.[24]

The second consequence I wish to raise is closely related to the first. The FPH requires all linguistic variation to be located in the properties of functional categories, and Radford insists that children pass through a pre-functional stage in their acquisition of language. It follows that any systematic variation in children's speech pre-functionally cannot be *linguistically* motivated. At first, this sounds like an implausible suggestion, but I believe that it can be defended.

What sort of variation are we talking about in this connection? The single obvious candidate is word-order. It is a standard observation in the acquisition literature (e.g. Brown, 1973) that in languages where word-order is fairly fixed, children rapidly use this word-order with very small numbers of errors (but see Braine, 1976, for word-order errors in the speech of children acquiring English). For languages where word-order is more flexible, there are differing reports. Thus, Slobin (1966) cites the case of a Russian-speaking child who first systematically used the occurring but non-dominant SOV order before switching to SVO. Clancey (1985) reports that Japanese-speaking children postpose constituents after the verb from an early age, this being a pragmatically motivated and frequently occurring phenomenon in the spoken language. Bowerman (1973) and Slobin (1982) note the early use of a number of word-orders permitted in the adult language by children acquiring Finnish and Turkish respectively. Hickey (1990), in a recent study of Irish, notes that children acquiring this VSO language exercise the option of using subject-initial utterances much more frequently than their mothers. Undoubtedly, it seems that there is variation cross-linguistically, and whether it is possible to account for it outside a parameter-setting, linguistically motivated framework is an important question. Noting that the FPH conjoined with Radford's position predicts that it must be, I shall put off further discussion of the issue until our final chapter.

10.5 Summary

This chapter has introduced functional categories and attempted to give an idea of the important role they play in current grammatical theories which adopt the principles and parameters perspective. While the notion of 'functional category' has intuitive appeal, it will be important for future research to articulate precise criteria for membership in this set. This is particularly true if the FPH is to be pursued with vigour. We have discussed examples which appear to confirm this hypothesis, but it would be foolish to underestimate the tasks confronting a wide-ranging investigation of its plausibility.

That children acquiring English appear to pass through a pre-functional stage is supported by Radford's work, but it is easy to neglect difficulties which can be raised for this approach because of our incomplete grasp of the basic notions. For example, consider negation. Negatives occur in the data on which Radford bases his claims, but are they members of a lexical or a functional category? To maintain his position, Radford has to claim that they are lexical, but to do this begins to strain the identification of lexical elements as 'thematic'. Does *not* assign a Θ-role to its 'argument'? If so, what is it? These are not questions I shall attempt to answer here. I raise them merely to indicate that a great deal of understanding needs to be achieved before we can be confident in tackling the issues raised in this chapter. At the end of the chapter, we raised some consequences of our discussion which are rather provocative. In the last chapter, I shall worry away at these a bit more, as well as summarize the main conclusions we can draw from the book.

11   Final Thoughts

One theme of this book has been to try to establish how PPT, viewed as a theory of acquisition, contrasts with one of its predecessors, ST, these contrasts being examined against a background of learnability. This is done in a preliminary way in chapters 1–3, and the remainder of the book is an exploration of issues, general and specific, which arise once PPT is interpreted in the acquisition context. Specific issues raised included the setting of the parameter which licenses null subjects (chapter 4), the detailed formulation of Binding Theory parameters and their implications for acquisition (chapter 5) and experimental investigation of when children's grammars can be confidently seen as constrained by particular principles (chapter 6). General issues were the question of epistemological priority in the primary linguistic data (chapter 7), the nature of developmental mechanisms (chapter 8), and the necessity for producing a constrained theory of parameters (chapters 9 and 10). Of course, the specific and the general have interacted at numerous points. Thus, in chapter 4, we were led to consider what properties of the data lead to a resetting of the parameter licensing null subjects, itself a question about primary linguistic data; in chapter 5, we considered the Subset Principle, a principle which embodies claims about developmental mechanisms; in chapter 10, we were forced to think again about the licensing of null subjects in the context of seeking to restrict parameters to properties of functional categories; and so on.

I believe that this interaction between specific linguistic proposals and general developmental questions represents a healthy state of affairs, and if the reader is persuaded to contemplate language acquisition in new ways on the basis of the book, I shall be well satisfied.

What have we actually established as well-founded claims about the process? I believe that the list in (1) contains some of the most important conclusions we are justified in drawing:

(1)   a. Where carefully collected evidence is available, children's grammars are constrained by remarkably abstract principles from a rather early age.

     b. The setting of parameters ought to be construed as a learning process, albeit one in which the child is not simultaneously evaluating a set of competing hypotheses against each other.

c. If parameter-setting is a learning process, the same cannot be said for the development of principles. If these are not available immediately, there is nothing incoherent in the suggestion that they mature according to a genetically determined schedule.

d. The epistemological priority question is an extremely difficult one, and it would be wildly optimistic to suggest that a solution to it is at hand. However, the convergence of ideas developed by linguists working on LRs and developmentalists such as Pinker is encouraging. I foresee an intensive period of collaboration in tackling this question.

e. It would be unwise to take the validity of The Subset Condition as a constraint on parameters as axiomatic. The domain of application of its procedural offspring, the Subset Principle, remains a largely open question.

f. The Degree-*n* Condition on possible parameters is worth continued investigation for some suitably small value of *n*. The suggestion that complexity might be definable in structural terms distinct from degree of embedding is another interesting issue in this area.

g. The juxtaposition of the FPH and the suggestion that children begin word-combination with a lexical 'thematic' grammar raises some thought-provoking issues. Again, these are likely to occupy suitably minded researchers in the immediate future.

To close, I want to look again at some of the problems arising out of (1g) in the context of two types of study which have not concerned us up to now. The first of these examines the characteristics of the gestural systems of communication developed by congenitally deaf children of hearing parents (Feldman, Goldin-Meadow and Gleitman, 1978; Goldin-Meadow and Mylander, 1984, 1990). The children in these studies received no significant aural input because of their deafness, and their parents, as well as not being signers, did not encourage signing behaviour in their children, as it was felt that this might inhibit any progress they might make with spoken language.

Under these extraordinary conditions, the deaf children *created* gestural systems of communication, known as Home Sign, with a range of identifiable characteristics. Summarizing, the authors recognized two major categories of signs in these created systems: 'points', which involved the child in pointing to some object in the environment, and 'characterizing signs' which were typically mimetic and predicational. Thus, points could be identified with arguments and characterizing signs with predicates. Further, the children combined these signs into 'utterances', clearly signalling the end of such a structured unit. Notably, they did this in such a way as to convince the investigators that they could not have *learned* the characteristics of the system from their parents; the latter's attempts at sign combination were inept when compared to the children's. So, not only are there arguments and predicates in this system, but there are also predicate–argument structures. Finally, the 'content' of the children's signed 'utterances' was remarkably similar to that of the average hearing 2-year-old, i.e. they communicated about the here-and-now, using a restricted set of predicates with the arguments interpretable in terms of such Θ-roles as Agent, Patient, Goal and Location. In short, what these children appear to have been doing was externalizing internally represented predicate–argument structures in a non-conventional way.

Additionally, as Goldin-Meadow and Mylander (1990, p. 336) put it:

> Ordering regularities were based on the position that a gesture for a particular thematic role tended to occupy in a sentence. The children tended to order gestures for patients, acts and recipients in a consistent way in their two-gesture sentences.

I suggest that this observation is highly significant in the light of the observations we made about pre-functional variations in word-order at the end of Section 10.4. To appreciate this significance, recall our discussion of Fassi-Fehri (1989) in Section 10.2. He accounts for the difference between SVO word-order in English and VSO word-order in Arabic by suggesting that I assigns nominative Case rightwards in Arabic but leftwards in English. As I is a functional category, this is an example of functional parameterization; and as parameter-setting requires learning, exposure to English or Arabic is required to fix this parameter. From this we might be tempted to predict that there will be no systematic word-order differences in the speech of English and Arabic children who have pre-functional grammars. But suppose there are such differences. What can we conclude from them?

One obvious possibility is that the FPH is incorrect, as there is at least one parameter already set in pre-functional grammars. But perhaps this conclusion is hasty. The deaf children display consistent sign-orders *in the absence of any linguistic input*, from which it follows that there are also non-linguistic principles at work in determining these orders. Of course, we can speculate about what these might be in terms of notions like 'discourse' and 'cognitive salience', but so long as they exist at all (and the signing of the deaf children suggests that they do), they can in principle provide us with a way of accounting for word-order which is not *linguistically* motivated.

With this possibility in mind, consider now Radford's (1990a) analysis of (2) as (3):

(2)   Hayley draw it

(3)   [$_{VP}$Hayley [$_{V'}$draw it]]

In (3), we have of course placed the lexical items in the appropriate order, but if the FPH is correct, this order will not actually be specified in the child's representation. As far as this latter is concerned, the orders in (4) are equivalent to (3):

(4)   a. [$_{VP}$ Hayley [$_{V'}$it draw]]
     b. [$_{VP}$ [$_{V'}$draw it] Hayley]
     c. [$_{VP}$ [$_{V'}$it draw] Hayley]

So, how does the English-speaking child come to produce (2) on the basis of a representation which is neutral between (3) and (4a, b, c)? Let us concentrate on the relative position of subject and predicate, and ignore the ordering within the V'.[1] As a possibility, consider the fact that the child is surrounded by utterances in which the subject precedes the predicate. Of course, for the adult producing such utterances the order is linguistically motivated via parameterization of direction of nominative Case-assignment from I. By assumption, the child has no I yet, so this linguistic motivation is not available to him or her. But I can see no reason why such a child should not use the language he or she hears to effect a linearization strategy. The intriguing thing is, of course, that when I enters the child's system enabling the appropriate parameter to be set, a word-order which has been used continues to be used but is now linguistically motivated. A fundamental change in the internal system of representation has no overt consequences for this aspect of the child's linguistic behaviour.

This suggestion may strike some as fanciful, but now recall Clahsen's (1986) claim (referred to in chapter 4) that German children produce large numbers of word-order errors at early stages of development and that these show a dramatic decrease at a certain point. Suppose this point corresponds to the emergence of functional categories and the German child's setting of the parameters which determine word-order in main clauses. Then the correct word-order becomes linguistically motivated. What about before this point? One can only speculate, but it is perhaps significant that SOV word-order is required in German subordinate clauses. If the children were trying to figure out the word-order on the basis of the order of the lexical categories to which they were exposed, the distribution of errors reported by Clahsen might not be unexpected.

I am suggesting, then, that a range of options may be accessible to children enabling them to use one or more word-orders before these word-orders are required by parametric settings in their linguistic system. The deaf children obviously avail themselves of one of these, although it is not at all clear which one.[2] The ambient language (not available to the deaf children) provides a skeleton of ordered lexical categories which might form the basis for another, and undoubtedly there are more, involving notions such as discourse prominence. There is as yet no compelling reason to abandon the conjunction of FPH and Radford's claims on the basis of systematic pre-functional word-order differences.

A second feature of Home Sign which is worthy of note here is the questionable existence in it of functional categories. In discussing Radford's thesis, we adopted his suggestion that functional category systems mature. Given this, we might expect that they will also mature for the congenitally deaf children, but apart from some rather tentative remarks on inflectional morphology, Goldin-Meadow and Mylander offer no hints of developed functional category systems. Is there any reason to expect this?

Assume for the sake of argument that the parameters with which we are concerned do not have unmarked default values. If this is so, exposure to primary linguistic data is a necessary condition for a parameter to have any value at all.[3] It is plausible to suggest that functional categories for which the parameterizable properties do not have fixed values are inert in the grammar. In short, the deaf children do not create that for which hearing children require evidence.[4]

It could well be that consideration of factors such as these will provide a way of coming to terms with the precocious development of inflectional systems in Italian and Polish children (Hyams, 1986, 1987a). Radford's suggestion that functional categories (including I) mature might be seen as committing him to the view that inflectional systems will emerge at about the same time cross-linguistically. But this would be a mistaken commitment.

To say that a representational capacity, in this case a grammar including functional categories, matures at *t* does not entail that the child will exhibit full competence with functional categories at *t*. He or she has still to determine how the system of functional categories is *realized* in the grammar being acquired, and there is no reason to believe that the complexity of this task will be uniform across grammars. Thus, it is not implausible to suggest that the rich inflectional paradigms in Italian and Polish provide the ideal circumstances for children to work out the properties of I in these languages and to display these properties in their own speech.

Although I am familiar with no relevant observations on Italian, the following comment by Smoczyńska (1985, p. 617) on the acquisition of Polish is quite consistent with the existence of a pre-functional stage:

> At the one-word stage there is no evidence for productive use of inflected forms, *with no significant changes being observed in this respect in the earliest two-word combinations.* (my emphasis – MA)

It thus appears that for at least one language in which inflections develop early, there is an identifiable period during which they are lacking.[5]

Further tentative support for the position we are outlining here can be gleaned from the classic study of the effects and non-effects of Motherese, conducted by Newport, Gleitman and Gleitman (1977) (see also Furrow, Nelson and Benedict, 1979, for an attempt to dispute the conclusions of the earlier study, and Gleitman, Newport and Gleitman, 1984, for a response which leaves these conclusions intact). What these authors did was collect samples of mothers' speech to their children on which they defined a number of measures, thereby providing a profile of individual differences between mothers. They also collected a sample of the children's speech at this time, followed up by a second sample six months later. Again, a number of measures were defined on these samples, enabling Newport et al. to compute *growth scores* for a number of aspects of the children's development. What was of interest was whether there were any significant correlations, positive or negative, between the scores defined on the data provided by the individual mothers and their child's development during the subsequent six months.

Without going into the elaborate but justified statistical work that Newport et al. report, we can caricature some of their major findings as follows. For basic predicate–argument structure, there were no discernible effects of variations in the speech of individual mothers. To put it concretely, it did not seem to matter whether mothers produced longer or shorter sentences, whether they asked lots of questions, whether they produced lots of imperatives and so on; as far as their abilities to combine nominal expressions and predicational expressions went, their children appeared to develop in the same way at the same rate.

However, a quite different outcome was reported for verbal complexity, defined by the number of verbal elements (including modals and auxiliaries) appearing in the verbal complex. Growth scores for this measure were positively correlated with the mothers' tendency to ask yes–no questions. In the terms that we have been using here, we might say that the development of an I-system was affected by variations in maternal speech. Now, as Newport et al. note, yes–no questions in English are characterized by a modal or other auxiliary appearing in initial position, and it is perhaps reasonable to suggest that this position is perceptually salient for the young child. That is, mothers who ask large numbers of yes–no questions could be viewed as providing ideal conditions for the child to begin to sort out the properties of the I-system and its interaction with the C-system.

Obviously related to the above finding was the negative correlation between mothers' use of imperatives and the children's development of verbal complexity. Affirmative imperatives contain *no* overt reflexes of the I-system (negative imperatives, of course, contain the dummy *do* in initial position), so it is perhaps not surprising that profligacy in their use appeared to have an inhibitory effect on the children's progress in this area.[6]

Overall, the correspondences between the studies of the deaf children and Newport et al.'s work on Motherese are quite striking. Hearing children appear to be insensitive to variations in maternal speech in exactly that domain where deaf children seem to be capable of creating a communication system. However, in certain limited domains, variations in maternal speech do appear to affect the hearing child's development; and deaf children show little evidence of creating systems in these domains. These domains, I suggest, are just those of functional categories.

If all of this is correct, we arrive at an admittedly incomplete but rather satisfying overview of the development of syntax in first language acquisition. The discontinuity marked by the emergence of functional category systems coincides with the onset of the only significant linguistic learning which needs to take place. This learning – establishing the properties of functional categories by fixing the values of parameters – can be facilitated or inhibited (presumably within certain limits) by the characteristics of the target grammar and by the distribution of primary linguistic data in the child's ambient environment, i.e. the language itself and others' use of the language can both play a part in determining the rate of acquisition at this point. Filling all of this out constitutes an extensive research programme, which I fully anticipate will be a focus of activity in this area during the coming years.

Notes

Introduction

1 Throughout, I follow the standard practice of indicating syntactic ill-formedness with an asterisk. One or more question marks preceding a string indicates that its syntactic status is questionable.

Chapter 1 Laying the Foundations

1 To get some idea of the poverty of the behaviourist framework, it is instructive to consult ch. 2 of Bloomfield (1933). Even he, with his sophisticated awareness of the complexities of language structure, was reduced to extraordinarily crude suggestions when considering first language acquisition, and it is difficult to see his account as an improvement on that of the linguistically ignorant Watson (1928).

2 That *semantic* aspects of Skinner's programme may be revivable in extensively modified form, as part of a 'naturalized' account of meaning, has been suggested by Fodor (1990).

3 Specifically, conjunctive concepts such as RED AND GREEN are easier to learn in these circumstances than disjunctive concepts such as RED OR GREEN. Readers familiar with Fodor (1975) will know that this observation, coupled with the logical equivalence of expressions employing conjunction and others employing disjunction and negation, provides one pillar of the argument for the 'Language of Thought' having a syntax.

4 For discussion of a different example involving the identification of sets of integers, see Osherson, Stob and Weinstein (1986, pp. 1–3).

5 In fact, Gold construes this space as containing grammars, but the latter are simply identified with *names* for languages and not as mentally represented *structures*, so no serious error is involved in the assumption in the text. See Section 1.5 for discussion of the significance of this issue.

6 It is noteworthy that transferring this definition into the sphere of natural language acquisition does not immediately render it implausible. Children acquiring English and other natural languages clearly do so on the basis of exposure to different data sequences however this latter notion is construed. For more discussion, see Section 1.5.

7 For a Characterization Theorem of classes of languages for which this result obtains, see Wexler and Hamburger (1973), Wexler and Culicover (1980, p. 46).

8 There are alternative ways of imposing restrictions on rule-types which will not concern us here. The interested reader is referred to textbooks on mathematical linguistics, such as Wall (1972), Partee (1975).

9 For a formal statement of this Superset Theorem, see Wexler and Culicover (1980, p. 49).

10 Note that this does not deny the *possibility* that all natural languages are in L_2 for example. It does deny that *all* languages in L_2 are natural languages. From the non-learnability of L_2, *nothing* follows about the non-learnability of its subsets.

11 See Fodor, Bever and Garrett (1974) for extensive discussion of neo-behaviourist psycholinguistics and its debt to American structuralism.

12 For an overview of different approaches to a priori constraints in cognitive development generally, see Keil (1990).

13 Given the dubious status of E-language as outlined in the text, it is necessary to rephrase this observation along the following lines: the child is confronted by utterances which are not an accurate reflection of the utterer's I-language (performance errors) and by utterances which provide inconsistent clues to the nature of I-language (environments which contain a variety of dialects/E-languages). Recognition of this latter possibility is the motivation for the idealization to a homogeneous speech community (Chomsky, 1965).

14 More recently, a number of studies have reopened the issues investigated by Brown and Hanlon with varying results. For example, Hirsh-Pasek, Treiman and Schneiderman (1984), Demetras, Post and Snow (1986), Penner (1987) and Bohannon and Stanowicz (1988) have all succeeded in identifying some feature of maternal behaviour which appears to be contingent on grammatical ill-formedness for *some* children at *some* time. However, it is unlikely that such claims justify the conclusion that children receive systematic information about non-sentences. For elaboration of this perspective, see Pinker (1989, pp. 9ff.), Morgan and Travis (1989), Grimshaw and Pinker (1989).

15 This is not to take issue with Hornstein and Lightfoot's more detailed arguments for UG. They themselves predicate these on what they see as more important deficiencies in the data to which the child is exposed (see also Hornstein, 1983).

16 To show that a single class of languages L^* has this property does not, of course, establish the general proposition that the set of informant-identifiable classes of languages properly contains the text-identifiable classes. Since it is obvious that *any* text-identifiable class is also informant-identifiable, however, the general proposition is readily derived.

17 In fact, Osherson et al. make a weaker assumption than this, merely requiring the learner not to increase the complexity of the current hypothesis beyond a certain bound in the face of a datum which is consistent with that hypothesis. The result described in the text is still obtained if the stronger, and perhaps more plausible, assumption of conservatism is adopted.

Chapter 2 Standard Theory and Language Acquisition

1 Explicit in (1) is the claim that semantic interpretation is determined entirely by deep structures, the Katz–Postal Hypothesis. The recognition that this was difficult to maintain was already present in Chomsky (1965) and later led to the waging of what Newmeyer (1980) describes as the 'linguistic wars' between generative and interpretive semantics.

2 The mnemonic value of the symbols here is fairly obvious: S = sentence, NP = noun phrase, AUX = auxiliary verb, VP = verb phrase, D = determiner, N = noun, C = complementizer, PP = prepositional phrase, P = preposition. In fact,

the rules in (3) and (4) do not produce (5), since, with the exception of *to*, they do not introduce the lexical items. We return to lexical insertion below.

3   I gloss over here the genuine distinctions between the model developed in Chomsky (1957) and ST, since they are not relevant in the present context.

4   This formulation follows Chomsky (1965) in assuming that the deep structure for a passive contains a *by*-phrase, with the object of the preposition *by* being filled by a 'dummy' NP. In this respect, the ST treatment of passives differs fundamentally from earlier versions.

5   Strictly speaking, we should pay much more attention to the *structure* which results from the operation of the rule. However, for our purposes it will be sufficient to note that we get the right linear order for the expressions in the passive sentence.

6   Again, the deep structure is actually a phrase structure tree, but for the purposes at hand, a linear representation will suffice.

7   As might be expected, there are many much more elaborate illustrations of the necessity for the Principle of the Cycle than that given here (see, for example, Akmajian and Heny, 1975, pp. 356–69). For simplicity, I have assumed that S is the only domain in which transformations operate, but many of the relevant discussions acknowledge that NP is also a *cyclic node*.

8   Readers familiar with recent linguistic theory will recognize the paradigm in (32)–(35) as providing part of the evidence for the Empty Category Principle. This will be discussed in ch. 3. Of course, children do produce a range of errors as they acquire a language and some of these may be seen to represent an inappropriate inductive generalization based on what they perceive. Particularly well known in this respect are the morphological errors in connection with irregular past-tense forms of verbs, when children produce such expressions as *goed* and *comed* instead of *went* and *came*, thereby overextending the regular past-tense formation rule (*jump/jumped*, etc.) to inappropriate contexts (see Brown, 1973; Kuczaj, 1977; Bybee and Slobin, 1982, for discussion of this phenomenon in naturalistic and experimental contexts; Clark, 1987, for theoretical discussion; and Morgan and Travis, 1989, for a study of indirect negative evidence in this connection). But such productive errors, while comprising some of the earliest evidence for the child taking an active and creative role in language acquisition, are of much less significance in recent work than errors which do not occur, despite the fact that they would be predicted by simple generalization mechanisms.

9   Probably the best-known such constraint from the period is that which prohibits the deletion of material which is not 'recoverable'. Consideration of such details would take us too far afield here (see Chomsky, 1965, for discussion).

10   Many readers will no doubt be familiar with the notion of a Language Acquisition Device (LAD) in Chomsky's writings. In (37) this is to be identified with UG, i.e. the set of universals and the evaluation measure.

11   Chomsky (1975) has defended the idealization, pointing to the uniformity of the mature state in the face of variations in input data. This uniformity suggests that it is not damagingly misleading to assume that the child has simultaneous access to the full range of data which determine the nature of the mature state. Wexler and Culicover (1980, pp. 525–8) have raised doubts about the soundness of this defence, and have also pointed to the dangers of oversimplifying the child's task by making the assumption. They see a theory of UG *which is not rich enough* as a possible consequence of this.

12   A theory of UG which accounts for the selection of a correct grammar on the basis of primary linguistic data is *explanatorily adequate* in terms of the levels of

adequacy discussed in Chomsky (1965). If the theory meets further empirical constraints such as the correct grammar being selected in a 'reasonable' time, it approaches the more demanding requirement of *feasibility*. See Wexler and Culicover (1980) for extensive discussion.

13   One way in which this might be justified is if there were a single universal base (apart from lexical insertion) for all grammars. If this Universal Base Hypothesis were true, then it could be assumed that it is available to the child in the initial state with no learning required. However, so long as our mode of data presentation remains text, the Universal Base Hypothesis is not helpful, since it is possible to define a class of unlearnable languages, the grammars of which include such a base. See Wexler and Culicover (1980, p. 52).

14   It is important to Wexler and Culicover's system that all transformations are *obligatory*. This is one respect in which they do not remain within the assumptions of ST; they themselves note this and emphasize the importance of studying the learnability of systems which include optional rules.

15   At this point, I switch to 'base structures' for 'deep structures', so as to maintain Wexler and Culicover's (b, s) notation. Nothing depends on this. It is reasonable to ask what justification there is for the assumption that children have access to such data. As far as b is concerned, the authors assume that children are often capable of working out what an utterance *means* without understanding its syntax. A transparent mapping between semantic interpretations and base structures might then enable the child to determine such structures. These issues are discussed at considerable length, but inconclusively, in ch. 7 of Wexler and Culicover (1980) under the rubric of the Invariance Principle. We shall consider a similar idea in ch. 7 below. For s, there is no difficulty in accepting the view that children are presented with surface *strings*. Indeed, as we shall see in the next section, it is likely that they are also presented with aspects of surface *structures*. Wexler and Culicover dismiss this possibility, saying (p. 82): 'Although children hear surface sentences . . . there is not much reason to believe that they are presented with information about what the surface phrase marker is.'

16   In fact, issues are considerably more complex than this, since Wexler and Culicover wish to limit the hypothesization of transformations to those which would have produced a correct result had they applied *on the highest cycle* in the derivation. Their reasons for this are partly to minimize the computational load for the learner.

17   Note that this is another example of the interaction between the components of the system illustrated by our discussion of 'simple data' (pp. 25–6). Here we are making the learning procedure less powerful. As a consequence, some other component of the model has to be modified.

18   A little clarification is perhaps appropriate here for readers not familiar with probabilistic concepts. We have an infinite set on which is defined a probability distribution with each member of the set being assigned a non-zero probability. The sum of these probabilities is 1. Consider a finite subset of this set. We can go through this, listing the probabilities assigned to each member under the distribution. One of these will be the smallest; call it p. We can then say that the probability assigned to any member of this finite subset is *bounded* by p, where p is greater than 0. For the infinite residue, however, this procedure is not possible. If p_i is the probability assigned to some element in this residue, it will always be possible to find another element assigned probability p_j such that p_j is less than p_i, i.e. there is no lower bound greater than 0 on the probabilities assigned to members of an infinite set.

19 I have glossed over the notion of 'correctness' assumed. In fact, Wexler and Culicover do not require that the selected transformational component be identical to that of the target grammar. A component will be 'correct' in their terms if it performs the appropriate mapping from base structures to surface strings. It need not produce the right surface *structures*. Transformational components which perform the same base structure–surface string mapping are referred to as *moderately equivalent*.

20 Note that it is merely a bracketing and not a labelled bracketing that the hypothesis assumes. That is, Morgan does not suppose that the child has access to categorial information.

21 Female genealogical terminology such as 'sister', 'mother' and 'aunt' is often used to describe the relationships between nodes in trees. The interpretation of this terminology is transparent.

22 In fact, this simple illustration, which is intended merely to exhibit how different assumptions about data can lead to different classes of detectable errors, is not an accurate representation of the Wexler and Culicover system. This system allows misadjunction errors of this type to be propagated up a tree. What the Raising Principle requires is that a transformation cannot 'look inside' a raised node and affect part of its contents. If the Raising Principle did not hold, it would be possible for a misadjunction error to be introduced at some point in a derivation, propagated up the tree by successive raisings of the node dominating the error, then revealed by a rule affecting part of the material in the successively raised node. With this situation, errors would no longer be detectable on degree-2 data. If, however, the node dominating the error continues to be raised in its entirety, the error will never be detectable and will continue to belong to the learner's grammar. It is for this reason that Wexler and Culicover's proof only guarantees the learnability of moderately equivalent grammars (cf. note 19).

23 A point of some interest here is an observation of Newport cited by Morgan that the mean number of S-nodes per utterance in a sample of mothers' speech to their children was 1.08. This suggests that degree-2 data are not frequent in the speech addressed to the child, and constitutes a prima facie case for a system which does not require such data (see also Section 9.3).

24 This is a conservative strategy which does not, of course, address the productive aspect of the alternation. See Section 7.4 for further discussion.

25 Note that in removing the ordered option from UG, we also address the basic quantitative problem of there being too many grammars. If UG does not permit statements ordering rules, all grammars containing such statements are immediately removed from consideration. The parallel observation holds for the next issue raised in the text.

26 There are two ways in which this observation might be responded to. The first is that adopted in Principles and Parameters Theory and simply assumes that all operations are optional. The second invokes the logic of markedness in a style reminiscent of Chomsky and Lasnik's (1977) defence of filters which, though part of UG, are not universal. In this context, the logic would require that obligatoriness should be the unmarked option in UG, with the child assuming that any operation is obligatory unless he or she is supplied with evidence to the contrary. For the optional rule in (53), this evidence would consist of exposure to the well-formed (53a, b). This logic, extended to the argument about rule ordering, would require that any pair of rules occurring in a derivation should be taken as ordered as they appear in that derivation until the child receives evidence that they are unordered.

27 For an example of such a failure, see Williams' (1981c) discussion of Jackendoff's (1977) use of a shortness evaluation measure in connection with English phrase-structure rules.

Chapter 3 Principles and Parameters Theory

1 Recall that in the previous chapter (p. 54), we pointed out that an unrestricted theory of phrase-structure rules would permit configurations in which the notion of projection cannot be understood in this way. Obviously, the structures in (1) are presupposing a more constrained theory of phrase structure (see Section 3.3).

2 In fact, this is not quite accurate, since Chomsky's definition of c-command does not even refer to branching node. What distinguishes it from his definition of m-command (identical to (6) in the text) is merely that the latter stipulates that γ is a maximal projection. These differences are not important for our present purposes.

3 Chomsky (1986b) suggests that γ in his definition of c-command should involve reference to branching node for purposes of Binding Theory, one of the modules which will be introduced in section 3.3.

4 In fact, the reference to 'no maximal projection' in (7) is too strong, but it would be inappropriate to go into the reasons for this here. See Aoun and Sportiche (1983), Chomsky (1986b), M. Baker (1988a) for extensive discussion. Additionally, there is nothing incoherent about defining a notion of government in terms of Reinhart's c-command. The ultimate questions are empirical: precisely which configurational relations play which roles in the theory of grammar?

5 Note that this is a distinct sense of *projection* from that introduced in the previous section. There we were concerned with lexical categories projecting into phrasal categories of the same syntactic type within a level of representation. Here we are conceiving of projection as the relation between two levels of representation. This usage of the same term is unfortunate, but it should not lead to confusion.

6 The structure in (14) is a (partial) labelled bracketing rather than a labelled tree, and it is customary (and space-saving) to use such bracketings when the example is reasonably transparent. The two systems of notation are entirely equivalent.

7 In the terminology of Chomsky (1986a), s-selection (semantic selection) predicts c-selection (categorial selection or subcategorization).

8 A word of caution is necessary here, because of the well-known *wanna* contraction phenomenon. Briefly, the sentence in (i) is ambiguous depending on whether it is derived from (ii) or (iii):

    (i)   Who do you want to visit?
   (ii) You want to visit who
  (iii) You want who to visit

In many English dialects, it is possible to contract *want to* to *wanna*, yielding (iv):

  (iv) Who do you wanna visit?

It is claimed that (iv) can only be interpreted as if derived from (ii), with *who* originating as d-structure internal argument of *visit*. This is then accounted for by assuming that *wanna*-contraction, a PF rule, is blocked by an empty category between *want* and *to*. Thus, it cannot apply to the s-structure in (v):

(v)   Who$_i$ do you want e_i to visit

If this is correct, *some* PF processes must be able to detect the presence of empty categories. However, this does not impinge on the point in the text (see Postal and Pullum, 1982; Lasnik, 1989, for discussion of arguments surrounding this phenomenon).

9   Of course, the co-referentiality indicated by the co-indexing in (20a, b, c) is not obligatory, i.e. each of these sentences is well-formed with the pronoun interpreted as referring to someone other than John, and (20d) is also well-formed under these circumstances. It is the *possibility* of co-referentiality that concerns us, a possibility which is not present in (20d).

10 Note that since *wh*-words are not referential, it is not strictly appropriate to talk about the co-indexing as indicating co-referentiality here. Rather what we are considering are possibilities for *bound variable anaphora*. The point established by whether the co-indexing is possible is that whereas (23a) can be interpreted as: 'who is the x such that x likes x's mother?', (23b) cannot be interpreted as: 'who is the x such that x's mother likes x?'

11 In these representations, we assume that the *wh*-word or phrase has moved even when it originates in the d-structure external argument position, as in (24a, c). This is not required by observations of linear order, but it is the standard view. As it does not affect the argument here, we adopt the assumption without further comment.

12 The *wh*-examples also have LF representations. For them, the mapping from s-structure to LF is trivial, ensuring that at LF the parallels between the two sets of structures are transparent.

13 At this stage it is appropriate to point out that there are various proposals for the principles of X-bar Theory which differ in detail from (36). For example, Jackendoff (1977) maintains that a third level of projection, (X'''), is necessary, and others (e.g. Emonds, 1985) have proposed that there are differences in the levels to which individual lexical categories project.

14 Recall note 5 on the two senses of 'projection'. Here we are concerned with the original use, as it occurs in 'maximal projection'.

15 In this respect, they have a similar status to the notions 'subject-of' and 'direct object-of' as these are understood in ST (Chomsky, 1965).

16 In these examples, no movement has taken place, so the appropriate d-structure will also be the appropriate s-structure. A number of issues are being ignored, such as the genitive -'s marker in *the enemy's*, and the *of* which introduces the complement of *destruction* (and of *proud* in (41b)). See the discussion of Case Theory below for the latter. The analyses of AP and PP suggested here will be modified in chs. 6 and 10 when we take account of adjuncts and Small Clauses.

17 The necessity to be inconsistent regarding the sense of 'internal' is a reflex of the less than total parallelism between clause-structure and NP-structure referred to in the text.

18 A major omission in the above discussion of X-bar Theory is the status of *adjunct* phrases. There will be brief consideration of where these are accommodated in the system in ch. 6. Radford (1988a, ch. 4) provides a detailed treatment of the distinction between complements and adjuncts.

19 The fate of the Agent argument in passives raises a number of difficult issues which will not be pursued here. See Baker, Johnson and Roberts (1989), Manzini (forthcoming) for relevant discussion.

20 The difficulty with this simple illustration of structure preservation is that it is redundant in that Case Theory independently requires that the moved NPs should have NP-positions as their targets (see below). For discussion of different types of movement and their interaction with structure preservation and other principles of grammar, see Chomsky (1986b, pp. 4–7), Radford (1988a, Sections 10.4 and 10.5).

21 An exception is provided by pronouns which occur in tag questions such as (i):

    (i) John$_i$ likes Mary, doesn't he$_{i/*j}$

22 The use of 'subject' in connection with noun phrases is justified in the context of the parallels between noun phrases and clauses illustrated in our discussion of X-bar Theory above.

23 There are several formulations of the Binding Theory principles which take account of these complications. One of the earliest and clearest is Huang (1982). See Chomsky (1981) for the ideas on which Huang builds and Chomsky (1986a) for a rather different proposal.

24 Extensive discussion of the level of application of the Binding Principles appears in Belletti and Rizzi (1988). They conclude that, while Principles B and C are correctly located at s-structure, Principle A can be satisfied at eight d- or s-structure.

25 The inclusion of this *rule* in a principle-based system was again a reflex of the fact that clausal structure was not fully integrated with the X-bar framework until the mid-1980s.

26 We ignore here the question of the inversion of the subject and the auxiliary verb.

27 The above arguments rely on implicit assumptions about the contents of C which prohibit a *wh*-expression from moving into it. These were made explicit by stipulations such as the Multiply Filled COMP Filter (Chomsky and Lasnik, 1977) within this analysis. When C is assimilated to the X-bar system, more elegant accounts of these phenomena become possible.

28 This choice of terminology has its origins in formal logic, where *operators* such as quantifiers bind variables in the equivalent of A-positions. Recall from Section 3.2 that quantifiers and *wh*-expressions are both assumed to move to A′-positions (operator positions) at some level of syntactic representation.

29 For reasons why it is misguided to treat *arb* like a referential index and for a feature-assigning approach to arbitrary interpretation, see Rizzi (1986).

30 For a proposal that aspects of Control Theory should be accommodated by Binding Theory, see Manzini (1983).

31 This is loosely formulated and probably not convincing. However, the original discussions also had these properties! As well as being useful here, I shall need to refer to this type of analysis of I in ch. 4. Again, we shall see in ch. 10 how a more attractive analysis can be developed.

32 A good deal of debate has gone on about whether [+TNS] is the property of I which determines its status as a governor, or whether reference to AGR is more appropriate. For summary and discussion of a range of languages, see Koopman (1984), Tuller (1986).

33 I omit here discussion of *Exceptional Case Marking* constructions such as (i) and (ii):

    (i)   John believes [Bill to be happy]
    (ii) *John believes [PRO to be happy]

Since the subordinate clause is infinitival, we might expect to find PRO subjects here. However, the fact that we find a lexical NP (*Bill*) suggests that the position is 'exceptionally' governed by the matrix verb. See Chomsky (1986a, pp. 189ff.), for discussion.

34 I omit discussion of the complex topic of genitive Case-assignment (see Chomsky, 1986a.)

35 One way to make the notion of 'absorption' less metaphorical is to suppose that the objective Case is assigned to the passive morpheme *-en*. For relevant discussion, see Jaeggli (1986), Baker, Johnson and Roberts (1989), Manzini (forthcoming).

36 The type of Case-assignment we have described is known as *structural* Case-assignment. This is because the process is based entirely on structural considerations and is in no way concerned with the semantic properties of the arguments to which Case is assigned. The examples in (i) illustrate that nominative Case-assignment to the subject is indifferent to whether that subject is an Agent (ia), Patient (ib), Experiencer (ic) or Goal (id):

> (i) a. He kissed Mary
>   b. He was kissed by Mary
>   c. He saw Mary
>   d. He received a gift from Mary

In addition to structural Case, there is another category of Case, known as *inherent* Case. This differs from structural Case in being inherently associated with a particular semantic role in the LR of a Case-assigner and in being assigned at d-structure.

Consider (ii):

> (ii) John gave a book to Mary

Here *Mary* is a Goal, but the preposition *to* which precedes it has no semantic content over and above that supplied by the meaning of *give*. It could be maintained, then, that the Goal argument *Mary* is projected into d-structure as a bare NP, and assigned inherent Dative Case by the verb, this Case being realized at s-structure by the preposition *to*. For discussion of datives along these lines, see Hale and Keyser (forthcoming). Larson (1988) is a comprehensive analysis of English dative constructions which operates with rather different assumptions.

37 That (116) may be more clearly motivated in Predication Theory, a module we do not discuss here, is argued by Williams (1980) and Rothstein (1983).

38 The issue is considerably complicated by the existence of *implicit arguments* such as the external argument of *float* in (i):
(i) the company was floated to make a profit
In (i), the subordinate clause has a PRO subject. Furthermore, this PRO is controlled by the implicit external argument of *float*, i.e. whoever did the floating intended to make the profit. Conditions under which arguments can remain implicit is currently the subject of a good deal of research (Roeper, 1984; Brody and Manzini, 1988; Manzini, forthcoming).

39 The technical manoeuvre necessary to make this precise is to introduce the concept of a *chain*, which in this case consists of ($Mary_i$, e_i). Then the Θ-criterion is rephrased to require the assignment of unique Θ-roles to chains.

40 Some caution is necessary in connection with Chinese, as this language has no overt Tense and Agreement morphology (see Huang, 1989, for recent discussion of

the status of *pro* in Chinese).

41 Relevant discussion appears in Lasnik and Saito (1984), Aoun, Hornstein, Lightfoot and Weinberg (1987) and Rizzi (1990). Van Riemsdijk and Williams (1986, ch. 18) trace the historical development of the theoretical ideas.

42 See, for example, Greenberg (1963) for this type of work, and Williams (1981c) for one of the earliest attempts to accommodate it within a parameterized X-bar framework.

43 See Lasnik and Saito (1984) for a similar formulation of this condition.

44 The reader may have noted that this informal discussion is consistent with a further d-structure as in (i):

(i) $[_{S'}[_C+WH][_S$ John wonders$[_{S'}[_C+WH][_S$ Mary kissed who$]]]]$

However, this d-structure cannot give rise to a well-formed s-structure, since it contains *two* [+WH] Cs and only *one* *wh*-phrase. Wherever *who* ends up at s-structure, one of the [+WH] positions will remain unoccupied by a *wh*-phrase and the result will be inconsistent with (140).

45 Of course, whether or not a grammar includes (144) provides the content of the parameter.

46 For external arguments in clauses, government by the head does not obtain because of the intervening VP-maximal projection. Because of frequently cited examples like those in (i), it is usually claimed that the assignment of a Θ-role to the external argument is 'indirect' and mediated by the VP:

(i) a. John broke his arm
    b. John broke Mary's arm

In (ia), the most natural construal is that *John* receives the Experiencer role, whereas in (ib) assignment of Agent to *John* is required. If this is correct, it means that the verb cannot assign a role directly to its external argument position, but must do this 'compositionally' through the VP, thereby taking account of the contribution to role-determination of the NP in internal argument position. VP, of course, does govern the external argument position, allowing the proposition that Θ-role assignment takes place under government to be maintained. For an analysis which retains the direct/indirect distinction, but allows Θ-role assignment to take place within the government domain of the head, see Fukui (1986) and discussion in ch. 10 below.

47 Adpositions which do not Θ-mark their complements and which are motivated solely by Case requirements do not, of course, have to appear as d-structure postpositions.

48 For comprehensive discussion of a range of devices by which NPs can satisfy the Case Filter, see M. Baker (1988a, pp. 111ff.).

49 The lack of explicitness here is to be contrasted with the assumptions made in the learnability accounts in chs. 1 and 2.

50 Recall the work of Osherson et al., briefly mentioned in Section 1.6, in which they demonstrated that a reasonably plausible set of assumptions led to the conclusion that the class of learnable languages is finite. In fact, they are at pains to point out that finiteness in itself does not trivialize learnability problems. In the same paper, they show that there are finite collections of languages which are *not* learnable on slightly different assumptions. Chomsky has maintained a somewhat ambivalent attitude towards the significance of learnability results. He says (1987a, p. 10): 'If

universal grammar permits unlearnable languages, as it might, then they simply will not be learned.' Having expressed reservations about the significance of observations on parsability for the theory of grammar, he goes on (ibid.): 'In the case of learnability, the proposition that natural languages are learnable may very well be true, but if so, that is not a matter of principle, but rather a surprising empirical discovery about natural language. Recent work in linguistics suggests that it probably is true . . .' The optimism expressed at the end of this passage is born of the belief that the class of possible grammars is finite.

Chapter 4 Null Subjects in the Theory of Grammar and Language Acquisition

1   In what follows, I shall try to convey the general form of sets of theoretical proposals and ignore differences of detail.
2   Rule R is what was referred to as Affix-Hopping in earlier formulations of generative grammar.
3   The choice of the modal *can* in (15) is important. Null Subject Languages, such as Italian, allow lexical subjects as well as null subjects. Lexical subjects must be Case-marked by I to avoid the effects of the Case Filter. Therefore, for I to remain in a position in which it governs the subject must be an option in Null Subject Languages.
4   See Rizzi (1982, pp. 159ff.) for a particularly clear discussion.
5   A question is being begged in connection with (16). The assumption that the inverted subject is adjoined to VP raises the issue of what counts as a maximal projection for c-command and government in such configurations. See May (1985), Chomsky (1986a) for relevant discussion and definitions. The treatment of e_i in (16), which as a trace of movement is subject to the ECP, gives rise to the complications alluded to. Suffice it to say that the analysis offered generalizes to provide an account of (7)–(9), ensuring a unified treatment of the full range of null subject phenomena.
6   For systematic discussion of this and other factors suggesting that the PRO analysis is incorrect, see Rizzi (1982), Jaeggli and Safir (1989). For rather different perspectives on the relationship between PRO and null subjects, see Borer (1989), Huang (1989).
7   Again, I oversimplify considerably. In particular, I ignore the issue of how the inverted subject receives Case, since this must now be assigned to the [+pronominal] feature in I (see Rizzi, 1982, p. 133 for discussion). The treatment of examples like (7)–(9) within this set of assumptions is complicated by consideration of a range of subject–object asymmetries involving quantifiers in French and Italian. To deal with these complications, Rizzi assumes (1982, pp. 138f.) that movements in such cases are from *inverted* subject position.
8   Note that this government requirement on *pro* brings its licensing condition into line with those for traces of movement and PRO. Each empty category is now licensed by some sort of condition on government: traces must be properly governed (the ECP) and PRO must be ungoverned. For this observation and extension to occurrences of *pro* in object position in Italian, see Rizzi (1986).
9   Safir (1985) also develops an account of the phenomena in Section 4.1 which does not utilize a single parameter. His approach differs from that of Hyams in a number of important respects.
10 For controlled AG/PRO, Hyams discusses examples like (i) from Spanish:

(i) Ho visto Luisella che ballava come una matta
     'I saw Luisella that was dancing like a crazy person'

In (i), the complement clause contains a tensed verb *ballava* but has a null subject. Since in a tensed clause, the subject position is governed, the null subject cannot be PRO, and Hyams argues at length that it cannot be *pro* either. The alternative she adopts is to propose that it is a null expletive co-occurring with an object-controlled AG/PRO. Arbitrary AG/PRO is seen as occurring in examples like (ii), again from Spanish, which Hyams maintains is ambiguous between a definite and an arbitrary interpretation of the subject:

(ii) Bussano alla porta
      (They) are knocking at the door

The arbitrary possibility again requires an expletive subject with an uncontrolled AG/PRO in this case according to the arguments Hyams presents. For details, see Hyams (1986, pp. 35–46).

11 Some of the details of this process, traditionally referred to as Subject–Auxiliary Inversion, will concern us in ch. 10.

12 As further support for her account, Hyams notes Rizzi's (1982) observations on the possibility of inversion of subject and verbal auxiliary in gerundive and infinitival constructions. Such constructions do not allow *pro* subjects and Hyams' account requires that PRO does not occur in the AG of such constructions since AG/PRO licenses *pro* subjects. But then there is no need for PRO to remain ungoverned in AG and it is permissible for forms of *essere* and *avere* to be raised from the VP to I, whence they can be inverted with subjects.

13 The account of the late emergence of modal verbs sketched here is clearly 'formal'. Intuitively, it seems clear that the semantics of the modals is rather complex, being generally concerned with 'non-actuality', and it might be felt that this is the true source of difficulty for the child. Hyams notes that a semantically based proposal cannot be the whole story, as the 'semi-auxiliaries' *hafta* and *gonna* are used productively at the optional subject stage, despite largely sharing the semantics of *must* and *will*. To make this observation consistent with her assumptions, Hyams has to hold that the child *can* analyse these forms as main verbs. She suggests that this is plausible because they do exhibit *some* verbal properties – *hafta* inflects for person (*hasta*), and *gonna*, when articulated slowly, as it almost certainly is on occasions in the language the child hears, carries the progressive *-ing* suffix, *going to*.

14 Young Italian children also alternate between initial position and post-verbal position in their expression of overt subjects, a fact which suggests to Hyams the relatively early setting of the Rule R parameter to enable Agreement and Tense affixes to move in the syntax. She speculates that the initial setting of this parameter ought to restrict the applicability of Rule R to PF, its setting for English, since the presence of post-verbal subjects will signal to the Italian-speaking child that the more liberal setting is required. The prediction following from this suggestion is that Italian-speaking children should go through a stage during which they employ only pre-verbal subjects, but the available data did not allow this prediction to be adequately tested.

15 This is a very approximate description, but it matches that offered by Hyams. For extensive and detailed discussion of relevant aspects of the syntax of German, see Haider and Prinzhorn (1986).

16 As Jaeggli and Hyams point out, Spanish also tolerates a certain amount of inflectional homonymy in its verbal paradigms. This does not prevent it being a prototypical Null Subject Language.

17 In fact, this is an oversimplification for spoken German, which allows null subjects (and objects), when these appear in Topic position. See Huang (1984, pp. 546ff.) for relevant discussion.

18 Other languages, diverse in many aspects of their verbal paradigms, but consistent with the generalization introduced in the text, are French, Danish, Icelandic, Hebrew, Irish and Japanese. See Jaeggli and Hyams (1987), Jaeggli and Safir (1989) for more extended discussion.

19 For a different view on the licensing and identification of *pro* in Italian extended to tokens of *pro* in object position, see Rizzi (1986).

20 For initial exploration of the idea that topicalization involves A'-movement, see Chomsky (1977).

21 A difficulty with this characterization is that Huang explicitly assumes that topic-identification is available in German and is what is involved in the identification of null (referential) subjects and objects (cf. note 17). Jaeggli and Safir do not consider such null arguments. A measure of consistency can be imposed on the discussion by requiring Jaeggli and Safir's comments to concern only null subjects which are tokens of *pro*. German does not have these, and these require agreement-identification.

22 It is not clear that it makes any sense to see (41) as presenting a simple choice to whole grammars, since this would require languages to be consistently uniform or non-uniform across all their morphological paradigms. See Hyams (1987b) for more general discussion of the role of uniformity in the acquisition of inflection.

23 Hyams cites a range of further well-known phenomena which support the idea that the child's initial setting for (41) is [+uniform]. For example, acquisition of verbal inflections in richly inflected languages such as Italian and Polish is relatively early to develop. This is to be expected if a child is disposed to meet morphologically uniform languages and receives ample evidence that what uniformity amounts to is *uniformly complex*. English-speaking children do not receive such an abundance of evidence and so assume that uniformity in this case means *uniformly simple*. Furthermore, the avoidance of ϕ-affixation and the 'inflectional imperialism' documented by Slobin and his colleagues (1973, 1985) can be seen as consistent with these suggestions.

24 This proposal would be more convincing if some ontogenetic primacy could be ascribed to null pronominals over variables, and Hyams cites Roeper, Rooth, Mallis and Akiyama (1984) as supporting this proposition. She hazards the suggestion that the developmental course of the inventory of empty categories is maturationally fixed, which, if correct, predicts that in early Chinese empty categories should be *pro*. If this is so, early Chinese should exhibit the same subject–object asymmetry as is claimed for early English. I am familiar with no evidence bearing on this prediction.

25 Interestingly, the corresponding figure for subject pronouns of Italian children is of the order of 30%. Valian (1990a) presents a detailed set of studies investigating a range of predictions based on Hyams' proposals. For instance, alongside pronominal subjects, she also investigates the appearance of modals in the speech of the same group of English-speaking children, concluding that it is not the case that a surge in modal-usage accompanies the disappearance of null subjects (see also O'Grady, Peters and Masterson, 1989). The use of expletive subjects is *very* infrequent even in children who have progressed to using obligatory subjects.

Valian suggests that it is therefore difficult to conclude anything from their non-occurrence at earlier stages. We shall return to some of the issues raised in this paper in ch. 10.

26 Jordens (1990) has disputed Clahsen's claim that the switch to correct VO order is indicative of the acquisition of V-movement. It is not clear to me that the point made here is affected by this issue.

27 Valian (1990a) reports analyses similar to Bloom's on a larger sample of subjects which failed to reveal significant differences.

28 Elsewhere Valian (1990b) has expressed reservations about an implementation of parameter-setting which regards one parameter value as unmarked. Specifically, she discusses Hyams' (1986) assumption that children start off with the 'Italian value' and questions its coherence by invoking the Subset Principle. This principle will be introduced in some detail in the next chapter. The child embarking with the 'English value' faces a different problem: the occurrence of subjectless utterances such as (i) in the linguistic environment:

> (i) Can't do it

Such utterances might be expected to lead the child to adopt the 'Italian value', since he or she has no means of knowing that, strictly speaking, they are grammatically ill-formed. Note that this is an example of the child's environment containing ungrammatical strings which are not labelled as such. See also Roeper and Weissenborn (1990).

Chapter 5 Parameterized Binding Theory and the Subset Principle

1 Yang also formulates a set of parameters for describing this variation. Since these are often somewhat opaque, we shall not consider them here. All examples in this section are from Yang's paper.

2 This complexity has two sources. First, Manzini and Wexler (1987) operate with a version of the Binding Theory which allows it to be extended to account for control phenomena as originally proposed in Manzini (1983). Second, the fact that the distributions of anaphors and pronouns are not quite complementary (see Section 3.3) requires that the reference to 'subject' in Principle A be replaced by 'accessible SUBJECT', where a SUBJECT can be either a subject or AGR and accessibility is a somewhat complex locality condition.

3 All examples in this section are from Wexler and Manzini (1987) or Manzini and Wexler (1987).

4 For the possibility that a sixth value may be necessary to accommodate reflexive clitics, see Koster (1986).

5 How this is achieved will not concern us here, but we might suppose that systematic exposure to simple sentences like (i), used in appropriate contexts, is an important factor:

> (i) John hurt/kicked/punched/hit himself

6 A word about how 'language' is to be interpreted here is in order. Clearly, it abstracts away from lexical forms, since no sentence of English is a sentence of

Korean. What we have in mind, then, is something like a set of indexed configurations such as those in (i):

(i) a. . . . . [$_S$antecedent$_i$ . . . anaphor$_i$]
    b. . . . . [$_S$ . . . antecedent$_j$. . .[$_S$NP$_j$ . . . anaphor$_i$]

English includes configurations like (ia) as does Korean, but only Korean allows (ib). That linear order must also be abstracted away from is obvious, but I will not speculate further on how we might represent the sets of objects which enter into the inclusion relationships in (21). From now on, in this context, I shall use 'language' and 'sentence' with the presupposition that these abstract configurations provide the appropriate referents.

7   It is important to be clear that (30) has a quite different status from that of the the Subset Principle: (30) constrains parameter values and, as such, must be viewed as part of UG. The Subset Principle, as noted, is a principle of the learning module. The interaction between UG and the learning module envisaged by Wexler and Manzini can be encapsulated by noting that UG parameters must satisfy the Independence Principle if the Subset Principle is to work. Cf. discussion of the Subset Condition in the next section.

8   Note that this reformulation does not affect the presumed universal status of Principles A and B.

9   Like the Independence Principle, the Subset Condition is a constraint on possible parameters. As such, it imposes an extremely strong restriction on UG.

10 I would not wish to be accused of invoking functional criteria for constraining parameter values here. In a peculiar sense, Wexler and Manzini are doing that. My point is that if we are to pursue that strategy, the functional criteria we invoke might as well be sensible!

11 This is not to suggest that the formulation of such a parameter is the correct way to proceed. We are merely noting that one apparently principled reason for not adopting this strategy cannot be relied upon.

12 The choice of name for this hypothesis can be understood from the schemas in (47). In (47a, b), the positions of possible antecedents *span* the whole structure. The Spanning Hypothesis requires this to be the case.

13 For detailed discussion of the necessity to reformulate the Spanning Hypothesis, see Newson (1990a). The matters he raises do not affect the text discussion.

14 I have omitted discussion of empty categories here. Manzini and Wexler (1987, pp. 441–2) offer some initial and somewhat tentative speculations about NP-trace and PRO.

15 Interestingly, Chomsky (1987a, p. 29) notes the importance of this issue. He says: 'Conceivably, there might be some significance to some notion of E-language in the theory of learnability, if [the] 'subset principle' plays a role in this theory as has been plausibly argued.'

16 Note that Newson does not pursue this course. I adopt it here because it greatly simplifies presentation of what I take to be the most important aspects of his proposals for our current concerns.

Chapter 6 The Child's Knowledge of Principles of Grammar

1 Subsidiary results were: (i) the range of complement types represented in (1) did not lead to significant differences in error scores. Specifically, there was no advantage for tensed complement clauses over infinitival clauses and gerundives; (ii) the children preferred a conjoined noun phrase as antecedent for *each other* to a plural noun phrase.

2 It might be interesting from this perspective to repeat Matthei's experiment with a simple change: rather than requiring the child to 'make *them* do it', the instruction would refer to the subordinate subject, i.e. 'make *the pigs* do it'. This should ensure that the Agent-role of the matrix subject is ignored, leaving the child with the choice of making the pigs tickle the pigs, in accordance with Principle A, or making the pigs tickle the chickens, which could then be more plausibly viewed as a violation of Principle A.

3 It is my experience, when discussing these matters, that a significant number of people have an unshakeable faith in *the* data as the ultimate arbiters of psychological reality claims, where *the* data are typically collected by psycholinguists or sociolinguists. One aim of this chapter is to undermine this faith a little.

4 Strong Crossover is distinguished from Weak Crossover, introduced in Section 3.2, in terms of the structural relationship between the pronoun and the *wh*-trace. In cases of Strong Crossover, the pronoun c-commands the trace, and the ill-formedness of the structure follows immediately if variables are subject to Principle C. For Weak Crossover, the pronoun does not c-command the trace, so some additional constraint is necessary to rule out the structures. See Section 3.2 for references.

5 Jakubowicz attempts to account for her results by claiming that children mistakenly treat pronominals as anaphors. She then proposes to account for her data theoretically using a version of the Subset Principle. For a convincing demonstration that this enterprise is misguided, see Wexler and Manzini, 1987.

6 In particular, as illustrated by (16), the subordinate clause was either finite or non-finite. This variable did not significantly affect the children's responses (cf. Solan, 1987).

7 They are not attracted by the possibility that Principle B must be *learned*, however, since they cannot conceive of how its content could be induced from primary linguistic data. They speculate that a maturational process may be involved.

8 But see the results of Tavakolian (1978) briefly discussed in the previous section.

9 An obvious difficulty with this argument is that it applies equally to sentences involving anaphors on which children performed rather well. Grimshaw and Rosen are aware of the problem and speculate that the children may utilize a task-specific strategy for anaphors which does not engage the Binding Theory.

10 Note that this proposal begins to approach a difficulty noted in Section 3.3, with the VP-analysis having some of the properties of clause-structure. We continue to put off further discussion of this until Ch. 10.

11 It is important that the reader not get the impression that this is a restricted and unimportant set of items. It obviously includes prenominal adjectives, and, although we do not have the space to go into it here, a large number of expressions which follow the head in English but cannot be analysed as complements. See Radford (1988a) for very detailed discussion.

12 All examples in this discussion are selected from the large numbers supplied by Radford (1990a).

13 Lust's work is not straightforwardly related to the PPT framework for a number of reasons. First, as she acknowledges (e.g. Lust and Mazuka, 1989, p. 667), the Principal Branching Direction Parameter is not to be identified with the Head Direction Parameter, but it is unclear what the relationship between these notions is. Second, much of her work is concerned with children's *preferences* regarding direction of anaphora, and is therefore more plausibly linked to processing strategies than to representational issues. Third, she operates with an extended sense of 'anaphora' which embraces conjoined structures such as (i):

    (i) John φ and Mary left

In (i), φ marks the site of an understood VP (*left*) and is interpreted as anaphoric in this extended sense.

14 One way in which this can be done is to replace the reference to lexical government by a reference to Θ-government or Θ-marking. Ultimately, if Θ-marking induces co-indexation, a formulation of the ECP referring only to government and co-indexing can be derived. See, for example, M. Baker (1988a, p. 39). Since verbs do not θ-mark adjuncts, the required result follows immediately.

15 The account I offer here is incomplete in a number of ways. Most notably, I omit discussion of the government of adjunct positions from C. This is a difficult and contentious area of grammatical theory, and the interested reader is referred to Chomsky (1986b), M. Baker (1988a) for relevant discussion.

16 In fact, the most common answer to sentences like (59b) consisted of (incorrect) attempts to answer the subordinate *who* question, and accounting for this behaviour constitutes a focus of the paper. However, the important difference reported in the text does exist, and, if nothing else, this study establishes the possibility of experimentally investigating an extremely abstract grammatical principle.

17 Regarding examples like (64), Lebeaux (1988, pp. 396ff.) has developed an interesting account, making use of the analysis of psych-verbs in Belletti and Rizzi (1988).

Chapter 7 Epistemological Priority and Argument Structure

1 To convey the style of Bloom's arguments for this conclusion, we can note that she draws attention to tokens of predicates collocated in her corpus with different arguments expressed with each token (see Ingram, 1989, pp. 276ff. for summary of Bloom's methodology). For use of similar techniques leading to the same conclusions with the manual systems of communication invented by congenitally deaf children, see Feldman, Goldin-Meadow and Gleitman (1978) and ch. 11 below.

2 To suggest that (5) has a structure like (6) raises the question of the syntactic status of the child's single-word utterances before the onset of word-combination. Atkinson (1985) argued that it would be inappropriate to treat these utterances as syntactic, a conclusion echoed in Radford (1990a). As we shall see in ch. 10 and 11, (6) is syntactic only in a rather restricted sense, and I now believe that it is probably appropriate to extend this restricted sense to the one-word stage. See also Lebeaux (1988).

3   In fact, things are not quite so straightforward as the above might suggest once we take account of optionally projected arguments which, when syntactically active, are referred to as *implicit arguments*(see also chapter 3, note 38). The Patient argument of *eat* in English is optionally projected, as witnessed by the alternation in (i):

(i)   a. John ate his breakfast
      b. John ate

However, this argument, when not projected, as well as being syntactically inactive has restricted interpretive possibilities – (ib) can only be used to convey that John ate food or a meal and not that he ate his hat or a newspaper. The syntactic inertness of this argument contrasts with the Agent argument of *sink* when this verb occurs in a passive such as (ii):

(ii) The boat was sunk [PRO to collect the treasure]

In (ii), PRO is controlled by the unprojected argument, i.e the agent of the sinking is also the agent of the collecting, and this shows that the implicit argument is not syntactically inert. Radford (1990a) considers *lexical saturation* as an alternative to *syntactic projection* for child grammars, concluding that there is no evidence bearing on the choice currently available. For relevant theoretical discussion, see Rizzi (1986), Brody and Manzini (1988), Manzini (forthcoming).

4   Recall that the learnability proof of Morgan (1986) required children to be presented with a surface bracketing *and* a base structure.

5   In ch. 11 we shall return to this issue of developmental discontinuity, suggesting that it might be correct in somewhat different terms from those envisaged by Gleitman.

6   An issue I do not have space to go into here is that of constraining semantic bootstrapping. One criticism which has been levelled against Pinker's original formulation of the hypothesis is that the assumptions he makes concerning semantics–syntax correspondences are extensive, and strain the condition of epistemological priority (see the table in Pinker, 1984, p. 41, for a list of these correspondences). Elliott and Wexler (1986, 1987) claim that a major failing in Pinker's account is that he does not avail himself fully of UG principles. They argue that if this is done, the role of semantic bootstrapping can be reduced to the postulation of a set of *Feature Realization Principles* such as (i):

(i)   G(rigid object) = [+COUNT]

These principles are restricted so as to take only values which are sub-categorial features of nouns, these being semantically fairly transparent. Supplementing these with the computational machinery of PPT, most notably Case Theory and Θ-Theory, Elliott and Wexler show how the child can assign an appropriate structure to some simple sentences. If the account we consider in ch. 10 is correct, the Elliott and Wexler proposals cannot be maintained, as they rely crucially on the involvement of Case Theory, a module we shall suggest is inoperative at the earliest stages of acquisition.

7   As regards (i), everyone's list of Θ-roles seems to include Agent, Patient, Theme, Goal and Source. But detailed syntactic investigation sometimes reveals that it is

inappropriate to regard these as unitary categories (cf. Belletti and Rizzi, 1988, who suggest that it is necessary to recognize two kinds of Theme). Hoekstra (forthcoming) maintains that no clear content can be given to such notions as Agent, Patient and Theme; if this is correct, endowing these notions with epistemological priority is unlikely to be justified. For (ii), M. Baker (1988b, forthcoming) and Bresnan and Kanerva (1989) have pursued an interesting debate in the context of the Bantu language family, with Baker defending analyses which maintain a single-valued CSR cross-linguistically.

8   It is customary to refer to this argument as a Theme (Belletti and Rizzi, 1988). However, Theme is normally understood as the role of the entity undergoing a change of location or state (Gruber, 1976), so it is not clearly applicable in such a case. Perhaps what we have here is motivation for the view of Hoekstra mentioned in the previous note.

9   The original suggestion was made by Perlmutter (1978). The widest range of published evidence for the analysis comes from languages other than English, e.g. Italian (Belletti and Rizzi, 1981) and Dutch (Hoekstra, forthcoming).

10   An increasingly popular response to this sort of difficulty is to abandon the idea that a simple set of Θ-roles provides the appropriate input to the projection mapping. For example, Levin and Rappaport Hovav (forthcoming) argue that the mapping must have access to the inherent semantic properties of verbs (e.g. whether a verb of motion is directional or not). As we shall see in the next section, Pinker (1989) adopts a similar perspective in the light of argument alternations. See also Tenny (1987); Hoekstra (forthcoming).

11   Again, so as to keep the discussion to a manageable length, I shall omit discussion of the alternation in structures including benefactive *for*-phrases as in (i):

(i) a. John bought a book for Mary
     b. John bought Mary a book

Such examples are usually assimilated with datives in theoretical treatments.

12   It should be made clear that Larson develops his account within the restricted PPT framework, seeing the double-object dative as derived by the operation of Move α constrained in ways which are similar to those operative in passive structures. The details of the analysis do not affect Pinker's point.

13   The proposals on semantic representations developed in Pinker (1989, ch. 5) are considerably more elaborate than (28). However, the vocabulary we use here captures the spirit of his analyses, and this simple formulation will serve for our purposes.

14   Given the sample of problems briefly presented in the previous section, Pinker's statement (p. 248) that 'this is not an attempt to sweep difficult problems under the rug' is perhaps a little misleading. He admits to not having a solution to the problem produced by ergative languages. See Bowerman (1990) for a less optimistic view of these matters.

15   Hale and Keyser (forthcoming) is a particularly interesting development in this area. They suggest that LRs, despite being formulated in terms of conceptual primitives (EVENT, THING, etc.) have a *syntax* which is strikingly similar to sentential syntax in that it manipulates the same configurational constructs (maximal projection, government, etc.) as sentential syntax and includes the possibility of *movement* in the derivation of the representation of such 'conflated' verbal forms as *shelve, saddle, winter*, etc. A difficulty I have with representational

systems like those of Jackendoff and Pinker is that they do appear to be subject to few constraints, and Hale and Keyser's proposals offer the hope that this may not be an insurmountable defect.

16 This coding scheme collapses conditions under which the object is explicitly referred to in the utterance (e.g. *see the dog*) and those where the identity of the object must be retrieved on the basis of context (e.g. *see*). Landau and Gleitman (1985, p. 214) indicate that taking account of this distinction does not affect their main conclusion.

17 The relationship between these contexts and those in which only *look* and *see* can occur is not one of identity. For example, *See NP* is included in this analysis, but the position preceding an NP is one in which several other verbs occur. This lack of correspondence is presumably what Gleitman (1989, p. 17) refers to when she says: '. . . we can – *with only a little fudging* – divide the environments of the vision-related verbs so as to pull apart those environments in which the NEARby-ness contextual cue holds, and those in which it does not' (my emphasis – MA).

18 This is certainly not an accurate characterization of Pinker (1984). Nor, I suspect, is it a position he would find attractive now.

19 None of this is intended to counter Gleitman's observations on the very real difficulties she perceives in the requirement that the child must extract semantic representations from the situation of utterance to make semantic bootstrapping work. The example of the blind child we have briefly considered only scratches the surface of this problem area (see Gleitman, 1989, pp. 6ff. for pertinent discussion).

Chapter 8 Developmental Mechanisms

1 The reference to 'taking to be' in this discussion is important. Suppose I am approached by a red London bus, *take it to be* (for whatever reason) a yellow banana, and as a consequence come to believe (for whatever reason) that London buses are red. This is doubly aberrant and hence doubly fanciful. However, if we did have evidence for such a causal route in the establishment of a belief about the colour of London buses, we would be reluctant to regard it as learning. The notion of 'content' assumed in the text discussion is what Fodor (1987, 1990) refers to as 'narrow content'. For extended discussion of the coherence of this notion, see several of the contributions to Loewer and Rey (1991).

2 Fodor (1981, p. 262) suggests that mechanisms as diverse as association in classic empiricist accounts and operations on logical notations in more recent formulations can fulfil this role.

3 It is noteworthy that ideas very similar to these were largely re-capitulated in Clark's (1973) original formulation of the Semantic Feature Hypothesis in connection with the development of word meaning.

4 Note that the use of 'sensorium' in (4) is strained, since a range of *non-sensory* concepts result directly from its operation. What is important is that it is the host to triggering mechanisms.

5 Others include the failure of some psycholinguistic experiments to find support for the on-line use of definitions (Fodor, Fodor and Garrett, 1975; Fodor, Garrett, Walker, and Parkes, 1980); the failure of positivism in philosophy of science; and the failure of bottom-up theories of visual perception (but see Fodor, 1983, for refinements). Not everyone has found Fodor's arguments compelling (see, for example, Katz, 1981; Jackendoff, 1983, 1989). For recent attempts to develop

accounts of concept acquisition and its relationship to lexical development, see Carey, 1985; Keil, 1989; Markman, 1989.

6 Piattelli-Palmarini (1989) likens parameter-setting to selective processes in biology and immunology, and his discussion of the recent history of these disciplines, focusing on the demise of instructive views, makes fascinating and convincing reading. However, extending this mode of talk into the cognitive domain of linguistics is not straightforward, since while it makes little sense to talk of an antibody being selected and *subsequently deselected* by antigens, the idea of a parameter being set and subsequently reset is certainly not unintelligible.

7 Koopman's (1984) re-analysis of Huang's data in terms of parameterized directionality of Case- and Θ-role assignment is subject to the same considerations, since she suggests that specification of the same direction for both parameters probably represents the unmarked case.

8 A different sense of determinism can be easily reconciled with a hypothesis-testing procedure, and it is likely that this sense is what Chomsky and perhaps also Borer and Wexler have in mind. According to this, at any stage in the child's development, there will be only a *single* grammar compatible with the primary linguistic data received so far and with the principles of UG, i.e. at no stage will the child employ anything analogous to the Evaluation Measure of ST to decide between competing hypotheses. This notion of determinism is clearly compatible with aspects of grammars being *re*determined by more extensive exposure to data.

9 I omit discussion of unstressed subject pronouns, since the form of the argument is identical for them.

10 Of course, this logic suggests that the child has an alternative to resetting the value of the AG/PRO Parameter, viz. abandoning the Avoid Pronoun Principle. This possibility is not considered by Hyams.

11 Note that we are not contemplating a more complex situation in which p_2 is set on the basis of a prior setting of p_1 *and* primary linguistic data. Presumably, so long as the relationship between p_1 and p_2 is arbitrary and we can establish that the setting of p_1 is a causally *necessary* antecedent for the setting of p_2, we would be justified in regarding this situation as triggering too, irrespective of the relationship between the primary linguistic data and p_2.

12 An exception to this conclusion, discussed in Section 5.6, is Newson's proposal for deductively linking anaphoric and pronominal parameter values.

   Note that the suggestion that parameter values may be deductively linked is one way in which a temporal dimension can be introduced into the model; if p_2 is deductively dependent on p_1, its value cannot be fixed until after p_1 is fixed. The next section is devoted to a second way in which such an outcome can be achieved, and it is appropriate here to draw attention to a third possibility which has been investigated in a number of publications by Roeper and his associates (Nishigauchi and Roeper, 1987; Roeper and de Villiers, 1989; Roeper and Weissenborn, 1990). This is motivated by the suggestion that children often receive apparently *contradictory* input relevant to a particular parameter setting (see Valian, 1990b, for discussion of null subjects in this light). One way to ensure that the effects of this are not disruptive is to enrich the model so that the child does not attempt to set some parameters until others are fixed. The idea is that these earlier settings will account for the apparently contradictory data, leaving the child with a consistent residue for the setting of the later parameters. The contrast between this suggestion and the one considered in this section is, in some ways, similar to the contrast between the Subset Principle as a principle of a learning module and the proposal that markedness orderings are directly represented in UG. It is a learning-theoretic perspective on the ordering of parameters. Since Roeper's ideas rely on a range of theoretical concepts, the bulk of which have not been introduced in this book, I shall not attempt to go more deeply into these important issues here.

13 In fact, as we shall see, *pace* the statement quoted in the text, Borer and Wexler do not adopt the position that *principles* mature, but rather *structures* to which principles apply. Chien and Wexler (1990, p. 254) make this clear when they adumbrate the notion of UG-Constrained Maturation as: . . . 'the most cons-trained theory that can be empirically held at the moment. All the instances that [Borer and Wexler] discussed are instances in which *structures* grow, but principles are in place from the beginning.' The reference to Borer and Wexler in this passage concerns unpublished work subsequent to the paper we are concerned with here. However, this latter adopts the same emphasis. Somewhat confusingly, then, Borer and Wexler's position is not opposed to the Continuity Hypothesis with respect to the presence of principles in children's grammars but rather with respect to the detailed nature of the representations available to the child. The issue of whether principles themselves mature will be returned to in ch. 10.

14 Borer and Wexler emphasize that the fundamental issue is that A-chain formation requires the *non-local* assignment of Θ-roles, i.e. a Θ-role assigned to the internal argument position of a verb must be transmitted to a position outside the verb's government domain.

15 Of course, the child would need *evidence* (primary linguistic data) to enable him or her to partition intransitive verbs appropriately. Quite what this evidence would be for a child acquiring English is not at all clear. Note that in Section 7.3 we noted that the Agent/Theme distinction was probably not predictive of the unergative/unaccusative distinction and that inherent semantic properties of verbs were probably referred to in the projection of d-structures. If this is so, Borer and Wexler's account appears to require that these can be overridden by syntactic demands following from the unavailability of A-movement.

Chapter 9 Constraining Parameters

1 I omit discussion of the parameterization of Rule R here. In Hyams' approach, its role is to license inverted subjects, and it is plausible to suggest that a grammar which allows Rule R to operate in syntax produces a superset of the sentences generated by a grammar in which Rule R is restricted to the phonology, i.e. the Subset Condition is satisfied (see Hyams, 1986, p. 154 for discussion).

2 A somewhat uncomfortable aspect of this argument is its reliance on the Avoid Pronoun Principle to account for the absence of expletive subjects in Null Subject Languages, i.e. the absence of such subjects does not follow solely from the +AG/PRO value of the parameter. If the Avoid Pronoun Principle were an unc ontroversial core grammatical principle, this would not be a problem, but its status in the theory of grammar is somewhat obscure.

Rizzi (1986), in a more general discussion of the licensing of *pro* in a variety of positions, suggests that UG supplies a set of potential licensers with particular languages selecting a subset from this set. English selects the empty subset and Italian selects {I, V}, the latter accounting for null objects. He says (p. 525): '. . . [the] Subset Principle appears to give the right result in this case; assuming that a given head is a licenser of *pro* amounts to increasing the set of well-formed structures that the system can produce; hence according to the Subset Principle, assuming that a given head is *not* a licenser represents the unmarked decision, the one the language learner adopts in the absence of evidence to the contrary.' In a subsequent footnote (p. 526), he goes on to assert that I being a licenser of *pro* is the marked option, and attempts to make this claim consistent with those of Hyams by speculating about the child's initial access to primary linguistic data.

3 It is not uncommon to find the Subset Principle being referred to as if it concerned *grammars*, rather than sets of structures or sentences. Thus, for example, in Nishigauchi and Roeper (1987, p. 105), we find: '. . . the new grammar is smaller than the earlier ones. In effect, it violates the subset principle. . . .' I assume that such usage is merely careless, although Lust (1986b) does explicitly attempt to interpret the principle as applying to grammars of different sizes. I believe that the consequences of this are incoherent, but will not pursue the matter here.

4 A word of caution is appropriate here. Valian (1990b) has pointed out that naturally occurring corpora of English will contain subjectless sentences such as those in (i):

> (i) a. Seems OK
>   b. Can't quite reach it

From the point of view of whatever parameter is responsible for null subjects, such data are misleading. Valian also notes that such constructions never occur in subordinate clauses:

> (ii) a. *John thought (that) seemed, OK
>   b. *John said (that) couldn't quite reach it

Roeper and Weissenborn (1990), arguing that subordinate clauses often contain more consistent cues to parameter values, suggest that such examples indicate the need for degree-1 data in sorting out the distribution of null subjects.

5 We set aside the case of Russian here. Obviously, if movement is even more restricted in this language than in English, the Russian value for the parameter should be the child's first hypothesis.

6 Italian presents a complication to which Lightfoot returns at the end of his paper. We shall avoid the issues surrounding this here.

7 There are, of course, questions begged by this account. For example, the child could respond to (22) by eliminating NP from the set of bounding nodes (see Wilkins, 1989). To rule out this possibility, it will be necessary for UG to contain the possible parameter settings which will indicate that NP is universally a bounding node (if it is).

8 Rizzi (1989), commenting on Lightfoot's article, suggests that a more perspicuous way to proceed might be to restrict the data necessary for the setting of parameters to *government domains*. Thus, in (32) if objective Case is to be assigned by *expects* to *him* under government, the government domain of *expects* must somehow be extended to include *him*.

9 Obvious difficulties are produced for degree-0 and for degree-0-plus-a-little by long-distance anaphors which can be bound in direct object position, as discussed in ch. 5.

10 Rizzi (1989, p. 355) contains a succinct statement of the atypicality of the bounding node parameter. Chomsky (1986b) includes much more extensive discussion.

11 Obviously, this observation generalizes to prepositions which also uniformly assign Case and Θ-role to the right in English. A word of caution is in order, however, as Safir (1987, p. 89) cites Dutch as a language which has both prepositions and postpositions. I am not familiar with any case in which a language partitions its verbs into leftward and rightward Case and Θ-role assigners.

12 It is important to be clear that such a conclusion is no way prejudices the status of the Subset Principle: *if* parameter values produce nested languages and if there are no negative data, the Subset Principle remains a necessary component of the learning module.

Chapter 10 Functional Categories and the Functional Parameterization Hypothesis

1 Here we restrict attention to 'ordinary clauses'. There is evidence to suggest that the clauses appearing as complements to Exceptional Case Marking verbs (see Section 9.3) lack a system of C-projections and are appropriately analysed as IPs. Small Clauses like the bracketed expressions in (i) appear to lack both a C-system and an I-system, and we shall return to their status in Section 10.3:

> (i) a. John considers [Mary intelligent]
>   b. John wants [Mary in his class]

For a comprehensive discussion of these different clause types, see Radford (1988a, ch. 6).

2 Earlier instances of Move α that we have considered have involved moving maximal projections (NPs or *wh*-expressions). Clearly Move α as stated can also apply to zero-level projections, and again the idea is that constraints on such movement will emerge from the interacting modules. The need to include the option of V-movement in the theory of grammar was argued for most comprehensively in Koopman (1984). For a wide-ranging discussion of X^0-movement in the context of syntactic incorporation structures, see M. Baker (1988a).

3 I say 'prima facie' here, because the possibility of the C being itself moved from initial to final position in such a language would have to be ruled out.

4 Abney (1987, pp. 290ff.) contains extensive discussion of specifier positions within DPs. We do not have space to go into these issues here.

5 They are, of course, consistent with an alternative conclusion: that bare determiners are NPs containing an empty head N. Abney (1987, p. 280) argues somewhat inconclusively against this alternative.

6 Alongside the lack of descriptive content, Abney offers the following diagnostics for the class of functional categories (1987, pp. 64–5):

> 1 Functional elements constitute closed lexical classes.
> 2 Functional elements are generally phonologically and morphologically dependent. They are generally stressless, often clitics or affixes, and sometimes even phonologically null.

    3 Functional elements permit only one complement, which is in general not an argument. The arguments are CP, PP and . . . DP. Functional elements select IP, VP and NP.

    4 Functional elements are usually inseparable from their complement.

7 All French examples cited in this discussion are from Pollock (1989).

8 That *pas* is the negative morpheme in French is justified on historical grounds and by modern usage.

9 The reader might note that requiring zero-level categories to satisfy the Head Movement Constraint is similar to requiring *wh*-expressions which move 'long distance' to pass through intermediate Cs. This latter requirement is motivated by the ECP, so it should come as no surprise that M. Baker (1988a) reduces the Head Movement Constraint to the ECP. See also Chomsky (1989).

10 The major motivation for decomposing categories into features is the role of the latter in expressing a range of generalizations. For example, we noted in Section 3.3 that verbs and prepositions are Case-assigners while nouns and adjectives are not. With the features in (42), this observation can be rephrased as: the Case-assigners are [−N]. Readers familiar with distinctive feature theory in phonology will be acquainted with this style of argument. Stowell (1981) provides fairly extensive justification for the system in (42). For an alternative, see Jackendoff (1977).

11 The reader familiar with the literature will no doubt have noticed that such a lowering operation violates the constraint that movement should always be to a c-commanding position. Chomsky (1989) contains discussion of this problem.

12 The status of [−finite] T in English cannot be determined in this respect, since the opacity of English AGR and the Head Movement Constraint ensure that English Θ-role-assigning verbs cannot move to T. Criticisms of Pollock's analysis appear in Iatridou (1990), Ouhalla (1990) and C. L. Baker (1991), but the first two of these retain some version of the opacity/transparency distinction.

13 Since Case-assignment takes place under government, it is necessary to suppose that I governs DP_1 in (50) despite the intervening VP maximal projection. See Chomsky (1986b) for discussion and justification.

14 Note that this suggestion is incompatible with the claim that V does not raise in English in the arguments from Pollock we have just discussed. This incompatibility is genuine, but since our task is simply to illustrate the *possible* roles of functional parameterization, we shall not seek to resolve it here.

15 Fassi-Fehri (1989) also considers word-order in gerundive constructions in English and Arabic which parallels that found in tensed clauses, as indicated by (i):

    (i) a. 'The enemy's bombing the city'

       b. qasf-u l-ᶜaduww-i l-madi:nat-a
          bombing-nom the-enemy-gen the-city-obj
          'The enemy's bombing of the city'

This is accounted for by assuming that these constructions have structures analogous to those of the corresponding clauses, except that they are headed by an abstract D which assigns genitive Case rightwards in Arabic and leftwards in English. Again, as D is a functional category, this is an instance of functional parameterization.

16   A further property of functional categories is *existence*. It is of some interest to note that Fukui (1986) has argued that Japanese completely lacks the categories D and C, and has a rather minimal I-system which lacks AGR. From this basis, Fukui deduces a range of surface differences between Japanese and English. Similarly, Aoun (1986) has suggested that Chinese lacks AGR, this being the third parameter considered by Lightfoot (1989) in his discussion of degree-0 learnability (see Section 9.3). Adopting an articulated theory of I, Ouhalla (1988) claims that grammars vary in terms of whether T 'dominates' AGR, as in English, or vice versa, Berber illustrating this possibility. Overall, there is a considerable variety of functional parameterization proposals.

17   See Lebeaux (1988) for similar observations within a somewhat different set of assumptions. We shall return to the significance of this claim in a more general context in the next section.

18   Valian (1990a) reports a study of English-speaking children with ages straddling their second birthday in which the usage of nominative Case-marked pronouns as subjects was well-established. It is possible that her subjects had already acquired D- and I-systems, and other results she presents are consistent with this conclusion. Evaluation of this issue will require intensive study of the period in question.

19   Xu (1986) has suggested that the grammar of Chinese might contain a *free empty category*, distinguishable from any of the orthodox empty categories, with a distribution determined by pragmatic factors (for a dissenting view, see Huang, 1987). The observation that null subjects are more *frequent* than null objects is not crucial in evaluating Hyams' proposals (see Radford, 1990b, pp. 210–11, n. 6 for a response to the suggestion that it is).

20   In principle, this suggestion ought to be testable. It maintains first that the presence of null arguments pre-functionally is irrelevant to the setting of the parameter, and second, that once functional categories appear, the initial setting of the parameter will be one which requires overt subjects. If this is the case, Italian children should pass through a (possibly very short) stage during which subjects are obligatory. Taking account of processing constraints, a (possibly very short) stage of greater-than-adult subject use would support the suggestion.

21   For some of the difficulties in applying Abney's (1987) criteria, see Radford (1990b, p. 197, n. 2). Despite these difficulties, we shall continue to operate with a 'descriptive'/'non-descriptive' or 'thematic'/'non-thematic' distinction in what follows. Lebeaux (1988), developing ideas which are strikingly similar to those discussed here, suggests that parameterization be restricted to 'closed class items' and he follows traditional grammar in including prepositions in this set. In terms of their thematic properties, prepositions are a mixed bag. Most prepositions are viewed as thematic, assigning a Θ-role to their object. However, *of* in derived nominals is clearly non-thematic, i.e. *the city* in (i) receives its Θ-role from *destruction*, and the function of *of* is purely formal:

   (i) destruction of the city

See Hale and Keyser (forthcoming) for arguments distinguishing prepositions as Θ-role assigners from prepositions as Case-markers and the intriguing suggestion that LRs, while syntactic, lack functional categories.

22   Demuth (1990b) argues that children acquiring Sesotho produce structures suggesting they have a C-system by the age of 2:5. It is not clear that this creates

any difficulties for Radford's suggestion, since he identifies the end of the lexical stage for English-speaking children at about 22 months.

23 It could, of course, be maintained that it is operative but its domain of operation is empty. It is not clear to me that there is an empirical issue in deciding between these two formulations.

24 The discontinuity alluded to here is reminiscent of that briefly mentioned in Section 7.2, when we discussed semantic bootstrapping. It is not, however, a semantics–syntax discontinuity, in that we are not suggesting that the child passes through a stage at which his or her grammar is defined on the semantic vocabulary of Agent, Patient, etc. It is perhaps not too misleading to suggest that the pre-functional child's grammar is 'semantic' to the extent that of the UG principles, the Projection Principle plays the central role, while the 'purely' formal principles are not operative.

Chapter 11 Final Thoughts

1 This is not an arbitrary decision, as the cynical reader may have guessed! The relative order of the verb and its complement(s) is standardly seen as involving parameterized directionality of Θ-role assignment and/or Case-marking (see Section 3.4). However, Θ-role assignment is a property of *lexical* heads and its direction ought not to be parameterizable on the FPH. Equally, objective Case is typically assigned by *verbs*, a lexical category. Lebeaux (1988) suggests that Cases and Θ-roles might themselves be regarded as 'closed class items', and this enables him to maintain his claim that parameterization is restricted to such items. Chomsky (1989), developing the ideas of Pollock we considered in Section 10.2, suggests that there are two AGRPs in I; one has a head AGR-S which includes subject agreement features and assigns Case to the subject and the other has a head AGR-O which fulfils the same function regarding the object. A desire not to convey more than the barest outline of these possibilities is the motivation for my decision!

2 Goldin-Meadow and Mylander (1990, p. 347) refer to a strategy 'to preserve the unity of the predicate', citing Ochs' (1982) claim that children acquiring Samoan prefer SVO or VOS order to the adult norm of VSO.

3 Cf. Freidin and Quicoli (1989), who distinguish between p-parameters and r-parameters – the former have unmarked values which they take on in the absence of primary linguistic data; the latter require encounters with data in order to be set at all.

4 It is tempting to speculate that if they do develop functional categories, this will be interesting evidence that functional parameters have unmarked values. Looking further afield, it might be interesting to contemplate Bickerton's (1984) bioprogram hypothesis in this light.

5 A similar point can be based on Lundin and Platzack's (1988) discussion of the acquisition of verb placement in Swedish and German. They replicate Clahsen's (1986) findings that correct verb placement appears to be contingent on the child acquiring the [±finite] distinction, but note that Swedish-speaking children produce the correct structures earlier than German-speaking children. This, they put down to the fact that (p. 54) 'the Swedish finite system is much less complex than the German finite system'.

6   Additionally, a significant positive correlation was obtained between the mothers'
    use of deixis – clearly referring to and drawing attention to objects or collections
    of objects in the child's immediate spatio-temporal environment – and the chil-
    dren's development of nominal inflections (specifically the plural inflection). This
    can be related to the D-system in fairly obvious ways, but I will not pursue this
    detail here.

Bibliography

Abney, S. P. 1987: The English Noun Phrase in its Sentential Aspect. MIT Doctoral Dissertation.

Akmajian, A. and Heny, F. 1975: *An Introduction to the Principles of Transformational Syntax*. Cambridge, Mass.: MIT Press.

Aldridge, M. 1989: The Acquisition of INFL. Indiana University Linguistics Club.

Aoun, J. 1985: *A Grammar of Anaphora*. Cambridge, Mass.: MIT Press.

Aoun, J. 1986: *Generalized Binding*. Dordrecht: Foris.

Aoun, J. and Hornstein, N. 1985: Quantifier types. *Linguistic Inquiry*, 16: 623–636.

Aoun, J., Hornstein, N., Lightfoot, D. and Weinberg, A. 1987: Two types of locality. *Linguistic Inquiry*, 18: 537–577.

Aoun, J., Hornstein, N. and Sportiche, D. 1981: Some aspects of wide-scope quantification. *Journal of Linguistic Research*, 1: 69–95.

Aoun, J. and Sportiche, D. 1983: On the formal theory of government. *The Linguistic Review*, 3: 211–236.

Atkinson, M. 1982: *Explanations in the Study of Child Language Development*. Cambridge: Cambridge University Press.

Atkinson, M. 1985: How linguistic is the one-word stage? In M. Barrett (ed.), *Children's Single-Word Speech*. New York: Wiley.

Atkinson, M. 1987: Mechanisms for language acquisition: parameter-setting, triggering and learning. *First Language*, 7: 3–30.

Atkinson, M. 1990: The logical problem of language acquisition: representational and procedural issues. In I. M. Roca (ed.).

Baker, C. L. 1970: Notes on the description of English questions: the role of an abstract question morpheme. *Foundations of Language*, 6: 197–219.

Baker, C. L. 1979: Syntactic theory and the projection problem. *Linguistic Inquiry*, 10: 533–581.

Baker, C. L. 1989: Some observations on degree of learnability. *Behavioral and Brain Sciences*, 12: 334–335.

Baker, C. L. 1991: The syntax of English *not*: the limits of core grammar. *Linguistic Inquiry*, 22: 387–429.

Baker, C. L. and McCarthy, J. J. (eds) 1981: *The Logical Problem of Language Acquisition*. Cambridge, Mass.: MIT Press.

Baker, M. 1988a: *Incorporation: A Theory of Grammatical Function Changing*. Chicago: University of Chicago Press.

Baker, M. 1988b: Theta theory and the syntax of applicatives in Chichewa. *Natural Language and Linguistic Theory*, 6: 353–389.

Baker, M. forthcoming: Thematic conditions on syntactic structures: evidence from locative applicatives. In I. M. Roca (ed.)

Baker, M., Johnson, K. and Roberts, I. 1989: Passive arguments raised. *Linguistic Inquiry*, 20: 219–251.

Belletti, A. and Rizzi, L. 1981: The syntax of *ne*: some theoretical implications. *The Linguistic Review*, 1: 117–154.

Belletti, A. and Rizzi, L. 1988: Psych-verbs and θ-theory. *Natural Language and Linguistic Theory*, 6: 291–352.

Berlin, B. 1978: Ethnobiological classification. In E. Rosch and B. Lloyd (eds), *Cognition and Categorization*. Hillsdale, N.J.: Erlbaum.

Berlin, B., Breedlove, D. E. and Raven, P. H. 1973: General principles of classification and nomenclature in folk biology. *American Anthropologist*, 75: 214–242.

Berwick, R. C. 1986: *The Acquisition of Syntactic Knowledge*. Cambridge, Mass.: MIT Press.

Berwick, R. C. and Weinberg, A. 1982: Parsing efficiency, computational complexity, and the evaluation of grammatical theories. *Linguistic Inquiry*, 13: 165–191.

Bickerton, D. 1984: The language bioprogram hypothesis. *Behavioral and Brain Sciences*, 7: 173–221.

Bloom, L. 1970: *Language Development: Form and Function in Emerging Grammars*. Cambridge, Mass.: MIT Press.

Bloom, L., Lightbown, P. and Hood, L. 1975: *Structure and Variation in Child Language. Monographs of the Society for Research in Child Development*, Vol. 40, no. 2.

Bloom, L., Lightbown, P. and Hood, L. 1978: Pronominal–nominal variation in child language. In L. Bloom (ed.), *Readings in Language Development*. New York: Wiley.

Bloom, P. 1990: Subjectless sentences in child language. *Linguistic Inquiry*, 21: 491–504.

Bloomfield, L. 1933: *Language*. New York: Holt.

Bohannon, J. N. and Stanowicz, L. 1988: The issue of negative evidence: adult responses to children's language errors. *Developmental Psychology*, 24: 684–689.

Borer, H. 1984: *Parametric Syntax*. Dordrecht: Foris.

Borer, H. 1989: Anaphoric AGR. In O. Jaeggli and K. Safir (eds).

Borer, H. and Wexler, K. 1987: The maturation of syntax. In T. Roeper and E. Williams (eds).

Bowerman, M. 1973: *Early Syntactic Development: A Cross-Linguistic Study with Special Reference to Finnish*. Cambridge: Cambridge University Press.

Bowerman, M. 1976: Semantic factors in the acquisition of rules for word use and sentence construction. In D. M. Morehead and A. E. Morehead (eds), *Normal and Deficient Child Language*. Baltimore, Md.: University Park Press.

Bowerman, M. 1978: Systematizing semantic knowledge: changes over time in the child's organization of word meaning. *Child Development*, 49: 977–987.

Bowerman, M. 1982: Reorganizational processes in lexical and syntactic development. In E. Wanner and L. R. Gleitman (eds).

Bowerman, M. 1990: Mapping thematic roles onto syntactic functions: are children helped by innate linking rules? *Linguistics*, 28: 1253–1289.

Braine, M. D. S. 1976: *Children's First Word Combinations. Monographs of the Society for Research in Child Development*, Vol. 41.

Bresnan, J. 1970: On complementizers: toward a syntactic theory of complement types. *Foundations of Language*, 6: 297–321.

Bresnan, J. (ed.) 1982: *The Mental Representation of Grammatical Relations*. Cambridge, Mass.: MIT Press.

Bresnan, J. and Kanerva, J. M. 1989: Locative inversion in Chichewa: a case study of factorization in grammar. *Linguistic Inquiry*, 20: 1–50.

Brody, M. and Manzini, R. 1988: On implicit arguments. In R. M. Kempson (ed.), *Mental Representations: The Interface Between Language and Reality*. Cambridge: Cambridge University Press.

Bromberger, S. and Halle, M. 1989: Why phonology is different. *Linguistic Inquiry*, 20: 51–70.

Brown, R. 1973: *A First Language: The Early Stages*. Cambridge, Mass.: Harvard University Press.

Brown, R. 1977: Introduction. In C. E. Snow and C. A. Ferguson (eds).

Brown, R. and Fraser, C. 1963: The acquisition of syntax. In U. Bellugi and R. Brown (eds), *The Acquisition of Language. Monographs of the Society for Research in Child Development*, Vol. 29.

Brown, R. and Hanlon, C. 1970: Derivational complexity and order of acquisition in child speech. In J. R. Hayes (ed.), *Cognition and the Development of Language*. New York: Wiley.

Burzio, L. 1981: Intransitive Verbs and Italian Auxiliaries. MIT Doctoral Dissertation.

Burzio, L. 1986: *Italian Syntax: A Government-Binding Approach*. Dordrecht: Reidel.

Bybee, J. L. and Slobin, D. I. 1982: Rules and schemas in the development and use of the English past tense. *Language*, 58: 265–289.

Carey, S. 1985: *Conceptual Change in Childhood*. Cambridge, Mass.: MIT Press.

Chien, Y.-C. and Wexler, K. 1985: Children's acquisition of the locality condition for reflexives and pronouns. *Proceedings of the West Coast Conference on Formal Linguistics*, 4.

Chien, Y.-C. and Wexler, K. 1990: Children's knowledge of locality conditions in binding as evidence for the modularity of syntax and pragmatics. *Language Acquisition*, 1: 225–295.

Chomsky, N. 1957: *Syntactic Structures*. The Hague: Mouton.

Chomsky, N. 1959: Review of B. F. Skinner's *Verbal Behavior*. *Language*, 35: 26–58.

Chomsky, N. 1963: Formal properties of grammars. In R. D. Luce, R. R. Bush and E. Galanter (eds).

Chomsky, N. 1965: *Aspects of the Theory of Syntax*. Cambridge, Mass.: MIT Press.

Chomsky, N. 1970: Remarks on nominalization. In R. Jacobs and P. S. Rosenbaum (eds), *Readings in English Transformational Grammar*. Waltham, Mass.: Ginn & Co.

Chomsky, N. 1973: Conditions on transformations. In S. Anderson and P. Kiparsky (eds), *A Festschrift for Morris Halle*. New York: Holt, Rinehart and Winston.

Chomsky, N. 1975: *Reflections on Language*. New York: Random House.

Chomsky, N. 1977: On Wh-Movement. In P. W. Culicover, T. Wasow and A. Akmajian (eds).

Chomsky, N. 1980: *Rules and Representations*. Oxford: Blackwell.

Chomsky, N. 1981: *Lectures on Government and Binding*. Dordrecht: Foris.

Chomsky, N. 1986a: *Knowledge of Language: Its Nature, Origin and Use*. New York: Praeger.

Chomsky, N. 1986b: *Barriers*. Cambridge, Mass.: MIT Press.

Chomsky, N. 1987a: On the Nature, Use and Acquisition of Language: Kyoto Lectures, I. Ms.

Chomsky, N. 1987b: Transformational Grammar: Past – Present – Future: Kyoto Lectures, II. Ms.

Chomsky, N. 1989: Some notes on economy of derivation and representation. *MIT Working Papers in Linguistics, 10: Functional Heads and Clause Structure*: 43–74.

Chomsky, N. and Halle, M. 1968: *The Sound Pattern of English*. New York: Harper and Row.

Chomsky, N. and Lasnik, H. 1977: Filters and control. *Linguistic Inquiry*, 8: 425–504.

Cinque, G. 1989: Parameter setting in 'instantaneous' and real-time acquisition. *Behavioral and Brain Sciences*, 12: 336.

Clahsen, H. 1986: Verb inflections in German child language: acquisition of agreement markings and the functions they encode. *Linguistics*, 24: 79–121.

Clancey, P. M. 1985: The acquisition of Japanese. In D. I. Slobin (ed.).

Clark, E. V. 1973: What's in a word? On the child's acquisition of semantics in his first language. In T. Moore (ed.), *Cognitive Development and the Acquisition of Language*. New York: Academic Press.

Clark, E. V. 1987: The principle of contrast: a constraint on language acquisition. In B. MacWhinney (ed.).

Cooper, W. E. and Paccia-Cooper, J. 1980: *Syntax and Speech*. Cambridge, Mass.: Harvard University Press.

Crain, S. in press: Language acquisition in the absence of experience. *Behavioral and Brain Sciences*.

Crain, S. and McKee, C. 1985: Acquisition of structural restrictions on anaphora. *NELS*, 16.

Crain, S. and Thornton, R. 1990: Levels of representation in child grammar. Paper presented at 13th GLOW Colloquium, Cambridge.

Culicover, P. W. 1976: *Syntax*. New York: Academic Press.

Culicover, P. W., Wasow, T. and Akmajian, A. (eds) 1977: *Formal Syntax*. New York: Academic Press.

de Haan, G. and Tuijnman, K. 1988: Missing subjects and objects in child grammar. In P. Jordens and J. Lalleman (eds), *Language Development*. Dordrecht: Foris.

de Laguna, G. 1927: *Speech: Its Function and Development*. New Haven, Conn.: Yale University Press.

Demetras, M. J., Post, K. N. and Snow, C. E. 1986: Feedback to first language learners: the role of repetitions and clarification questions. *Journal of Child Language*, 13: 275–292.

Demuth, K. 1989: Maturation and the acquisition of the Sesotho passive. *Language*, 65: 56–80.

Demuth, K. 1990a: Subject, topic and the Sesotho passive. *Journal of Child Language*, 17: 67–84.

Demuth, K. 1990b: Relative clauses, cleft constructions and functional categories in Sesotho acquisition. Paper presented to 5th Child Language Congress, Budapest.

Deutsch, W., Koster, C. and Koster, J. 1986: What can we learn from children's errors in understanding anaphora? *Linguistics*, 24: 203–225.

de Villiers, J., Roeper, T. and Vainikka, A. 1990: The acquisition of long distance rules. In L. Frazier and J. de Villiers (eds).

Elliott, W. N. and Wexler, K. 1986: A principle theory of categorial acquisition. *NELS*, 16.

Elliott, W. N. and Wexler, K. 1987: Principles and Computations in the Acquisition of Grammatical Categories. Ms., University of California, Irvine.

Emonds, J. 1976: *A Transformational Approach to English Syntax*. New York: Academic Press.

Emonds, J. 1985: *A Unified Theory of Syntactic Categories*. Dordrecht: Foris.

Evans, G. 1980: Pronouns. *Linguistic Inquiry*, 11: 337–362.

Fassi-Fehri, A. 1989: Generalised IP structure, Case and VS order. *MIT Working Papers in Linguistics, 10: Functional Heads and Clause Structure*: 75–112.

Feldman, H., Goldin-Meadow, S. and Gleitman, L. R. 1978: Beyond Herodotus: the creation of language by linguistically deprived deaf children. In A. Lock (ed.), *Action, Gesture and Symbol*. New York: Academic Press.

Ferguson, C. A. and Slobin, D. I. (eds), 1973: *Studies of Child Language Development*. New York: Holt, Rinehart and Winston.

Fillmore, C. J. 1968: The case for case. In E. Bach and R. J. Harms (eds), *Universals in Linguistic Theory*. New York: Holt, Rinehart and Winston.

Fodor, J. A. 1975: *The Language of Thought*. New York: T. Y. Crowell.

Fodor, J. A. 1978: Computation and reduction. In W. C. Savage (ed.), *Perception and Cognition: Minnesota Studies in the Philosophy of Science*, Vol. 9. Minneapolis: University of Minnesota Press.

Fodor, J. A. 1981: The present status of the innateness controversy. In J. A. Fodor, *Representations*. Hassocks: Harvester.

Fodor, J. A. 1983: *Modularity of Mind*. Cambridge, Mass.: MIT Press.

Fodor, J. A. 1987: *Psychosemantics: The Problem of Meaning in the Philosophy of Mind*. Cambridge, Mass.: MIT Press.

Fodor, J. A. 1990: *A Theory of Content and Other Essays*. Cambridge, Mass.: MIT Press.

Fodor, J. A., Bever, T. and Garrett, M. F. 1974: *The Psychology of Language*. New York: McGraw-Hill.

Fodor, J. A., Fodor, J. D. and Garrett, M. F. 1975: The psychological unreality of semantic representations. *Linguistic Inquiry*, 6: 515–531.

Fodor, J. A., Garrett, M. F., Walker, E. C. T. and Parkes, C. H. 1980: Against definitions. *Cognition*, 8: 263–367.

Frazier, L. and de Villiers, J. (eds) 1990: *Language Acquisition and Language Processing*. Dordrecht: Kluwer.

Freidin, R. and Quicoli, A. C. 1989: Zero-stimulation for parameter setting. *Behavioral and Brain Sciences*, 12: 338–339.

Fukui, N. 1986: A Theory of Category Projection and its Applications. MIT Doctoral Dissertation.

Furrow, D., Nelson, K. and Benedict, H. 1979: Mothers' speech to children: some simple relationships. *Journal of Child Language*, 6: 423–442.

Gazdar, G. 1982: Phrase structure grammar. In G. K. Pullum and P. Jacobson (eds), *The Nature of Syntactic Representation*. Dordrecht: Reidel.

Georgopoulos, C. 1991: Canonical government and the Specifier Parameter: an ECP account of Weak Crossover. *Natural Language and Linguistic Theory*, 9: 1–46.

Gleitman, L. R. 1981: Maturational determinants of language growth. *Cognition*, 10: 103–114.

Gleitman, L. R. 1989: The structural sources of verb meaning. *Papers and Reports on Child Language Development*, 28: 1–48.

Gleitman, L. R., Gleitman, H., Landau, B. and Wanner, E. 1988: Where learning begins: initial representations for language learning. In F. J. Newmeyer (ed.), *Linguistics: The Cambridge Survey (III. Language: Psychological and Biological Aspects)*. Cambridge: Cambridge University Press.

Gleitman, L. R., Newport, E. and Gleitman, H. 1984: The current status of the Motherese Hypothesis. *Journal of Child Language*, 11: 43–79.

Gleitman, L. R. and Wanner, E. 1982: Language acquisition: the state of the state of the art. In E. Wanner and L. R. Gleitman (eds).

Gold, E. M. 1967: Language identification in the limit. *Information and Control*, 16: 447–474.

Goldin-Meadow, S. and Mylander, C. 1984: *Gestural Communication in Deaf Children: The Effects and Non-Effects of Parental Input on Early Language Development. Monographs of the Society for Research in Child Development*, Vol. 49, nos 3–4.

Goldin-Meadow, S. and Mylander, C. 1990: Beyond the input given: the child's role in the acquisition of language. *Language*, 66: 323–355.

Goodluck, H. 1981: Children's grammar of complement-subject interpretation. In S. Tavakolian (ed.).

Goodluck, H. 1986: Language acquisition and linguistic theory. In P. Fletcher and M. Garman (eds), *Language Acquisition* (2nd edn.). Cambridge: Cambridge University Press.

Goodluck, H. and Behne, D. in press: Development in control and extraction. In J. Weissenborn, H. Goodluck and T. Roeper (eds).

Greenberg, J. H. 1963: Some universals of grammar with particular reference to the order of meaningful elements. In J. H. Greenberg (ed.), *Universals of Language*. Cambridge, Mass.: MIT Press.

Greenfield, P. and Smith, J. 1976: *The Structure of Communication in Early Language Development*. New York: Academic Press.

Grimshaw, J. 1981: Form, function, and the language acquisition device. In C.

L. Baker and J. J. McCarthy (eds).

Grimshaw, J. and Pinker, S. 1989: Positive and negative evidence in language acquisition. *Behavioral and Brain Sciences*, 12: 341–342.

Grimshaw, J. and Rosen, S. T. 1990: Knowledge and obedience: the developmental status of the Binding Theory. *Linguistic Inquiry*, 21: 187–222.

Gropen, J., Pinker, S., Hollander, M. and Goldberg, R. 1991: Syntax and semantics in the acquisition of locative verbs. *Journal of Child Language*, 18: 115–151.

Gropen, J., Pinker, S., Hollander, M., Goldberg, R. and Wilson, R. 1989: The learnability and acquisition of the dative alternation in English. *Language*, 65: 203–257.

Gruber, J. 1965: Studies in Lexical Relations. MIT Doctoral Dissertation.

Gruber, J. 1976: *Lexical Structures in Syntax and Semantics*. Amsterdam: North-Holland.

Guilfoyle, E. 1984: The Acquisition of Tense and the Emergence of Lexical Subjects. Ms., McGill University.

Guilfoyle, E. and Noonan, M. 1989: Functional Categories and Language Acquisition. Ms., McGill University.

Haegeman, L. 1991: *Introduction to Government and Binding Theory*. Oxford: Blackwell.

Haider, H. and Prinzhorn, M. (eds) 1986: *Verb Second Phenomena in Germanic Languages*. Dordrecht: Foris.

Hale, K. and Keyser, S. J. forthcoming: The syntactic character of thematic structure. In I. M. Roca (ed.).

Hamburger, H. and Crain, S. 1984: Acquisition of cognitive compiling. *Cognition*, 17: 85–136.

Hamburger, H. and Wexler, K. 1973: Identifiability of a class of transformational grammars. In K. J. J. Hintikka, J. M. E. Moravcsik and P. Suppes (eds).

Hamburger, H. and Wexler, K. 1975: A mathematical theory of learning transformational grammar. *Journal of Mathematical Psychology*, 12: 137–177.

Hammond, M. 1990: Parameters of metrical theory and learnability. In I. M. Roca (ed.).

Harris, R. 1989: Degree–0 explanation. *Behavioral and Brain Sciences*, 12: 344–345.

Hickey, T. 1990: The acquisition of Irish: a study of word-order development. *Journal of Child Language*, 17: 17–41.

Higginbotham, J. 1980: Pronouns and bound variables. *Linguistic Inquiry*, 11: 679–708.

Higginbotham, J. 1985: On semantics. *Linguistic Inquiry*, 16: 547–593.

Hintikka, K. J. J., Moravcsik, J. M. E. and Suppes, P. (eds) 1973: *Approaches to Natural Language*. Dordrecht: Reidel.

Hirsh-Pasek, K., Treiman, R. and Schneiderman, M. 1984: Brown and Hanlon revisited: mothers' sensitivity to ungrammatical forms. *Journal of Child Language*, 11: 81–88.

Hoekstra, T. 1990: Markedness and growth. In I. M. Roca (ed.).

Hoekstra, T. forthcoming: Aspect and theta-theory. In I. M. Roca (ed.).

Horgan, D. M. 1975: Language Development: A Cross-Methodological Study. University of Michigan Doctoral Dissertation.

Hornstein, N. 1983: *Logic as Grammar*. Cambridge, Mass.: MIT Press.

Hornstein, N. and Lightfoot, D. 1981: Introduction. In N. Hornstein and D. Lightfoot (eds).

Hornstein, N. and Lightfoot, D. (eds) 1981: *Explanation in Linguistics: The Logical Problem of Language Acquisition*. London: Longman.

Hsu, J. R., Cairns, H. S., Eisenberg, S. and Schlisselberg, G. 1989: Control and coreference in early child language. *Journal of Child Language*, 16: 599–622.

Huang, C.-T. J. 1982: Logical Relations in Chinese and the Theory of Grammar. MIT Doctoral Dissertation.

Huang, C.-T. J. 1984: On the distribution and reference of empty pronouns. *Linguistic Inquiry*, 15: 531–574.

Huang, C.-T. J. 1987: Remarks on empty categories. *Linguistic Inquiry*, 18: 321–337.

Huang, C.-T. J. 1989: *Pro*-drop in Chinese: a generalized control theory. In O. Jaeggli and K. Safir (eds).

Hyams, N. 1986: *Language Acquisition and the Theory of Parameters*. Dordrecht: Reidel.

Hyams, N. 1987a: The setting of the null subject parameter: a reanalysis. Paper presented to the Boston University Conference on Child Language Development.

Hyams, N. 1987b: The Acquisition of Inflection: A Parameter-Setting Approach. Ms., University of California, Los Angeles.

Hyams, N. 1987c: The theory of parameters and syntactic development. In T. Roeper and E. Williams (eds).

Hyams, N. and Sigurjonsdottir, S. 1990: The development of 'long distance anaphora': a cross-linguistic study with special reference to Icelandic. *Language Acquisition*, 1: 57–93.

Iatridou, S. 1990: About Agr(P). *Linguistic Inquiry*, 21: 551–577.

Ingram, D. 1989: *First Language Acquisition: Method, Description and Explanation*. Cambridge: Cambridge University Press.

Jackendoff, R. 1972: *Semantic Interpretation in Generative Grammar*. Cambridge, Mass.: MIT Press.

Jackendoff, R. 1977: *X-Bar Syntax: A Study of Phrase Structure*. Cambridge, Mass.: MIT Press.

Jackendoff, R. 1983: *Semantics and Cognition*. Cambridge, Mass.: MIT Press.

Jackendoff, R. 1987: The status of thematic relations in linguistic theory. *Linguistic Inquiry*, 18: 369–411.

Jackendoff, R. 1989: What is a concept, that a person may grasp it? *Mind and Language*, 4: 68–102.

Jaeggli, O. 1982: *Topics in Romance Syntax*. Dordrecht: Foris.

Jaeggli, O. 1986: Passive. *Linguistic Inquiry*, 17: 587–622.

Jaeggli, O. and Hyams, N. 1987: Morphological uniformity and the setting of the null subject parameter. *NELS*, 18.

Jaeggli, O. and Safir, K. (eds) 1989: *The Null Subject Parameter*. Dordrecht: Kluwer.

Jaeggli, O. and Safir, K. 1989: The null subject parameter and parametric theory. In O. Jaeggli and K. Safir (eds).

Jakobson, R., Fant, G. and Halle, M. 1952: *Preliminaries to Speech Analysis*. The Hague: Mouton.

Jakubowicz, C. 1984: On markedness and binding principles. *NELS*, 14.

Joos, M. (ed.) 1957: *Readings in Linguistics*. Washington: American Council of Learned Societies.

Jordens, P. 1990: The acquisition of verb placement in Dutch and German. *Linguistics*, 28: 1407–1448.

Katz, J. J. 1981: *Language and Other Abstract Objects*. Oxford: Blackwell.

Katz, J. J. and Fodor, J. A. 1963: The structure of a semantic theory. *Language*, 39: 170–210.

Katz, J. J. and Postal, P. 1964: *An Integrated Theory of Linguistic Descriptions*. Cambridge, Mass.: MIT Press.

Kayne, R. 1981: ECP extensions. *Linguistic Inquiry*, 12: 93–133.

Kayne, R. 1983 Connectedness. *Linguistic Inquiry*, 14: 223–249.

Kazman, R. 1988: Null arguments and the acquisition of Case and Infl. Paper presented at the University of Boston Conference on Language Acquisition.

Keil, F. C. 1989: *Concepts, Kinds and Cognitive Development*. Cambridge, Mass.: MIT Press.

Keil, F. C. 1990: Constraints on constraints: surveying the epigenetic landscape. *Cognitive Science*, 14: 135–168.

Koopman, H. 1983: ECP effects in main clauses. *Linguistic Inquiry*, 14: 346–350.

Koopman, H. 1984: *The Syntax of Verbs*. Dordrecht: Foris.

Koopman, H. and Sportiche, D. 1982: Variables and the bijection principle. *The Linguistic Review*, 2: 135–170.

Koopman, H. and Sportiche, D. 1988: Subjects. Ms, University of California, Los Angeles.

Koster, J. 1986: *Domains and Dynasties: The Radical Autonomy of Syntax*. Dordrecht: Foris.

Kuczaj, S. A. II 1977: The acquisition of regular and irregular past tense forms. *Journal of Verbal Learning and Verbal Behavior*, 16: 589–600.

Landau, B. and Gleitman, L. R. 1985: *Language and Experience: Evidence from the Blind Child*. Cambridge, Mass.: Harvard University Press.

Larson, R. K. 1988: On the double object construction. *Linguistic Inquiry*, 19: 335–391.

Lasnik, H. 1981: Learnability, restrictiveness and the evaluation metric. In C. L. Baker and J. J. McCarthy (eds).

Lasnik, H. 1985: On Certain Substitutes for Negative Data. Ms., University of Connecticut.

Lasnik, H. 1989: The nature of triggering data. *Behavioral and Brain Sciences*, 12: 349–350.

Lasnik, H. and Crain, S. 1985: On the acquisition of pronominal reference. *Lingua*, 65: 135–154.

Lasnik, H. and Saito, M. 1984: On the nature of proper government. *Linguistic Inquiry*, 15: 235–289.

Lebeaux, D. 1987: Comments on Hyams. In T. Roeper and E. Williams (eds).

Lebeaux, D. 1988: Language Acquisition and the Form of the Grammar. University of Massachusetts Doctoral Dissertation.

Levelt, W. M. 1974: *Formal Grammars in Linguistics and Psycholinguistics, Vol. 3: Psycholinguistic Applications.* The Hague: Mouton.

Levelt, W. M. 1975: *What Became of LAD?* Lisse: Peter de Ridder.

Levin, B. 1984: Lexical semantics in review: an introduction. *Lexicon Project Working Papers*, 1. MIT Center for Cognitive Science.

Levin, B. and Rappaport, M. 1986: The formation of adjectival passives. *Linguistic Inquiry*, 17: 623–661.

Levin, B. and Rappaport Hovav, M. forthcoming: The lexical semantics of verbs of motion: the perspective from unaccusativity. In I. M. Roca (ed.).

Levy, Y. 1983: It's frogs all the way down. *Cognition*, 15: 75–93.

Lightfoot, D. 1989: The child's trigger experience: 'degree–0' learnability. *Behavioral and Brain Sciences*, 12: 321–334.

Loewer, B. and Rey, G. (eds) 1991: *Meaning in Mind: Fodor and His Critics.* Oxford: Blackwell.

Luce, R. D., Bush, R. R. and Galanter, E. (eds) 1963: *Handbook of Mathematical Psychology,* Vol. 2. New York: Wiley.

Lundin, B. and Platzack, C. 1988: The acquisition of verb inflection, verb second and subordinate clauses in Swedish. *Working Papers in Scandinavian Syntax*, 42: 43–55.

Lust, B. 1981: Constraints on anaphora in child language: a prediction for a universal. In S. Tavakolian (ed.).

Lust, B. 1986a (ed.): *Studies in the Acquisition of Anaphora,* Vol. 1. Dordrecht: Reidel.

Lust, B. 1986b: Remarks on the psychological reality of the Subset Principle: its relation to Universal Grammar as a model of the initial state. Paper presented to Cognitive Science Conference, Amherst, Mass.

Lust, B. and Chien, Y.-C. 1984: The structure of coordination in first-language acquisition of Mandarin Chinese: evidence for a universal. *Cognition*, 17: 49–83.

Lust, B. and Mangione, L. 1983: The Principal Branching Direction Parameter in first language acquisition of anaphora. *NELS*, 13.

Lust, B. and Mazuka, R. 1989: Cross-linguistic studies of directionality in first language acquisition: the Japanese data – a response to O'Grady, Susuki-Wei and Cho 1986. *Journal of Child Language*, 16: 665–684.

McCarthy, D. 1954: Language development in children. In L. Carmichael (ed.), *Manual of Child Psychology.*, New York: Wiley.

Macnamara, J. 1982: *Words for Things.* Cambridge, Mass.: MIT Press.

McNeill, D. 1966: Developmental psycholinguistics. In F. Smith and G. A. Miller (eds).

MacWhinney, B. (ed.) 1987: *Mechanisms of Language Acquisition.* Hillsdale, N.J.: Erlbaum.

Manzini, R. 1983: On control and control theory. *Linguistic Inquiry*, 14: 421–446.

Manzini, R. forthcoming: The Projection Principle(s): a re-examination. In I. M. Roca (ed.).

Manzini, R. and Wexler, K. 1987: Parameters, binding theory and learnability. *Linguistic Inquiry*, 18: 413–444.

Maratsos, M. 1979: How to get from words to sentences. In D. Aaronson and R. W. Rieber (eds), *Psycholinguistic Research: Implications and Applications*. Hillsdale, N.J.: Erlbaum.

Maratsos, M. 1982: The child's construction of grammatical categories. In E. Wanner and L. R. Gleitman (eds).

Maratsos, M. 1983: The acquisition of syntax. In J. Flavell and E. Markman (eds), *Carmichael's Handbook of Child Psychology*. New York: Wiley.

Maratsos, M. and Chalkley, M. 1980: The internal language of children's syntax: the ontogenesis and representation of syntactic categories. In K. Nelson (ed.), *Children's Language*, Vol. 2. New York: Gardner.

Markman, E. M. 1989: *Categorization and Naming in Children: Problems of Induction*. Cambridge, Mass.: MIT Press.

Matthei, E. 1981: Children's interpretation of sentences containing reciprocals. In S. Tavakolian (ed.).

Matthei, E. 1982: The acquisition of prenominal modifier sequences. *Cognition*, 11: 301–332.

May, R. 1977: The Grammar of Quantification. MIT Doctoral Dissertation.

May, R. 1985: *Logical Form: Its Structure and Derivation*. Cambridge, Mass.: MIT Press.

Mazurkewich, I. and White, L. 1984: The acquisition of the dative alternation: unlearning overgeneralizations. *Cognition*, 16: 261–283.

Miller, G. A. and Chomsky, N. 1963: Finitary models of language users. In R. D. Luce, R. R. Bush and E. Galanter (eds).

Milsark, G. 1987: Singl-*ing*. *Linguistic Inquiry*, 18: 611–634.

Morgan, J. L. 1986: *From Simple Input to Complex Grammar*. Cambridge, Mass: MIT Press.

Morgan, J. L. 1989: Learnability considerations and the nature of trigger experiences in language acquisition. *Behavioral and Brain Sciences*, 12: 352–353.

Morgan, J. L. and Travis, L. 1989: Limits on negative information in language input. *Journal of Child Language*, 16: 531–552.

Naigles, L. 1990: Children use syntax to learn verb meanings. *Journal of Child Language*, 17: 357–374.

Newmeyer, F. J. 1980: *Linguistic Theory in America*. New York: Academic Press.

Newport, E., Gleitman, L. and Gleitman, H. 1977: Mother, I'd rather do it myself: some effects and non-effects of maternal speech style. In C. E. Snow and C. A. Ferguson (eds).

Newson, M. 1990a: Questions of Form and Learnability in Binding Theory. University of Essex Doctoral Dissertation.

Newson, M. 1990b: Dependencies in the lexical setting of parameters: a solution to the undergeneralisation problem. In I. M. Roca (ed.).

Nishigauchi, T. and Roeper, T. 1987: Deductive parameters and the growth of empty categories. In T. Roeper and E. Williams (eds).

Ochs, E. 1982: Ergativity and word order in Samoan child language. *Langu-*

age, 58: 646–671.

Oehrle, R. 1985: Implicit Negative Evidence. Ms., University of Arizona.

O'Grady, W. 1987: *Principles of Grammar and Learning*. Chicago: University of Chicago Press.

O'Grady, W., Peters, A. M. and Masterson D. 1989: The transition from optional to required subjects. *Journal of Child Language*, 16: 513–529.

Osgood, C. 1963: On understanding and uttering sentences. *American Psychologist*, 18: 735–751.

Osherson, D., Stob, M. and Weinstein, S. 1982: Learning strategies. *Information and Control*, 53: 32–51.

Osherson, D., Stob, M. and Weinstein, S. 1984: Learning theory and natural language. *Cognition*, 17: 1–28.

Osherson, D., Stob, M. and Weinstein, S. 1986: *Systems that Learn*. Cambridge, Mass.: MIT Press.

Osherson, D. and Weinstein, S. 1982: Criteria of language learning. *Information and Control*, 52: 123–138.

Otsu, Y. 1981: Universal Grammar and Syntactic Development in Children: Toward a Theory of Syntactic Development. MIT Doctoral Dissertation.

Ouhalla, J. 1988: The Syntax of Head Movement: A Study of Berber. University College, London, Doctoral Dissertation.

Ouhalla, J. 1990: Sentential negation, relativised minimality and the aspectual status of auxiliaries. *The Linguistic Review*, 7: 183–231.

Parodi, T. 1989: The Acquisition of Word-Order and Case Morphology. Ms., Hamburg University.

Partee, B. H. 1975: *Fundamentals of Mathematics for Linguistics*. Dordrecht: Reidel.

Penner, S. 1987: Parental responses to grammatical and ungrammatical child utterances. *Child Development*, 58: 376–384.

Perlmutter, D. 1978: Impersonal passives and the Unaccusative Hypothesis. *Papers from the Berkeley Linguistic Society*, 4.

Pesetsky, D. 1982: Paths and Categories. MIT Doctoral Dissertation.

Piattelli-Palmarini, M. (ed.) 1980: *Language and Learning: The Debate Between Jean Piaget and Noam Chomsky*. Cambridge, Mass.: MIT Press.

Piattelli-Palmarini, M. 1989: Evolution, selection and cognition: from 'learning' to parameter setting in biology and in the study of language. *Cognition*, 31: 1–44.

Pinker, S. 1979: Formal models of language learning. *Cognition*, 7: 217–283.

Pinker, S. 1981: Comments on the paper by Wexler. In C. L. Baker and J. J. McCarthy (eds).

Pinker, S. 1982: A theory of the acquisition of lexical interpretive grammars. In J. Bresnan (ed.).

Pinker, S. 1984: *Language Learnability and Language Development*. Cambridge, Mass.: Harvard University Press.

Pinker, S. 1987: The bootstrapping problem in language acquisition. In B. MacWhinney (ed.).

Pinker, S. 1989: *Learnability and Cognition: The Acquisition of Argument Structure*. Cambridge, Mass.: MIT Press.

Platzack, C. 1990: A Grammar without Functional Categories: A Syntactic Study of Early Swedish Child Language. Ms., Lund University.

Pollock, J.–Y. 1989: Verb movement, universal grammar, and the structure of IP. *Linguistic Inquiry*, 20: 365–424.

Postal, P. 1964: Limitations of phrase-structure grammars. In J. A. Fodor and J. J. Katz (eds), *The Structure of Language: Readings in the Philosophy of Language*. Englewood Cliffs, N.J.: Prentice Hall.

Postal, P. 1974: *On Raising*. Cambridge, Mass.: MIT Press.

Postal, P. and Pullum, G. K. 1982: The contraction debate. *Linguistic Inquiry*, 13: 122–138.

Pye, C. 1990: The acquisition of ergative languages. *Linguistics*, 28: 1291–1330.

Radford, A. 1988a: *Transformational Grammar: A First Course*. Cambridge: Cambridge University Press.

Radford, A. 1988b: Small children's small clauses. *Transactions of the Philological Society*, 86: 1–46.

Radford, A. 1990a: *Syntactic Theory and the Acquisition of English Syntax: the Nature of Early Child Grammars in English*. Oxford: Blackwell.

Radford, A. 1990b: The syntax of nominal arguments in early child English. *Language Acquisition*, 1: 195–224.

Read, C. and Schreiber, P. 1982: Why short subjects are hard to find. In E. Wanner and L. R. Gleitman (eds).

Reinhart, T. 1976: The Syntactic Domain of Anaphora. MIT Doctoral Dissertation.

Rizzi, L. 1982: *Issues in Italian Syntax*. Dordrecht: Foris.

Rizzi, L. 1986: Null objects in Italian and the theory of *pro*. *Linguistic Inquiry*, 17: 501–557.

Rizzi, L. 1989: On the format for parameters. *Behavioral and Brain Sciences*, 12: 355–356.

Rizzi, L. 1990: *Relativized Minimality*. Cambridge, Mass.: MIT Press.

Roca, I. M. (ed.) 1990: *Logical Issues in Language Acquisition*. Dordrecht: Foris.

Roca, I. M. (ed.) forthcoming: *Thematic Structure: Its Role in Grammar*. Dordrecht: Foris.

Roeper, T. 1973: Theoretical implications of word order, topicalization and inflections in German language acquisition. In C. A. Ferguson and D. I. Slobin (eds).

Roeper, T. 1984: Implicit Arguments and the Projection Principle. Ms., University of Massachusetts.

Roeper, T. 1988: Grammatical principles of first language acquisition: theory and evidence. In F. J. Newmeyer (ed.), *Linguistics: The Cambridge Survey (II. Linguistic Theory: Extensions and Implications)*. Cambridge: Cambridge University Press.

Roeper, T. and de Villiers, J. 1989: Ordered decisions in the acquisition of Wh-questions. Draft of chapter to appear in J. Weissenborn, H. Goodluck and T. Roeper (eds).

Roeper, T., Rooth, M., Mallis, L. and Akiyama, A. 1984: The Problem of

Empty Categories and Bound Variables in Language Acquisition. Ms., University of Massachusetts.

Roeper, T. and Weissenborn, J. 1990: Making parameters work. In L. Frazier and J. de Villiers (eds).

Roeper, T. and Williams, E. (eds) 1987: *Parameter Setting*. Dordrecht: Reidel.

Rosch, E., Mervis, C. B., Gray, W. D., Johnson, D. M. and Boyes-Braem, P. 1976: Basic objects in natural categories. *Cognitive Psychology*, 8: 382–439.

Rosen, C. 1984: The interface between semantic roles and initial grammatical relations. In D. Perlmutter and C. Rosen (eds), *Studies in Relational Grammar*. Chicago: University of Chicago Press.

Ross, J. R. 1967: Constraints on Variables in Syntax. MIT Doctoral Dissertation.

Rothstein, S. D. 1983: The Syntactic Forms of Predication. MIT Doctoral Dissertation.

Safir, K. 1985: *Syntactic Chains*. Cambridge: Cambridge University Press.

Safir, K. 1987: Comments on Wexler and Manzini. In T. Roeper and E. Williams (eds).

Saleemi, A. P. 1990: Subjects, markedness and implicit negative evidence. In I. M. Roca (ed.).

Saleemi, A. P. forthcoming: *Universal Grammar and Language Learnability*. Cambridge: Cambridge University Press.

Schlesinger, I. M. 1971: Production of utterances and language acquisition. In D. I. Slobin (ed.), *The Ontogenesis of Grammar*. New York: Academic Press.

Schlesinger, I. M. 1977: *Production and Comprehension of Utterances*. Hillsdale, N.J.: Erlbaum.

Skinner, B. F. 1957: *Verbal Behavior*. New York: Appleton-Century-Crofts.

Slobin, D. I. 1966: The acquisition of Russian as a native language. In F. Smith and G. A. Miller (eds).

Slobin, D. I. 1973: Cognitive prerequisites for the development of grammar. In C. A. Ferguson and D. I. Slobin (eds).

Slobin, D. I. 1977: Language change in childhood and in history. In J. Macnamara (ed.), *Language Learning and Thought*. New York: Academic Press.

Slobin, D. I. 1982: Universal and particular in the acquisition of language. In E. Wanner and L. R. Gleitman (eds).

Slobin, D. I. (ed.) 1985: *The Cross-Linguistic Study of Language Acquisition*, Vol 1: *The Data*. Hillsdale, N.J.: Erlbaum.

Smith, F. and Miller, G. A. (eds) 1966: *The Genesis of Language: A Psycholinguistic Approach*. Cambridge, Mass.: MIT Press.

Smoczyńska, M. 1985: The acquisition of Polish. In D. I. Slobin (ed.).

Snow, C. E. 1977: Mothers' speech research: from input to interaction. In C. E. Snow and C. A. Ferguson (eds).

Snow, C. E. and Ferguson, C. A. (eds) 1977: *Talking to Children: Language Input and Acquisition*. Cambridge: Cambridge University Press.

Solan, L. 1983: *On The Acquisition of Pronominal Reference*. Dordrecht: Reidel.

Solan, L. 1987: Parameter setting and the development of pronouns and reflexives. In T. Roeper and E. Williams (eds).

Sportiche, D. 1981: On bounding nodes in French. *The Linguistic Review*, 1: 219–246.

Sportiche, D. 1988: A theory of floating quantifiers and its corollaries for constituent structure. *Linguistic Inquiry*, 19: 425–449.

Stowell, T. 1981: The Origins of Phrase Structure. MIT Doctoral Dissertation.

Stowell, T. 1982: The tense of infinitives. *Linguistic Inquiry*, 13: 561–570.

Tavakolian, S. 1978: Children's comprehension of pronominal and missing subjects in complicated sentences. In H. Goodluck and L. Solan (eds), *Papers in the Structure and Development of Child Language. University of Massachusetts Occasional Papers*, 4.

Tavakolian, S. (ed.) 1981: *Language Acquisition and Linguistic Theory*. Cambridge, Mass.: MIT Press.

Tenny, C. 1987: Grammaticalizing Aspect and Affectedness. MIT Doctoral Dissertation.

Travis, L. 1984: Parameters and Effects of Word Order Variation. MIT Doctoral Dissertation.

Truscott, C. 1984: On Boundedness in Government-Binding Theory. University of California, Irvine, Doctoral Dissertation.

Tuller, L. 1986: Bijection Relations in UG and the Syntax of Hausa. University of California, Los Angeles, Doctoral Dissertation.

Valian, V. 1989: Children's production of subjects: competence, performance and the null subject parameter. *Papers and Reports on Child Language Development*, 28: 156–163.

Valian, V. 1990a: Syntactic Subjects in the Early Speech of American and Italian Children. Ms., Hunter College, New York.

Valian, V. 1990b: Null subjects: a problem for parameter-setting models of language acquisition. *Cognition*, 35: 105–122.

van Riemsdijk, H. and Williams, E. 1986: *Introduction to the Theory of Grammar*. Cambridge, Mass.: MIT Press.

Wall, R. 1972: *Introduction to Mathematical Linguistics*. Englewood Cliffs, N.J.: Prentice-Hall.

Wanner, E. and Gleitman, L. R. (eds) 1982: *Language Acquisition: The State of the Art*. Cambridge: Cambridge University Press.

Wasow, T. 1977: Transformations and the lexicon. In P. W. Culicover, T. Wasow and A. Akmajian (eds).

Wasow, T. 1989: Why degree–0? *Behavioral and Brain Sciences*, 12: 361–362.

Watson, J. B. 1928: *Behaviorism*. Chicago: Norton.

Weinberg, A. 1987: Comments on Borer and Wexler. In T. Roeper and E. Williams (eds).

Weissenborn, J., Goodluck, H. and Roeper, T. (eds) in press: *Studies in Theoretical Psycholinguistics: Papers from the Berlin Workshop*. Hillsdale, N.J.: Erlbaum.

Wexler, K. 1982: A principle theory for language acquisition. In E. Wanner and L. R. Gleitman (eds).

Wexler, K. and Chien, Y.-C. 1985: The development of lexical anaphors and pronouns. *Papers and Reports on Child Language Development*, 24: 138–149.

Wexler, K. and Culicover, P. W. 1980: *Formal Principles of Language Acquisition*. Cambridge, Mass.: MIT Press.

Wexler, K. and Hamburger, H. 1973: On the insufficiency of surface data for the learning of transformational languages. In K. J. J. Hintikka, J. M. E. Moravcsik and P. Suppes (eds).

Wexler, K. and Manzini, R. 1987: Parameters and learnability in Binding Theory. In T. Roeper and E. Williams (eds).

White, L. 1981: The responsibility of grammatical theory to acquisition data. In N. Hornstein and D. Lightfoot (eds).

Wilkins, W. 1989: Why degree–0? *Behavioral and Brain Sciences*, 12: 363.

Williams, E. 1980: Predication. *Linguistic Inquiry*, 11: 203–238.

Williams, E. 1981a: Argument structure and morphology. *The Linguistic Review*, 1: 81–114.

Williams, E. 1981b: A readjustment in the learnability assumptions. In C. L. Baker and J. J. McCarthy (eds).

Williams, E. 1981c: Language acquisition, markedness and phrase structure. In S. Tavakolian (ed.)

Williams, E. 1987: Introduction. In T. Roeper and E. Williams (eds).

Williams, E. 1989: Linguistic variation and learnability. *Behavioral and Brain Sciences*, 12: 363–364.

Xu, L.-J. 1986: Free empty category. *Linguistic Inquiry* 17: 75–93.

Yang, D.-W. 1983: The extended binding theory of anaphora. *Language Research*, 19: 169–192.

Index